WORKS ISSUED BY
THE HAKLUYT SOCIETY

Series Editors
Gloria Clifton
Joyce Lorimer

THE STRUGGLE FOR THE SOUTH ATLANTIC:
THE ARMADA OF THE STRAIT, 1581–1584

THIRD SERIES
NO. 31

THE STRUGGLE FOR THE SOUTH ATLANTIC

THE ARMADA OF THE STRAIT, 1581–1584

Edited by

CARLA RAHN PHILLIPS

Published by
Routledge
for
THE HAKLUYT SOCIETY
LONDON
2016

First published 2016 for the Hakluyt Society by
Routledge
2 Park Square, Milton Park, Abingdon, Oxon OX14 4RN

and by Routledge
711 Third Avenue, New York, NY 10017

Routledge is an imprint of the Taylor & Francis Group, an informa business

British Library Cataloguing in Publication Data
A catalogue record for this book is available from the British Library

Library of Congress Cataloging in Publication Data
CIP data applied for

ISBN: 978-1-908145-15-4 (hbk)
ISBN: 978-1-315-40614-5 (ebk)

Typeset in Garamond Premier Pro
by Waveney Typesetters, Wymondham, Norfolk

Routledge website: http://www.routledge.com
Hakuyt Society website: http://www.hakluyt.com

Printed in the United Kingdom
by Henry Ling Limited

CONTENTS

vii

DOCUMENTS APPENDED TO RADA'S *RELACIÓN*

LIST OF MAPS

PREFACE, ACKNOWLEDGEMENTS, AND DEDICATION

The Armada of the Strait first interested me in a general way long before I decided to focus on it as a topic of research. The James Ford Bell Library at the University of Minnesota holds a copy of a minor epic poem written about the expedition in 1584. In the course of other research, I read the poem and wondered why the armada was so little known. Years later, when the Huntington Library in southern California purchased Pedro de Rada's *Relación*, Bill Frank, then Curator of Hispanic, Cartographic, and Western Historical Manuscripts at the library, wrote a detailed synopsis of it in the *Huntington Spectator* (Fall, 1999). That reawakened my interest. I spent some time with Rada's manuscript during my next visit to the Huntington and decided to write a book about the armada, using Rada's *Relación* as one of the sources but not as the book's focus. Thereafter, I made several other visits to the library, both for research and to teach summer seminars in Spanish palaeography, sponsored by the Andrew W. Mellon Foundation.

The Huntington Library is unique in featuring a world-class art collection and botanical garden in addition to a world-class archive and library, all in a gorgeous 100-acre setting near the foothills of the San Gabriel Mountains. Researchers as well as casual visitors appreciate the unparalleled environment of the Huntington. I appreciate it more than most, as my ancestors settled in the area in the late eighteenth century, and it has always felt like home to me. I was able to spend the academic year 2005–6 at the Huntington as the Fletcher C. Jones Foundation Distinguished Senior Fellow, devoting my time to Rada's manuscript and its historical context. A sabbatical from the University of Minnesota for the academic year 2008–9, with additional support from the Bush Foundation, gave me more time to focus on the Armada of the Strait. The more I learned, the more I was struck by the discrepancies between Rada's account and virtually every published mention of the armada. To set the record straight, Rada's previously unknown manuscript deserved to be better known. In 2010 I approached the Hakluyt Society as an ideal venue for its publication. Fortunately, the Hakluyt Society Council agreed and its series editors were patient while I finished my research.

All of the professionals at the Huntington Library were very helpful to me, but Bill Frank above all. His thirty-two-year tenure there was marked by significant acquisitions of Spanish-language manuscripts, maps, and other materials. Bill was an extraordinary resource for my palaeography students as well, sharing his deep knowledge of the Huntington's Spanish-language manuscripts in our show-and-tell sessions. He truly embodied the old saying that 'the best catalogues are on two legs'. Soon after Pedro de Rada's *Relación* arrived at the Huntington Bill made a full transcription of it, and he provided me with an electronic copy when I began my research. With rare exceptions, my transcription agreed with his. Bill continued to take a keen interest in the progress of my project for the Hakluyt Society, but he steadfastly refused to accept any credit for the initial transcription. I regret that my introduction and translation took so long to complete; I regret even more that Bill did not live to see the finished product, which is dedicated to his memory.

The documentary sources for the Armada of the Strait are richer and deeper than I could have imagined at the outset, both in published and in manuscript form. Moreover, under the aegis of Spain's Ministry of Culture, archivists have created a computerized database called PARES (Portal de Archivos Españoles / Port of Spanish Archives), which went online in 2007 (www.PARES.mcu.es). PARES is a searchable record of the holdings in Spanish state archives, based on manuscript catalogues and inventories from the eighteenth century on, plus published finding aids. PARES enables researchers online to locate persons, places, and things such as ships in a variety of archives and sections therein. The database includes summaries of particular documents and their context within a given archival section. Some of the documents have been digitized in full, so that a researcher can consult images of the documents online, with the ability to enlarge, enhance, rotate and download those images. The work of digitization is ongoing, and the website provides regular updates of the progress made. PARES made it possible for me to find information about many of the men and ships of the armada, which would have been much more time-consuming otherwise.

The Archive of the Museo Naval in Madrid was also crucial for my research. As part of the Ministry of the Navy, its holdings are not included in the PARES database, but they are exceptionally well catalogued in both written and computerized forms. The military and civilian staff members and a succession of directors have made my sojourns there both pleasant and productive. I would also like to thank the professional staff at the Biblioteca Nacional de España and the Archivo Histórico Nacional, both in Madrid, and the Archivo General de Simancas, who provide essential support for researchers from around the globe. Finally, I would like to thank the Hakluyt Society for allowing me to be a part of their distinguished series of editions, and especially Joyce Lorimer, honorary joint series editor, who shepherded this project through every stage with unfailing expertise, patience and good humour.

Carla Rahn Phillips
Professor of History, *Emerita*,
University of Minnesota, Twin Cities (USA)

LIST OF ABBREVIATIONS

ABNRJ	*Annaes da Bibliotheca Nacional do Rio de Janeiro*
AGI	Archivo General de las Indias, Seville
AGS	Archivo General de Simancas, Valladolid
AHN	Archivo Histórico Nacional, Madrid
AMN	Archivo del Museo Naval, Madrid
ARCV	Archivo de la Real Chancillería de Valladolid
BA	Biblioteca de Ajuda, Lisbon
BNE	Biblioteca Nacional de España, Madrid
BNF	Bibliothèque Nationale de France
BL	British Library
CODOIN	*Colección de documentos inéditos para la historia de España*
CSP	*Calendar of State Papers*
doc.	*documento*
leg.	*legajo*
lib.	*libro*
N.	*Número*
ODNB	*Oxford Dictionary of National Biography*
OM	*Ordénes Militares*
PN1	*The Principall Navigations* (1589)
PN2	*The Principal Navigations* (1598–1600)
PN(M)	*The Principal Navigations* (1903–5)
R.	*Ramo*
TNA	The National Archives, Kew

WEIGHTS, MEASURES, AND CURRENCY

almud	a dry measure with a volume from 2 to 21 quarts, according to region, period, and the item measured. To reduce the measure to weight, many scholars use the figure of 4 kg per *almud*.
alquer	an ancient Portuguese dry measure [*alqueire*], varying considerably from place to place.
arroba	a Castilian weight of 11.5 kg.
azumbre	a liquid measure equal to about 2 litres.
braza	a linear measure equal to 2 *varas* or 1.67 m.
cruzado	a Portuguese gold coin first issued in the mid-fifteenth century in aid of a crusade against the Turks, who had captured Constantinople in 1453.
ducado	[ducat]: a gold coin worth 11 *reales* or 375 *maravedís* in money of account.
legua	5,000 *varas* or 3 *millas*, equivalent in modern terms to about 2.6 miles or 4.2 km.
legua náutica	unit of distance at sea, variable between 3.2 and 4.2 modern nautical miles.
libra	pound; a unit of weight in Spain and Portugal equal to about 460 g or 16 oz troy weight; also known in Portuguese as an *arratel*.
libreta	also *libreta carnicera* or 'flesh pound', weighing 32 oz.
maravedí	the least monetary unit of account in the sixteenth century: 1 *real* = 34 *maravedís*; 1 escudo = 340 *maravedís*; 1 ducat = 375 *maravedís*.
milla	mile.
milréis	1 *milréis* = 1,000 *réis* in Portuguese accounting, which seems to have been worth slightly more than 1,000 Spanish *reales*.
pipa	a large barrel for transporting and storing various liquids and comestibles; equal to about 27.5 *arrobas* in the late sixteenth century.
quartillo	a liquid measure equal to 504 ml.
quintal	a hundredweight (cwt); in Castile equal to 100 Castilian *libras*, about 101.47 lb, or 46.03 kg; in Portugal equal to 128 Portuguese *libras*, about 129.54 lb, or 58.75 kg.
real	a Spanish silver coin, worth 34 *maravedís* in money of account; 10 *reales* = 1 *escudo*; 11 *reales* = 1 ducat. A silver coin worth 8 *reales* was called a *peso de a ocho*, or piece of eight.
tonelada	equal to 2 *pipas* of 27.5 *arrobas* each in southern Spain, according to Juan Escalante de Mendoza in 1575.
vara	a yard, each one equal to about 0.84 m.

INTRODUCTION

1. Overview

The Armada of the Strait under Captain General[1] Diego Flores de Valdés (hereafter Flores) set out from south-western Spain in the fall of 1581, with twenty-three ships and 3,500 people, including officers, royal officials, sailors, soldiers, and settlers with their families. The year before, as Philip II of Spain made good his claim to the Portuguese throne,[2] he planned the armada to demonstrate Habsburg authority in the Americas, in response to Francis Drake's incursions into the South Atlantic and Pacific oceans in 1577–9. He had been persuaded that a strong armada could bolster the defences of Portuguese Brazil and Spanish Chile and Peru, and defend the Strait of Magellan with forts and a colony.[3] Despite careful planning, the expedition suffered terrible losses from the very beginning and hardships throughout. Hundreds of people drowned in shipwrecks and hundreds more perished from disease and privation. Several ships were lost or so damaged by storms that they could not continue. A contingent of the armada finally was able to establish 338 persons at the Strait, following two earlier failed attempts.[4] Other contingents from the armada skirmished with an English expedition under Edward Fenton, expelled French interlopers from north-eastern Brazil, and improved the defences of several coastal regions.[5] The armada officially ended when Flores arrived back in Spain

[1] The supreme commander of a Spanish fleet was a captain general. Although this was the equivalent of an English admiral, the English equivalent should not be confused with the second-in-command of a Spanish fleet – the almirante.

[2] King Sebastião I of Portugal, Philip II's nephew, died without issue in North Africa in August of 1578. For a detailed summary of Philip II's accession to the throne of Portugal and its empire, see Merriman, *Rise of the Spanish Empire*, vol. 4, pp. 344–406. In Portugal, the new king was known as Philip I; to avoid confusion he will be referred to as King Philip when dealing solely with affairs relating to Portugal.

[3] For the context of Spanish politics and diplomacy in the late 16th century, see Phillips and Phillips, *Concise History of Spain*, pp. 143–53.

[4] Sources differ about the total numbers and their distribution. An official document reported a total of 338 persons: 177 soldiers; 48 mariners; 2 friars; and artisans and other settlers, including 13 women and 10 children. Sarmiento, *Viajes al Estrecho,* vol. 2, p. 343.

[5] Richard Hakluyt first published a brief contemporary summary of the armada and its encounter with Fenton's expedition, written by the Portuguese Lopez Vaz, as 'An extract out of the discourse of one Lopez a Spaniard before spoken of, touching the foresayd fight of M. Fenton with the Spanish ships together with a report of the proceeding of M. John Drake after his departing from him', in PN1(1589), pp. 673–4. This was republished as 'An extract out of the discourse of one Lopez Vaz a Portugal, touching the fight of M. Fenton with the Spanish ships, with a report of the proceeding of M. John Drake after his departing from him to the river of Plate', in PN2 (1600), vol. III, pp. 727–8. Hakluyt published the full 'Discourse of the West Indies and South Sea written by Lopez Vaz a Portugal' in PN2, III, pp. 778–802. These are most easily accessible in PN(M), the 12-volume edition of PN2 published in Glasgow, 1903–5, vol. XI, pp. 92–5, 227–90. Vaz summarizes the activities of the armada, pp. 249, 266–73.

with five ships and some 600 men in July of 1584. In September of that year, another three ships and 200 men arrived with the armada's second in command, Almirante Diego de la Rivera,[1] who had carried the colonizers to the Strait.

2.   Documentation of the Voyage and Pedro de Rada's *Relación*

Despite a wealth of extant archival material and the extraordinary efforts required to plan and carry out its three-year mission, the Armada of the Strait has been largely ignored or misrepresented in standard histories of Spanish overseas ventures. Detailed records were kept of the ships, men, and provisions amassed for the armada, as well as for the planned settlement and fortifications at the Strait.[2] During the expedition, the chief scribe, Pedro de Rada, wrote thousands of pages of official documentation. Other individuals also wrote reports and letters about their experiences. Shortly after Flores returned to Spain in July of 1584, the king requested all of Rada's records.[3] The documentation he submitted included recruitment papers of soldiers and sailors on the five ships owned by the crown, along with lists of their supplies and armament. Rada also recorded the last wills and testaments of those who died during the expedition, with after-death inventories of their belongings. His other papers included orders for the various officers in the fleet; letters, petitions, and testimonies to and from officials in Brazil; and records of legal proceedings against wrongdoers.

Rada noted that the documents he conveyed to the crown were 'all those that have been made in this expedition of Magellan, beyond which I have no other'.[4] Nonetheless, he had also written a *Relación* or report covering the entire voyage, with copies of various official documents appended. Rich in detail and human drama, Rada's *Relación* provides a unique perspective on the events and personalities involved in the Armada of the Strait, opening a new window onto the geo-politics of the time and its human cost. It is not clear for whom he wrote the report or for what purpose, and he presumably did not consider it part of the official documentation. He does not appear to have submitted his *Relación* to the crown, and it was not deposited in the Archivo General de Simancas in north-central Spain, where most official documents for overseas ventures from the sixteenth

---

[1] Rivera sometimes appears in contemporary documents as Ribera.

[2] The Armada of the Strait is one of the best-documented expeditions in the whole of Spanish history, with countless bundles of official papers extant in Spanish archives. Historians such as Martín Fernández de Navarrete; Pablo Pastells and Constantino Bayle; Clements R. Markham and Ángel Rosenblat transcribed many volumes of those documents, some of which are available in modern editions. See also *CODOIN*, vols 34 and 94; Navarrete, *Colección de documentos*, esp. vol. 20, pts 1 and 2. The original manuscript volumes of the Navarrete collection are in the AMN in Madrid. They were copied from various state and private archives at the end of the 18th century and carefully proofread in order to compile a record of documents pertaining to maritime affairs. The modern publication of facsimiles made the full collection of 39 volumes more widely available, and many academic libraries worldwide own the set. Although most of the original documents still exist in Spanish state archives, the Navarrete collection is much more accessible, so it will be cited by preference here. Selected documents also appear in Sarmiento, *Narratives of the Voyages*; Sarmiento, *Viajes al Estrecho*, 2 vols; Landín, *Vida y viajes de Pedro Sarmiento*, pp. 213–88; Pastells and Bayle, *Descubrimiento del Estrecho de Magallanes*.

[3] Secretary Juan de Ledesma to Rada, late July 1584, in Navarrete, *Colección de documentos*, vol. 20, ff. 365r–366v.

[4] Rada to Secretary Ledesma, c.1 Aug. 1584, in Navarrete, *Colección de documentos*, vol. 20, f. 366v.

century resided until they were moved in 1785 to the newly established Archivo General de las Indias in Seville. Instead, Rada's *Relación* remained in private hands for centuries, until the Henry E. Huntington Library in San Marino, California, purchased it in 1999 and effectively moved it into the public sphere.

Until Rada's *Relación* surfaced, the Armada of the Strait was known largely from the point of view of Pedro Sarmiento de Gamboa (hereafter Sarmiento), the governor-designate of the future colony at the Strait and an implacable enemy of Captain General Flores. Their contemporary Richard Hakluyt was interested in the possibilities of founding English colonies in the area south of the Río de la Plata in the 1580s,[1] and his *Principall Navigations* included material about the Armada of the Strait.[2] Over time, Sarmiento's emotional and opinionated version of events overwhelmed all other voices regarding the armada and influenced generations of historians. In 1895, the Hakluyt Society published translated excerpts from Sarmiento's voluminous writings, edited by R. Clements Markham.[3] The publication, in the mid-twentieth century, of documents from Fenton's voyage clarified many aspects of his failed expedition but did little to alter the historiography of the Armada of the Strait.[4] By contrast, Pedro de Rada's *Relación* provides the reader with an official, dispassionate voice to contrast with the self-serving accounts by Sarmiento. More broadly, Rada's narrative complements other sources and adds important new information about French and English interests in Brazil at a crucial period in the European rivalry for overseas territory, especially the complicated struggle for the South Atlantic in the late sixteenth century.

Above all, Rada's first-hand account, together with the extensive Spanish documentation about the preparations for the voyage, clearly shows how the most meticulous plans for overseas ventures could be wrecked by the hazards inherent in sailing into largely unknown waters – in this case, the often-terrifying South Atlantic. Those plans could also be jeopardized by personal conflicts that had entirely human causes. In modern histories of early exploration and colonization mention of personal antagonisms is generally avoided as a petty distraction from the central, heroic narrative. Likewise, Rada's laconic account only hints at the ongoing clash between Flores and Sarmiento. Nonetheless, by reading Rada's journal in the light of other contemporary documentation, we can understand the extraordinary logistical efforts required to launch the expedition in the first place and to carry out at least some of its objectives. We can also understand the difficulties posed by the enmity between Sarmiento and Flores and appreciate what the expedition was able to accomplish despite that enmity.

3. Rada's Manuscript

In its present state, Rada's account of the voyage, and the copies of various official documents which he included, covers ninety-three numbered folio sheets of paper (300 × 210 mm), for a total of 194 written pages. The paper is in good condition, apart from

---

[1] Andrews, 'Drake and South America', p. 55, citing Taylor, *Original Writings*, p. 142.

[2] See above, p. 1, n. 5.

[3] Sarmiento, *Narratives of the Voyages*.

[4] For example, Donno, *Diary of Richard Madox,* pp. 51–4, 121–7; Taylor, *Troublesome Voyage, passim*; Andrews, *Elizabethan Privateering*, pp. 203–5. See also McDermott, 'Fenton'.

damp stains, ink-bleed, or worm holes on some leaves. The foliated pages are bound in 'contemporary Spanish blind-stamped calf with gilt sprigs', with minor chipping and wear on the spine.[1] A watermark on some pages shows a cross with wide equal arms within a shield shaped like a drop of water.[2] The handwriting is a clear, sixteenth-century Spanish script generally called *cortesana* (courtly script). The text presents few difficulties to transcribe, despite frequent abbreviations, variable orthography, and a virtual lack of punctuation and paragraphing. A table of contents at the beginning of the volume refers to the numbered leaves or folios for sections of the narrative and the copies of official documents that follow. Overall, the physical appearance and organization of the volume suggest that the text and accompanying documents were written before being copied onto folios and bound. At the end of the last copied document, Rada adds his signature and personal rubric, in the same hand as the rest of the volume. In short, the whole appears to be an original manuscript written by Pedro de Rada, but the condition of the paper does not suggest that it spent much time at sea. Rather, it seems likely that Rada made a fair copy of his original log, as well as the various documents that follow it, after the expedition returned in July of 1584.

The only variant handwriting appears in the endorsements of ownership, written at the beginning and end of the bound manuscript. These indicate that a family named Chópite owned the manuscript in 1742. It eventually found its way into the library of James P. R. Lyell, but there is no indication of its location or ownership before its acquisition by Lyell. Bernard Quaritch, a London dealer in rare books and manuscripts, acquired the manuscript in 1951, along with many others from Lyell's library. The Huntington Library purchased the manuscript from Quaritch in 1999.

4. Brazil as a Venue for European Rivalries

Despite its official designation, the Armada of the Strait was to spend most of its time and energy in Brazil, bolstering Portuguese defences, ensuring the loyalty of local officials to King Philip, and expelling other European interlopers.

Although the Treaty of Tordesillas (1494) between Castile and Portugal had allotted Brazil to the latter, for the first three decades of the sixteenth century the Portuguese presence in Brazil was confined to periodic reconnaissance expeditions and casual trade with the coastal tribes for dye woods and other exotic commodities. While individual Portuguese seamen had married native women and settled in indigenous communities, the first permanent Portuguese colonies were not founded until the early 1530s. Between 1534 and 1536 the Portuguese crown divided the vast territory into largely independent hereditary captaincies, with little coordination among them. A map attributed to Luís Teixeira shows the boundaries of the various captaincies, along with the names of hundreds of settlements, nearly all of them along the coast.[3] The Portuguese crown did

---

[1] From the catalogue description of the manuscript from the dealer in rare books Bernard Quaritch. Quaritch catalogue 1257, item 167.

[2] Ibid. According to the catalogue entry, the watermark is similar to Briquet, *Filigranes*, items 5681, 5682 and 5683, dated 1561–82, and Heawood, *Watermarks*, item 968, dated Seville 1571.

[3] The map is part of a codex in the Ajuda Library in Lisbon. *Roteiro de Todos os Sinaes conhecimientos, fundos, baixos, Alturos, e derrotas que ha na costa do Brasil desdo Cabo de Sāto Agostinho até o estreito de Fernão de*

not impose direct royal government over Brazil until 1549, when King João III installed the first governor-general at Bahia,[1] reclaiming ultimate authority from the captaincies. Thereafter, the expansion of Portuguese settlements and the establishment of permanent sugar plantations created a new demand for food supplies and Indian labour which, together with epidemic disease, ravaged the indigenous groups along the coast and exacerbated local conflicts and the capture and trade in slaves. The presence of French settlements and individual adventurers also complicated Portuguese interaction with local tribes.

Faced with the linguistic, social, and locational complexity represented by the numerous, politically fragmented coastal peoples of Brazil, early European observers classified them into two general groups which they differentiated as 'Tupi' and 'Tapuia'. They identified the 'Tupi' as having more sedentary settlement and developed horticulture, with warfare, ritual sacrifice of captives and cannibalism central to their culture. The language of the 'Tupi', categorized by the Portuguese as the *lingua geral da costa* (general language of the coast), was one of several associated dialects of Tupi-Guaraní spoken by many peoples along the coast. The 'Tapuia', also cannibals and categorized as primitive hunter-gathers, were Gê-speakers. Portuguese interactions were largely with the Tupi-Guaraní speakers settled along the coast between the Río de la Plata and the Amazon. Recent scholarship has again combined the many disparate polities into two broad groups, identifying those to the south of São Vicente as Guaraní, and those northward to the Amazon as Tupinambá.[2] Some tribes made alliances with either the French or the Portuguese exclusively; others shifted their loyalties to their best advantage.[3] The most powerful and dangerous Indian tribes were those usually grouped together as 'Tupi' – all of them cannibals – who killed their foes for sacrificial

---

Magalhão. It shows the general state of settlement in Brazil up to the mid-1580s, though some elements date from decades earlier. See Alegria, 'Portuguese Cartography', p. 990. Teixeira represents the demarcation line between Portuguese and Spanish spheres of influence, established by the Treaty of Tordesillas in 1494, about 10 degrees too far to the west, which would have placed the Río de la Plata region within the Portuguese sphere. The current scholarly consensus dates the map as finished *c.*1585–6, but the donataries named on the map for several captaincies had died before 1585, and there is no indication of the forts built by the Armada of the Strait in 1583 in Santos and in 1584 near the Paraíba River. The map has appeared in several modern publications, most accessibly in J. B. Harley, D. Woodward et al., *History of Cartography*, vol. III, pt one, plate 33. For a digitalized image, manipulated for legibility and with the scale of latitudes slightly altered, see J. Pimentel Cintra, 'Reconstruindo o Mapa', pp. 11–45. I thank Joyce Lorimer for locating this article. Both the original and the digitalized image appear on various websites on the internet.

[1] For the full name of this city, see below, pp. 46, n. 1, 59, n. 1.

[2] For extended discussion of the complex identities and relationships of Brazilian tribes and linguistic families in the 16th century, see Monteiro, 'Crises and Transformations', pp. 973–7; and Wright and da Cunha, 'Destruction, Resistance, and Transformation', pp. 287–94, 299, 314–18, 324–6, 328–9, 334–6, 340–41, 347–9, 363, 370–78. Wright and da Cunha include a map (19.1) of the location of 52 ethnic groups.

[3] Travellers' accounts of Brazil discuss these relationships in detail. The German Hans Staden wrote from a personal perspective as a captive of a French-allied group, and his *Warhäftig Historia* (1557) was one of the first captivity narratives in European literature. The most recent English edition of Staden's *True History* was edited by Neil L. Whitehead and Michael Harbsmeier (2008). Boucher, *Les Nouvelles Frances*, pp. xvii–xxi, lists virtually all the contemporary accounts of France's overseas ventures in the early modern period. The best-known are Léry, *Voyage* (1578), and its English translation, Léry, *History of the Voyage* (1990); and Thevet, *France antarctique* (1558), and its English translation, Thevet, *Antarctik* (1568).

rituals and for food. The various 'Tupi' tribes were each associated with a particular area, and the rivalries of contiguous groups kept Brazil in a state of almost continual conflict.[1]

French traders had made incursions into Brazil from as early as 1503, challenging the validity of Portuguese claims based on the Treaty of Tordesillas. The great prize was brazil wood, the raw material for a brilliant red dye (*brazilin*) valued by the European textile industry.[2] Europeans had encountered a similar species of tree in Asia, with wood the colour of a burning ember (*brasa* in Portuguese).[3] In 1500, Pedro Álvares Cabral named the land he discovered south of the Equator in the Western Hemisphere the 'Terra do brasil' (Land of brasil) for the similar trees that grew there; the name Brazil soon came to apply to the land itself.

Although the Portuguese claimed exclusive rights to exploit the dye wood,[4] French seafarers, merchants, and settlers soon established a regular trade with the coastal tribes. By 1529 textile-manufacturers in Rouen were receiving Brazilian dye wood from Dieppe traders, and artists sailing in the Dieppe vessels depicted the land, its inhabitants, and French trading factories. This information was transferred onto the decorative maps produced by the so-called Dieppe school of cartography from the late 1530s to the 1550s.[5] Spain was also interested in the promise of Brazil and collected information about the towns, ports, and local inhabitants.[6] Some English trade with Brazil also occurred from 1530 to 1542, but very little thereafter until a renewal of interest in the late 1570s.[7] French interest persisted, despite setbacks. In 1555 Nicolas Durand de Villegaignon settled a mixture of Calvinists and recruits from French prisons on an island in Guanabara Bay and on the opposing mainland, near the future site of Rio de Janeiro. Although hunger and dissension among the colonists facilitated their expulsion by the Portuguese in 1567, successive rulers of France continued to plan for colonies in Brazil, referred to as 'la France antarctique'.[8]

During the late sixteenth century, virtually the whole of coastal Brazil was involved in a series of battles and skirmishes that became known as the 'Brazil Wood Wars', as Portuguese settlers, French interlopers, and other Europeans formed a complicated and shifting network of alliances with local tribes. Portuguese colonial officials spent much of the sixteenth century trying to consolidate their control of the Brazilian littoral. During

---

[1] Monteiro, 'Crises and Transformations', pp. 986–9, analyses the central importance of warfare to the various 'Tupi' groups.

[2] Due to its beauty, strength, and flexibility, brazil wood (*Caesalpinia echinata*) also became popular in 17th-century Europe for making bows for stringed instruments.

[3] Known as sappanwood (*Caesalpinia punctata*), the tree grows widely in East Asia.

[4] In the early 16th century, the Portuguese crown allowed anyone to harvest brazil wood in exchange for a fee of 1 *cruzado* per *quintal*. By the late 16th century, however, would-be exporters had to contract with the crown for a licence that cost about 40,000 *cruzados* for 10,000 *quintales* per year. Anyone without an official licence was an illegal interloper; Brandao, *Great Things of Brazil*, p. 223. For French incursions into Brazil, see Johnson, 'Portuguese Settlement of Brazil', pp. 258–61.

[5] Jean Rotz produced perhaps the most famous Dieppe atlas, the *Boke of Ydrography*, presented to Henry VIII of England in 1541. See Wallis, *Maps and Text of the Boke of Ydrography*. See also Buisseret, *Mapmakers' Quest*, p. 42 and pl. X; Brunelle, 'Dieppe School', pp. 237–8.

[6] For example, see the report by the pilot Juan Sánchez de Vizcaya, dated c.1543, AGI, Patronato, leg. 28, doc. 45.

[7] Andrews, *Trade, Plunder and Settlement*, pp. 59–60, 138–45.

[8] Thevet, *France antarctique* (1558). Dickason, *Myth of the Savage*, pp. 181–93, discusses the history of French settlement and interactions with local tribes in Brazil.

the 1560s and 1570s, the Portuguese and their Indian allies managed to push several rival native groups inland away from the coast. They even arranged a truce with their long-term enemies the Potiguara from 1560 to 1574, though warfare resumed thereafter as the French supplied weapons to the Potiguara and taught them how to build European-style defensive works. At least two French expeditions were planned to conquer Brazil in the aftermath of the death of King Sebastião I of Portugal, one in 1579 and another in 1582, despite the current civil wars in France.[1] Spain's European rivals continued to hope that Brazil would be open for foreign incursions if Philip II could not make good his claim to the Portuguese throne.

5.   The Spanish Response to Drake's Passage through the Strait of Magellan

The accession of Philip II of Spain as King Philip I of Portugal in 1580 offered the possibility of increased defences for Portuguese Brazil, but Spain's control of the area south of Brazil was tenuous at best. Spanish exploration of the Pacific after Magellan's time had proceeded from New Spain or Peru, rather than directly from Spain. Even after Spaniards had conquered the Inca Empire in Peru in the 1530s, the route through the Strait held little appeal. In addition to the distance and logistical challenges involved in sailing from Europe through the Strait, the south-western Atlantic features some of the roughest seas and strongest winds on Earth. It was preferable to communicate with Peru by way of the Caribbean and the Isthmus of Panama, trusting to the natural defences of the South Atlantic to keep European rivals from entering the Pacific through the Strait of Magellan. That trust vanished when Francis Drake attacked both Iberian empires.

Rada devotes several folios to Drake's raids as the genesis of the Armada of the Strait.[2] The viceroys of both Peru and New Spain[3] wrote to Philip II and to each other immediately after the raids, but it took months for the news to arrive. The viceroy of Peru

---

[1] A map of Brazil by Jacques de Vau de Claye (1579) included the coat of arms of Filippo Strozzi, a cousin of Catherine de Medici, queen mother of France. The map showed areas in north-eastern Brazil where Strozzi could supposedly recruit 10,000 Indian allies to fight against the Portuguese; BNF, Cartes et Plans Rés, GE D 13871. Catherine planned that Strozzi would sail to the Azores to support Dom António, the Prior of Crato, head of the Order of the Knights of St John of Jerusalem and a rival claimant to Philip II for the Portuguese throne. Dom António claimed the Portuguese throne after the death of Cardinal Henry, who reigned in Portugal from 1578 to 1580, despite the latters's decision, before his death in January 1580, to support the claims of Philip II. Merriman, *Rise of the Spanish Empire*, vol. 4, pp. 351–4. It was planned that, after securing the throne for Dom António, Strozzi would conquer Brazil. He carried letters from Catherine de Medici appointing him lieutenant general or viceroy of unnamed lands overseas, which the Spanish understood to mean Brazil. Strozzi was killed in 1582 at the Battle of Terceira in the Azores, when Spanish forces defeated the French, but that did not end the French threat to Brazil. See Roncière, 'Carte française', p. 590; Buisseret, *Monarchs, Ministers, and Maps*, p. 106; Safier, *Measuring the New World*, pp. 81–2.

[2] See below, pp. 62–4.

[3] In the late 16th century, Nueva España (New Spain) included the area from Mexico south to Panama. Spain's fleet system was organized around voyages to New Spain and to Tierra Firme, effectively the northern coast of South America, but by extension all of South America apart from Brazil. The Viceroyalty of Peru in the late 16th century had jurisdiction over that vast extended territory. For a good general overview of colonial Spanish America, see Burkholder and Johnson, *Colonial Latin America*, pp. 79–97; Bethell, *Cambridge History of Latin America*, vol. 1. Spain's Atlantic fleet system in the 16th century is discussed in Phillips, *Six Galleons*, pp. 8–15.

at the time, Don Francisco Álvarez de Toledo, arranged an expedition to search for Drake southward along the Pacific coast, assuming that he would return to England and unaware that he had headed northward. The viceroy's expedition included two ships with four pilots, fifty-two mariners, and forty soldiers, all well-provided with arms and munitions. The ships left Callao, the port of Lima, on 11 October 1579, under the command of Pedro Sarmiento. To explore in the shallower depths of the Strait, they carried a disassembled *bergantín*, which they put together after reaching its western mouth.[1] According to Sarmiento's letter to the king, the viceroy had ordered him not only to pursue Drake, but

> more especially to examine the Strait of Magellan by which the said robber had entered [into the Pacific], to survey it and proceed to give a report to Your Majesty setting forth the needs of that land and applying for a remedy, that Your Majesty might order it to be settled and fortified, so that this way might be closed, for the security of the Indies and of the other lands of your Majesty situated on the shores of the Southern Sea [Pacific Ocean].[2]

Sarmiento entered the western mouth of the Strait on 22 January 1580 and produced a detailed map of his trajectory before exiting from the eastern mouth on 24 February. The other ship in the expedition, under Juan de Villalobos, separated from Sarmiento shortly after reaching the Strait, and Sarmiento wrote to the viceroy that Villalobos had deliberately deserted the expedition. During a sojourn in Chile, Villalobos and his men helped to quell an Indian uprising and then returned to Lima. Meanwhile, Sarmiento continued across the Atlantic Ocean, stopping briefly in Cape Verde, where he sent one of the pilots back to Peru, by way of Panama, to report to the viceroy. The pilot arrived in Lima in early September of 1580.[3] The viceroy took Villalobos into custody, based on Sarmiento's accusations.[4] During the investigation, however, soldiers with Villalobos testified that fierce storms had forced them to turn back north from the Strait.[5]

By the time that Sarmiento reached Spain on 19 August 1580, the government had been discussing the response to Drake's raids for more than a year. When Philip II first learned of the attacks, he wrote to Viceroy Toledo to ask his opinion. The viceroy responded, in a letter dated 27 November 1579, that he had thought long and hard about the matter and had consulted various experts and royal officials in Lima. Based on those consultations, he reiterated his earlier opinion that in the short term the best defence would be to build several galleys to patrol the entrance to the Strait. He also reported on the expedition he had sent to the Strait a month and a half earlier. Although the viceroy did not mention Sarmiento by name, he noted that he had appointed 'a person of much

---

[1] Sarmiento, *Viajes al Estrecho,* vol. 1, p. 44; Sarmiento, *Narratives of the Voyages,* pp. 59–60. In the late 16th century, a *bergantín* was a small, light skiff with a single lateen sail and open deck. Later ships called brigantines had very different characteristics.

[2] Sarmiento, *Narratives of the Voyages,* p. 227. Viceroy Toledo's detailed instructions to Sarmiento appear on pp. 8–17. The volume, edited and translated by Clements R. Markham, makes some of the documents of the voyage accessible to English-speaking readers. Only a small number of the extant documents are included, however, and most are excerpted. Moreover, the translations are not consistently reliable. When Markham's translations are consistent with Spanish-language editions, they will be cited here. Otherwise, passages will be cited and/or translated from Spanish editions.

[3] Sarmiento, *Viajes al Estrecho,* vol. 1, p. 194.

[4] Ibid., vol. 1, pp. 81–2, n. 1.

[5] AGI, Patronato, leg. 33, N. 2, R. 10, cited in Landin, *Vida y viajes de Pedro Sarmiento,* pp. 234–5.

intelligence in matters of the sea and a great mathematician and cosmographer' to lead the expedition and told the king to expect his arrival at court.[1]

Philip II referred the viceroy's letter to the Council of the Indies to consider. The council reported back on 30 June 1580, summarizing the viceroy's main points and supporting his short-term plan to build galleys to patrol the entrances to the Strait. The council urged the king to sign the royal *cédulas* (orders) that had been prepared to that effect. In fact, the king had already authorized the building of such galleys in a letter to the viceroy on 2 December 1578, but a lack of funds had stalled their construction.[2] The king pondered the council's advice regarding the Strait for much of the summer of 1580, but he had other things on his mind related to the volatile political situation in Europe. Spain was increasingly involved in the chaotic series of struggles known as the 'French Wars of Religion' as well as a rebellion in the Netherlands. Moreover, England's Queen Elizabeth I was increasingly perceived as an enemy after Drake's raids, although she was careful not to provoke Spain openly.[3]

Despite his other concerns, it was clear to Philip II and his councillors that something had to be done quickly to safeguard the Americas. Drake's bold attacks had demonstrated the vulnerability of both Spanish and Portuguese colonies, and intelligence reports indicated that other English adventurers hoped to replicate Drake's successful melding of trade and plunder. Presumably, they hoped to gain support from Englishmen who lived in Brazil and farther south along the coast towards the Strait.[4] Despite their small numbers, English settlers would play a role in the unfolding drama of the expedition chronicled by Pedro de Rada.

6.   Personal Conflict in the Armada of the Strait: Sarmiento versus Flores

Like any large enterprise, the Armada of the Strait was bound to have a range of personalities and a certain amount of disagreement and friction among its participants. Nonetheless, one ongoing clash all but defined the Armada of the Strait: the enmity between Pedro Sarmiento, governor-designate of the colony to be planted at the Strait, and Don Diego Flores de Valdés,[5] captain general of the armada as a whole. Their continual wrangles began during the planning stages of the armada in 1581 and continued after the expedition ended in 1584. Historians know quite a bit about their disagreements, and virtually everyone who has written about the voyage has taken the side of Sarmiento.[6] One likely reason is that Sarmiento wrote much of the documentation published to date, endlessly arguing his own side of the story; praising his own actions; and accusing Flores of numerous character flaws, mistaken judgment, evil intent, incompetence, and fraud. In

[1] Viceroy Don Francisco de Toledo to Philip II, 27 Nov. 1579, in Navarrete, *Colección de documentos*, vol. 20, f. 110r–v.

[2] Navarrete, *Colección de documentos,* vol. 20, f. 111v.

[3] MacCaffrey, *Queen Elizabeth and the Making of Policy, 1572–88*, pp. 130, 253–5, 268–74, 281–2, 288, 316–23.

[4] Sarmiento wrote about the presence of Englishmen on both the east and west coasts of South America in the chronicle of his voyage through the Strait in 1579–80. Sarmiento, *Derrotero al Estrecho*, pp. 42, 196, 198–200, 209–10. See also Sarmiento, *Narratives of the Voyages*, pp. 179–95.

[5] Hereafter referred to as Flores.

[6] For example, Pastells and Bayle, *Descubrimiento del Estrecho de Magallanes*, pp. 251–312.

the published historical accounts that mention the voyage and the attempt to plant a colony at the Strait, Sarmiento emerges as a hero – flawed, as all heroes are – but a hero nonetheless. Flores emerges as a villain – or at best, as an inept foil for Sarmiento's heroic actions.[1] Even the great historian of Spain's Atlantic fleets, Pierre Chaunu, was inclined to accept Sarmiento's version of events, although he noted that another prominent historian 'gave too much credence to his documents ... and Sarmiento failed in the end'.[2] Because Pedro de Rada does not mention the conflict between Sarmiento and Flores, and because it is crucial to understanding the history of the Armada of the Strait, some background is necessary here.

The enmity between the two men began with the king's decision to appoint Flores as captain general. Sarmiento's biographers suggest that he deserved the post because he was the one who had persuaded the king to send an armada to the Strait. Nonetheless, Flores was the logical choice for the position, given the prior careers of both men. Sarmiento, born in Alcalá de Henares near Madrid, built his career in the rough-and-tumble atmosphere that followed the Spanish conquest of the Americas. He was in New Spain by 1555 but fled to Peru two years later, though it is not clear why. Well-versed in astronomy, history, geography, and cosmography, he ran afoul of the Inquisition in Lima at least twice, but the inquisitors did not find sufficient evidence to convict him. Sarmiento evidently influenced the decision of the interim viceroy of Peru, Don Lope García de Castro (1565–9), to send an expedition into the Pacific in search of the legendary Solomon Islands. Instead of appointing Sarmiento as its captain general, however, the viceroy chose his nephew, Álvaro de Mendaña, and sent Sarmiento as the expedition's cosmographer. During what proved to be a successful voyage in 1567, Sarmiento quarrelled with the twenty-five-year-old Mendaña and maintained a protracted legal battle against him thereafter.[3] Nonetheless, Sarmiento continued to serve as a soldier in Peru, helping to suppress Inca resistance to Spanish rule. He gained the support of the new viceroy, Don Francisco Álvarez de Toledo (1569–81), who urged him to write a history of the Incas in 1572, which chronicled and justified the Spanish conquest.[4] Sarmiento continued his work as a cosmographer in Peru until Viceroy Toledo sent him to the Strait in pursuit of Drake in 1579. Despite his undoubted learning and intelligence and his experience as a soldier and cosmographer, Sarmiento could not match the social status of Flores or his decades of naval service to the crown.

Diego Flores de Valdés was born between 1530 and 1535, the son of Juan Flores and Doña Urraca de Valdés; both families had impeccable noble credentials in Asturias in

---

[1] In the index to Sarmiento, *Narratives of the Voyages*, p. 392, virtually every mention of Flores is a litany of prejudicial language. Setting the tone, Markham's introduction (p. xxvii) mentions 'the disgraceful conduct of Diego Flores, of Sarmiento's inexhaustible patience and determination, of the final establishment of two settlements in the Straits of Magellan, and of the subsequent misfortunes and adventures of Sarmiento'.

[2] Chaunu, *Séville et l'Atlantique*, vol. 3, p. 296, referring to Pablo Pastells, a member of the Society of Jesus and a tireless researcher in the Archive of the Indies in Seville. Despite his reservations, Chaunu lists the Armada of the Strait as the 'armada going to the Strait of Magellan, under the direction of Pedro Sarmiento de Gamboa, captain general, Diego Flores de Valdés'; ibid., vol. 3, p. 292. In fact, the armada was not under Sarmiento's direction, though he claimed as much. See below, pp. 16, 18–19, 21–2, 27–8, 57, n. 5, 65.

[3] See Mendaña, *Discovery of the Solomon Islands*, vol. 2, pp. 502–12.

[4] The book remains an important source of information about Peru and its people. Modern editions are available in Spanish and English. See Sarmiento, *Historia de los Incas* and *History of the Incas*.

northern Spain. One of Diego's maternal uncles was Pedro Menéndez de Avilés, a distinguished naval commander in Spain's Atlantic fleets.[1] As soon as Philip II came to the throne in 1558, he and his advisers had to deal with incursions by interlopers and corsairs near what they called La Florida. Pedro Menéndez became indispensable to that effort. Menéndez's instructions from the crown in 1562–3 reflected the need for heightened security and royal control of Spain's Atlantic fleets.[2] In 1564, the king named Menéndez as the *adelantado* of La Florida, which gave him responsibility for conquering and settling the area and protecting Spain's claims to exclusive control of that important outpost in North America.[3]

Diego Flores, like his uncle and many other members of their clan, would make his career in royal service at sea, undoubtedly aided by his noble status and service to the royal family. In 1554, when the future Philip II – then heir to the throne as Prince of Asturias – married Mary Tudor, Diego Flores was part of the entourage accompanying the prince to England.[4] Diego and the prince were close in age, Philip having been born in 1527, which may have fostered the trust and loyalty that seems to have characterized their relationship. Flores reinforced Philip II's trust by his long years of service and his competence as a naval officer. He went to sea quite early in life, according to his uncle, though he left no trace in the sparse official records for the 1540s and 1550s.[5] Nonetheless, in 1565 Menéndez wrote that Diego Flores had already served the crown for fifteen years, and Flores corroborated that several years later.[6] During those long years at sea, he acquired familiarity with Atlantic sailing, attaining the rank of captain, and demonstrated his commitment to royal service and imperial defence.

Captain Diego Flores was second in command to Pedro Menéndez de Avilés in the 1565 expedition that ousted the French from La Florida and made clear that interlopers would not be tolerated.[7] Menéndez dispatched Flores to Spain with news of the victory, praising him and asking the king to honour his efforts with admission to a military order and financial rewards.[8] The king was well pleased with news of the victory and with the emissary. To reward his service, Philip II nominated Flores to the military Order of Santiago on 31 March 1566, setting in motion the legal process required for his

[1] Hereafter referred to as Menéndez. See Lyon, *Enterprise of Florida*, pp. 71–7, for the Menéndez family clan in Asturias. I have not been able to locate records of Diego Flores's baptism.

[2] Chaunu, *Séville et l'Atlantique*, vol. 3, p. 268; Navarrete, *Colección de documentos*, vol. 21, ff. 349r–353v.

[3] The designation *adelantado* (lit., one sent on ahead) referred to someone given authority in an area not yet firmly held by the crown, such as the frontier regions in medieval Spain during the ongoing wars against the Muslims. La Florida, which included much of what is now the south-eastern United States, was a similar frontier territory in the 16th century.

[4] Martin and Parker, *Spanish Armada*, p. 26.

[5] As late as the 1560s, the records provide little detail about the fleets, according to Chaunu, whose multi-volume work on Spain's Atlantic fleets remains a fundamental resource. Chaunu, *Séville et l'Atlantique*, vol. 2, p. 587.

[6] Menéndez to Philip II, 15 October 1565, in Menéndez de Avilés, *Cartas sobre la Florida*, p. 154, copied from AGI, Santo Domingo, leg. 231. In 1570, Flores noted that he had already served the crown for 23 years. Flores to Philip II in Navarrete, *Colección de documentos*, vol. 22, f. 155v.

[7] For a detailed analysis of that campaign and its participants; see Lyon, *Enterprise of Florida, passim*. See also Meide and de Bry, 'Lost French Fleet', pp. 79–82.

[8] Menéndez to Philip II, 15 Oct. 1565, in Menéndez de Avilés, *Cartas sobre la Florida*, p. 154, from AGI, Santo Domingo, leg. 231.

admission.[1] In addition, during a hunting expedition in the forest of Segovia on 4 August 1566, the king granted Flores an award of 2,000 ducats for his service in La Florida.[2]

Thereafter, Flores joined the ranks of the principal naval commanders in Spain's Atlantic fleets. He first served as captain general of the Tierra Firme fleet in 1567,[3] and did so again in 1569, 1570, and 1572. Each time, he was in charge of several dozen vessels and thousands of men. In the 1569 fleet, Flores transported the newly appointed viceroy of Peru, Francisco Álvarez de Toledo, the count of Oropesa, to Panama, from whence he would continue on to Lima.[4] It is worth noting that even such a distinguished royal appointee had no authority in the fleet, and, indeed, none except what courtesy demanded, until he reached his viceroyalty.

In command of the Tierra Firme fleets of 1570 and 1572, Flores helped to pioneer a revised sailing schedule for Spain's Atlantic fleet system. To protect the ever-larger merchant contingents sailing from New Spain and Tierra Firme, both fleets would rendezvous in Havana before sailing back to Spain with an escort of armed warships – the Armada de la Guardia, or guard squadron – first commanded by Pedro Menéndez de Avilés, then by Diego Flores in 1574–5.[5] Pedro Menéndez Márquez, another nephew of Pedro Menéndez de Avilés, served as the squadron's captain general in 1576. The following year, the king conveyed command of the squadron to Cristóbal de Eraso, another noble veteran of the Atlantic fleets, but Flores was given command again in 1580. This series of events may help to explain the rivalry between Eraso and Flores and his clan, which would surface in preparations for the Armada of the Strait.[6] By 1580, the guard squadron consisted of one large galleass of 700 *toneladas*,[7] named *San Cristóbal*;

[1] AHN, OM, Pruebas de Santiago, 1566, expediente 3107. The Órden de Santiago was arguably the most prestigious of Spain's military orders, established during the medieval reconquest of territory from Muslim control. Acceptance as a *caballero* (lit., horseman; knight) in one of the military orders raised a simple nobleman (*hidalgo*) to the middling ranks of the Spanish nobility.

[2] BNE, MS 781, parte 389, f. 95r–v, Royal order to pay Diego Flores de Valdés 2,000 ducats, 4 Aug. 1566.

[3] AGI, Indiferente, leg. 738, R. 8; Chaunu, *Séville et l'Atlantique,* vol. 3, pp. 105, 126; Navarrete, *Colección de documentos*, vol. 21, f. 443 and vol. 22, ff. 495r–498v.

[4] Chaunu, *Séville et l'Atlantique*, vol. 3, pp. 128–35. Until the founding of Portobelo in 1597, the Tierra Firme fleet used the port of Nombre de Dios on the Isthmus of Panama to transfer goods, passengers, and revenue to and from the Viceroyalty of Peru.

[5] Chaunu, *Séville et l'Atlantique*, vol. 3, pp. 146–53, 168–77, 194–205, 217. Chaunu describes the returning squadron in 1574 as the 'galleons of Pedro Menéndez de Avilés', but Flores was their captain general. His uncle lay ill in Santander and died on 16 September 1574, likely from typhus. See Menéndez de Avilés, *Cartas sobre la Florida*, p. 290, n. 401. Chaunu, *Séville et l'Atlantique*, vol. 3, p. 232, mistakenly gives the year of his death as 1576. See also Navarrete, *Colección de documentos*, vol. 22, f. 511r–v. Together, the fleets for New Spain and Tierra Firme contained an average of 150 or more large vessels each year in the late 16th century. See Chaunu, *Séville et l'Atlantique*, vol. 3, *passim*, for lists of commanders, ships, and tonnages in Spain's Indies fleets from 1561 to 1595.

[6] Don Cristóbal de Eraso had experience as a soldier in the armies of Flanders and Italy before serving the crown at sea. He was appointed captain general of several Indies fleets in the 1560s and early 1570s. Eraso had once served in the royal household , and he has also been called the first Spanish military engineer to reach the New World, where he began the fortifications at San Juan de Ulúa to guard Veracruz. See Buisseret, 'Spanish Military Engineers', p. 46, citing Moncada Maya, *Ingenieros militares*, p. 20.

[7] The Spanish *tonelada* was an indication of both a ship's volume and carrying capacity. In southern Spain in the later 16th century, the *tonelada* was equal to two *pipas* (barrels) of 27.5 *arrobas* each, according to Juan Escalante de Mendoza writing in 1575; Escalante, *Itinerario de navegación*, pp. 461–2. For *arroba*, see above, pp. xiv, 164, n. 2. As an approximate equivalent in modern terms, I use the figure of 1.42 cubic metres per *tonelada*; Phillips, *Six Galleons*, p. 259, n. 50.

and three *fragatas* of 80 *toneladas* each – *Nuestra Señora de Guadalupe*, *La Magdalena*, and *Santa Isabel* – all belonging to the crown.[1] Flores knew the ships well and would command them again in the Armada of the Strait.[2]

Through his extensive service in the fleets, Flores developed an expert's knowledge of ships and the defensive needs of Spain's Atlantic empire. From 1570, when he noted that he had already served the king for twenty-three years, Flores wrote frequent reports regarding the construction of ships, their ideal measurements, and the best ways to defend Spanish trading vessels along the extensive coastlines of the Americas. In those reports, Flores often mentioned that the Spanish colonies and their shipping lanes needed much better security. Ports such as Havana and Cartagena, as well as the coasts of La Florida and the Caribbean, were crucial for the network of communication that supported Spain's transatlantic trade and colonial defence.[3] The tone of Flores's letters to the king is professional and respectful, but also frank and somewhat informal, suggesting that its author was accustomed to addressing his sovereign, and one whose judgment the king trusted.[4] Flores relied on that trust, not only to further his own career but also to promote the careers of men who served him well. For example, in command of the 1570 fleet to Tierra Firme, he praised the exemplary service of one of his captains, Gregorio de las Alas, who would later accompany him in the Armada of the Strait.[5] By 1580, Diego Flores had served the crown at sea for more than three decades. He arrived back in Sanlúcar de Barrameda in the early autumn, escorting the Tierra Firme fleet with the four armed ships of the guard squadron, and then travelled on to Seville.[6]

[1] A *fragata* (lit., frigate) in late 16th-century Spain was a light, armed fighting ship. With a shallow draft and oars as well as sails, a *fragata* was versatile, fast, and manoeuvrable in a variety of situations. In the prologue to Sarmiento, *Viajes al Estrecho*, vol. 1, p. xxxiv, the editor, Ángel Rosenblat, refers to the *fragatas* in the Armada of the Strait as *carabelas* (caravels). Sarmiento, however, consistently refers to those same vessels as *fragatas*, as does Rada. Rosenblat may have meant that they had a half-deck aft of the main-mast as well as one full deck which were characteristics of early caravels. In the absence of contemporary descriptions or depictions of the *fragatas*, however, that cannot be assumed, and Rosenblat's discussion of caravels on p. xvi is also misleading. See Phillips, *Six Galleons*, pp. 37–8, and below, pp. 178–9. Later *fragatas* and ships called frigates in a variety of other European languages were also fighting ships, but they had far different characteristics from late 16th-century *fragatas*.

[2] Chaunu, *Séville et l'Atlantique*, vol. 3, pp. 276–83. Pedro Menéndez de Avilés and Cristóbal de Eraso had also used these ships in the Armada de la Guardia, sometimes in combination with other vessels. Both men experimented with using various types of ships in the squadron, including small, fast *fragatas*, galleasses, and even galleys; ibid., pp. 248–51, 272–5. Pedro Menéndez de Avilés invented and built a very large galleon or galleass that used oars as well as sails, the *San Pelayo*, for the expedition to La Florida in 1565. It was at least 600 *toneladas*, and perhaps much larger; Lyon, *Enterprise of Florida*, pp. 26, 30, 36, 48. Such hybrids might be known as *galeones agaleradas* (galley-like galleons) for the larger sort, or as *galizabras*, for smaller versions. See Phillips, *Six Galleons*, p. 29; and Fernández Duro, *Disquisiciones náuticas*, vol. 5, pp. 25–6. For discussions of Indies defence and debates about the relative effectiveness of galleons and galleys for that purpose, see Navarrete, *Colección de documentos*, vol. 22, docs 38–42. In the 17th century, the guard squadron for the transatlantic fleets would use mid-sized galleons almost exclusively, because of their proven versatility; Phillips, *Six Galleons*, *passim*, esp. pp. 31–3, 42–6.

[3] For example, 'Memorial presentado al Rey por Diego Flores de Valdes, capitán general de la Carrera de las Indias sobre la seguridad y guarda de la navegación, cabos y puertos dellos' in Navarrete, *Colección de documentos*, vol. 22, ff. 153r–155v; also in Calvar et al., *Batalla del Mar Océano*, vol. 1, pp. 50–51 .

[4] Navarrete, *Colección de documentos*, vol. 21, ff. 554r–555v.

[5] Ibid., vol. 22, ff. 498v–501r. For the career of Gregorio de las Alas, see below, pp. 16, 71, 106–7.

[6] Flores wrote to the king from Havana on 7 June 1580 that, with other treasure expected from Nombre de Dios, he would be escorting the richest fleet that had ever left Cartagena. Navarrete, *Colección de documentos*, vol. 22, ff. 552r–553r.

Pedro Sarmiento was already in Spain, having arrived with the New Spain fleet on 9 September 1580. After successfully traversing the Strait of Magellan from west to east, he sailed across the Atlantic to the Azores. There, local officials supporting Dom Antonio's claim to the Portuguese throne arrested and held him briefly, but the arrival of the fleets from New Spain and India established King Philip's authority; Sarmiento made the last leg of his long journey to Spain in company with the New Spain fleet.[1] Although he was unknown at court, he had first-hand knowledge of the Strait and a plan to ensure the security of the southern Atlantic. Sarmiento went to Badajoz to present his plan to the king, who was on his way to Portugal to consolidate his claim to the throne. Sarmiento's arrival at the king's travelling court came at a propitious time. Royal authorities from Spain to Manila needed royal guidance to respond to Drake's unprovoked peacetime attacks. Rather than sending a few galleys to patrol the Strait, as Viceroy Toledo advised, Sarmiento urged the king to send an armada to the Strait, build forts to guard the entrance on the Atlantic side, and establish a permanent settlement to sustain them. Despite King Philip's concerns about expense, he found the notion of sending a large armada to the Strait appealing on both military and political grounds. An armada would allow him to demonstrate his will to protect both Portuguese Brazil and Spanish Peru. Some of his concern about financing the expedition dissipated when Sarmiento offered to fund the settlement in the Strait from his own fortune and to recruit the settlers himself.[2] With both Iberian empires in the Americas under threat, the king was pleased to accept Sarmiento's offer and to speed the preparation of a large military and colonizing expedition.

7. Planning and Early Preparations for the Armada of the Strait

Philip II submitted the matter to the Council of the Indies in Madrid for discussion, while he continued on the road towards Lisbon.[3] The king or the council may have asked for advice from other knowledgeable persons, including Diego de Robles. In a lengthy memorandum that reads like a direct response to Sarmiento's proposal, Robles discussed the idea that building two forts in the Strait would protect the whole Pacific coast. The most crucial issue was whether there was more than one entrance and exit to the Strait of Magellan and thus more than one passage from the southern Atlantic into the southern Pacific. The best European geographical opinion postulated a vast southern continent (Terra Australis) south of the Strait of Magellan. However, recent exploration led Robles to question that notion. He briefly discussed the voyages by Magellan, García Jofre de Loaísa, the Bishop of Plasencia, and Captain Juan de Ladrillero, who was sent to the Strait by the third marquis of Cañete, Peru's viceroy.[4] The latitudes recorded by those voyages placed the mouth of the Strait farther than 53°40′S, in modern terms, with the narrowest

---

[1] Chaunu, *Séville et l'Atlantique*, vol. 3, pp. 286–8.

[2] Sarmiento, *Viajes al Estrecho*, vol. 1, p. 194.

[3] Sarmiento's proposal appears in Navarrete, *Colección de documentos*, vol. 20, ff. 121r–125r. Although there is no place or date given in the document, the contents are consistent with later discussions of Sarmiento's proposal by the Council of the Indies and other royal officials.

[4] The 3rd marquis of Cañete, Don Andrés Hurtado de Mendoza, was Viceroy of Peru from 1556 to 1560. Captain Ladrillero made the voyage in 1558.

point estimated at two to three and a half leagues wide. By contrast, the ship that had recently come through the Strait and its chief pilot had found the mouth at 52°30′S, with the narrowest point no more than half a league wide.[1] Because of those discrepancies, Robles wrote, 'it can be taken as a certain thing that there is more than one channel through which one can exit the Strait'.[2] Forts and settlements would be worthless if enemy ships could simply avoid them by following an alternative route. On the other hand, Robles acknowledged that, if there was only one mouth and one strait, forts could indeed prevent enemy ships from passing through to the Pacific. He did not doubt the existence of a north-west passage into the Pacific via Labrador, but he judged it too difficult to navigate.

Robles also raised serious questions about the best ways to defend settlements and trading vessels on the coasts of Chile and Peru. He argued that winds and currents made the use of galleys impractical for voyages southward from Panama, implicitly rejecting Viceroy Toledo's preference for galley patrols. He also questioned whether a settlement and forts in the Strait could defend all of the viceroyalty of Peru. Instead, Robles favoured the use of convoys protected by armed ships for coastal trade along the lengthy Pacific coast. Above all, he questioned the immediate dispatch of a large expedition to the Strait when so little was known about its geography and characteristics. With all due deference, he urged the king to consider sending a small, relatively inexpensive expedition at first, deferring any major efforts at fortification and colonization.[3]

If the council members, or the king, saw Robles's memorandum, they did not pay it much heed. After deliberating the matter, the council wrote to the king on 3 November 1580, basing their advice on the report from Viceroy Toledo regarding Drake's raids and a summary of the memorandum that Sarmiento had presented to the king. They had not seen the memorandum itself, nor had Sarmiento gone to Madrid to meet with them. Nonetheless, by then, Bernardino de Mendoza, Spain's ambassador in England, had confirmed Drake's return with booty from the Spanish Indies and had warned the council that English and French adventurers would surely try to replicate Drake's voyage. To meet that threat, the council urged the king to send a military force to Chile under an experienced general, as well as a strong armada of twelve to fifteen ships to expel any enemy forces they found in the Strait, to establish a settlement and build forts at the most propitious point, and to then sail into the Pacific to patrol the coasts of Chile and Peru.[4]

In the next few months, the king and his advisers in Portugal continued to study the matter, while the Council of the Indies deliberated in Madrid. Sarmiento's advice weighed heavily in all the planning. On 18 February 1581, shortly before leaving Lisbon to meet the Portuguese Cortes[5] at Thomar, Philip II asked the council in Madrid to provide advice

---

[1] In other words, the ship of Sarmiento and the pilot Antón Pablos.

[2] Robles, 'Discurso acerca el poblar a Estrecho de Magallanes', in Navarrete, *Colección de documentos*, vol. 20, f. 99r.

[3] For the whole discourse, see ibid., ff. 98r–108v. Robles refers to the Pacific throughout, as the *Mar del Sur* (Southern Sea) and to the Atlantic as the *Mar del Norte* (Northern Sea), which is consistent with many contemporary maps and documents.

[4] Sarmiento, *Viajes al Estrecho*, vol. 2, pp. 281–2.

[5] In Portugal, as in Castile, the representative legislative body was known as the Cortes; in Aragon it was the Corts. In each venue, the representatives were called into session by the monarch to consider specific proposals, to swear loyalty to a new monarch in exchange for concessions granted, or to deal with other matters. The Cortes of Thomar would perform all these functions.

about the logistics involved in sending an armada to the Strait. The document explaining his decision was dated in Elvas on 23 February.[1] By then, the king had already appointed Diego Flores de Valdés as the armada's captain general,[2] though other posts were still under consideration. Flores's memorandum of 26 February included a list of men whom he recommended as captains for the armada, which was planned to go directly to the Strait, accomplish what it had to do there, and then patrol the coasts of the Indies looking for corsairs. He also advised assigning eight small warships (*navíos*) to patrol between Cape Finisterre in north-western Spain and Cape St Vincent and the Azores to protect incoming Indies fleets.[3]

From Madrid, the Council of the Indies sent the king a long memorandum dated 1 March 1581, reporting on its progress in planning the expedition to the Strait. They discussed Sarmiento's advice that the ships chosen should be small enough to easily navigate the Strait and his assurance that two forts built at the mouth of the Strait could 'close the door of the entrance to the whole strait'.[4] They also noted Sarmiento's strong argument that civilians and clerics, in addition to soldiers, be settled at the Strait. Soldiers could be expected to behave badly towards the local inhabitants, whereas colonists and religious would temper their excesses and work towards the conversion of the inhabitants. According to Sarmiento, settlers would be able to provide the food necessary for their own sustenance as well as for the forts. The council accepted his proposal and nominated Sarmiento as governor of both the settlement and the forts in the Strait.

In the same memorandum of 1 March, the council mentioned that the compensation the king proposed for Flores – 4,000 ducats – could easily be covered from royal funds in Lima or Mexico City. In addition, they discussed various candidates to serve as Flores's second in command, or almirante.[5] Among the names discussed:

> those for whom there were the best reports were Captain Pedro de Rada and Don Antonio Enríquez and Captain Gutierre de Solís. And Captain Pedro de Rada had and continues to have [the reputation] of being very well qualified, and no one on the council knows anything but the good reports about him, and thus he was put in first place.[6] And in addition to those nominated, there is Diego de la Rivera, who at present is treasurer of the armada, a man who has much experience in matters of warfare and who served many years with Pedro Menéndez in warfare, and after that he served with Don Cristóbal de Eraso, and he is a knowledgeable man and a good person. And it seems that Captain Gregorio de las Alas will be a good officer, and he also served for much time with Pedro Menéndez in the armada, and after that with Don Cristóbal [de Eraso], and he has acquitted himself well and enjoys good approval.[7]

---

[1] AMN, Sanz Barutell, MS 377, ff. 285r–286r, Philip II to the Council of the Indies, 23 Feb. 1581.

[2] To distinguish him from subordinate captains, he was often referred to as the general.

[3] AMN, Sanz Barutell, MS 388, ff. 143r–144r, Flores to Philip II, 26 Feb. 1581. The word *navío* could be used generically for a sailing ship. In the 16th century, however, it most often denoted a mid-sized, well-armed sailing ship. Rada uses *navio* fairly consistently to refer to specific ships in the fleet, though he rarely includes the accent on the 'i'. The meaning of the word changed over time. By the late 17th and early 18th centuries, *navío* most often denoted a very large armed ship and could be used interchangeably with the word *galeón* or galleon.

[4] Sarmiento, *Viajes al Estrecho,* vol. 2, p. 283. The full text of memorandum appears in vol. 2, pp. 283–8.

[5] See above, p. 1, n. 1.

[6] Captain Pedro de Rada declined to serve in the Armada of the Strait, possibly because the compensation offered was insufficient; AGI, Indiferente, leg. 739, N. 322, Report of the Council of the Indies to Philip II, 8 May 1581.

[7] Sarmiento, *Viajes al Estrecho,* vol. 2, pp. 285–6.

After reviewing the council's recommendations, the king chose Diego de la Rivera as almirante of the Armada of the Strait. As chief scribe of the expedition he named Pedro de Rada, who already held the post of escribano mayor (chief scribe) of the Guard Squadron of the Indies. Captain Pedro de Rada was another man, though the two may have been related.[1] The king had already appointed Don Alonso de Sotomayor as the governor of a military contingent destined for Chile. Because enemy forces might already have established themselves in Chile, the council urged the king to dispatch Sotomayor as quickly as possible, in company with the Tierra Firme fleet. He and his men could then cross the Isthmus of Panama and march down the coast to Chile, 'without stopping in Peru or Lima' or anywhere else. The council urged the king not to send Sotomayor's contingent with the Armada of the Strait, 'because the journey would be very long, doubtful and dangerous, and very costly'.[2] The councillors were correct in their assessment, but the king had already made up his mind.

Back in Lisbon, the duke of Alba, one of Philip II's senior military advisers, wrote to the king on 4 March, agreeing that building two forts in the Strait would be of paramount utility, if indeed they could be built, and if two forts alone could protect the Strait as a whole.[3] Those were the key issues. Alba's letters reached the king on the road to Thomar, and he answered each of them immediately. On 12 March, he wrote to Alba to send several ships to Seville for the expedition as quickly as possible. He also told Alba to 'summon Pedro Sarmiento to discuss the matter of the fortification of the Strait'.[4] At that moment, however, Sarmiento's continued participation was by no means assured. He seems to have assumed that he would command the expedition, and he was deeply disappointed to learn that Diego Flores had been appointed as captain general. In a letter to the king on 6 March, Sarmiento asked to be allowed to return to his home in Peru, because the king evidently had no further need for his services and he had depleted his finances in his previous odyssey eastward through the Strait from Peru to Spain.[5] The king denied Sarmiento permission to return to Peru but accepted his earlier offer to finance and establish a settlement at the Strait, appointing him governor and captain general-designate of that settlement, on recommendation from the Council of the Indies. That meant Sarmiento would be responsible for making arrangements for the settlers and would assume authority once they arrived on land at or near the site of the settlement.

Sarmiento wrote to the king again on 13 March, thanking him for the appointments, but either misunderstanding or deliberately misrepresenting what the Council of the Indies in Madrid had conveyed to him. As Sarmiento phrased it:

> The Licenciado Gasca ordered that I be told that [the council] would do me the favour that I would travel in the armada, and jointly with Diego Flores, general of it, [that I] would order and govern everything that be fitting and necessary for the good direction and service of His

[1] Both men were fined for carrying unregistered silver back from the Indies in 1579, and the documents clearly identify them as two separate individuals; AGI, Indiferente, leg. 739, N. 239. Lacking this document, I mistakenly conflated the two men in Phillips, 'Spanish Mariners', p. 248.

[2] Sarmiento, *Viajes al Estrecho,* vol. 2, p. 284.

[3] Fernando Álvarez de Toledo y Pimentel, 3rd duke of Alba to Philip II, 4 March 1581, in *CODOIN*, vol. 34, p. 767; also in Sarmiento, *Viajes al Estrecho,* vol. 2, pp. 289–90.

[4] Philip II to Alba, 12 March 1581, in *CODOIN*, vol. 34, pp. 116–17.

[5] Sarmiento to Philip II, 6 March 1581, in Navarrete, *Colección de documentos,* vol. 20, f. 141r–v.

Majesty, and without my counsel and opinion that nothing should be done; and that I would bear the name of governor and settler of the places that are to be peopled in the Strait.[1]

When the king received Sarmiento's letter in Thomar, he questioned the description of the appointment and the responsibilities that went with it. The king's secretary, Antonio de Eraso, noted on 20 March:

His Majesty conceded to Pedro Sarmiento the title of governor for the time when there be population in the Strait, and ordered that he go in the armada that is now being formed around the person of General[2] [Flores] .... His Majesty has now given orders to confirm that this is what he wrote to the council, and that they send [those orders] back [to him] with an official copy of the letters of Pedro Sarmiento, so that the one and the other can be seen [and compared], since it seems that it is different from what [Sarmiento] says has been said to him.[3]

In the same letter of 13 March, Sarmiento also discussed the financial compensation promised him, complaining that it was inadequate. He described that compensation as:

3,000 ducats in income from the fruits of the land, and 100 ducats of salary or subsidy (*ayuda de costa*) each month while the expedition lasts, with another 3,000 ducats in income for two lifetimes in Peru from the first vacancies in the distribution of Indian labour that occur, and that [these payments be made on] the order of His Majesty, and another 2,000 in subsidy, of which one-third should be paid to me here and two-thirds in Peru.[4]

On this matter as well, Secretary Eraso clarified the terms offered. Sarmiento would receive '100 ducats of *entretenimiento* per month for the time that the voyage lasts, and ... 3,000 ducats in income from whatever source seems best to the council, and another 3,000 in salary for the governorship, payable from the fruits of the land, and 2,000 ducats in subsidy, the majority of it paid there, or at least half'.[5] The term *entretenimiento* typically referred to sums provided for the maintenance of distinguished passengers who had no official post on a voyage, such as members of the entourage of a captain general or other high official. Defining Sarmiento's compensation on the voyage as an *entretenimiento* indicated that he had no official role for its duration. Sarmiento's redefinition of the payment as a salary or subsidy for expenses allowed him to maintain the fiction that he was the co-commander of the armada. That was clearly not the intent of the king or of the Council of the Indies.

Pedro de Rada's *Relación* does not discuss the implications of the appointment of Diego Flores as captain general and Diego de la Rivera as his second in command,[6] but they would have been obvious to anyone familiar with Spain's Atlantic fleets. By appointing Flores, an experienced military commander, to the position of captain general,

[1] Sarmiento to Philip II, 13 March 1581, in Navarrete, *Colección de documentos*, vol. 20, ff. 141v–142r.

[2] See above, p. 1, n. 1.

[3] Secretary Eraso to the king, 20 March 1581, in Navarrete, *Colección de documentos*, vol. 20, ff. 143v–144r. The editors of Sarmiento, *Viajes al Estrecho,* do not include either Sarmiento's letters to the king of 6 and 13 March 1581, or Secretary Eraso's note of 20 March.

[4] Navarrete, *Colección de documentos*, vol. 20, ff. 141v–142r.

[5] Navarrete, *Colección de documentos*, vol. 20, f. 144r. The index to the Navarrete collection does not mention Sarmiento's claim to coequal status with Flores, his complaints about his proposed compensation, or Secretary Eraso's doubts about Sarmiento's formulation of the agreements. Instead, the author of the index writes that 'as a consequence of having been ordered to go on the same expedition jointly with Diego Flores de Valdés, general of [that armada], Sarmiento comments regarding the difficulties and impossibilities he understood there would be in carrying it out'. See Vicente, *Indice de la colección*, item 2354, p. 332.

[6] See above, p. 16, and below, pp. 18–19, 21–2, 27–8, 57, n. 5, 65.

the king gave him supreme command of the whole expedition, outranking everyone else while the armada was at sea, and on land as well, wherever he was in port. In fact, the captain general of a Spanish fleet outranked even a viceroy, if both happened to be in the same place at the same time.[1] Spanish fleets, regardless of their orders or destination, had virtually the same command structure, which functioned well most of the time. When the structure became dysfunctional, it was invariably because of the personalities involved. For the Armada of the Strait, from the moment that the king chose Diego Flores as captain general, Sarmiento became a constant source of complaint and often of open insubordination towards Flores, despite the importance of the armada as the first demonstration of the king's resolve to defend both Iberian empires from European rivals.

Meanwhile, the king remained in Thomar, meeting with the Portuguese Cortes.[2] In mid-April, he directed Sarmiento to consult with the duke of Alba in Lisbon to discuss the plan further.[3] Sarmiento and the Italian engineer, Giovanni Battista Antonelli, an expert on fortifications, met with Alba to discuss logistics and review plans for the forts and watchtowers. Antonelli had worked for Philip II since 1559 and had extensive experience building forts in Spain and North Africa, as well as designing other projects.[4] Alba also invited other military experts to attend the discussions, including Tiburcio Spanocchi, another Italian military engineer who had recently entered Philip II's service. Despite Sarmiento's assurances, information about the Strait was incomplete at best, and neither Antonelli nor Spanocchi had first-hand knowledge of conditions there. Alba was particularly worried about the strong current at the narrows and the flat terrain in the area for the planned forts. Nonetheless, it was clear that the king was determined to go ahead with the project, and Alba added his military expertise to the ongoing discussions. Spanocchi drew up plans for the forts, which he estimated would cost about 12,000 ducats to build, plus another 6,000 ducats for their complement of men and arms.[5]

By late April, Alba wrote to the king that he had examined the plans and had formed an opinion.[6] Giovanni Battista Antonelli proceeded to Thomar to present the details of Alba's proposal to the king. The duke based his opinion on Sarmiento's report that the navigable channel for large ships was quite narrow at the point proposed for the forts,

---

[1] Phillips, *Six Galleons*, pp. 120–22; Olesa Muñido, *Organización naval*, vol. 1, pp. 591–603.

[2] On 16 April 1581, Philip II of Spain took his official oath as King Philip I of Portugal, promising to follow the laws and customs of the Portuguese kings before him. He also accepted responsibility to defend the Portuguese Empire. Representatives of the Portuguese political establishment presented various petitions at Thomar, based on a set of fundamental principles that had been agreed upon by Philip's representatives and the aged Cardinal-King Henry, the uncle and successor of the late King Sebastião, when he gave his support to the Habsburg succession. On 12 November 1582, Philip would grant virtually all those petitions in a *carta patente* (letter patent) outlining how he would govern Portugal and its empire. The language was designed to consolidate support for his accession and to reassure the Portuguese that their trade to Brazil and the rest of their overseas empire would continue unchanged. For a full discussion of the concessions made to Portugal, see Merriman, *Rise of the Spanish Empire*, vol. 4, pp. 370–76.

[3] *CODOIN*, vol. 34, pp. 238–9.

[4] Giovanni Battista Antonelli was born in Gatteo, Italy, in 1528, and died in Toledo, Spain, in 1588. See Gasparini, *Los Antonelli*, pp. 31–6.

[5] Spanocchi was born in Siena and entered Philip II's service *c.* 1580. See Sarmiento, *Viajes al Estrecho*, vol. 2, pp. 289–305; Navarrete, *Colección de documentos*, vol. 20, ff. 134r–139r; and Buisseret, 'Spanish Military Engineers', p. 47. Spanocchi's diagrams appear in the locations cited above in Sarmiento and Navarrete.

[6] Alba to Philip II, 21 April 1581, in *CODOIN*, vol. 34, pp. 262–6. Clissold, *Conquistador*, p. 137, mentions Alba's positive comments but omits the many difficulties he noted with the proposal.

with a very strong current. To prevent enemy ships from sailing through the channel too quickly for artillery to damage them, Alba proposed building three *barcones*[1] for each fort, pointed at both ends and strong enough to carry one or two cannons. When the watchtower at the mouth of the Strait signalled the approach of enemy ships, the boats would be rowed out in single file in the shallows, three on each side of the enemy and more than one harquebus-shot apart. They would fire their guns from a safe distance until the enemy ships came within range of the artillery at the forts. Then, a chain of heavy timbers linked by iron rings and attached to pillars in the shallows would be deployed to stall the enemy ships where the forts' heavy guns could sink them.[2]

The plan described by Antonelli depended on the navigable channel at the narrowest point in the Strait 'not being more than five-hundred-and-something paces' wide,[3] which was presumably what Sarmiento had told him. Five hundred paces would be, at most, half a kilometre.[4] In Sarmiento's initial memorandum, he had estimated the narrowest point in the Strait at only 'one *verso*-shot wide from one hill to the other' – roughly 25 metres.[5] Diego Robles had heard that the narrows were half a league (*legua*) wide, presumably also drawing on information provided by Sarmiento.[6] Although the definition of a league could vary considerably and might refer with different definitions to land or sea, to a Spaniard such as Robles, half a league would presumably mean a distance between 2.1 km by land or 2.9 km by sea. The huge discrepancy in the estimates could not be resolved until the armada actually reached the Strait, and it was not even mentioned in the written discussions of the defensive works proposed. In modern terms, the narrowest point in the Strait, known as Punta Delgada, is about 4.6 km or 2.5 nautical miles from shore to shore. Given that reality, Sarmiento's plan was doomed from the start, though no one knew it at the time.

In Sarmiento's later writings about the expedition, he emphasized the settlement and fortification of the Strait as its primary purpose. In his words, the king appointed

> Diego Flores de Baldés, an Asturian, of the Order of [Santiago], as general of the armada, which he ordered to be powerful and very well supplied with ammunition and provided with men, arms, and provisions for any peril, believing that there might be enemies in the Strait, ordering Diego Flores, with the men he brought, to establish and build two forts, facing one another, in the narrowest part of the Strait, and to put in them four hundred men of war, soldiers, who would draw wages, with two hundred soldiers in each, and that he not come away from there until leaving them finished and readied to perfection, together with their structures.[7]

Philip II's instructions to Flores defined the objectives of the voyage rather differently. In a memorandum dictated on 1 May 1581 in Thomar, he laid out the rationale for the

---

[1] A *barcón* was a large, flat-bottomed boat, propelled by oars. Its pointed ends made for easier landing through surf.

[2] *CODOIN*, vol. 34, pp. 275–7; also in Sarmiento, *Viajes al Estrecho*, vol. 2, pp. 299–300.

[3] Ibid., p. 276.

[4] See Arnold et al., *Nautical Archaeology of Padre Island*, pp. 240–43.

[5] Navarrete, *Colección de documentos*, vol. 20, f. 124r. A *verso* was a small, rail-mounted swivel gun, breechloaded with small shot and with a very limited range. It was an anti-personnel weapon, not designed for long-range firing but generally used in the 16th century against fighters trying to board a vessel.

[6] Navarrete, *Colección de documentos*, vol. 20, f. 99r.

[7] Sarmiento, *Viajes al Estrecho*, vol. 1, pp. 194–5.

armada and provided Flores with detailed instructions about its purpose.[1] Using the familiar form of address, as was habitual for kings addressing their subjects, the king first noted that for many years after Magellan's voyage, there was no need to use the strait named for him. It had remained almost hidden until the English corsair Francis Drake sailed through it and assaulted Spanish ports from Chile to New Spain. Because this had encouraged others in England and France to think about replicating Drake's exploits, it was necessary to defend and fortify the Strait and, more importantly, to search for and punish any interlopers with rigour.

Although the king mentioned the fortification of the Strait, he placed the greatest emphasis on the armada's principal military goal 'to punish the said corsairs'. Flores was to seek out and destroy any fortified places that the corsairs had built, either at the Strait or elsewhere along the Atlantic coast. Should he have to disembark in pursuit of the enemy, he was to leave the fleet in control of his second in command, the almirante. By questioning local inhabitants through interpreters,[2] Flores was to determine if any more corsairs had passed through the Strait into the Pacific and, if so, with how many ships, men, and weapons. Only if there was evidence that they had done so was he to sail through the Strait, given the risk that some of his men might desert once they arrived in Chile. In the case he had to chase corsairs into the Pacific, he was to leave enough men at the Strait to fight the corsairs, should they elude him and double back.

Because the dangers of the Strait were well known to the maritime community in Spain, the king ordered Flores to maintain secrecy about the armada's destination and purpose, not only to avoid alerting enemies, but also so that 'the men go with better will'.[3] Flores was to say only that the armada aimed at guarding the Indies, and to do everything possible to enlist seasoned veterans of the guard squadron of the Indies fleets. The king's plans called for 1,400 soldiers – 1,000 for the fleet and 400 to be divided between the two forts planned for the Strait – and 600 sailors, all to be Spaniards. Following recommendations of the Council of the Indies, the king noted that all of the men should be able to help build the forts, so that they could be completed as quickly as possible. He also specified the armament for each fort – four cannons, four culverins, and some smaller arms and munitions – supervised by one captain of artillery and one engineer. He also mentioned the arms, shields, and munitions that the seaborne soldiers should carry.

The king's instructions made clear that Flores was in supreme command. Sotomayor's contingent of 500–600 men would sail in designated ships with their equipment, provisions, and arms. That way, they could sail on to Chile without inconvenience to the fleet as a whole. The king noted that, 'although the said Don Alonso travels in command of [his men], it is understood that this is in order to govern them, because in matters of war all have to be subordinated to you, and to obey you and comply with your orders'.[4] The king urged Flores to work closely with Pedro Sarmiento, given the latter's knowledge of the Strait, and to consult with him, Sotomayor, and 'other persons of intelligence and quality who will sail in the armada, and to take resolution with mature counsel and

---

[1] Rada's *Relación* does not include the king's instructions to Flores.

[2] In Spanish documents of the period, interpreters are referred to as *lenguas* (lit., tongues).

[3] Navarrete, *Colección de documentos*, vol. 20, f. 130v. The king wrote to the Council of the Indies on 27 Feb. 1581 giving the same rationale. Landin, *Vida y viajes de Pedro Sarmiento,* p. 116.

[4] Navarrete, vol. 20, f. 132r.

deliberation in all that has to be done'.[1] Almirante Diego de la Rivera should of course be consulted, along with the captains, pilots, and knowledgeable officers in the armada. Such consultations were standard procedure on Spanish fleets, in part as a matter of courtesy, but mainly for their practical value. However, the consultations never signified a divided command, despite the assumptions of many scholars regarding the Armada of the Strait.[2] Rivera, Sotomayor, and all the other officials in the fleet – everyone except Sarmiento – behaved in accordance with the proper chain of command. Although Sarmiento had to acknowledge Flores's status as captain general, he would continue to act as if he held joint command.

Despite the king's careful planning, he knew that circumstances might cause Flores to deviate from his instructions. In the last of his seventeen points, after telling Flores to govern the fleet according to the rules of the Armada de la Guardia, he noted:

> This instruction contains what can be said with respect to the principal intent for sending you on this expedition, but you already know how differently things can happen from what is imagined. Thus, no more clarity can be given to you except to remit to your prudence and intelligence the execution of matters as the opportunity and character of things require. As you know how important it is to succeed, and the reputation that would be lost in the contrary case, you should proceed in all things with much circumspection, industry, and diligence, having always before you God, our Lord, whom we supplicate for your protection and help, that he give the good outcome that is suitable and that we desire in His holy service, having as intercessors the Virgin, Our Lady, his blessed mother, and the glorious Apostle Santiago.[3]

Flores continued to oversee preparations for the fleet in Seville, a process filled with difficulties from the start. Everything, especially money, was in short supply.[4] Pierre Chaunu commented that launching the Armada of the Strait in 1581 exceeded the physical capabilities of Spain's Atlantic fleet system even more than its financial capabilities. He further suggested that the effort exceeded late sixteenth-century technological capabilities in general.[5] The previous fleets for New Spain and Tierra Firme had not yet returned. Nineteen ships would leave for New Spain in the fleet of 1581, plus another nine that sailed individually across the Atlantic. The regular fleet to Tierra Firme would not sail at all, in part because ships, men, and supplies were diverted to the Armada of the Strait. This cannot have pleased the House of Trade.[6] A military expedition had little possibility of making a commercial profit, and the dangers involved increased the risk of losing ships and men. Flores could not acknowledge the armada's purpose, destination, or urgency, even while the need for ships, men, and provisions competed with the regular fleets for New Spain and Tierra Firme.[7]

---

[1] Ibid., *Colección de documentos*, vol. 20, ff. 130r–132v.

[2] For example, Clissold, *Conquistador*, p. 137; Landin, *Vida y viajes de Pedro Sarmiento*, p. 117; Cerezo, *Armadas de Felipe II*, pp. 186–7; Chaunu, *Séville et l'Atlantique*, vol. 3, p. 296.

[3] Navarrete, *Colección de documentos*, vol. 20, ff. 132v–133r.

[4] Flores to Antonio de Eraso, Seville, 13 April 1581, in *CODOIN*, vol. 94, pp. 528–30.

[5] Chaunu, *Séville et l'Atlantique*, vol. 3, pp. 295–6.

[6] The *Casa de la Contratación* (House of Trade) in Seville, was founded in 1503 and and came to oversee virtually every aspect of Spain's Atlantic fleets and the trade goods and passengers that they carried.

[7] Chaunu, *Séville et l'Atlantique*, vol. 3, pp. 292–3 includes a list of 23 ships in Seville that were assigned to the Armada of the Strait, based on documents in AGI, CT, leg. 2899, lib.1, which include additional information about many of the vessels and their officers.

Flores had to depend on the officials of the House of Trade to supply his fleet, but his relations with them were not always smooth. The person in charge of supplying all the Indies fleets was Francisco Duarte, a member of the city council of Seville and a factor in the House of Trade.[1] From Lisbon, Philip II wrote often to Duarte to assemble the necessary ships, men, and provisions as quickly as possible.[2] Duarte had been in charge of such matters for many years; he was used to doing things his own way and in his own time, without interference or oversight. Flores, however, unlike many of his peers, was not content to leave preparations entirely in other hands. Based on his long experience, Flores thought that a captain general should pay close attention to the soundness of the vessels chosen for a particular fleet, as well as to the outfitting and provisioning of those vessels.[3] Flores's active participation in the preparation of his armada in the late spring and summer of 1581 was bound to create disagreements with factors, purveyors, and ship owners in southern Spain.[4]

Flores tried to supply the armada on credit, but he wrote to Secretary Eraso on 13 April that it was virtually impossible to do so, as previous supplies had not yet been paid for. It would be much easier if the king paid what was owed, he argued, using revenue from the Indies. To underscore his difficulties, Flores wrote, 'It alarms me that anyone would have told His Majesty that supplies could be had on credit, as the only way that could happen would be to take them by force. Merchants will not provide supplies on credit, and they hide what they have.' Presumably in response to complaints from Francisco Duarte, Flores agreed to leave the provisioning in his hands, accepting that, with the king's encouragement, '[Duarte] will do marvels', but he worried greatly about the pace of the preparations.[5] The best time to depart for the Strait would have been March, and that was already past.

[1] The officials on the city council of Seville were known as veinticuatros (twenty-fours) for their legal number. According to Juan Carlos Mercado, who edited a volume of letters by Pedro Menéndez de Avilés, *Cartas sobre la Florida*, p.120, n. 94, Francisco Duarte was an enemy of Menéndez. If that is true, Duarte's enmity may have extended to the Menéndez clan as a whole, which included Diego Flores.

[2] For example, AMN, Sanz Barutell, MS 377, f. 304r, Philip II to Francisco Duarte, 12 June 1581.

[3] In 1570, Flores wrote a lengthy memorandum arguing that captains general should inspect all of the ships assigned to them in Seville to make sure that they were fit and appropriate for service, even countersigning the reports prepared by the royal inspectors (visitadores) of the fleet. He also argued that the judicial officials who inventoried the ships and their contents in Sanlúcar de Barrameda should not proceed unless the captain general was present, in order to avoid fraud on the part of the masters of rations of the various vessels. Among Flores's most controversial recommendations was that local judges should not be allowed to handle incidents that occurred in the fleets. Instead, Flores argued that the captain general should have supreme authority over all such incidents, not even coordinating with the local judiciary; otherwise, he thought the sailors would try to take advantage of jurisdictional disputes. Based on the commercial fleets he had observed, Flores maintained that the captain general, not the ship owners, should name the captains of the ships in his fleet. He noted that owners tended to choose captains who would maximize profits by overloading ships, so that the artillery could not be used properly and the munitions could not be stowed in their proper place. Diego Flores to Philip II in Navarrete, *Colección de documentos*, vol. 22, ff. 42r–43v.

[4] While preparations for the fleet went ahead in the summer of 1581, Captain General Flores and other experienced mariners, including Pedro Sarmiento, commented on configurations for galleons to be built on the Vizcayan coast. Those ships were designed to strengthen the defence of the Indies from enemy attack, but they would take several years to build. In the interim, the Armada of the Strait would provide some measure of additional defence.

[5] Flores to Antonio de Eraso, 13 April 1581, in *CODOIN*, vol. 94, pp. 528–30.

At the same time, Pedro Sarmiento was recruiting one hundred households to settle at the Strait. Once he had assurance of his official role as governor general-designate, he threw himself into the preparations with great enthusiasm. His efforts were crucial for the planned settlement and he bought supplies and provisions from the same local vendors who supplied the fleets in general. With cash in hand, he had an advantage over royal officials, and this was supplemented by his persistence and single-mindedness. Sarmiento sent a steady stream of letters to the House of Trade in Seville, to the Council of the Indies in Madrid, and to the royal secretaries with the king in Portugal, complaining that Flores was failing to do his job, that he himself was having to take up the slack (always to great effect), that Flores resented his 'interference',[1] and that without his zeal the expedition would founder. Interestingly, Sarmiento did not complain about Francisco Duarte, perhaps because he dared not antagonize the man who controlled supplies for the fleets.

Despite Sarmiento's complaints, Flores continued to keep a close eye on all the preparations, travelling back and forth between Seville and Sanlúcar de Barrameda during the last two weeks in April. He wrote to Secretary Eraso again on 1 May, clearly annoyed at the endless complaints, though he did not mention Sarmiento by name. Flores assured Eraso that any delay in outfitting the ships was due to a lack of money, which the king should remedy. For his part, he said he was working night and day to finish the preparations, and that even Francisco Duarte could not find workers for the Armada of the Strait without cash in hand. Flores added bitterly that 'men who are tired and used up from serving [nonetheless] do not lack those who envy them'.[2] Presumably, Flores included Pedro Sarmiento in that company. At about the same time, Sarmiento wrote directly to the king, asking to be ennobled. He reminded Philip II of his past service to the crown in Peru and the Pacific and noted that, 'I am of well born parents, and my works have not been lacking'.[3] The king's response is not known, but he obviously did not grant the request. Sarmiento remained a commoner for the rest of his life.

Flores wrote to Secretary Eraso again on 20 May 1581, frustrated with the House of Trade, which, he claimed, was taking up his time 'all day in [meetings], and nothing is accomplished'. He also complained that everything had to have the approval of Francisco Duarte, who raised '100,000 doubts' about everything he proposed. Flores noted that preparations for the New Spain fleet always took precedence over the Armada of the Strait, but even so, and with cash in hand, the preparations for the New Spain fleet were taking far too long. The Armada of the Strait would need twenty-four ships or more, and there was still no cash available to outfit them.[4]

The rest of Flores's long letter of 20 May dealt with salaries and wages. He agreed that it was crucial that Antón Pablos sail with the fleet, as he was the pilot who had guided Sarmiento through the Strait and presumably knew it well. Flores nonetheless questioned the high wages that Pablos had evidently demanded and been promised, though the wages would be paid to him in Peru, not in Seville. Flores would have preferred Juan Ramos as chief pilot, a Spaniard with more than twenty years' experience on Atlantic voyages. Nonetheless, he was resigned to working with Antón Pablos, whom he did not yet know, with Ramos appointed in another capacity, preferably as an adviser

---

[1] Sarmiento, *Narratives of the Voyages*, p. 230. See also Sarmiento, *Viajes al Estrecho*, vol. 1, pp. 201–5.
[2] Flores to Antonio de Eraso, 1 May 1581, in *CODOIN*, vol. 34, pp. 530–32.
[3] Sarmiento to Philip II, spring 1581, in *CODOIN*, vol. 94, p. 533.
[4] Flores to Antonio de Eraso, 20 May 1581, in *CODOIN*, vol. 94, pp. 534–5.

to Pablos.[1] Flores noted that word had got around Seville of Pablos's promised salary, and 'all those approached to go on this expedition try to get the same as Antón Pablos, and even the sailors, with my having offered them two ducats more [per month] than the ordinary wages, I can find none but those who want even more money'.

Flores might have said the same about himself. He asked for the same salary that other captains general such as the Adelantado Pedro Menéndez de Avilés and Cristóbal de Eraso had received on earlier voyages, amounting to 6,000 ducats per year. This voyage was no less important than theirs, he wrote to Secretary Eraso, and had no possibility of profit, nor were his services less deserving than those of his precursors. He said that Secretary Juan Delgado had promised that the king would grant what he asked, because His Majesty surely would not allow the Council of the Indies to treat him so badly. If it did, he would not accept the post of captain general and would fulfil his duty to the king as a simple harquebusier on the voyage. That presumably empty threat nonetheless got Secretary Eraso's attention. His marginal note said he would consult the king about paying Flores the full amount he requested.[2]

8.   Recruiting Sailors and Soldiers

Captain General Flores and his senior officers, along with officials of the House of Trade, were responsible for enlisting sailors and soldiers for the fleet. Even Sarmiento recognized that fact, noting that he would not intervene in such matters, though he observed them carefully and wrote to the king complaining about standard procedures and their expense.[3] Flores and the other officials had to raise 2,500 *gente de mar y guerra* (men of sea and war), which was far from easy in the summer of 1581. As Flores wrote to the king in Portugal, there were already three royal fleets at sea, serving the trade to New Spain and Tierra Firme, plus armies in Flanders and Italy.[4] Subtracting the men needed for the 1581 New Spain fleet, few able-bodied sailors or soldiers remained who were willing to sign on for an expedition whose destination was still supposed to be secret, but which must have been the subject of ominous rumours.

Flores had sent agents north to the ports of Santander, Vizcaya, and Guipúzcoa, which were traditional recruiting grounds for sailors. He was working on recruitment in the south-west himself, with help from his subordinates and from the duke of Medina Sidonia, the king's factotum in the south.[5] Reports from one royal official in the north,

---

[1] In the event, Captain Juan Ramos would sail on the flagship as a consejero (senior adviser) in matters of navigation.

[2] Flores to Antonio de Eraso, 20 May 1581, in *CODOIN*, vol. 94, pp. 536–8. Flores had made a similar threat in 1566, while preparing his first Tierra Firme fleet. On that occasion, he offered to serve as a common sailor rather than captain general, if the king did not accept his advice regarding more men and arms to confront corsairs. Flores to Philip II, 14 October 1566, in Navarrete, *Colección de documentos*, vol. 21, f. 552v.

[3] Sarmiento, *Viajes al Estrecho*, vol. 1, p. 204.

[4] Flores to Philip II, undated but presumably July 1581, in Navarrete, *Colección de documentos*, vol. 20, ff. 154r–155r. The 1580 New Spain fleet of Francisco de Luxán, with 34 ships, would not return to Spain until September of 1581, along with the 10 ships of the 1580 Tierra Firme fleet of Antonio Manrique. Another 8 ships would return singly; Chaunu, *Séville et l'Atlantique*, vol. 3, pp. 300–305.

[5] Don Alonso Pérez de Guzmán (1550–1615), the 7th duke of Medina Sidonia, was one of the most distinguished members of the Spanish nobility. By long tradition, the ducal house of Medina Sidonia served the crown in recruitment and other military matters in south-western Spain.

Pedro de Ledesma, noted that few recruits had signed on, largely because the advances on future wages and other financial incentives were too low.[1] With the king's approval, the council authorized Ledesma to offer the men four ducats in wages per month, with three advance payments, plus one *real* per day to buy food until embarkation. They also told Ledesma to work closely with the men that Flores had sent north – Domingo Martínez de Avendaño and Rodrigo de Rada – who knew how to recruit men for seaborne duty.[2] The councillors urged Ledesma to recruit the men 'with all delicacy and blandishment',[3] a reminder that the Spanish crown rarely used force to enlist men for the navy, even in times of great need.[4] Nonetheless, when the 1580 fleets of New Spain and Tierra Firme returned to Spain in September of 1581, some of their men were forcibly reassigned to the Armada of the Strait, which confirms the desperation of royal officials to recruit sufficient men in time. Their arrival, together with the enhanced compensation and official blandishments to voluntary recruits, had the desired effect. By the time the ships were ready to sail from Sanlúcar de Barrameda, they carried a full complement of sailors and soldiers.[5]

9. Final Preparations

In addition to myriad concerns regarding the fleet, Flores had to worry about retaining the king's support as delays mounted. At least one rival, Don Cristóbal de Eraso, evidently wanted Flores's job.[6] From Portugal, King Philip closely followed preparations for the armada, corresponding with Francisco Duarte, the duke of Medina Sidonia, and other

---

[1] Ledesma to the Council of the Indies in Madrid, 7 and 8 July 1581, in Navarrete, *Colección de documentos*, vol. 20, f. 153r.

[2] Both Martínez de Avendaño and Rodrigo de Rada would serve as captains in the Armada of the Strait. It is not clear whether Captain Rada was related to the armada's chief scribe, Pedro de Rada.

[3] Navarrete, *Colección de documentos*, vol. 20, ff. 153r–154r. Regarding recruitment, see also AMN, Sanz Barutell, MS 377, f. 313r, Philip II to Francisco Duarte, 19 July 1581.

[4] See Phillips, 'Life Blood of the Navy', pp. 423–7, 438–41.

[5] AMN, Sanz Barutell, MS 388, f. 192r–v, Francisco Duarte to Antonio de Eraso, 18 Sept. 1581. In all, some 280 men were forcibly recruited. To prevent their fleeing or otherwise drifting away, they were held and fed in the jail in Sanlúcar de Barrameda until they could be distributed among the ships that still needed men. The treasurer of Flores's armada received 1,000 ducats to buy clothing for the sailors. Once out to sea beyond the sandbar at Sanlúcar, officers would enlist the forced recruits and pay them the four ducats in advance that the voluntary recruits had already received. The 672 mariners voluntarily recruited included 24 pilots – 2 on the *capitana* (flagship) and one for each other ship – and 26 officers, as well as common sailors, apprentice seamen, and pages; ibid., ff. 198r–201r.

[6] Cristóbal de Eraso to Philip II, 1 July 1581, in Navarrete, *Colección de documentos,* vol. 20, ff. 145–148r, stating 'although Diego Flores de Valdés understands things of the sea, he has no experience of war, never having been a soldier, nor having been anywhere in Italy or Flanders or in any other *presidio* (garrison)'. Those historians who accept Sarmiento's version of events often quote Eraso's comments as an objective analysis, failing to note that he ended his letter by offering to replace Flores as captain general. Eraso, like many other successful captains general, was adept at advancing his own career and those of his relatives. See Pérez Mallaína, *Spain's Men of the Sea*, pp. 32–3. It is nonetheless surprising that he would attempt to undercut Flores with preparations so far advanced and the command structure set months before. He did not succeed, and his letter may have damaged his own career. Although Eraso would serve with distinction in the Battle of Las Terceiras in 1583, which consolidated King Philip's control of the Portuguese Azores, he never again commanded a large Indies fleet. See Chaunu, *Séville et l'Atlantique*, vol. 3, pp. 272–400.

officials to work as quickly as possible.[1] Intelligence reports indicated that France was preparing a large expedition to attack Brazil and other parts of the Iberian empires in the Americas. Moreover, rumours reached the king that various members of the English elite were interested in financing expeditions to the Strait in imitation of Drake's voyage. The sooner Flores and his armada departed, the sooner those challenges could be met and surmounted. Moreover, sailing conditions from southern Europe to the South Atlantic also demanded a rapid departure. The Portuguese pilot Pedro Díaz de Lagos wrote to the king from Seville on 16 August 1581, stressing the need for getting past the sandbar at Sanlúcar de Barrameda before the first of September.[2] Díaz had long experience with the Río de la Plata region and would accompany the Armada of the Strait as pilot of the *almiranta* (the second ship in the chain of command). With the ships assembled in Sanlúcar, Flores and Rivera moved downriver to oversee their final outfitting. Sarmiento remained in Seville, occupied with preparations for the settlement he intended to plant at the Strait. He was outraged when Flores left Seville before all the arrangements for the colony had been completed.[3] Nonetheless, it was standard procedure for the captain general and almirante of an armada to concentrate on readying the ships.

The king pressed Flores and all the officials involved to finish preparations by 1 September,[4] but that proved impossible. At the end of August, the king wrote to the duke of Medina Sidonia to consider whether six or seven ships, rather than ten, would be sufficient for the contingent going to the Strait, given that there was no news of English corsairs departing for that destination.[5] To prepare a response, on 5 September the duke met with Captain General Flores and Almirante Rivera in Bonanza, a small river port between Seville and Sanlúcar. Don Francisco Tello and Dom Pedro de Tarsis[6] witnessed the meeting. Despite the need to conserve money and supplies, Flores and Rivera argued strongly that ten ships were necessary to carry out the mission to the Strait and deal with any corsairs already there. They noted that Don Alonso de Sotomayor's men would sail on the four smallest ships, which were the most suitable for traversing the Strait to Chile, while Sarmiento and his settlers and supplies would travel in the six larger ships. The largest vessel would be broken up before they entered the Strait; any other ships broken up thereafter would provide munitions and supplies for the forts at the Strait. No fewer than ten ships would suffice.

In the most controversial part of their argument, Flores and Rivera proposed that the ten ships destined for the Strait sail from Spain on their own, with Pedro Sarmiento as their captain general and Don Alonso de Sotomayor sailing with him for defence and consultation. The other thirteen ships assembled for the armada, under Flores and Rivera, would carry out the military mission of clearing the coasts of corsairs and assuring the

---

[1] See AMN, Sanz Barutell, MS 388, f. 304r, Philip II to Francisco Duarte, 12 June 1581; ibid., f. 173r–v, Duarte to Philip II, 3 July 1581; MS 377, f. 315r–v, Philip II to Duarte, 10 Aug. 1581; MS 496, ff. 69r–71v, Philip II to Medina Sidonia, 23 and 29 Aug. 1581.

[2] Pedro Díaz to Philip II, 16 Aug. 1581, in Navarrete, *Colección de documentos*, vol. 20, f. 157r–v. The pilot is sometimes referred to as Pero Díaz or Díez.

[3] Sarmiento, *Narratives of the Voyages*, pp. 231–2.

[4] See AMN, Sanz Barutell, MS 377, f. 315r–v, Philip II to Duarte, 10 Aug. 1581.

[5] AMN, MS 496, ff. 69r–71v, Philip II to Medina Sidonia, 29 Aug. 1581.

[6] Don Francisco Tello was treasurer (tesorero) and judge (juez) of the House of Trade in Seville. Dom Pedro de Tarsis was a member of the Portuguese noble military order of Santiago, the counterpart of the military order in Spain to which Flores belonged; see below, pp. 35, 45, 62, 65–6, 77, n. 5.

safety of the returning Indies fleets. Clearly, Flores saw the voyage to the Strait as separable from his mission to clear the coast of corsairs, and it is likely that his ongoing contention with Sarmiento played a part in his reasoning. The duke of Medina Sidonia was presumably aware of that contention and the potential conflicts between the military mission of the armada and the settlement and fortification of the Strait. He agreed that twenty-three ships were necessary for the diverse goals the king had defined, regardless of how the ships were deployed, and he expressed no disagreement with the proposal by Flores and Rivera to split the fleet into two contingents. The duke sent the proposal to the king on 5 September.[1]

As soon as he received it, the king rejected the idea of splitting the fleet. He wrote to the duke on 12 September, saying that 'the said armada should depart, leave, and go all together to the Strait, with all of its ships and men of sea and warfare, and with [those who have] been gathered as pioneers and settlers, as was agreed upon'.[2] This interchange appears to be one source for the notion that the king split command of the armada between Flores and Sarmiento. In fact, the proposal to split the fleet – not the command – came from Flores himself, supported by Rivera, and the king rejected it.[3]

The king also sent a packet of letters for Flores, the most important being missives directed to the governor of Brazil, Lorenzo de Vega (Lourenzo da Veiga), instructing him to aid Captain General Flores and Governor Sarmiento in the expedition to the Strait. The packet also contained letters to Portuguese officials in Santiago on the island of Cape Verde, and Funchal on the island of Madeira, which were standard ports of call on the way to and from Brazil. Another six letters left the names of the addressees blank for Flores to fill in as needed, and there were six other letters addressed to the local citizenry of various Brazilian towns.[4]

10.   The Disastrous First Departure from Spain

The armada was finally ready to leave Sanlúcar de Barrameda in late September of 1581. By then, the contention between Sarmiento and Flores had erupted into open – and sometimes ludicrous – conflict. Sarmiento did not arrive in Sanlúcar de Barrameda with his settlers until 15 September.[5] According to Sarmiento, from that point, Flores did everything possible to keep them from accompanying the fleet, stalling for nine days, deciding that Sarmiento's baggage was too heavy to load until the ship designated to carry it had crossed the treacherous sandbar at Sanlúcar, and subsequently still refusing to load all the baggage when the ship was anchored in twenty fathoms of water. Sarmiento further complained that, while the excess baggage was being returned to shore, much of it was lost

---

[1] AMN, MS 496, ff. 78r–81v, Medina Sidonia to Philip II, 5 Sept. 1581.

[2] Ibid., ff. 88r–89r, Philip II to Medina Sidonia, 12 Sept. 1581.

[3] Martín Fernández de Navarrete reflects that mistaken notion in his introduction to the section of letters related to the Armada of the Strait, where he describes it as 'the armada that left in the year 1581 from the port of Sanlúcar for the Strait of Magellan, under command of the generals Pedro Sarmiento and Diego Flores Valdés and of the Almirante Diego de Ribera', ibid., f. 147r–v.

[4] AMN, Sanz Barutell, MS 377, ff. 317r–321v, Philip II to Flores, 12 Sept. 1581.

[5] The king would have preferred to embark the settlers in Cádiz, but that proved impractical. AMN, MS 496, ff. 69r–71v, Philip II to Medina Sidonia, 29 Aug. 1581.

or ruined by rain in open launches, and some was stolen. Sarmiento later claimed that he
'embarked in spite of Diego Flores' and, despite being so abused, decided 'to avoid an
altercation with Diego Flores' in the interest of the king's service.[1] Sarmiento habitually
refers to himself in the third person in his writings, and, if we believe his account, Flores
was less than accommodating. Nonetheless, the captain general was well within his
authority to refuse loading excess baggage, and he clearly knew that he could not leave
without Sarmiento, the settlers and their families, and their necessary supplies. Rada says
nothing about the contretemps, noting only that, once everyone was aboard, the armada
was ready to depart.[2]

Bad weather delayed the departure for nearly a week, until the duke of Medina Sidonia
and other officials deemed it safe. On 24 September, Flores issued instructions for the
captains, pilots, and masters of the various ships in the armada.[3] The destination and
purpose of the armada were still unstated, though the sailors and soldiers probably knew
by then where they were going.[4] Francisco Duarte assured Secretary Eraso that, in fifty
years serving the king, he had never seen a fleet better supplied.[5] On 25 September, the
armada officially sailed out of port with twenty-three ships and some 3,500 people,
though it took two more days for all the ships to get beyond the sandbar at Sanlúcar. No
one could know what disasters lay ahead.

The armada sailed for several days with favourable winds. Then, on 3 October, a fierce
storm arose when the ships were near Cádiz, about thirty-five leagues (105 miles) from
Sanlúcar de Barrameda. With most of the sails lowered, and nosed into the wind, the
armada rode out the tempest for three days, but the winds blew so hard on 6 October
that Flores had to jettison some cargo to save the *capitana*.[6] Sarmiento would later claim
that he had countermanded Flores's order to jettison, and that his own heroic actions had

---

[1] Sarmiento, *Narratives of the Voyages*, p. 233.

[2] See below, pp. 65–6.

[3] For copies of those instructions, see below, pp. 131–4.

[4] Rumours had spread widely in Sanlúcar de Barrameda, so that even Englishmen who were in port at the time knew the destination was the Strait of Magellan. See 'Relación de carta de fray Juan de Rivadeneira al Gobernador de Tucumán', in *CODOIN*, vol. 94, pp. 549–50.

[5] Duarte nonetheless complained that 'so many hands' had commented on the preparations and about the difficulty of pleasing Captain General Flores, no matter how hard he and his son worked at sending the '100,000 little things' that Flores requested for the fleet. See AMN, Sanz Barutell, MS 388, f. 192r–v, Duarte to Antonio de Eraso, 18 Sept. 1581. Don Cristóbal de Eraso also had sour words about Flores, whose command he had coveted. He complained to another royal secretary, Juan Delgado, that 'although it is certain that His Majesty likes the general, those who know him definitely do not. May it please God that everyone gains as much as he has from this expedition, although he has always complained and shown ingratitude', ibid., f. 192r–v, Cristóbal de Eraso to Juan Delgado, 27 Sept. 1581. Once the armada was poised to depart, Don Francisco Tello prepared preliminary accounts of the crown's expenses. Only 5 of the 23 ships in the armada belonged to the crown: the galleass serving as flagship and named *San Cristóbal*; 3 *fragatas*; and the ship that Sarmiento had sailed from Peru through the Strait, named *Nuestra Señora de Buena Esperanza*. The crown had leased the other 18 ships from their owners for 6½ *reales* per *tonelada* per month – the standard fee paid for private ships leased by the crown in the Indies fleets. Altogether, the crown contracted to pay an estimated 54,600 *reales* per month for the 8,400 *toneladas* comprised by those ships. However, the crown had paid for repairing and refitting the ships with sails, rigging, and other equipment; those costs plus the wages owed to carpenters, caulkers, and other shipwrights would be deducted from the fee due to the ship owners. Tello noted that the total spent in preparing each vessel would likely equal the leasing fee. See ibid., Financial account of Francisco Tello, 30 Sept. 1581, ff. 198r–201r.

[6] See below, p. 68. Rada generally refers to the flagship *San Cristóbal* as the *capitana*, the *galeaza capitana*, or the *galeaza*, referring to its function and type rather than its name.

saved the ship. In Sarmiento's words: 'Diego Flores ordered the cargo and anchors to be thrown overboard. Pedro Sarmiento prevented this from being done ... The large galleass would certainly have been lost in the port, if the anchors had been thrown overboard, as Diego Flores desired.'[1]

That Sarmiento would try to countermand an order from Captain General Flores on his own flagship was a breath-taking breach of military hierarchy, to say the least. Sarmiento had no authority at sea, and certainly not on the flagship. Moreover, Flores knew the vessel well, having sailed on it as part of the guard squadron of the Indies fleets a few years earlier. The *galeaza capitana* survived what followed, as did the *nao almiranta*.[2] Don Alonso de Sotomayor lost twenty-five men, but otherwise his contingent for Chile survived the storm, for which he thanked God in his report to the king's secretary.[3] Hundreds of others were not so fortunate. Rada's spare narrative captures the horror of the events in heart-breaking detail, describing the loss of four ships and nearly 800 men, women, and children.[4] One of the lost ships was *Nuestra Señora de Esperanza*, which had carried Sarmiento through the Strait of Magellan in 1579.

Sarmiento's report on the disaster focused on Flores, accusing him of cowardice, incompetence, and malfeasance, and congratulating himself on his own exemplary services to the crown.[5] Rada's narrative provides no support for Sarmiento's accusations. Nonetheless, Flores was undoubtedly devastated by the deaths of so many people, including several members of his extended family who had served as officers on the lost ships. For some days, as the surviving ships straggled into ports along the southern coast, Flores seemed paralysed by grief and unable to function. On top of everything else, he fell seriously ill, hardly able to leave his bed. In mid-October, he told Don Francisco Tello to ask the king to relieve him of command, because he would not have the necessary resources to serve, and that the surviving ships needed too many repairs to depart in a timely fashion.[6] Concerned, Tello sent word to the king and engaged two physicians to visit Flores in his lodgings in Cádiz. They examined him daily for several days and filed a notarized report on 21 October regarding his condition. The senior physician, Doctor Cuéllar, reported that Flores was suffering from an acute attack of kidney stones, 'urinating nothing but blood and other thick matter'. He was also experiencing great pain in his loins and running a fever every afternoon. Although the doctor and his colleague had tried various remedies, Flores seemed no better, and Cuéllar judged that 'the illness posed a great risk and danger to his life'. Doctor Cuéllar's colleague, the Licenciado Antonio Crespo, was also a physician, though he held a lesser academic degree in medicine (*licenciatura*) than Cuéllar's doctorate. Crespo gave the same diagnosis: an acute, life-threatening attack of kidney stones, with severe pain, daily sweats, and afternoon fever. He could not predict when, or if, the attack

[1] Sarmiento, *Narratives of the Voyages*, p. 234.

[2] Like the designation *galeaza capitana* for the flagship, *nao almiranta* defined the vessel on which the armada's second-in-command (almirante) sailed; see above, p. 22. Although the ship's proper name was *San Juan Bautista*, it is almost always referred to as the *nao almiranta*. In Spanish usage, the word *nao* could refer generically to any large sailing ship, either armed or unarmed. It could also denote a merchant vessel as opposed to a warship. Rada's *Relación* and other contemporary documents use the word *nao* in both senses.

[3] AMN, Sanz Barutell, MS 388, f. 206r, Sotomayor to Antonio de Eraso, 16 Oct. 1581.

[4] See below, pp. 68–9.

[5] Sarmiento, *Narratives of the Voyages*, pp. 234–7.

[6] AMN, MS 496, ff. 98r–100v, mentioned in a letter of Philip II to Medina Sidonia, 22 Oct. 1581. Rada makes only an oblique reference to Flores's request to be replaced. See below, pp. 69–70.

would subside.[1] Despite the official diagnosis, Sarmiento would later claim that Flores had feigned his illness and was simply afraid to go on the voyage.[2]

At the same time, Philip II wrote to the duke of Medina Sidonia to assess the situation and decide whether Flores should be replaced. The king also noted, however, that both he and the duke should write to Flores and other officials saying that there was no change in the orders or in the command structure, 'as to do otherwise would make the men feel disheartened and abandoned, which would cause notable harm'. To prevent the men from deserting, they were not allowed ashore.[3] Given the unsettled situation in Cádiz, the king formed a *junta* (committee) of advisers in Lisbon to consider the future of the armada. News had reached Portugal that the French were arming corsairs to attack the Brazilian coast, which made the repair and departure of the armada even more urgent. The report of the *junta* on 27 October advised the king to dispatch the armada as soon as possible and arrange for it to spend several months in Brazil, awaiting favourable weather for sailing to the Strait. From Rio de Janeiro, the armada would be able to respond to threats from any corsairs along the coast. Moreover, news that the governor of Brazil had died raised the possibility of unrest among the population. That was an additional reason to send the armada to Brazil for an extended stay.[4]

The *junta* noted that the area around Rio de Janeiro had abundant supplies of meat, fresh water, various crops, and a good-sized population, but the armada would still need additional supplies of biscuit and wine sent from Iberia. Assuming that the remaining ships could not depart until mid-November at the earliest, the *junta* thought the armada should plan for a stay in Rio de Janeiro of seven months, during which the 2,000 men would need an estimated 7,000 *quintales* (hundredweights) of biscuit. The *junta* suggested that the armada carry merchandise to sell in Brazil and use the proceeds to buy supplies, given the shortage of cash on hand, and that the king could send other supplies directly to the Strait. The contingents led by Don Alonso de Sotomayor and Pedro Sarmiento would carry their own supplies and provide for the layover in Brazil separately.[5] On 29 October 1581, two days after the *junta* wrote its report in Lisbon, and presumably after the king had received the doctors' report about Flores, he wrote to Medina Sidonia to oversee repairs to the remaining ships in Cádiz, aided by Don Francisco Tello and Dom Pedro Tarsis.[6]

11. Definitive Departure of the Armada of the Strait

Medina Sidonia and his colleagues completed the repairs and provisioning of the ships by the end of November, by which time Flores had regained his health. On 23 November, the king sent him the official order to sail to Brazil and remain there until October of 1582, when the

---

[1] AGS, GyM, leg. 109, doc. 394.

[2] Sarmiento, *Viajes al Estrecho*, vol. 1, p. 208.

[3] AMN, MS 496, ff. 98r–100v, Philip II to Medina Sidonia, 22 Oct. 1581. Juan Gutiérrez de Palomar, one of the senior captains in the fleet, offered to substitute for Flores should he be unable to continue. AMN, Sanz Barutell, MS 388, f. 208r–v, Gutiérrez to Antonio de Eraso, 23 Oct. 1581.

[4] The *junta* consisted of Cristóbal de Mora, Pedro de Alcazaba, Miguel de Mora, Luis César, Santiago Delgado, Juan Núñez de Illescas, and Antonio de Eraso. The deceased governor of Brazil was Lourenzo da Veiga. See, AMN, Sanz Barutell, MS 388, ff. 210r–212v, Deliberations and report of the *junta*.

[5] Ibid.

[6] AMN, MS 496, ff. 101v–104v, Philip II to Medina Sidonia, 29 Oct. 1581.

start of summer in the South Atlantic would provide better weather for the voyage to the Strait.[1] The armada left the Bay of Cádiz on 2 December, but its bad luck continued. A powerful wind came up from the east, battering the ships for four days and threatening to sink several of them. The *fragata Guadalupe* lost its battle with the sea, although it was moored next to the bulwark of San Felipe in the Bay of Cádiz. Fortunately, all the crew and passengers and part of the supplies and munitions were saved, thanks to heroic efforts by the crew of the *fragata*, aided by other ships. The rest of the armada lost only some cables and anchors.[2] Rada does not mention that the captain of the battered *fragata* was Flores' own son-in law, Álvaro del Busto. Sarmiento mentions the relationship but later claimed that no help would have been offered to the crew and passengers of the doomed *fragata* if he had not reminded the captain general of his duty – a claim that is difficult to credit.[3]

In this incident, as in earlier events, Sarmiento not only flouted the chain of command, he tried to frame the tragedy in terms that would favour himself and condemn Flores. In the days that followed the narrowly-averted loss of life, Flores and his captains readied their ships for departure once again. Sarmiento busied himself on shore, gathering together more equipment and supplies for his proposed colony, evidently without asking permission or even consulting with Flores. When Sarmiento tried to find boats to carry the extra cargo to the armada, neither Almirante Rivera nor any of the captains would help him. Even Sarmiento's staunchest defenders acknowledge that by then he had so alienated the captains in the fleet that none would offer him aid. He later wrote indignantly that he had to hire a boat on his own to load the supplies, and that

> Diego Flores laughed when he saw the boatman being paid, for he always rejoiced at the troubles and expenses of Pedro Sarmiento, who considered all well spent in the service of Your Majesty, even life itself. ... [W]hen Diego Flores saw this, he departed without waiting for Pedro Sarmiento, leaving him on shore and going to sea without him. In order to catch up with him, Pedro Sarmiento hired a *bergantín*, which cost him more money, and went in chase some considerable distance outside [the port].[4]

If we can believe Sarmiento's account, the captain general did not behave in an entirely professional manner in this instance. Nonetheless, Sarmiento's predicament provided comic relief after so much tragedy. Rada, as usual, says nothing about the clash between Sarmiento and Flores, noting only that the armada finally sailed from the Bay of Cádiz on 9 December 1581.[5] Two days earlier, officials in Cádiz made a brief report of the ships and persons on board – sixteen ships and 2,408 persons.[6] With the Armada of the Strait out of sight, the royal bureaucracy again totted up the costs.[7]

---

[1] See below, p. 70.

[2] See below, p. 70.

[3] Sarmiento, *Viajes al Estrecho*, vol. 1, pp. 211–12; Sarmiento, *Narratives of the Voyages*, p. 237.

[4] Sarmiento, *Narratives of the Voyages*, pp. 238–9.

[5] See below, pp. 70–71.

[6] See Appendix 1. The same list appears in several manuscript and printed sources, with variant spellings of names and discrepancies in numbers. Appendix 1 is a composite of the various sources, with the names made consistent with common usage, and the numbers corrected for mathematical accuracy. All the sources agree about the total number of ships and persons. See Navarrete, *Colección de documentos*, vol. 20, ff. 161r–165r; AMN, *Sanz Barutell*, MS 388, ff. 220r–224r; Sarmiento, *Narratives of the Voyages*, pp. 219–22; Sarmiento, *Viajes al Estrecho*, vol. 1, pp. 335–7. The earlier census of potential ships for the armada from AGI, CT, leg. 2899, lib. 1, appears in Chaunu, *Séville et l'Atlantique*, vol. 3, pp. 292–3.

[7] Don Francisco Tello filed accounts for the repair and resupply of the armada in Cádiz, as well as for paying

12.   From Cádiz to the Cape Verde Islands

With generally good weather, the armada sailed south-west from Iberia and arrived at the port of Santiago in the Cape Verde Islands on 11 January 1582. Portuguese officials greeted the arrival warmly, anxious to show loyalty to their new Habsburg king. Captain General Flores carried letters from King Philip that directed local officials to provide the armada with meat, salt, and firewood. While workers butchered and salted the meat, Flores and the local Portuguese officials entertained one another, and Rada describes the festivities in considerable detail.[1]

Flores wrote to the king on 24 January 1582, noting that he had purchased additional supplies in Santiago for the two-month voyage to Brazil, which had cost most of the 13,000 ducats that he carried.[2] That left very little to provide for the '3,000' people in the armada during their long layover in Brazil, which worried him greatly.[3] He told the king that he planned to leave Brazil for the Strait in early October of 1582 and requested that additional supplies be sent from Iberia to arrive sometime in August or early September in Rio de Janeiro or Bahia, but not at the Strait, as the Council of the Indies had suggested. Captain General Flores also wrote to the governors of the cities in Brazil where the armada planned to layover, sending those messages with a caravel heading to Brazil.

As a reminder that his mission was diplomatic as well as military, Flores told the king that there were opponents as well as strong partisans to his accession in Santiago.[4] Others might well move into opposition if the rival claimant, Dom Antonio, gained strength. Flores wrote that he had endeavoured to quiet the opposition, and he strongly urged increased fortifications in Santiago as a show of royal support for the inhabitants. To consolidate their loyalty, Flores urged the king to aid the completion of the principal church in Santiago, which remained unfinished years after construction began. He also noted that he had made a tour of inspection of the island and had directed 'the engineer who travels in this armada',[5] to draw up plans to fortify the area from the town of Santiago

---

the officers and men aboard. In all, Tello's accounts totalled more than 29,500 ducats (11,063,758 *maravedís*). Nearly half that amount comprised the cash – some 13,000 ducats – that accompanied the armada in an *arca de tres llaves* (three-keyed strongbox), to purchase additional supplies in ports of call. As the name implies, that type of strongbox required the simultaneous turning of three keys to open the lock. Each key was entrusted to a different individual to guard against malfeasance. Clearly, the strain of preparing so many ships in 1581 had made it imperative to regularize fleet preparation. From Lisbon, Philip II wrote to the Council of the Indies in Madrid on 18 Dec. 1581, establishing rules to better organize preparation of the various Atlantic fleets. Among other points, the king ordered the captains general and almirantes appointed for each fleet to be present in Seville to oversee its preparation, and then in Sanlúcar de Barrameda to oversee its final lading; Navarrete, *Colección de documentos*, vol. 22, ff. 336r–337r. Diego Flores had urged that requirement and other elements in the new rules since 1570.

[1] See below, pp. 72–3.

[2] Flores to Philip II, 24 Jan. 1582, from Santiago de Cabo Verde, in *CODOIN*, vol. 94, p. 540.

[3] The official count of the armada when it left Spain was 2,408. See above, p. 72, and Appendix 1.

[4] According to Sarmiento, the Bishop of Santiago, Don Bartolomé Leitão, was initially opposed to the resolution which proclaimed Philip of Habsburg as king of Portugal, but Francisco and Gaspar de Andrada persuaded him to change his mind; Sarmiento, *Viajes al Estrecho*, vol. 1, p. 214.

[5] That is, Battista Antonelli, whom the Spaniards call Bautista Antoneli (b. Gatteo, Italy, 1547, d. Madrid, 1616). Battista's older brother, Giovanni Battista, had served Philip II since 1559, and the two brothers collaborated on several engineering projects in Spain before 1580. See above, pp. 19–20. Although Giovanni Battista advised the duke of Alba about fortifications for the Strait, he excused himself from accompanying the

to the beach, a distance of about two leagues (some six miles on land), and to provide heavier artillery for coastal defence. He recommended that the king send two galleys to patrol the area between the islands and Guinea, both to protect trade and to guard against French and English incursions.

Sarmiento later wrote that he examined the fortifications of Santiago along with Captain General Flores and the local governor and that he, not Flores, had asked Battista Antonelli to sketch plans to fortify the island, which the governor sent to the king. Sarmiento complained that he gave a copy to Flores to accompany the general's own report, but that 'Diego Flores chose to lose it, in order that nothing might arrive that would give your Majesty satisfaction connected with the services of Pedro Sarmiento'.[1] Rada does not directly contradict Sarmiento, but he emphasizes the care taken by Captain General Flores to ensure that his report arrived safely by sending copies on two caravels, one via the Canary Islands and the other directly to Lisbon.[2]

13. Arrival and Layover in Brazil, 25 March–26 October 1582

Having loaded their additional supplies, the armada left Santiago on 2 February 1582 and sailed directly across the Atlantic toward Brazil. Rada provides a meticulous record of their progress day by day, and of the winds, currents, and weather that the armada encountered. Although such records are repetitive, they are valuable for historians of the maritime world, and also for scholars of historical climate patterns. The ships anchored in the port of Rio de Janeiro[3] on the night of 25 March. The next day, they received a cordial reception from local officials and the inhabitants of the coast, as well as their Indigenous allies.[4] Captain General Flores presented a letter from King Philip to the local governor, Salvador Correa de Saa, directing him to help the armada secure necessary supplies. In the days that followed their arrival, some of the officers and officials in the armada were able to arrange lodgings on land in the houses of local citizens. The rest of the large expedition built makeshift huts (*chozas*) in which to live, or lodged on farmsteads in the vicinity. Repairs began on the ships, while their sails, guns, and other crucial equipment were disembarked and warehoused on land, to avoid deterioration in the hot and humid climate.[5]

---

expedition. Instead, Battista and an assistant named Gaspar de Sampier, along with two servants, made the voyage; see Sarmiento, *Narratives of the Voyages*, p. 223. During his long and distinguished career in service to the Spanish crown, Battista would design most of the important Spanish fortifications in the Caribbean. See Gasparini, *Los Antonelli*, pp. 37–88 for discussion of his career and numerous photographs of his fortifications. Unfortunately, Gasparini mistakenly identifies the head of the Armada of the Strait as Álvaro Flores de Valdés and refers to him as the almirante, rather than the captain general; see pp. 38–9.

[1] Sarmiento, *Narratives of the Voyages*, p. 240.

[2] See below, p. 73. It was standard practice to send multiple copies of important dispatches by different carriers and routes to guard against mishaps at sea, particularly when corsairs were active.

[3] The port is located at 22°54′S, 43°14′W.

[4] See below, pp. 74–5.

[5] Sarmiento, *Viajes al Estrecho*, vol. 1, pp. 182, 221. Tropical shipworms (various species of the genus of molluscs called *Teredo*) would bore into many of the ships' hulls during the long layover; the five ships that belonged to the crown were protected by thin lead sheathing below the waterline. See Sarmiento, *Narratives of the Voyages*, p. 246.

The climate also threatened the health of the people in the armada, but they were better off on land than during the voyage. In less than two months at sea between the Cape Verde Islands and Brazil, some 150 people had sickened and died. Sarmiento noted that many of the afflicted complained of stomach pains and thirst as soon as the armada entered tropical climes.[1] It is impossible to determine what sickened them, but perhaps they had contracted some malady or maladies during their sojourn in the Cape Verdes. In addition to those who died at sea, many others died after arriving in Rio de Janeiro. Members of a local religious confraternity, the *Cofrades de la Misericordia* (Brethren of Mercy), did their best to care for the sick, but they had limited resources and personnel. Sarmiento wrote that some 200 more people died after arriving in Rio de Janeiro. He also accused Flores of great indifference toward the sick, claiming that he refused to give them extra rations of water at sea and even laughed at their plight.[2] It is impossible to test those accusations; Rada mentions nothing more than the total deaths before reaching Brazil.[3]

To supply the large expedition for nearly eight months before they departed for the Strait represented a huge challenge for local resources. Rio de Janeiro had only recently begun to develop economically, after the Portuguese ousted the French in 1567. The arrival of the Armada of the Strait must have overwhelmed the small settlement and its available resources. In late June of 1582, Captain General Flores sent Almirante Rivera and other officers south to Santos y São Vicente, the oldest Portuguese port and settlement in Brazil, to buy additional supplies. While awaiting their return and additional supplies from Spain, Flores and other officials continued to prepare for the voyage to the Strait. On 8 August 1582, Flores received news from Spain that the king had granted him an *encomienda* (commandery) in the Order of Santiago, the prestigious noble military order to which he already belonged.[4] This suggests that Philip II continued to have confidence in his captain general, despite the steady stream of vitriol that Sarmiento had been sending to court since long before the armada's departure. In the same packet of letters, officials in Spain reported the departure of French corsairs bound for Brazil, and authorities elsewhere in Brazil reported the presence of three large armed ships on the coast – a reminder of the armada's military mission to combat corsairs and interlopers.[5] At that juncture, Flores could not be sure if the armed vessels on the coast were the corsairs who had departed from France or other potential enemies.

In contrast to Rada's *Relación*, Sarmiento's account of the layover in Rio de Janeiro is an indictment of nearly everyone connected with the armada, from Captain General Flores down to unnamed common seamen and soldiers.[6] One complaint involved the construction of storehouses for the supplies he had collected for the Strait. Sarmiento arranged for local Indians to cut wood from the forest into planks, promising to compensate them with linen shirts and loose trousers (*zaragüelles*) for three months' work. The governor supplied slaves from one of his islands to help cut and transport the

---

[1] Sarmiento, *Viajes al Estrecho*, vol. 1, pp. 180–82.

[2] Ibid., pp. 218–21.

[3] See below, p. 75. Don Francisco de Vera later noted that some 300 persons had died on the voyage, presumably including those who died after reaching Rio de Janeiro; see below, p. 166.

[4] AHN, OM, Carpeta 247, N. 7.

[5] Sarmiento, *Viajes al Estrecho*, vol. 1, pp. 241–2.

[6] Sarmiento to Philip II, 30 Oct. 1582, in Sarmiento, *Viajes al Estrecho*, vol. 1, pp. 179–90. Sarmiento's expanded account of the voyage, dated 1 June 1583, appears in vol. 1, pp. 206–90.

wood.[1] Sarmiento later wrote that after the settlers had completed one storehouse, under his constant supervision, Flores halted construction and used the wood for other purposes.[2] Even worse, according to Sarmiento, when it came time to pay the Indians for their labour, Flores opened the bales of clothing brought for the settlers and gave 'the best items' to the Indian sawyers. Sarmiento further claimed that:

> [Flores] also took 2,400 yards of linen that I carried for the settlers and sent it to São Vicente to pay for the victuals purchased there. The general also used much of the iron and steel for the settlement to make certain gun carriages and tools for cutting kindling, and they say that to buy flour from the Indians, he has also taken the garments that I carried for the Indian sawyers.[3]

If Sarmiento's allegations are true, Flores no doubt behaved in a high-handed manner, though he was within his authority as captain general to do so.

Sarmiento criticized the rest of the military contingent as well, presenting himself as the only true guardian of the king's interests. He complained that the ships' masters refused to load roof tiles and other additional supplies for the Strait, while at the same time buying and loading brazil wood for eventual sale in Europe. Sarmiento singled out one captain, 'the brother of the almirante'[4] for loading brazil wood on the *almiranta*. Sarmiento claimed that he complained so loudly and publicly about these goings-on that Captain General Flores had no choice but to order 'between his teeth, that the dye wood should be landed'.[5] According to Sarmiento, the master and crew members of one of the affected ships, the *San Esteban* of Arriola:

> seeing that Pedro Sarmiento has been the cause that the order was given to land the dye wood, publicly declared that they would throw all the stores for the Straits into the sea; and they did throw a quantity overboard, it being the property of your Majesty. Diego Flores disliked what Pedro Sarmiento did to preserve the property of your Majesty and to check the proceedings of the thieves; and although he made an appearance of doing the same, he dissimulated too much, and in reality did nothing.[6]

Sarmiento also decried the widespread pilferage of food and ships' stores and their sale in Rio de Janeiro. He accused two of the officers of complicity: Captain Francisco de Cuéllar of the king's *fragata Santa Catalina*, and Captain Gonzalo Meléndez de Valdés, of the *nao Santa Marta*.[7] When accused of stealing the king's provisions, according to Sarmiento, the men said they had to do so in order to survive, and there is no reason to doubt either Sarmiento's accusations or the men's justification. Sarmiento's complaints about pilferage and waste extended to the use of gunpowder for military drill, although that was part of the routine for enlisted soldiers. He also expressed outrage that three men from the armada received very light punishment from Flores for crimes against his settlers – one for

---

[1] Sarmiento, *Viajes al Estrecho*, vol. 1, p. 183.

[2] Ibid., pp. 182–3.

[3] Ibid., pp. 188–9. The tools for cutting kindling were *hocinos*, a kind of hatchet with a hooked blade.

[4] Presumably, Captain Alonso de las Alas; Sarmiento, *Narratives of the Voyages*, p. 248.

[5] Ibid.

[6] Ibid. Markham excerpted Sarmiento's letter of 1 June 1583 in *Narratives of the Voyages*, but he failed to indicate which parts he omitted. The full text of the very lengthy letter appears in Sarmiento, *Viajes al Estrecho*, vol. 1, pp. 206–90.

[7] Ibid., p. 230.

rape, one for refusing to marry a settler's daughter whom he had seduced, and one for murder.[1] Assuming the accusations were true, it would seem that Flores thought the costs of harsher punishments outweighed the benefits. He had some 2,000 men under his command during the long layover. Maintaining generally good discipline among them required a deft use of his power. It is telling that when Sarmiento's accusations led to firmer measures, such as the order to unload brazil wood, the men turned against Sarmiento and not Flores. Sarmiento acknowledged that reality at several points in his lengthy narratives.[2] According to Sarmiento, Suero Queipo de Llano, captain of the king's *fragata Santa Isabel*, even urged Flores to have Sarmiento executed.[3]

On 3 October 1582, Flores issued general orders for all the officers in the armada who were going to the Strait, though they could not depart until Almirante Rivera returned from São Vicente.[4] He and his contingent had left Rio de Janeiro on 25 June to purchase additional supplies, but they did not return until 17 October, due to bad weather and high seas. When they finally arrived, Flores had the armada ready to depart, though he still hoped to wait until promised relief supplies arrived from Spain. Those hopes vanished on 24 October, when a party of Franciscan friars and their leader, Commissary Juan de Rivadeneira, arrived after a five-month journey from Spain.[5] They informed Flores that a fleet of four or five ships, laden with his relief supplies, had instead been diverted to the island of Terceira in the Azores, where the king had sent a fleet to defeat opposition to his accession to the Portuguese throne.[6] Hearing that, Flores gave orders to set sail from Rio de Janeiro, writing to the king that he would return from the Strait as soon as possible to patrol the Brazilian coast in pursuit of corsairs.[7]

14.   The Best Laid Plans Go Awry: The First Attempt to Enter the Strait

Up to that point, the Armada of the Strait followed the objectives and timetable established by Philip II. Thereafter, circumstances repeatedly thwarted those aims and disrupted the timetable, while the ongoing contention between Sarmiento and Flores complicated every aspect of the armada's activities. Rada's spare narrative never mentions that conflict directly, though his records of several consultations among the senior officers suggest that Sarmiento disagreed with virtually everyone else. His one goal was to have the armada deliver the settlers to the Strait and build the fortifications that he had envisioned. Anything and everything that delayed that goal he blamed on Flores, recording his criticism in an endless stream of vituperation sent to Madrid. Rada's narrative provides an implicit response to Sarmiento's complaints, giving detailed evidence of the great difficulties that the armada faced in reaching the Strait.

---

[1] Ibid., pp. 238–9.

[2] Ibid., pp. 187–9, 229–31.

[3] Ibid., p. 227.

[4] See below, pp. 135–6.

[5] The comisario (commissary) in this context was an official of the Catholic monastic order of St Francis, charged with conducting a group of his fellow friars to a mission in the Río de la Plata.

[6] In fact, the relief fleet was not diverted, but it had left for Brazil after Rivadeneira's departure. AMN, MS 496, f. 141r–v, Philip II to Medina Sidonia, 29 July 1582; MS 498, doc. 337.

[7] See below, p. 77.

As captain general, Flores must have been as anxious as Sarmiento to reach the Strait, so that he could focus on the armada's primary military mission. Prior to the departure from Rio de Janeiro, Flores ordered Sarmiento to move from the *capitana* to another ship of his choice, along with his supplies for the Strait. The *capitana* was the largest ship in the armada at 700 *toneladas*; everyone knew it could not navigate in the Strait, even under the best conditions. It was logical to move Sarmiento and his stores to one of the ships small enough to enter the Strait, though the contention between the two men may have influenced Flores's decision. Sarmiento took the order as a personal attack and tried to enlist the support of the armada's chief accountant, Andrés de Eguino, in protesting Flores's decision. Sarmiento interpreted the king's instruction that he and Flores should consult with one another as an absolute mandate for them to stay together. Eguino told Sarmiento that there was nothing more to be done, as the captain general had given his orders. Sarmiento then tried the same approach with Rada, asking him to tell the general not to disobey the king so 'exorbitantly'. According to Sarmiento, Rada spoke to the general but returned to say that there was no remedy for the decision. Asking Rada to witness that he absolved himself from blame if anything went wrong thereafter, Sarmiento concluded that Flores had 'conceived such hatred for Pedro Sarmiento on account of his efforts, that contrary to the orders of Your Majesty that they should be together for mutual help, he separated himself, and made Pedro Sarmiento embark on another ship, where there was scarcely room for his stores'.[1] That ship was the *nao Santa María de Begoña*.

The armada first set sail from Rio de Janeiro with seventeen ships on 26 October 1582, then definitively on 2 November with sixteen. Rada chronicles the voyage south in harrowing detail. With the weather alternating between middling good and very bad, the ships were assailed by brutal winds and high seas.[2] No amount of planning in Madrid could compensate for the treacherous conditions in the South Atlantic, even in summer. Nonetheless, Sarmiento later blamed Flores for every mishap.[3] He was also outraged that Flores and Antón Pablos, the chief pilot of the armada, had set the course for the Strait without consulting him, though Sarmiento had never sailed that coast. He viewed the chief pilot's collaboration with Flores as a betrayal, after he had secured the position for him and had 'done him more friendship and good in other things than if I were his father. And in payment of this, he concerted with Diego Flores against me.' Sarmiento further accused Pablos of spreading the notion that he, Pablos, was responsible for the best information about the Strait and that the charts Sarmiento had prepared for the voyage in Seville were inaccurate.[4]

The farther south the armada sailed, the worse the weather and seas became. Sarmiento later wrote that the settlers on the *Begoña* blamed him for bringing them to such a pass, voicing 'a million blasphemies against him', while the friars and royal officials stirred up the settlers' fears. One ship was lost during a terrible storm at the end of November, with 220 persons and most of the supplies for the settlement in the Strait. On 2 December, a south-west wind was forcing the armada on a course towards the north-east, farther from the Strait. During a lull in the wind, when the armada was at

---

[1] Sarmiento, *Narratives of the Voyages*, pp. 248–9; Sarmiento, *Viajes al Estrecho*, vol. 1, pp. 246–7.
[2] See below, pp. 78–82.
[3] For example, Sarmiento, *Viajes al Estrecho*, vol. 1, p. 253.
[4] Ibid., pp. 244–5.

36°S, Don Alonso de Sotomayor asked Captain General Flores's permission to take his damaged ships into the nearby Río de la Plata and march his men overland to Chile, rather than attempting to sail through the Strait. Flores agreed with his reasoning but told Sotomayor not to leave the armada without his express orders to do so.[1] On 5 December, the wind slackened enough for Flores to call a general meeting of the principal officers and officials in the armada. After due deliberation, they agreed to head for the Río de la Plata or the first accessible port to repair their ships, instead of trying to continue south. Following standard procedures, everyone present at the meeting, including Sarmiento, signed a statement to that effect.[2] Nonetheless, Sarmiento later represented the official consultation as nothing more than a pro forma confirmation of a prior decision. He alleged that Flores, 'supported by all the Asturians and the others who had never wanted to make this trip', had decided without consultation to head for a port such as the Río de la Plata or São Vicente, due to their cowardice in the face of bad weather. He acknowledged that the damaged ships needed repairs, but he blamed Flores for leaving Rio de Janeiro too early and sailing too far off the coast on a course recommended by Antón Pablos. When Pablos learned that he was being blamed for setting a faulty course, 'he said a thousand bad things about Pedro Sarmiento', which the latter 'suffered in silence, because he wanted to do the right thing'.[3]

15. Encounters with the Expedition of Edward Fenton

Nearing Río de la Plata on 15 December, they saw the sails of a small ship, which turned out to be carrying the Franciscan commissary Juan de Rivadeneira with six friars, Don Francisco de Vera, and thirteen other passengers.[4] They had left Rio de Janeiro the same day as the armada, heading for the Río de la Plata, but an English expedition had captured and held them for six days at the port of Dom Rodrigo.[5] Vera and Rivadeneira described the two large English ships in that port as well gunned, manned, and outfitted. The English were careful not to identify their leader, but the Spaniards later learned that he was Edward Fenton.[6] The English interrogated Vera and Rivadeneira at length and took most of the food and clothing that their bark carried, but otherwise they treated their

[1] See below, p. 81.
[2] See below, pp. 81–2. The transcript of the meeting appears on pp. 145–9.
[3] Sarmiento, *Viajes al Estrecho*, vol. 1, pp. 258–9. Sarmiento frequently complained about the numerous men from Flores's home region of Asturias on the expedition, accusing them of concerted plotting against him.
[4] See below, pp. 82–5.
[5] The port of Dom Rodrigo, today's Garopaba Bay, is located at approximately 28°10′S, just south-west of Santa Catarina Island. The modern city of Florianopolis, capital of the state of Santa Catarina, includes the northern portion of the island.
[6] Fenton had participated in several overseas ventures in the 1570s. His official instructions for this voyage were to establish trade with rulers in the Far East friendly to Portugal and to follow up Drake's contacts with the Moluccas. Notes were also prepared for him regarding trade with Brazil. See Andrews, 'Latin America', in Quinn, *Hakluyt Handbook*, vol. 1, p. 241, citing TNA, SP 12/153, f. 43. Even in the planning stages, however, veterans of Drake's voyage and those of like mind hoped to plunder Portuguese and Spanish targets, creating conflict with the merchants accompanying the voyage, which marked the enterprise from beginning to end. See Taylor, *Troublesome Voyage*; Donno, *Diary of Richard Madox*; Andrews, *Elizabethan Privateering*, pp. 203–5; McDermott, 'Fenton'.

prisoners well. Rivadeneira would later note, however, that all but four or five of the English notables had wanted to kill them, though the minority eventually prevailed and they were released.[1] During their captivity, Vera and Rivadeneira told the English everything they knew about the Armada of the Strait, but they did not know where it was at the time. Likewise, Flores did not know the whereabouts of the English, but there was a chance that they were still in the vicinity.

Rada took full statements from Vera and Rivadeneira. The latter surmised that the English were headed to the Río de la Plata and planned to stay there until the Spanish armada had left the Strait and then traverse it themselves on their way to the Moluccas. Flores consulted his principal officers and decided to go to Santa Catarina Island, some six leagues north of the port of Dom Rodrigo, to make repairs and decide which of the ships were still fit to continue south. In a few days, the men repaired nine of the ships at Santa Catarina well enough for a second attempt at the Strait, aware that they might encounter the English on the way.[2] After consultation, Flores left the *almiranta* and two other ships at Santa Catarina for more extensive repairs, under the command of Accountant Andrés de Eguino. Making sure they had provisions and weaponry for their sustenance and defence, Flores ordered Eguino to repair the ships sufficiently to transport soldiers, sailors, and settlers who were too weak or sick to continue to the Strait, back to Rio de Janeiro or another accessible port to recover. Along the way, Eguino was to search for the English and engage them, if by chance they had headed north.[3]

As Rivadeneira and Vera had surmised, Fenton's expedition sailed south after releasing them. They knew the total size and strength of Flores's armada when it left Rio de Janeiro for the Strait on 2 November. They did not know its subsequent movements or whereabouts. When Fenton reached 33°15′S, several degrees north of the entrance to the Río de la Plata on 21 December, he called a council of his senior officers to discuss their options. Luke Ward, his second in command, later testified that Fenton asked them to consider whether to continue on to the Strait, 'considering the force of the enemy, which we knew to be there before us', which would thwart their plans to repair their ships and resupply at the Strait before proceeding into the Pacific. There were also potential problems in resupplying at the Río de la Plata. Given those difficulties, Fenton decided to turn north and resupply on the Brazilian coast before proceeding anywhere else. John Drake disagreed with that decision and slipped away the next night for the Río de la Plata with the pinnace *Francis* and eighteen crew members.[4]

Fenton sailed his two remaining ships north to Santos y São Vicente, arriving on 20 January 1583. There are hints that the English considered forcing the community to

---

[1] 'Relación de carta de fray Juan de Rivadeneira al Gobernador de Tucumán', in *CODOIN,* vol. 94, pp. 549–52. Richard Madox, physician, cosmographer and chaplain of Fenton's expedition, provides detailed commentary on the capture and interrogation of the bark's passengers, confirming that some of his colleagues wished to kill them without cause. Donno, *Diary of Richard Madox*, pp. 246–58.

[2] See below, pp. 86–9.

[3] See below, pp. 136–9, for Flores's detailed instructions for Eguino and the other officers. Sarmiento later criticized every aspect of the decisions at Santa Catarina, claiming that the ships left for repairs were perfectly sound, and that Flores wanted nothing more than to return to Spain to enjoy the honours the king had given him. Sarmiento, *Viajes al Estrecho*, vol. 1, pp. 264–8.

[4] Taylor, *Troublesome Voyage*, pp. 248–50. See also below, pp. 101–2.

trade with them, but in the end they seem to have decided to move on.[1] The arrival of Andrés Eguino changed their plans. Eguino's men had finished repairs sooner than expected on the three ships that Flores left behind in early January. They had departed from Santa Catarina on 18 January, bound for Rio de Janeiro.[2] Along the way, Eguino followed Captain General Flores's orders to search for the English corsairs. He found them on 24 January in Santos.[3] Eguino later described the two English ships as a galleon of 450 *toneladas*, and another vessel of 350 *toneladas*, both of them well armed and well manned.[4] His own hastily repaired ships included the *almiranta San Juan Bautista* at 500 *toneladas*, *La Concepción* at 400, and *Santa María de Begoña* at 230.[5] The *Begoña* carried the weakened settlers and presumably did not have room for a full complement of soldiers.

Although Eguino was officially the contador (accountant) of the Armada of the Strait, he was also experienced in warfare. After consulting his officers, he organized a night-time attack that began about 10 o'clock. Fighting continued through the night and into the next day, but the Spaniards were ultimately outgunned. The *Begoña*, flying the flag of the *almiranta* in the encounter, sank after splitting apart from heavy artillery fire, though most of the people aboard survived. *San Juan Bautista*, flying the flag of the *capitana*, and *Concepción* suffered heavy damage as well.[6] Though the English clearly had the advantage, they disengaged and sailed away the next morning, and the two remaining Spanish ships were too damaged to pursue them. According to observations from shore, the English ships had sustained damage as well, and one Portuguese witness, Antonio Chavero, reported that they had also suffered heavy casualties.[7] At the time of the battle, Rada was on the *capitana* with the contingent making a second attempt at the Strait, so his account relied on later information from Eguino and other eyewitnesses.[8] Rada explicitly declined to comment on why the English sailed away when they had the advantage,[9] a question that would feature prominently in later inquiries in England.[10] Nor did he comment on

---

[1] Antonio Chavero, a Portuguese resident of Brazil, said the English put men ashore to forcibly take provisions after the governor refused to trade. 'Relación del suceso de la armada que fué al Estrecho de Magallanes' in *CODOIN*, vol. 94, p. 553. Eguino also claimed that the English had 'occupied the port and terrorized the inhabitants'; Taylor, *Troublesome Voyage*, p. 252.

[2] See below, p. 99.

[3] Bradley, *British Maritime Enterprise*, p. 378, writes that Flores's armada surprised Fenton at Santos, unaware that the armada had been split into several contingents by then.

[4] See below, pp. 99–100.

[5] Chaunu, *Séville et l'Atlantique*, vol. 3, pp. 292–3, provides the tonnages of the Spanish ships from a list made in Seville in 1581.

[6] Taylor, *Troublesome Voyage*, pp. 255–6, 286–7. The Portuguese named Juan Pinto witnessed the battle from one of the English ships and later told the Spanish ambassador in London that the English had sunk the *capitana* of Flores's fleet. Ambassador Bernardino de Mendoza duly reported the bad news to Philip II. Although Pinto was an eyewitness, he mistook what he saw. *San Juan Bautista*, the *almiranta* of the armada as a whole, flew the flag of the *capitana* for the three Spanish ships in the battle. *Begoña*, the ship that sank, flew the *almiranta*'s flag. Reflecting that confusion, King Philip replied that it was known that Flores's *almiranta* (i.e. *San Juan Bautista*) had fought, but not whether it had sunk. Philip II to Mendoza, 12 Sept. 1583, in Calvar et al., *Batalla del Mar Océano*, vol. 1, doc. 334.

[7] 'Relación del suceso de la armada que fué al Estrecho de Magallanes' in *CODOIN*, vol. 94, pp. 552–4.

[8] See below, pp. 99–102.

[9] See below, pp. 101–2.

[10] Donno, *Diary of Richard Madox*, pp. 38–40.

the controversy regarding the conduct of the Spanish officers during the battle and their responsibility for the Spanish losses.[1] A few days after the battle, Portuguese authorities asked Eguino to build a fort at Santos, as they had no proper defences. Work commenced in late January of 1583.

Meanwhile, after making repairs on 25 and 26 January, the English sailed to the nearby island of Queimada Grande, where they anchored for two days to collect water and firewood.[2] During that interval, Captain Luke Ward on the *Edward Bonaventure* separated from Fenton and sailed back to England; he would later report that the wind and seas gave him no choice.[3] Fenton then sailed the *Leicester* to the small port of Espírito Santo at 20°S.[4] In late February, just as he thought the local authorities would sign an agreement permitting him to trade, they received news about the Battle of Santos.[5] At that point, Fenton hurriedly left Espírito Santo and headed out to sea, without being able to replenish his supplies. He may have planned to sail to Newfoundland, and some of his ship's company may have hoped to plunder in the Caribbean, but ultimately Fenton set a course for England.[6] His expedition no longer posed a threat to Spanish and Portuguese interests, but they did not know it, either in Brazil or in Iberia.

After their release by Fenton and their re-encounter with the Armada of the Strait, Commissary Rivadeneira and his friars eventually arrived at the Río de la Plata, following a further series of misadventures. Rivadeneira immediately wrote to the king and to the governor of Tucumán with news about the armada and the English. The governor forwarded the information, along with his own comments, to the viceroy of Peru.[7] Rivadeneira noted that the English ships carried 350 men and 12,000 ducats' worth of merchandise, including many bibles and works of popular literature, along with enough supplies to last for two years. He warned that they planned to attack Flores when he returned from the Strait and then to capture any forts that Flores had built there and then

---

[1] See below, pp. 101–2. Andrés de Eguino requested an official inquiry into the battle, which was conducted on 8–9 February in São Vicente. Several questions put to witnesses suggest that Eguino blamed the captain of the *Concepción*, Francisco de Cuéllar, for failing to fight vigorously during the night battle, dooming the *Begoña* and leaving the *San Juan Bautista* too damaged to pursue the English. A translation of the questionnaire appears in Taylor, *Troublesome Voyage*, pp. 322–3. Their legal battle continued when they returned to Spain. See AGI, Escribanía, leg. 1069B. I thank Francis Kelly of University College, Cork, Ireland, for sharing his research notes on Francisco Cuéllar and his quarrel with Eguino.

[2] The island, located at 24°28′59″S, 46°40′48″W, is a rare habitat of the golden lancehead (*fer-de-lance*), one of the deadliest snakes on earth; at present there may be as many as three snakes per square metre. None of the English accounts mentions seeing snakes on the island, which was a rare piece of good luck for Fenton's expedition. Taylor, *Troublesome Voyage*, pp. 129–33.

[3] Ward arrived back in Plymouth on 29 May 1583. Bradley, *British Maritime Enterprise*, pp. 378–9. See also Taylor, *Troublesome Voyage*, pp. 158–9.

[4] In about 1570, the captaincy of Espírito Santo held about 180–200 Portuguese households; McAlister, *Spain and Portugal in the New World*, pp. 280–81.

[5] Testimony of Juan Pérez (Richard Carter), a resident of the Río de la Plata, whom Fenton had captured along with the Franciscan friars and Don Francisco de Vera; in Navarrete, *Colección de documentos*, vol. 25, f. 186v. After releasing most of their prisoners, the English had continued to hold Pérez for his knowledge of the area. Taylor, *Troublesome Voyage*, p. 234, n. 1, surmises that he was released at Espírito Santo, which is accurate.

[6] Fenton left Brazil on 19 May 1583 and arrived in England on 29 June, having accomplished none of his aims; Taylor, *Troublesome Voyage*, pp. l–liv.

[7] Don Martín Enríquez de Almanza served as viceroy of Peru from 23 Sept. 1581 to 13 March 1583, when he died in office.

proceed into the Pacific. In contrast to his earlier debriefing by Flores, Rivadeneira's letter did not speculate about English plans to sail to the Moluccas.[1]

The news from Rivadeneira arrived in Peru at the end of April by the difficult overland route across the Andes. In Lima, the interim viceroy, Cristóbal Ramírez de Cartagena, President of the Audiencia, consulted his colleagues and then wrote his own note to the king at the beginning of May.[2] By then, local authorities both in the Río de la Plata and in Lima had heard that the few ships remaining in the armada were badly damaged, and that Captain General Flores and his officers were very pessimistic about overtaking the corsairs. According to the interim viceroy, Flores 'had no plans to pass through the Strait, nor was he able to do so'. With good weather, the corsairs could continue unhindered, he warned, 'and no one would be able to resist [their] designs'. He concluded that if the English planted a colony in the Strait, it would be very bad, but if they continued into the Pacific, it would be even worse, as they would certainly do harm to the viceroyalty.[3] His dismal prognosis reflected the judgment of various local officials who had little recent news about the English and only bad news about the armada.

16.   The Second Attempt to Reach the Strait, January–February, 1583

After entrusting the three damaged ships to Eguino at Santa Catarina, on 7 January 1583 Flores had left with the nine ships that were deemed fit to sail. He aimed to overtake the English if they were headed south, and to follow them through the Strait if necessary, after depositing Sarmiento and some of the settlers. With the *almiranta* undergoing repairs at Santa Catarina, Flores transferred Almirante Rivera to the *capitana* along with Sarmiento, whose ship *Begoña* also remained behind. Flores himself moved to the small, agile *fragata Santa Isabel*, which could reconnoitre ports and potential hiding places for the English. Rada remained on the *capitana*, which means that his journal recorded events largely from the perspective of that vessel. One ship ran aground departing from Santa Catarina and was left behind; the other eight continued south, battling winds and stormy weather.[4]

Near the Río de la Plata, Flores summoned the principal officers to his *fragata* on 19 January to discuss their situation. They agreed that the armada might not be able to return to sea in a timely fashion if all the ships sailed into the broad, shallow estuary. Flores

[1] A summary of Rivadeneira's letters was prepared for Philip II by his secretaries and dated 19 March 1583. Presumably, that was the date of Rivadeneira's correspondence, not the date of the summary. See 'Relación de carta de fray Juan de Rivadeneira al Gobernador de Tucumán' in *CODOIN*, vol. 94, pp. 549–52; also in Calvar et al., *Batalla del Mar Océano*, vol. 1, doc. 313. In his letters, Rivadeneira reported on the arrival of Don Alonso de Sotomayor and his men at the Río de la Plata, which occurred in late January 1583; see below, p. 104. He also included information about both the armada and Fenton's expedition that he had not known the previous December. Some of the additional information may have come indirectly from Juan Pérez (Richard Carter), who gave a statement to local authorities in Espíritu Santo after Fenton released him in February 1583; see 'Relación que dió Juan Perez' in Navarrete, *Colección de documentos*, vol. 25, ff. 184r–186v. Assuming that Rivadeneira wrote on 19 March, 1583, his letters would not have reached Madrid until at least a month or so later.

[2] After the death of of Viceroy Enríquez in March of 1583, Ramírez served as interim viceroy until a successor arrived.

[3] Interim Viceroy Ramírez to Philip II, 3 May 1583, in Navarrete, *Colección de documentos*, vol. 26, ff. 83r–84r; also in Calvar et al., *Batalla del Mar Océano*, vol. 1, doc. 316.

[4] See below, pp. 103–4. The ship left behind was the *San Esteban* of Soroa.

ordered Don Alonso de Sotomayor to take the three ships that carried his infantrymen into the Río de la Plata, and to continue overland to Chile – the option that Sotomayor had favoured for weeks. Two of the vessels carrying Sotomayor's men would remain in the Río de la Plata. The newest ship of the three – the *Trinidad* – would return to Rio de Janeiro carrying extra munitions and supplies for the settlers preparing to go to the Strait.[1]

Flores's five remaining vessels continued south towards the Strait on 19 January 1583, but once again they ran into fierce midsummer weather in the South Atlantic. Rada chronicled their day-to-day progress, dutifully recording the direction of the winds, the course that the ships followed, the reckoning of their position, and the various mishaps that befell them as they proceeded towards the mouth of the Strait at 52°30′S. As they prepared to enter the Strait on 17 February, the wind began to blow from the west and west-south-west with such strength that it forced them more than twenty leagues out to sea again. For the next several days, they fought to return to the mouth of the Strait, with supplies running low and fierce winds and waves battering all the vessels.[2] The wind died down on 23 February, just as they again reached the mouth of the Strait, and it looked as if they might be able to enter. The next day, however, the wind from the west-south-west returned, howling out of the Strait with renewed force. With one ship missing and the situation critical, the four remaining ships abandoned the attempt to enter the Strait and headed north, fighting strong winds and seas through the 'roaring forties'.[3] Flores and the *fragatas Santa Isabel* and *Santa Catalina* were separated from the other three vessels as they continued north.

On Easter Sunday, 31 March, the armada's *capitana*, under the command of Almirante Rivera, with Rada and Sarmiento aboard, arrived at the port of Santos, along with the *nao María de Villaviciosa* and the *fragata Magdalena*. Work on the fort at Santos was still continuing, and Almirante Rivera took charge from Eguino as the senior officer.[4] Captain General Flores arrived with the two *fragatas* on 15 April.[5] After arranging for the completion and manning of the fort, Flores left Santos y São Vicente on 28 April with the seven ships remaining in the armada – the five that returned from the Strait and the two that survived the Battle of Santos. They all arrived safely in Rio de Janeiro on 9 May 1583, greeted by the relief mission sent from Spain under Don Diego de Alcega.[6]

17.   The Relief Mission Joins the Armada

Captain General Alcega had left Spain late in summer 1582 with additional supplies for the Armada of the Strait. He reached Rio de Janeiro on 21 December, irritated to discover

---

[1] See below, p. 104.

[2] See below, pp. 91–5.

[3] See below, pp. 95–6. Sarmiento later claimed that the decision to head north was unwarranted, that the ships could have made their way into the Strait with God's help, and that virtually everyone but himself was cowardly and lacking in dedication to duty; Sarmiento, *Viajes al Estrecho*, vol. 1, pp. 276–9.

[4] See below, pp. 99, 102.

[5] Sarmiento, *Viajes al Estrecho*, vol. 1, pp. 280–81, later accused Flores of deliberately separating from the other ships, 'being so anxious to flee back to Brazil and Spain to enjoy his honours, ... and hoping that the *capitana* would sink with all aboard'. See below, pp. 97, 102–3, for a very different version of the events.

[6] See below, p. 104. For the preparations for the relief fleet, with Alcega as its captain general, see AMN, MS 496, f. 141r–v, Philip II to Medina Sidonia, 29 July 1582.

that Captain General Flores had departed for the Strait on 2 November without waiting
for him. He heard from the local governor that the armada was well supplied and
equipped for the voyage, which may have added to his irritation. On 22 December, Alcega
and his senior advisers agreed to remain in Rio de Janeiro until Flores returned. In their
notarized accord, they criticized Flores's decision to leave before their arrival and his failure
to leave proper instructions, either for them or for the governor.[1] They did not know that
Flores had left only after hearing that the relief fleet had been diverted to the Azores. On
28 January 1583, Alcega wrote a letter to the king. By then, he had learned that Flores had
in fact left orders for the collection of additional supplies, and Alcega reported on the
progress of those efforts. He also reported that Flores planned to return to Rio de Janeiro
in March, after completing one of the forts in the Strait.[2] March and April came and went
with no word from Flores. By early May, Alcega was about to return to Spain when Flores
and the remnant of the armada finally arrived; he was very pleased to see them.[3] The two
men – Flores and Alcega – had more in common than their naval careers in royal service.
Both men belonged to the Order of Santiago, an affiliation that could help to ameliorate
differences of opinion between them.

Alcega conveyed timely information from Philip II to Flores about English designs on
the Strait. Although Queen Elizabeth I tried to keep the details of Francis Drake's voyage
of circumnavigation secret, Ambassador Mendoza had heard that Drake had ventured
into another passage south of the western mouth of the Strait. He sent that information
to Spain in April of 1582, and Alcega carried the news to Brazil.[4] If there was more than
one way into the Pacific, the forts that Pedro Sarmiento proposed for the Strait of
Magellan could not prevent interlopers from reaching the viceroyalty of Peru. Flores
already doubted the wisdom of Sarmiento's enterprise. The information from Mendoza
must have reinforced those doubts.

18.   The Third Attempt to Reach the Strait, and Sarmiento's Complaints

On 13 May, Flores held a consultation to discuss the next phase of the expedition. In
attendance were Flores and Alcega; Pedro Sarmiento; Diego de Rivera and Juan de
Medina,[5] almirantes of their respective armadas; royal officials; and Pedro de Rada, who
included the record of their discussion in his *Relación*.[6] The consensus of the meeting was

[1] Accord in Rio de Janeiro, 22 December 1582, in Navarrete, *Colección de documentos*, vol. 20, ff. 177r–179r.
[2] Alcega to Philip II, 28 Jan. 1583, in Navarrete, *Colección de documentos*, vol. 20, f. 181r–v.
[3] See below, p. 104. Flores outranked Alcega once he arrived in Rio de Janeiro, because his armada was senior
to that of Alcega.
[4] According to Helen Wallis, Mendoza's informant had heard Francis Drake say that Tierra del Fuego 'was
not continent but only very large islands, and there was the open sea beyond'. See Wallis, 'Cartography of Drake's
Voyage', p. 134, citing Mendoza's letter to Philip II, 20 April 1582, in *CSP Spain*, vol. III, item 248, p. 341. Nuño
da Silva, a Portuguese pilot whom Francis Drake had captured in Santiago, Cape Verde, mentioned sailing as far
as 57°S after exiting the Strait. Silva made his report in Mexico City, dated 20 May 1579, after Drake left him
in Guatulco on the Mexican coast. See Navarrete, *Colección de documentos*, vol. 26, ff. 48v–49r. It is not clear if
Mendoza saw Silva's report, though there would have been sufficient time for it to reach him. Kelsey, *Sir Francis
Drake*, pp, 125–35, examines in detail the possible sources for this notion, including Silva.
[5] Juan Gómez de Medina, almirante of Alcega's small armada.
[6] See below, pp. 149–52.

that Almirante Rivera would lead a third attempt to land Sarmiento and his settlers at the Strait. Captain General Alcega would return to Spain. Captain General Flores and the remnant of the Armada of the Strait would look for corsairs along the Brazilian coast and winter over in the Bahia de Todos os Santos[1] before returning to Spain.

According to Sarmiento's accounting, 154 settlers remained for the Strait. Flores designated five ships and 500 men from the armada to transport and help them in establishing their colony. He also wrote detailed instructions for Almirante Rivera, including the directive to disembark Sarmiento and his settlers in 'the best and most comfortable place', leaving them with one or two ships and 300–350 soldiers. Despite Sarmiento's repeated complaints that Flores tried to discourage and undermine his efforts, the captain general made ample provisions to assure their success – at least in the short term.[2] For the longer term, Flores had serious concerns about the ability of the colonists to survive, as his later reports make clear.[3]

Sarmiento wrote several lengthy letters to the king from Rio de Janeiro, all of them dated 1 June 1583; he presumably sent them to Spain with Captain General Alcega. One letter names all the settlers and their assigned ships, together with comments about the difficulties they had endured.[4] Another letter provides a detailed record of the voyage to that point.[5] The third letter is an extended personal attack on Captain General Flores for his every decision and action during the expedition, especially the failure to enter the Strait. According to Sarmiento, the horrendous winds, seas, and storms during the two failed attempts were minor irritations that could easily have been overcome with God's help and the force of will. Throughout his narrative, which covers nearly 100 folios in manuscript and 100 pages in a modern printed edition, Sarmiento repeatedly accuses Flores of cowardice, dishonesty, dereliction of duty, greed, and implacable enmity towards him.[6]

Many historians have used bits and pieces of Sarmiento's writings to condemn Flores, but virtually no one has examined those writings for what they reveal about Sarmiento. Some, claiming to take a neutral stance regarding his quarrel with Flores, acknowledge that both men shared the blame, but they rarely acknowledge that Flores was not his only perceived enemy. According to Sarmiento, nearly everyone turned against him at various times, including the settlers, the friars, and even his hand-picked advisers, such as the chief pilot Antón Pablos. Sarmiento's intemperate rants about persons and events tell us more about his personal view of the world than about the persons and events in question. In any case, in May of 1583 Flores effectively withdrew from the ongoing quarrel by placing

---

[1] This is the name of the bay where the capital of Brazil was established in 1549. Rada refers to the city itself as Bahia or Salvador. In 1570, the captaincy of Bahia held 1,000 to 1,100 Portuguese householders (*vizinhos*, variant *vecinos*), for a total Portuguese population of about 5,000 or 6,000. Estimates for the total depend upon whether the multiplier chosen to convert households to total population is 5 or 6. See McAlister, *Spain and Portugal in the New World*, pp. 280–81.

[2] See below, pp. 105–7. The provisions and equipment that Flores left in Rio de Janeiro and sent from Bahia for the Strait are listed in Navarrete, *Colección de documentos*, vol. 20, ff. 357r–358r, and in Pastells and Bayle, *Descubrimiento del Estrecho de Magallanes*, pp. 658–60.

[3] See below, pp. 47–8.

[4] Sarmiento, 1 June 1583, in Navarrete, *Colección de documentos*, vol. 20, ff. 189r–204v.

[5] Ibid., ff. 309r–341r. The word used is *derrotero* (rutter), which can mean the day-to-day log of a ship's position and weather conditions. It can also mean a narrative description of a voyage, including a ship's position, landmarks, and other aids to navigation; or a collection of sea charts.

[6] Ibid., ff. 207r–304r; printed in Sarmiento, *Viajes al Estrecho*, vol. 1, pp. 206–90.

Almirante Rivera in charge of depositing the governor-designate and his settlers at the Strait. Sarmiento strongly opposed that decision and did not sign the accord reached on 13 May by all the other senior officers. Despite Sarmiento's objections, once the captain general made his decision, he had no recourse.

19.   Flores Focuses on the Armada's Military Mission

Captain General Flores and the remnant of the armada left Rio de Janeiro on 4 June 1583, accompanied by Captain General Alcega, with six *naos*, and a dispatch boat. The small *nao* carrying Alcega was separated from the others during a storm on 13 June. After searching for him without success, Flores continued northward with the other ships, fighting winds, seas, and storms all the way. On 30 June, they anchored at the port of Tinaja, about twelve leagues south of Bahia. Flores sent word to the governor of Brazil, Manuel Tellez Barreto, asking for a pilot to guide them into Bahia; General Alcega had already arrived there safely. Most of the armada would remain in Bahia for the rest of the winter. During their stay, Flores consulted with local officials regarding coastal defences and the growing presence of the French in Pernambuco to the north. Word arrived that the French were fortifying the entrance to the Paraíba River, and the governor of Paraíba asked Governor Barreto for assistance.[1] He and other Portuguese officials gratefully accepted Flores's offer of help in the effort to oust the French.[2]

Once established in Bahia, Flores wrote two long letters to the king, both of them dated 5 August 1583, reporting on the actions of the armada since arriving in Brazil.[3] The first letter is a straightforward chronicle. In the second, Flores discusses the accomplishments of the armada to that point. He excuses himself for not carrying out the fortification of the Strait, arguing that it was not only impractical but impossible:

> From what I have seen of the Strait, I believe that it will not be possible to effect the [building of the] forts that Your Majesty ordered done, for one thing because Your Majesty was not given a true relation of the distance between the two points at the narrowest part. There is about one league of channel, without counting the distance to the places where the forts have to be situated, and the artillery will be able to have little effect; and because of the strong current at the narrowest point, any *navío* would be able to pass through easily without [the artillery] doing it any damage. The other reason is that the land is so empty and flat from one part to the other that there is nowhere to take shelter, which, for a land with such extreme cold, is of great inconvenience for the people who have to live there, because there is neither firewood nor water, except 40 leagues away at the Río de San Juan, which is very close to the second narrow place, where I understand they will establish the settlement. And for these reasons and the many others that there are, it would be of great cost to Your Majesty to sustain [the settlers], and of great cost in people, and it would accomplish nothing.[4]

---

[1] The Paraíba River (Tupi for non-navigable) was in the captaincy of Pernambuco in north-eastern Brazil, north of Bahia. In 1570, the captaincy held about 1,000 Portuguese householders, or 5,000 to 6,000 individuals; McAlister, *Spain and Portugal in the New World*, pp. 280–81.

[2] See below, p. 111.

[3] Flores to Philip II, Bahia, 5 Aug. 1583, in Sarmiento, *Viajes al Estrecho*, vol. 2, pp. 315–28. As Flores's version of events since the armada left the Cape Verde Islands, his report provides a crucial counterpoint to Sarmiento's version.

[4] Flores to Philip II, Bahia, 5 Aug. 1583, in Sarmiento, *Viajes al Estrecho*, vol. 2, pp. 323–4.

Flores advised Philip II to abandon the notion of forts and a colony near the entrance to the Strait. Instead, he urged the king to deploy a small force of galleys to defend the passage, which could be supplied and dispatched in rotation from secure bases farther north and could use the many shallow inlets in the Strait to intercept enemy ships. Any settlers should live where they could best survive.[1]

Flores's analysis of the dismal prospects for establishing a colony and forts at the Strait would prove to be deadly accurate, but there was nothing he could do to stop it. He wrote to Sarmiento on 14 September 1583, wishing him well and sending him a map, supposedly drawn by an English pilot who had sailed with Francis Drake in 1577.[2] Almirante Rivera and Governor-designate Sarmiento were in Rio de Janeiro with the ships, sailors, soldiers, and settlers destined for the Strait. They would remain there for another six months, collecting additional supplies and awaiting favourable weather conditions before heading south again.[3]

20. The Battle of Paraíba and the Return to Iberia

Captain General Flores's offer to help Portuguese authorities and settlers in Brazil to oust the French from Paraíba meant that the work of the Armada of the Strait was far from over. If historians remember the expedition for anything besides Sarmiento's self-serving claims, it is because of the Battle of Paraíba in April of 1584.[4] In that encounter, Flores's men, with the forces he organized in Bahia and Pernambuco, drove the French from the area and demonstrated the king's support for his Portuguese subjects and their colonies overseas. With his authority as captain general, Flores could simply have taken control of the coastal defences away from local officials, but that would have risked alienating them from King Philip's service. Instead, he persuaded local officials to join their forces with his own to carry out a successful Hispano-Portuguese effort against a common enemy. Rada chronicles the genesis and events of the Paraíba expedition in considerable detail and inserts copies of pertinent documents that Flores dictated in the aftermath of the battle.[5] After the successful action at Paraíba, Flores and the remnant of his fleet, along with two Portuguese ships also bound for home, set sail on 1 May 1584 and arrived at the island of Terceira in the Azores on 26 June. After remaining there for about a week to take on needed supplies, the ships departed on the last leg of their journey. Captain General Flores and five ships of the armada arrived in the Bay of Cádiz on 19 July 1584. Another three ships under Almirante Rivera arrived on 21 September.[6]

---

[1] Ibid.

[2] See below, pp. 112–13.

[3] See Navarrete, *Colección de documentos*, vol. 20, ff. 357r–358r, for a report on the settlers and supplies in Rio de Janeiro from June to early December 1583. The report is neither signed nor notarized, but its general tone of complaint suggests Sarmiento was the author.

[4] Various references to the battle in modern histories are mistaken about the year in which it occurred. Rada's *Relación* makes clear that it took place in 1584. See below, pp. 117–18.

[5] See below, pp. 116–24, 158–62. Gabriel Soares de Sousa, a Portuguese explorer, lived in Brazil at the time of the battle and wrote about it a few years later. His account of the battle agrees well with Rada's *Relación*; Sousa, *Derrotero de la costa del Brasil*, ch. 12.

[6] For the fate of all the ships from the armada, see Appendix 2.

21. Aftermath

As soon as Flores reached Spain, the Armada of the Strait officially ended. Rada tells us that Don Francisco Tello, the treasurer of the House of Trade in Seville, arrived on 21 July to inspect the fleet. He praised the men for their actions during the expedition and then dismissed them from royal service. In other words, from that day forward the 600 or so men who returned with Flores would no longer earn wages or be given rations at the king's expense. They had not been paid any wages at all to that point, apart from the advance paid at their recruitment, and they had been on short rations for some time because of diminishing supplies in the fleet. In a long, surprisingly emotional passage, Rada relates that Flores, seeing how needy the men were, sold the loads of brazil wood that had been confiscated from the French at Paraíba and arranged to distribute the profits among his sailors and soldiers.[1] They would have to travel to Seville to receive their shares, and collecting their back wages would be even more difficult, given that the royal treasury was more over-extended than usual. In the interim, Philip II told officials at the House of Trade to enlist the men for service in the galleys that were being dispatched to meet the returning fleets from the Indies. Although that would have allowed them to receive rations, almost none of the men signed up, despite pressure and blandishments from the recruiters. Instead, in August, officials at the House of Trade gave each man a small stipend from the royal treasury to pay for food, because of 'their nakedness and want'. The officials informed the king of their actions after the fact.[2] When Almirante Rivera arrived with the other three ships from the armada in mid-September, the president of the House of Trade wrote that the men were roaming around Seville in bands, demanding to be paid.[3] Almost two years later, at least a dozen of the officers from the Armada of the Strait signed on for service in the Indies fleets for 1586, in order to collect part of the monies owed them and the promise to receive the balance in the near future.[4]

Despite their suffering and sacrifices on behalf of the crown, the Armada of the Strait in which they had served had very mixed results and achieved few of its immediate goals. Captain General Flores did not build forts in the Strait, though he arranged to disembark Sarmiento and his remaining settlers there. In retrospect, the Battle of Paraíba seems the only obvious success of the three-year expedition, even though the men left in charge there soon quarrelled, the fort was abandoned in the face of Indian attacks, and the French trickled back into the vicinity. Nonetheless, in 1585 a mixed force of Portuguese, Spaniards, and Indians reconquered the area and re-established the settlement at Paraíba. In the longer term, the French failed to establish themselves in the north-east, and by the end of the century Portuguese forces were able to arrange a lasting peace with several Indian groups and to defeat others.[5]

---

[1] See below, pp. 129–30.

[2] According to officials in the House of Trade, the back pay amounted to more than 70,000 ducats; AMN, Sanz Barutell, MS 389, f. 158r–v, Report of officials in the House of Trade to the king, 24 Aug. 1584.

[3] AMN, Sanz Barutell, MS 389, f. 184r, Diego de Zúñiga to Philip II, 24 Sept. 1584.

[4] AGI, Patronato, leg. 33, N. 3, R. 65, Memorandum from the Council of the Indies to Philip II, 14 June 1586.

[5] For overviews of 16th-century Brazilian history, see Hemming, *Red Gold*, pp. 162–82, and Mauro, 'Portugal and Brazil', pp. 441–6.

As for the English, the presence of the Armada of the Strait probably persuaded Edward Fenton to abandon plans to replicate Francis Drake's voyage. Believing it likely that Flores and Sarmiento had already reached the Strait, Fenton continued southward as far as the Río de la Plata, but turned north again when John Drake abandoned the expedition. After the battle at Santos, he gave up any attempt at the Strait. According to Peter Bradley, 'of the various reasons given, the late season, decay of food and goods, loss of men due to fierce conflicts with the openly hostile Portuguese, and fear of the fleet of Flores de Valdés off the Brazilian coast, the last seems the most decisive' in his reasoning.[1] Bernardino de Mendoza, the Spanish ambassador in London, wrote to Philip II on 16 July 1583 that both Fenton and Luke Ward had to answer charges,

> for not having continued the voyage. These ships have not plundered … All the money spent on this expedition has been lost, and the merchants say the English cannot make the voyage in ships of less than 1000 tons burden, as they have to sail loaded with victuals, considering the way Englishmen eat, and they can only bring half a cargo home for the same reason. Even a cargo of spices will not pay under these circumstances, the voyage being so long.[2]

In English historiography, Fenton's expedition is known as 'the troublesome voyage' for good reason. Moreover, Kenneth Andrews argues that, 'The years of the Fenton and Hawkins expeditions, 1582 and 1583, can thus be seen on reflection as a turning point at which South American hopes faded and North American ambitions began to gather strength – a significant shift of focus in the prehistory of the British Empire'.[3]

Scarcely a week after Flores's fleet anchored in Cádiz, a soldier with the armada obtained an exclusive licence to print and sell an epic poem he had written about the engagement with the French at Paraíba. Juan de Pedraza's verse praised all involved in the action, including the captain general.[4] Flores presented his own report to Philip II on 24 August at the new Escorial palace in the foothills north-west of Madrid. The king had remained in Portugal throughout the planning for the Armada of the Strait and for much of its time overseas, but he was back in Spain when Flores returned. Despite Sarmiento's efforts to denigrate him, Flores continued to enjoy royal favour. When Philip II decided to send a great armada against England in 1588, he chose Diego Flores to head the Squadron of Castile. The captain general of the expedition was to be the same duke of Medina Sidonia who had worked with Flores to prepare the Armada of the Strait; Flores would serve as his chief naval adviser. On the king's direct orders, Flores sailed with Medina Sidonia, rather than on the flagship of the Squadron of Castile.[5] When the armada failed, Flores had to take the blame. As punishment, he was sent to the castle of Burgos, where he was imprisoned until January of 1590.[6] By then he was about sixty years old and retired to his birthplace in Asturias. He died in 1595.[7]

Don Alonso de Sotomayor, the governor-designate of Chile, travelled overland from the Río de la Plata to Lima – a route relatively new at the time but increasingly important.

---

[1] Bradley, *British Maritime Enterprise*, p. 409.

[2] Mendoza to Philip II, 16 July 1583, in Taylor, *Troublesome Voyage*, doc. 68, p. 287.

[3] Andrews, 'Drake and South America', p. 58. See also Andrews, *Elizabethan Privateering*, pp. 203–5.

[4] Pedraza, 'Relación cierta y verdadera' in Fernández Duro, *Disquisiciones náuticas*, vol. 6, pp. 465–74. An English translation is found in Estelle, '*Battle of Paraíba*'.

[5] Martin and Parker, *Spanish Armada*, p. 24.

[6] AGS, GyM, leg. 264; also, *CODOIN*, vol. 81, pp. 233–4.

[7] Flores's last will and testament is dated 9 Jan. 1595, AGS, CME, leg. 227, N.16.

He served as governor and captain general of Chile from 1583 to 1592.[1] He was appointed captain general of Panama in 1595, and in that capacity he organized the successful defence against the attack of Drake and Hawkins.

Pedro Sarmiento de Gamboa founded his settlement at the Strait in February of 1584 with 338 colonists, craftsmen, and soldiers, well-provisioned with food and other supplies for the short term. For the longer term, it quickly became clear that the colony could not survive without continual provisioning from outside, as Flores had warned. Sarmiento left his colony at the Strait in May and wrote to the king from Brazil for help. After trying unsuccessfully to deliver additional supplies to the Strait, he sailed for Spain to plead his case in person. On the way, he was captured near the Azores by two English ships belonging to Sir Walter Ralegh and held for ransom in 1586. After borrowing the ransom money, he set out for Spain but was captured again in France. When he finally reached Spain, he begged Philip II to send re-supply missions to the Strait, as well as lobbying for recognition and rewards for himself.[2] By then, as Lopez Vaz noted at the time:

> the king was sore displeased at Pedro Sarmiento, because hee made him beleeve that the narrowest place of the Streights was but a mile over: and that it might be fortified so that a boate could not passe: whereas Diego de Ribera, and others certified the king, that it was above a league broade, and that if a ship came with winde and current, all the Ordinance in the world could not hurte it. Wherefore the king thought that Pedro Sarmiento had deceived him, in making him to lose so many men, and so much charges to no effect.[3]

Despite his displeasure, the king sent additional provisions to the colony and planned to send more, but it was too late. When the English corsair, Thomas Cavendish,[4] passed through the Strait in January of 1587, only sixteen men and three women remained alive, the rest having perished of starvation and disease. Cavendish took one young soldier aboard for questioning and then sailed away with him, leaving the other survivors to their fate. That young soldier, Tomé Hernández, escaped when Cavendish stopped in southern Chile and eventually made his way to Lima. In 1620, at the age of sixty-two, Hernández gave an extraordinary deposition at the viceroy's request, recounting his experiences as a soldier in Flores's armada and in the doomed colony at the Strait. His testimony supplied poignant evidence of the tragedy, which must have haunted him for the rest of his life.[5]

As for Pedro de Rada, thanks to the manuscript purchased by the Huntington Library, his voice can join the other eyewitnesses who wrote about the Armada of the Strait. Rada's hitherto unknown *Relación* chronicles an expedition that was launched with extraordinary effort at a critical period in Spanish exploration and colonization. Despite all the careful planning that preceded its departure, the armada suffered more calamities than many other expeditions, partly due to chance, but also due to the irrational schemes of Pedro Sarmiento, whom so many historians have praised as a visionary hero. Rada's

---

[1] See Andrews, *Last Voyage, passim*.

[2] Letters and reports about sustaining the colony are in Navarrete, *Colección de documentos*, vol. 20, ff. 449r–470v. Accounts of Sarmiento's misfortunes on the way back to Spain appear in Sarmiento, *Viajes al Estrecho*, vol. 2, pp. 354–63.

[3] Vaz, 'Discourse of the West Indies' in PN(M), vol. XI, p. 272.

[4] In some sources, he is listed as Thomas Candish.

[5] Navarrete, *Colección de documentos*, vol. 20, ff. 551r–566v. An English translation appears in Sarmiento, *Narratives of the Voyages*, pp. 352–75. A ship from Bristol picked up another man at the Strait in 1589, but he and Tomé Hernández seem to have been the only two survivors of the colony that Sarmiento planted.

sober narrative captures the horrors faced by the men and women who sailed with the Armada of the Strait and helps to counter the voluminous writings of Sarmiento, which have dominated the historiography far too long.

22. Notes to the Translation

It is difficult to retain the sentence structure of sixteenth-century manuscripts in translation without sacrificing meaning. As noted above, Rada rarely includes punctuation, and what marks he provides often seem eccentric or out of place to a modern reader. Some sentences go on for dozens, or even hundreds, of words without an obvious break. To make sense of his narrative, my translation breaks unduly long passages into separate sentences, or at least into separate subordinate clauses separated by semi-colons, and supplies commas when necessary.

Referring to dates, Rada will often use a phrase such as 'from 2 of November ... until 7 of December'. In such cases, the translation renders this as 'from the 2nd ... until the 7th of December'. In describing events in his *Relación*, Rada continually switches verb tenses, often using a verb in the past tense with words that imply immediacy, such as *hoy* (today). To avoid confusion, *hoy* is translated as 'this day' and other ambiguous pairings of subject and verb tense are altered for clarity. Otherwise, the translation follows Rada's wording as closely as possible, aiming to convey his voice without sacrificing meaning.

Some words denoting common, generic ship types, such as galleon (*galeón*) and bark (*barca*), are given in English throughout, with a footnote at the first instance explaining what the word meant in sixteenth-century Spanish. Other words for ship types – such as *bergantín, fragata, nao,* and *navío* – have been left in the original Spanish since they refer to specific types of shipping of late sixteenth-century Spain and they should not be confused with later vessels with the same classification. Both *nao* and *navío* could sometimes be used generically to mean 'ship' and at other times could refer to specific ships or to ship types; it is useful to know how and when Rada uses each word. The word *fragata* (frigate) was rarely used generically in the late sixteenth century, but it denoted a far different sort of ship than a frigate of later times; to avoid confusion, it is left untranslated. A footnote at the first appearance of each ship classification left in Spanish in the translated text explains its meaning and usage in sixteenth-century Spanish. Words with little or no ambiguity in their definition, such as *ducado* (ducat) and *cañón* (cannon) are given in English throughout the translated text. Spanish and Portuguese units of measure, such as *arroba, almud,* and *braza,* and most monies, such as *maravedí, real,* and *milréis,* are left in the original language. Definitions are provided in the list of 'Weights, Measures, and Currency' and explained further in footnotes where necessary.

Rada generally denotes place names in Brazil and elsewhere with their Spanish spelling, which is retained in the translation; the accepted modern national spelling is supplied throughout the footnotes, and in this introduction and the maps. Rada's spelling and variants of proper names of persons and ships are also retained in the translated text, and annotated, with exceptions for common place names such as England, Spain, Lisbon, or Seville. Rada generally, but not always, omits accents and other diacritical marks in the names of persons, places and things. The translation follows the original, rather than trying to be consistent or to follow modern norms. However, in footnotes throughout, as in the text of this introduction, diacriticals are supplied for Spanish and Portuguese words and names.

Rada frequently abbreviates words and personal names in his *Relación*, with or without superscripts. Since this is a translation, as opposed to a transcription, the extensions have been supplied but not indicated by italics as long as there is no ambiguity. Footnotes explain any peculiarities, as in Rada's spelling of the names of non-Spaniards, such as the Italian engineer Battista Antonelli (Bautista Antoneli in Spanish). Rada's spelling is retained in the translation, but the footnotes and this introduction use the native spelling of such names.

Foreign job titles, offices, and military ranks have been translated, excepting only those where translation does not provide the reader with an appropriate equivalent. In these cases the Spanish form has been retained but not italicized (following Hakluyt Society practice). The range of duties of these positions are indicated in footnotes. Many of the titles of sixteenth-century Spanish military, legal, or bureaucratic records, or administrative structures and procedures, have been absorbed into contemporary historical usage and have been retained in their Spanish form, with the explanation of the nature and purpose of each record or procedure explained in the footnotes. Rada's spelling here, as elsewhere, is erratic and many of the words in the categories discussed in this paragraph have numerous variants, some close to accepted modern spelling. For the ease of the reader they have all been reduced to modern spelling, with Rada's variants footnoted at the first occurrence together with modern standardized spelling and the diacriticals not supplied in Rada's text. Further information about the conventions used in the translation and footnotes is provided in 'Abbreviations' and 'Weights, Measures, and Currency'.

Relacion of the success of the Royal Armada of His Majesty, which he ordered brought together in the river of Seville and the port of San Lucar de Barrameda for the Estrecho de Magallanes, with Captain General Diego Florez, knight of the Order of Santiago in the past year of 1581.[1] Written and seen by me, Pedro de Rada, its chief scribe,[2] which is as follows.

[1] The date is written as 'i℧dlxxxi' In Spanish documents of the period, the placeholder for thousands, called a *calderón*, was variously written, often Ø, U or ℧. In Rada's manuscript, the *calderón* is represented by ℧.

[2] Escribano mayor.

[f. ir] I belong to Pedro de Chopite;[1] and now to Domingo de Chopite, the eve of San Pedro, the year of 1742[2]

[f. iir]

— 1581 —

Table of contents of the route taken and discourse of the success of the Royal Armada of His Majesty that went to the coasts of Brasil[3] and the Estrecho de Magallanes,[4] under Captain General Diego Florez de Baldes,[5] which departed from San Lucar de Barrameda[6] on the 25th of September of the year 1581, until the 17th of July of 1584, when it returned to the Baya de Cadiz.[7]

The reason that moved His Majesty to send this armada and how it was gathered in the port of San Lucar, and what was done to outfit and prepare it before it made sail will be seen from leaves 1 to 3.

What happened from the 25th of September of 1581, when it made sail from the port of San Lucar until the 7th of October of that year, when after a storm it returned and entered the Baya de Cadiz, and what was done there will be seen from leaves 3 to 5.

The navigation that it made from the 9th of December of 1581, when it left from the Baya de Cadiz, until the 11th of January of 1582, when it arrived at the island of Sanctiago de Cavo Berde,[8] and what it did there will be seen from leaves 5 to 7.

---

[1] A note inside the bound volume, which is in a different hand from Rada's. The surname is Basque in origin (Txopite, modern spelling Chópite). A man named Pedro de Chópite married Josepha de Camino Goitia on 1 Jan. 1727 in Ondarroa, a town in the Basque province of Vizcaya (Biscay). There is no proof that this was the owner of the Rada manuscript, but that is a possibility. See *rootsweb, The Vital Records Index* at http://wc.rootsweb.ancestry.com/cgibin/igm.cgi?op=GET&db=bo7156&id=I51724&style=TABLE. There is no listing for Domingo de Chópite.

[2] St Peter's Day is 29 June.

[3] Brazil; elsewhere Rada uses the variant Brasill. The table of contents for Rada's Relación, found above pp. viii–ix, is based on Rada's list, but the wording is abbreviated and the spelling of place names is modernized for the convenience of the reader.

[4] Strait of Magellan; elsewhere Rada uses the variants Magallanes, strecho de Magallanes.

[5] Diego Flores de Valdés. Elsewhere Rada uses the variants Florez de Valdes, Florez. As capitán general (captain general), equivalent in rank to an English admiral, Flores held supreme command of the Armada of the Strait. Contrary to the assertions of many historians, his command was neither shared nor divided. See above, pp. 16, 18–19, 21–2, 27–8, and below, p. 65.

[6] Sanlúcar de Barrameda; elsewhere Rada uses the variant San Lucar de Barameda.

[7] Bahía de Cádiz (Bay of Cádiz). Elsewhere Rada uses the variants Baya, Bayya, Vayya meaning bay. An oval leather bookplate inscribed '*ex libris* of Jacobi P. R. Lyell' is affixed to the right margin of the manuscript here. J. P. R. Lyell (1871–1946) was a solicitor, bibliophile, and bibliographer whose impressive collection of books and manuscripts was sold and dispersed from about 1942 on. The Bodleian Library at Oxford University purchased many of his medieval manuscripts, some of which contain the same oval leather bookplate as found in Rada's *Relación*.

[8] Elsewhere Rada uses the variants Cabo Berde, Cabo Verde, Cavo Verde. Ilha Santiago de Cabo Verde is the largest island in the Cape Verde chain, 15°04′N, 23°38′W.

The navigation that it made from the 2nd of February of 1582, when it left from Sanctiago de Cavo Berde until the 25th of March, when it arrived at the Rio de Jenero,[1] and what occurred there will be seen from leaves 7 to 12.

What happened to the armada from the 2nd of November of the year 1582, when it set sail from the Rio de Jenero on course to the Estrecho de Magallanes, until the 17th of December of the said year, when with a storm it turned to arrive at the port of Sancta Catalina,[2] and what it did there will be seen from leaves 12 to 17.

[f. iiv] The navigation that it made and what happened to it from the 7th of January 1583, when it left again from the port of Sancta Catalina, until the 19th of the aforesaid when it arrived near the Rio de la Platta,[3] where Don Alonso de Sotomayor was sent with three *naos*[4] from the armada in order to disembark his men in Buenos Ayres,[5] will be seen from leaves 17 to 19.

From the 19th of January 1583, when it left from the mouth of the Rio de la Platta until the 17th of February of that year, when it arrived at the Estrecho de Magallanes, and the storms that it experienced there, and how it could not disembark the people and was forced to turn back toward port, until the 31st of March of the said year, when it arrived at San Vicente,[6] and what was done there, will be seen from leaves 19 to 27.

From the 28th of April of 1583, when it departed from the port of Sanctos[7] y San Vicente, until the 9th of May, when it arrived at the Rio de Jenero, where Don Diego de Alcega[8] was found, and what was done and agreed upon about the five *navios*[9] that remained there in order to return to the Strait will be seen from leaves 27 to 32.

From the 2nd of June 1583, when it made sail from the Rio de Jenero, until the 13th of July,

---

[1] Rio de Janeiro; elsewhere Rada uses the variant Jenero. The total population of Rio de Janeiro *c.*1580 is not clear. Contemporary estimates range from 140 to 400 Portuguese *vizinhos* (householders), depending on whether a given figure refers to the immediate area near the port or to the entire captaincy. See McAlister, *Spain and Portugal in the New World*, pp. 280–81, citing contemporary estimates by Pedro de Magalhães de Gandavo and Juan López de Velasco. Standard practice uses a multiplier of 5 or 6 persons per household to calculate total population. Throughout, Rada uses the Spanish word *vecinos* or *vezinos*, equivalent to the Portuguese *vizinhos*, to denote the legal heads of household in a given place, in contrast to temporary residents without the rights and responsibilities of householders.

[2] Santa Catarina island extends from 25°57′41″S to 29°23′55″S and from 48°19′37″W to 53°50′W, with various coves and potential ports.

[3] Río de la Plata; elsewhere Rada uses the variants Plata and Palata.

[4] See above, p. 30, n. 3, for the definition of a *nao* in contemporary usage.

[5] Buenos Aires. Spaniards founded the town on the Río de la Plata in 1536 but abandoned it in 1541 because of insufficient food supplies, dissension, and Indian attacks. It was re-established in 1580 by an expedition led by Juan de Garay. See Burkholder and Johnson, *Colonial Latin America*, pp. 62–3; Angelis, *Fundación de la ciudad de Buenos-Aires*, 'Discurso preliminar'; Brown, 'Outpost to Entrepôt', pp. 3–4.

[6] São Vicente, a port on the west end of the island of the same name at 23°57′48″S, 46°23′32″W, was the oldest Portuguese settlement in Brazil and head of the captaincy of São Vicente. Taylor, *Troublesome Voyage*, includes a manuscript chart of the settlement from a Portuguese rutter dated *c.*1570, opposite p. 128. In about 1570, the captaincy of São Vicente was estimated to have 500 Portuguese householders; see McAlister, *Spain and Portugal in the New World*, pp. 280–81, citing contemporary estimates by Pedro de Magalhães de Gandavo and Juan López de Velasco.

[7] The settlement of Santos was very close to São Vicente. Rada often mentions them together as Santos y San Vicente. In later centuries, both were absorbed by the growing city of São Paulo.

[8] Elsewhere Rada uses the variants Alciega, Alzega.

[9] See above, p. 16, n. 7, for the definition of a *navío* in contemporary usage.

when it arrived at the Baya del Salvador de Todos Sanctos,[1] where Don Diego de Alcega was dispatched to come to Spain, and the rest that was done there will be seen from leaves 32 to 37.

From the first of March of 1584, when the armada left from the Baya del Salvador, until the 19th of the aforesaid, when it arrived at Pernambuco, and what was done there will be seen from leaves 37 to 40.

From the 16th of April 1584, when it departed from Pernambuco until arriving at the port of la Paraiba,[2] and how it was won from the French and the fort that was made there, with the rest that happened will be seen from leaves 40 to 48.

[f. iiir] From the first of May of 1584, when it departed from the port of la Paraiba, until the 26th of June, when it arrived at the island of La Tercera,[3] and what was done there will be seen from leaves 48 to 50.

From the 3rd of July 1584, when it departed from La Tercera until the 17th of the aforesaid, when it arrived at the Baya de Cadiz, and what was done there will be seen on leaves 50 to 52.

The *instruccion*[4] that was given to the captains, pilots and masters[5] of the armada about navigation and the good order of war, in the port of San Lucar on the 25th of September 1581, will be found from leaves 52 to 56.

The *instruccion* that was given to the said captains, pilots and masters in Sanctiago de Cavo Berde, on the 28th of January 1582, will be found at leaves 56 to 57.

The *instruccion* that was given to the said captains in the Rio de Jenero on the 4th of October 1582, in order to go to the Estrecho de Magallanes, will be found at folio 57.

The *instruccion* that was given to the accountant[6] Andres de Eguino on the 5th of January 1583 in the port of Sancta Catalina, in whose charge remained three *naos* of the armada, will be found at leaves 58 to 60.

What was agreed upon on the 19th of January of 1583, at the mouth of the Rio de la Platta, about the departure of Don Alonso de Sotomayor with three *naos*, and the *acuerdo*[7]

---

[1] Elsewhere Rada uses the variants Baya, Bayya, Baya del Salvador. The city of Salvador was designated the capital of all Brazil in 1549. Located on the north-eastern coast at 12°58′29″S, 38°28′36″W in the captaincy of Bahia, on the Bahia de Todos os Santos, the city was commonly referred to simply as Bahia; see Russell-Wood, *Fidalgos and Philanthropists*, p. 48. The captaincy of Bahia was estimated to have no more than 1,100 householders in about 1570. McAlister, *Spain and Portugal in the New World*, pp. 280–81, citing contemporary estimates by Pedro de Magalhães de Gandavo and Juan López de Velasco. See above, p. 58, n. 7.

[2] The estuary of the Paraíba River, is located at 9°37′S, 35°57′W. There was no permanent settlement there in 1584. In the aftermath of the Battle of Paraíba, a fort was built, though it had to be abandoned after a few months. In 1585 Portuguese and Spanish forces recaptured the area and founded a town called Filipéia that would later become the modern city of João Pessoa. The armada departed on 6 April; see below, p. 118.

[3] Ilha Terceira, in the Azores, 38°43″N, 27°03″W.

[4] An *instrucción* was an official directive about how to carry out an assignment or duties, often in the form of numbered paragraphs; Rada uses variant spellings of the phrase '*instrución y orden*' or its plural '*instrucciones y órdenes*', the equivalent of general orders.

[5] A capitán (captain) was the senior officer in charge of a ship. A piloto (pilot) was the ship's officer primarily in charge of setting its course, though he often consulted with the captain and other officers, including other pilots if a ship carried more than one. The pilot also gave orders to the crew for handling the ship and the sails. The maestre (master) in a Spanish maritime context was the officer in charge of keeping track of everything on board the ship, primarily provisions and equipment, but also crew and passengers.

[6] A contador (accountant) was in charge of keeping detailed financial records.

[7] An *acuerdo* (accord) could be a verbal or written agreement. Rada often uses the verb *acordar* in a generic sense, meaning 'to agree' or 'to resolve by common consent'. At other times he uses the noun *acuerdo* to denote a more formal agreement or consensus, whether or not the *acuerdo* was a signed document.

and *instruccion* that he was given to take them and disembark his men in Buenos Ayres will be found at leaves 60 to 62.

The *instruccion* that was given on the 26th of April of 1583 to Tomas Gari, alcaide of the fort[1] that was made in the port of Sanctos, about how it had to be governed, with the list of the artillery, arms, munitions and other things that were put in his hands, will be found at leaves 62 to 65.

What was agreed upon on the 5th of December of 1582,[2] the armada being at a latitude of 35 degrees,[3] with the opinions of Don Alonso de Sotomayor, Pedro Sarmiento, Diego de la Rivera, and the captains and pilots about what course to take[4] will be found from leaves 65 to 69.

[f. iiiv] What General[5] Diego Florez proposed in the Rio de Jenero on the 13th of May 1583 about leaving the five *navios* of the armada to return to the Strait, with the opinions given by Don Diego de Alcega, Pedro Sarmiento, the almirantes[6] Diego de la Rivera and Juan de Medina, and the royal officials will be found from leaves 69 to 73.

The *instruccion* that was given on the last day of May 1583 to Diego de la Rivera in the Rio de Jenero, about how he should govern the 5 *navios* that remained for him to return to the Strait, and how he received the original *instruccion* of His Majesty, with two letters from Don Bernardino de Mendoza about things regarding the said strait will be found from leaves 73 to 75.

The *requerimiento*[7] that the general issued to Manuel Tellez Bareto,[8] governor of the Baya del Salvador, on the 28th of November 1583 will be found at leaves 75 to 77.

The *instruccion* that was given to the captains, pilots and masters in the Baya del Salvador on the 27th of February 1584, regarding how to sail to Pernambuco and to la Paraiba, will be found at folio 77.

---

[1] In the Spanish world, an alcaide could be in charge of a fortress (*presidio*), castle (*castillo*) or other military establishment. Tomás Garri was originally appointed to serve as commander of one of the forts planned for the Strait of Magellan, presumably as a replacement for someone who died in the shipwrecks in early October of 1581; see AMN, MS 496, f. 104v, Philip II to Medina Sidonia, 29 Oct. 1581.

[2] Rada places this document out of chronological sequence.

[3] Latitude at sea was calculated by measuring the height of the sun above the northern horizon at midday, using an instrument such as an astrolable or a fore-staff. The angle read from the instrument was then adjusted according to published tables for the declination of the sun for that day of the year. If the sun was not visible, the latitude could not be calculated. Rada generally refers to the process as 'taking the *altura*' (lit., height), which will be translated as 'taking the latitude', but occasionally he refers to 'taking the sun'.

[4] The verb used is *arribarse*, which can mean to arrive at a port, or to change course at sea to aim the prow downwind and take advantage of a following wind to reach a port.

[5] Although Flores's proper title was captain general of the fleet, Rada often refers to him simply as General Flores, or as 'the general'. See above, pp. 18–19, for discussion of a captain general's authority.

[6] Diego de la Rivera was the almirante of Flores's Armada of the Strait. Juan (variant Jhoan) de Medina was the almirante of the 4 ships sent to Brazil with additional supplies under Don Diego de Alcega. For the definition of this rank here and in all subsequent ocurrences, see above, p. 1, n. 1.

[7] A *requerimiento* (lit. requirement) was a legal document mandating an action or actions that had to be carried out to avoid serious consequences. In the case of Governor Barreto, he would face royal disapproval. In the context of Spanish colonization and conquest overseas, the *requerimiento* written in 1512 by the jurist Juan López de Palacios Rubios, based on Christian doctrine and papal concessions, required newly-encountered peoples to accept Spanish rule. Those who did not submit faced war. Although other Spanish scholars would argue against the validity of the papal grants, they continued to be used to justify Spanish conquests. See Zavala, *Instituciones jurídicas*, pp. 79–80, 95–6, 487–97; Elliott, *Empires of the Atlantic World*, p. 11; Muldoon, *Americas in the Spanish World Order*, pp. 136–40.

[8] Usually rendered as Manoel Teles Barreto in Portuguese documents.

The *instruccion* that was given to Diego Baez de Vega[1] and to Captain Pedro Corea de la Cerda in the Baya del Salvador on the 29th of February 1584, that they sail in the two Portuguese *naos* with the armada to Pernambuco and la Paraiba, will be found from leaves 77 to 79.

The vow and pledge of homage[2] made byCaptain Francisco de Castrejon,[3] who remained as alcaide of the fort named Sant Felipe y Sanctiago that was built in the port of la Paraiba, with the *instruccion* that was given him and the *libranza*[4] to provide him with provisions from Pernambuco, with the list of the provisions, artillery, gunpowder and other munitions that remained with him will be found from leaves 79 to 82.

The report of the money that was carried from Spain, and what was given out and loaned on the coast of Brasill that the armada spent until returning to Spain will be found at leaves 82 and 83.

The report of the powder, lead and match-cord that was given to Juan de Urbina on 29 June 1584 on the island of La Tercera for its defence will be found at leaf 84.

[f. ivr] The report that Don Francisco de Bera[5] gave on the 15th of December 1582 at a latitude of 30 degrees about the two English galleons that captured him in the port of Don Rodrigo,[6] and what they interrogated him about, and the treatment of Friar Juan de Rivadeneira[7] by the general of those galleons will be found from leaves 84 to 90.

The official copies of the letters that this English general wrote in the port of Sanctos on the 20th of January 1583 to Governor Geronimo Leiton,[8] and to an Englishman who is married there, will be found at leaf 91.

The *derrotero*[9] that was taken in San Vicente from an Englishman who was in company with El Draque[10] on one of the *naos* that passed through the Strait into the Mar del Sur[11] and returned through the same strait will be found from leaves 91 to 93.

---

[1] Diogo Báez/Váez da Veiga, son of the deceased former governor of Brazil, Lourenzo da Veiga. Elsewhere Rada uses the variants Beiga and Vega.

[2] *Voto y pleito homenaje*; a vow and pledge of homage and obedience to orders.

[3] Francisco Castrejón arrived in Brazil in December 1582 as captain of the *nao Santa Cruz*, one of the 4 ships in the relief fleet under Don Diego de Alcega. See below, pp. 107, 110, 112, 118–19, 123, 158–61, and MacDonald, *Making of Brazil*, p. 125. Given that Captain General Flores named him as alcaide (see above, p. 60, n. 2) for the new fort at Paraíba, he presumably showed the necessary qualities of leadership to be trusted with that command.

[4] A *libranza* was an order to pay or to hand over.

[5] A variant of Vera, which is the standard modern spelling.

[6] Dom Rodrigo. See above, pp. 39–40.

[7] The Franciscan, commissary Juan de Rivadeneira, accompanied Juan de Garay at the refounding of Buenos Aires in 1580 and figured prominently in the early religious history of the Río de la Plata area. Elsewhere Rada spells the name as Riva Deneira or Rivadeneyra.

[8] Jerónimo Leitão. His name is often rendered as Leiton or Leitón in English and Spanish texts. Leitão was already well known for his military exploits against the French and their Indian allies. In the 1590s, he would be a leader in the marauding raids into the interior from São Paulo to capture Indians to enslave. See Hemming, *Red Gold*, pp. 136, 245–50.

[9] The word rutter and its equivalents in other languages (Sp., *derrotero*; Fr., *routier*) often refers to the written record of a voyage. Here *derrotero* refers to verbal testimony about the trajectory of a voyage, in the form of a legal deposition to local authorities in São Vicente.

[10] Francis Drake; elsewhere Rada uses the variants Drac, El Draq. See below, pp. 112–13, 173–5.

[11] In Spanish usage, the Mar del Sur (Southern Sea) referred to the Pacific Ocean. The Mar del Norte (Northern Sea), also known as the Mar Océano (Ocean Sea), referred to the Atlantic Ocean.

[f. 1r] *Relacion* of the success of the Royal Armada of His Majesty, which he ordered brought together in the river of Seville and the port of San Lucar de Barrameda for the Estrecho de Magallanes, with Captain General Diego Florez, knight of the Order of Santiago,[1] the past year of 1581. Written and seen by me, Pedro de Rada, its chief scribe, which is as follows:

So as not to tell anew the history of the discovery and the Estrecho de Magallanes, which is already written and I do not want to tire [the reader], I will only say in summary that Hernando de Magallanes, Portuguese, offered to the emperor of glorious memory[2] that he would discover the route through which he would pass from the Mar del Norte to that of the south, in order to go to the Malucas[3] and the Islas de la Especeria,[4] which would be a brief navigation. The emperor of glorious memory gave him an armada to do so, and he departed with it from San Lucar[5] on the 20th of September of 1519. And sailing with that aim, he discovered the strait that now is called Magallanes, through which he exited into the Mar del Sur and sailed to the Malucas, and there they killed him. Afterwards, others went to the said strait, but I do not mention them here.

His Majesty the king Dom Phelipe,[6] for some considerations and reasons, has not thought it in his service that his subjects and vassals should sail the said strait, and thus it was not dealt with, more than to have been discovered, until the past year of 1577. Then, on the 4th of December, Francisco Draque, English corsair, left from England with an armada of seven *navios*[7] with the motive of going with them through this strait into the Mar del Sur, and to rob and do whatever damage they could on the coasts of Piru.[8] And thus he sailed with these *navios* to the Islas de Cavo Berde, and in the port of Fuego[9] he found a Portuguese *nao* that was going to Brasil loaded with merchandise, and he captured it. And he carried with him the pilot who was called Nuño de Silba,[10] and from there he departed on his voyage on a course straight to the Rio de la Platta

---

[1] For Flores's admission to the Order of Santiago, see above, pp. 11–12.

[2] Holy Roman Emperor Charles V, also king Charles I of Spain.

[3] Moluccas Islands.

[4] Spice Islands.

[5] Sanlúcar de Barrameda.

[6] i.e. Philip II of Spain. It is perhaps significant that Rada uses the Portuguese honorific Dom, rather than the Spanish Don, given that King Philip had recently claimed the throne of Portugal.

[7] Rada's description of the events and dates in Drake's voyage is accurate in broad outline but differs in specific details from accepted scholarship. In fact, Drake's expedition first left Plymouth on 15 Nov., but bad weather drove it back to port. Drake definitively left with 5 ships on 13 Dec.; Drake, *World Encompassed*, pp. 7–8. For a recent biography of Drake, see Kelsey, *Sir Francis Drake*.

[8] Peru. With the blessing of Elizabeth I of England, Drake set out to follow the route that Magellan had pioneered into the Pacific. Although ostensibly a trading mission, Drake's voyage immediately turned to piracy and plunder, though England was at peace with both Portugal and Spain at the time.

[9] Fogo, one of the Sotavento group of the Cape Verde Islands, is located at 14°55′59″N, 24°22′59″W.

[10] Nuño da Silva carried charts, sailing directions, and nautical instruments, arguably more valuable to Drake than the merchandise on the ship. After accompanying Drake to Brazil, through the Strait and up the west coast of South America, he was released at the port of Guatulco in New Spain (Mexico) and later gave testimony about his experiences. The testimony, dated 20 May 1579, appears in Spanish in Navarrete, *Colección de documentos*, vol. 26, ff. 47r–54v, and in English in Hakluyt, *PN2*, III (1600), pp. 742–7. Silva's account remains one of the most detailed and trustworthy records of the first 2 years of Drake's 1577–80 voyage.

without touching [f. 1v] another port, where he arrived on the 3rd of April of the year of 1578; and from there he sailed toward the said strait. And being in the latitude of 38 degrees, he broke up two *navios* from those that he brought, because they were worn out, and the men from them passed to the other *navios*. And he arrived at the port of San Julian,[1] 50 leagues from the said strait,[2] where he was until the 17th of August of the year of [15]78, and where he broke up another two *naos* and killed an English gentleman who sailed in his company, for suspicion that he wanted to rise up with the *naos* and kill him.[3]

And on the 17th of the month of August, he left from that port with the three *naos* that remained to him and entered the mouth of the said Strecho de Magallanes on the 24th of the aforesaid and exited on the 6th of September with the three *naos*. And sailing into the Mar del Sur with them, on the 10th of the aforesaid he lost one in a great storm; and on the 8th of October in another powerful storm he lost another. This is understood from a report that I have from the ship that turned around to exit the mouth of the said strait in order to return to England.[4] And with only the *navio capitana* in which the said Draque sailed,[5] he was in many ports of Piru, New Spain and Nicaragua, where he did much damage and robbed gold, silver and merchandise from His Majesty as well as from individuals.[6] And with more than a million,[7] he left fleeing and sailed to the Malucas, and

[1] The port of San Julián is located at 49°18′S, 67°43′W.

[2] On land, the Spanish *legua* or league was set at 5,000 *varas* (yards), or three *millas* (miles), equivalent in modern terms to about 2.6 miles or 4.2 km. The *legua náutica* (nautical league) in use between 1400 and 1600 was supposedly equal to 4 Roman miles, or about 3.2 modern nautical miles, but it seems to have varied between 3.6 and 4.2 modern nautical miles. Rada's *Relación* uses the word *legua* for distances on both land and sea. Unless otherwise noted, this translation will assume that he had in mind the traditional *legua* of 5,000 *varas* or 3 *millas*.

[3] i.e. to organize a mutiny against Drake with the men from the ships. Rada refers here to the execution of Thomas Doughty, allegedly for treason, but more likely because the well-born Doughty represented a threat to the low-born Drake's authority. Scholars generally accept that the execution was not legally justifiable, but that Drake thought it necessary to reassert his absolute command of the expedition. See Cliffe, 'Voyage', pp. 278–9; Andrews, *Drake's Voyages*, pp. 63–8; Parry, 'Drake and the World Encompassed', pp. 5–6; and Kelsey, *Sir Francis Drake*, pp. 97–110.

[4] Drake sailed with 5 ships to the Cape Verde Islands, where he captured another vessel. After crossing the Atlantic, he scuttled 2 ships due to the loss of so many men on the crossing. He burned another ship at San Julián, leaving 3 to traverse the Strait. Rada is correct that one ship, the *Marigold*, was lost in a storm, though some of the crew may have survived. The *Elizabeth* under Captain John Wynter, who had served until that point as Drake's second-in-command, was separated from Drake in the next storm. After waiting unsuccessfully to rendezvous with Drake, Wynter and the *Elizabeth* turned back through the Strait. Thereafter they spent 4 months on the Brazilian coast before returning to England. Wynter was later imprisoned for having abandoned the expedition, but Harry Kelsey suggests that it was Drake who abandoned Wynter and that the latter was punished less for his own failings and more to enhance the evolving heroic legend of Drake's exploits. Kelsey, *Sir Francis Drake*, pp. 122–4.

[5] The *Pelican*, renamed the *Golden Hind*. See Kelsey, *Sir Francis Drake*, pp. 113–16.

[6] Along the coast of Chile, Nicaragua, and into New Spain, Drake sacked towns and captured ships, gold and silver, merchandise, food, and people with useful knowledge about the vicinity. The most valuable loot came from a richly laden though unarmed merchant vessel named *Nuestra Señora de la Concepción*, which he captured north of Guayaquil. Speculation and legend have coalesced around the notion that the ship's nickname was *Cacafuego* (*Shitfire*), though that is not certain. See Kelsey, *Sir Francis Drake*, pp. 142–71, for a detailed analysis of Drake's activities on the Pacific coast.

[7] Rada does not mention the monetary unit, but he presumably meant *pesos* worth 8 *reales* each. More than 360,000 *pesos* were captured from *Nuestra Señora de la Concepción* alone; Andrews, *Drake's Voyages*, p. 75; Kelsey, *Sir Francis Drake*, p. 157.

he was on the Ysla de Teranarte.[1] And he left for the Cabo de Buena Sperança[2] and arrived with all speed to England.[3]

The robberies of this corsair were known in all of Las Yndias.[4] By all the ways that they could borrow *navios*, they went in search of him; and Don Francisco de Toledo, who was Viceroy of Piru,[5] quickly dispached two *navios* with men of war and sea to go in his pursuit; and as the caudillo[6] and head of them, he sent Captain Pedro Sarmiento de Gamboa, to whom he gave orders to go in pursuit of the said Drac [f. 2r] and go directly to the said strait, where it was understood that [Drake] would return with the booty that he carried.[7] And thus the said Sarmiento departed with these two *navios* from the port of Callao of Lima[8] on the 11th of October of 1579, and he sailed thence until, near the mouth of the said strait, a great storm arose and one *navio* was thrown off course and returned to Callao, whence it had left. And the one in which Sarmiento was sailing entered into the said strait, and sailing through it he disembarked in some parts and places that seemed suitable to see the land and the disposition of it, and to know what Indian people inhabited it, and he found and saw there a great quantity of them, of different garb and nations. And he seized and took on board four barbarous Indians from among them and carried them with him, and some samples of precious stones and pearls; it is understood that the land will have mines of gold and silver and will be very fertile when cultivated. This done, he exited the mouth of the said strait and came to Spain, having experienced considerable risks. He entered into the port of San Lucar with this *navio* on the 10th of August of the year of 1580.

And after he and his men disembarked, he departed Seville with the four Indians for Badajoz, where His Majesty was at the time, and he told him in detail of all that had happened to him since he had left Lima in pursuit of this corsair, and of the disposition of the land of the said strait. And with this report, and others that His Majesty had of the incursion and robbery of the said Francisco Drac in the Mar del Sur, he resolved to send a powerful armada to the said Estrecho de Magallanes, so that [f. 2v] in the narrows therein – which the said Sarmiento said was less than half a league wide – two forts would be made, the one at one side and the other at the other, so that they correspond with one another, and that heavy reinforced guns and other necessary artillery and munitions for the defence of the said strait be carried for them, to secure that passage from other corsairs who would want to pass through it. [And the king resolved] as well to colonize, populate,

---

[1] Ternate an island in the Moluccas located at 0°47′13″N, 127°22′39″E.

[2] Cabo de Buena Esperanza (Cape of Good Hope). Elsewhere Rada uses the variant Cabo de Buena Esperança.

[3] Drake arrived back in Plymouth on 26 Sept. 1580.

[4] Las Indias (the Indies) was the Spanish designation for lands in the Western Hemisphere. News of Drake's raids spread quickly throughout administrative circles in Spanish America, and no doubt among the general population as well.

[5] Don Francisco Álvarez de Toledo held the office of Viceroy of Peru from November 1569 to September 1581.

[6] A caudillo is a commander or head officer in a military context.

[7] In other words, the viceroy assumed that Drake would sail south and return through the Strait to England. He did not know that Drake had already sailed north before crossing the Pacific.

[8] Callao, the port of Lima, was located 9.3 miles (15 km) west of the historic centre of Lima in the 16th century.

and cultivate those lands with people from Spain and to reduce those barbarous Indians to our holy faith.[1]

For this, he assigned the said Captain Pedro Sarmiento as governor of the forts and land of the said strait, and gave him licence to carry from Spain one hundred households as settlers and provided him with Franciscan friars to create a monastery. And His Majesty ordered that four hundred soldiers were to be brought as troops for the said forts, with two alcaides[2] and two captains. And His Majesty provided as captain general of this Armada of the Strait and for the guard and security of the coasts of Brasill, and for other effects, Diego Florez de Baldes, knight of the Order of Santiago, an expert with much experience in the things of the sea as well as of war, and for his almirante Diego de la Rivera. And he ordered [Flores] to travel to Seville, so that he would quickly prepare this armada and would then send the captains that would be assigned to raise two thousand and five hundred men of war and sea for the armada, which was done. And His Majesty sent orders to the president and judges of the House of Trade[3] of Seville that they help to prepare it, providing the supplies, artillery, [f. 3r] arms and munitions necessary for the expedition.

And having selected and careened the *navios* that were to go, they were assembled in the port of San Lucar de Barameda, where the general and almirante were, to outfit them and put them in order. And Don Francisco Tello, treasurer and judge of the said House [of Trade], went to the dispatch of this armada. And from Lisbon, where His Majesty was, he sent Don Diego Maldonado and Dom Pedro de Tarsis, knights of the Order of Santiago,[4] so they would help dispatch it. And he entrusted the duke of Medina Sidonia, who was in San Lucar, to assist at the dispatch of this armada, so that with his intervention and advice all would be provided, as was done;[5] and Don Xptoval de Erasso[6] helped in

---

[1] In Spanish, the verb *reducir* (to reduce) has several meanings, including to return something to its original or previous state, to bring back to obedience those who have disobeyed, and to persuade or attract someone with reasons and arguments. Rada's use of the word would seem to relate to the prevalent Spanish understanding that Christian evangelization would return the peoples of the Americas to their original state of grace, before the Devil had got hold of them. In the colonies of New Spain and Peru, native peoples were congregated – often forcibly – into settlements called *reducciones*, explicitly linking the resettlement with the aim of reducing the Indians to Christian belief and customs. See Elliott, *Empires of the Atlantic World*, pp. 74–5, for a comparison between the Spanish *reducciones* and the 'praying towns' in New England. In Portuguese Brazil from the mid-16th century, similar Indian settlements were known as *aldeias* (villages). See Hemming, *Red Gold*, pp. 99–109.

[2] See above, p. 60, nn. 2 and 3.

[3] See above, p. 22, n. 6.

[4] Órden de Santiago. Both Portugal and Spain had a military order with this name, Maldonado belonging to the Spanish and Tarsis to the Portuguese order. Although both orders were dedicated to the same saint, each had a separate history, membership, and administration. For Portugal, see Dutra, 'Order of Santiago', *passim*; and also above pp. 11–12. Maldonado in particular was knowledgeable about seafaring and ship design. Philip II had asked for his opinion, along with that of six others, about the design of several galleons being built for the crown in Vizcaya in February of 1581. See Navarrete, *Colección de documentos*, vol. 22, ff. 286r–329r, for the text of all the opinions. See also above, p. 27, for Tello and Tarsis.

[5] Alonso Pérez de Guzmán, 7th duke of Medina Sidonia, captain general of Andalusia, was the king's factotum in south-western Spain, enlisting soldiers and sailors for the crown and assisting in preparing and dispatching the Atlantic fleets. The ducal house of Medina Sidonia, whose seat was in Sanlúcar de Barrameda, had served the crown in such matters since the 13th century.

[6] Don Cristóbal de Eraso. See above, pp. 12–13. Spanish documents of the period often use a *crismón* or monogram of Christ (Xpo, from the Greek) to represent the letters *cristo*; thus, the name Cristóbal is often written as Xpobal.

this. And so as not to make a long report, I will not speak in detail about the work, diligence, and services that one and another did before the armada left from this port, in all of which I helped and found myself present. In addition, His Majesty resolved that there go in this armada Don Alonsso de Sottomayor, knight of the Order of Santiago,[1] whom he had provided as governor and captain general of the provinces of Chile, with six hundred men of war whom he brought in his command for the security and defence of the said provinces, so that once arrived at the said strait, the general[2] would give them the *navios* that were necessary for Don Alonso to carry his men to Chile.

And the armada being ready, and the provisions and the rest of the munitions and military supplies embarked, the captains arrived [f. 3v] with the men that they had gone to recruit and conduct. And Don Francisco Tello, with the general and royal officials[3] of the said armada, commenced to pay them on the 13th of September of 1581. And all the men of war and sea thereof being paid and embarked, and the said Don Alonso de Sotomayor with his men, and Governor Pedro Sarmiento and his settlers, on Monday the 25th of September of the said month and year, the duke of Medina and Don Francisco Tello, Don Diego Maldonado, and Dom Pedro de Tarsis agreed to dispatch the said armada from the port in continuance of its voyage, because it seemed to them that the weather for it was good and stable. [*margin:* The armada departed from San Lucar] And thus, in the morning the whole armada set sail, which included twenty-three seagoing *navios* with the captains and royal officials who were named beforehand, most of them old hands from the Royal Armada of the Guard Squadron of the Indies fleets,[4] with many important and distinguished people – altogether three thousand, five hundred men.[5] And as the armada was leaving, the wind calmed, and no more than five *navios* left port. The next day, Tuesday the 26th, another six left. The next day, Wednesday the 27th, the *galeaza capitana*[6] left with the *galeras*[7] towing her, and all the other *naos*. And having gone beyond the bank,[8] some provisions and artillery were embarked that had been taken off the large *naos*.[9]

---

[1] See above, pp. 11–12.

[2] i.e. Captain General Flores.

[3] For the final preparations for departure, Captain General Flores worked with land-based officials such as Don Francisco Tello, as well as with the men appointed to bureaucratic offices on his fleet, including Pedro de Rada, the chief scribe.

[4] This escort squadron for the Indies fleets was generally known simply as the Armada de la Guardia or Guard Squadron. Flores had served as its captain general several times since 1574. See above, pp. 10–13. Rada uses the word *biejos* (*viejos*: old ones), to denote the veterans of this squadron who were old in experience but not necessarily in years.

[5] Rada usually uses the word *gente* (people) to include both men and women who sailed on the armada. Here he uses the word *hombres* (men), though the total included women and children among the settlers for the Strait.

[6] The flagship *San Cristóbal* was a *galeaza* (galleass) of 700 *toneladas*, the largest vessel in the fleet, and the only galleass – i.e. a vessell carrying oars as well as sails. Rada usually calls the vessel the *capitana*, the *galeaza capitana*, or the *galeaza*, rather than the *San Cristóbal*. For *tonelada*, see above 'Weights, Measures, and Currency', p. xiv.

[7] *Galeras* (galleys) were long narrow vessels with a shallow draft, propelled primarily by oars, though they generally carried at least one sail as well. These galleys were based in the port to assist the fleets. They were not part of the Armada of the Strait.

[8] i.e. the sandbank at de Barrameda.

[9] Some provisions had been removed from the large *naos* so that they could get over the sandbar at Sanlúcar. Rada does not mention Sarmiento's complaints about Flores regarding the former's baggage and its final lading. See above, p. 70.

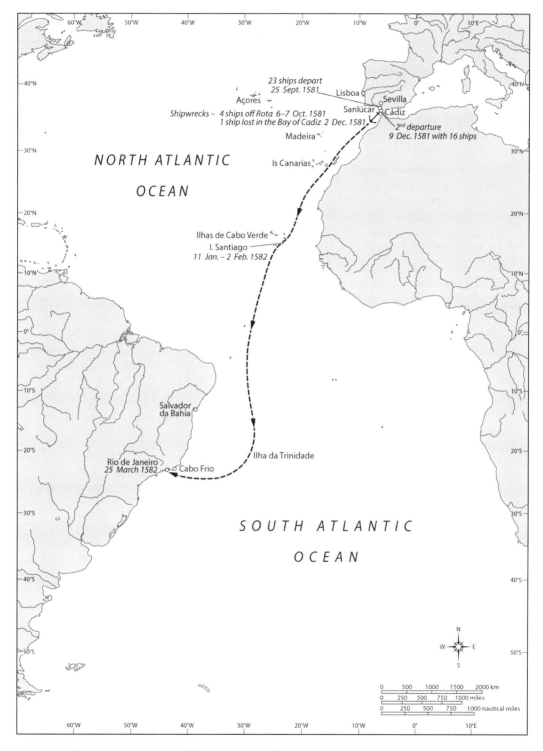

Map 1.   The outward voyage of the Armada of the Strait.

And at nightfall, the *capitana* set sail with all the armada in continuance of its voyage, [f. 4r] with the wind east, until Saturday the 30th of the aforesaid, which had a mild breeze south-south-west;[1] until Tuesday, the 3rd of October, the eve of San Francisco,[2] when we had sailed about 35 leagues from San Lucar, there began to be such strong wind from the south-south-west, with much shifting of the cargo, and things looked bad, so that it was indispensable that the armada take down its sails and heave to,[3] until Friday, the 6th of the aforesaid, when the weather had such force that the *galeaza capitana* had to jettison some things, which was done.[4] And the weather worsened so much on this day[5] that eight *navios* from the armada could not be seen. And the next day, Saturday the 7th, we found ourselves so off course that, though we were not ten leagues from the Baya de Cadiz, the pilots did not know where they were, and thus there were a thousand variations amongst them, until the *capitana* saw the land of Rotta[6] downwind,[7] and we found ourselves blown so far to leeward that, given the force of the weather, it was greatly feared that we would not be able to enter the Bayya de Cadiz. And thus we sailed toward it with great difficulty, close to the wind[8] because the wind and sea were excessive, the *galeaza capitana* entering with another fifteen *naos* that were going with her. In sight of the city of Cadiz, the *nao* named *Nuestra Senora de Guia*[9] whose captain was Martin de Quiros,[10] went to the bottom in a trice, and all who were on her drowned, which was the greatest misfortune to see without being able to succour even a single man, although it was four in the afternoon; and 150 men and some women and children settlers were on this *nao*.

[f. 4v] This day,[11] the *navio* named *Nuestra Señora de Buena Esperanza*, on which Pero Estebanez de las Alas sailed as captain, was lost near Roctta, which it could not get round.

---

[1] The Spanish is *sur y sudueste*. At other points in the manuscript, Rada uses the ambiguous *sueste*, rather than *sudeste* for south-east or *sudueste* for south-west. In ambiguous instances, the translation infers the proper direction from the context.

[2] The feast day of St Francis of Assisi is 4 Oct.

[3] The Spanish phrase is '*ponerse de mar entravés*', often translated as putting the ship in a beam sea or heaving to. This means to lower most or all sails and turn the ship so that it rides perpendicular to the direction of the waves, which then reach the ship on the side or beam, rather than head on or from the stern. A ship in this situation is often described in English as being hove to.

[4] Rada mentions nothing about Sarmiento's claim that he countermanded Captain General Flores's order to jettison. See above, p. 29.

[5] Rada often mixes present and past tense in the same sentence, presumably because his *Relación* is a fair copy of his previously written log. To avoid confusion, Rada's *hoy* (lit., today) is translated as 'this day'.

[6] Rota (variants Roctta and Rotta), a small town and prominent cape near the entrance to the Bay of Cádiz.

[7] *Sotavento* means leeward or downwind, the direction toward which the wind blows.

[8] Rada's phrase is '*metiendo de loo*', which means to luff or to sail close to the direction of the wind.

[9] *Nuestra Señora de Guía*.

[10] Martín de Quirós, a nephew of Pedro Menéndez de Avilés, had served the crown for 8 years by 1580. In addition to participating in military operations on land and sea in the Indies, he was appointed treasurer of La Florida in 1577, when Pedro Menéndez Márquez, another nephew of Pedro Menéndez de Avilés, was its captain general. Quirós had also sailed under Pedro Menéndez de Avilés, Diego Flores de Valdés, and Cristóbal de Eraso in the guard squadron of the Indies fleets. On 15 Nov.1580, Quirós was appointed to the rank of captain and assigned to serve either in a galley squadron in the Mediterranean or wherever he was needed; AGI, Patronato, leg. 261, R. 3. On 28 Feb. 1581, Diego Flores named him as one of the captains for the Armada of the Strait; AMN, Sanz Barutell, MS 388, f. 143r.

[11] i.e. 7 Oct. 1581.

The captain himself and one hundred other persons from this *navio* were drowned. This same day the *navio* named *San Miguel* was lost, whose captain, Hector Abarca, was drowned with another eighty persons. This same day the *nao* named *Sancti Yspiritu* was lost near the Rio del Oro in El Picacho.[1] The captain and owner was Juanes de Villaviciossa Lizarza, who had remained in San Lucar and did not go on the expedition, because he was given too little money as subsidy;[2] and Captain Alvaro Romo sailed in her and was drowned with another 120 persons.[3] The *nao almiranta*,[4] in which Diego de la Rivera sailed, entered into the bay the next day, Sunday the 8th of October, after nearly being lost next to Arenas Gordas.[5] Another two *naos* entered San Lucar with great difficulty, one in which Don Alonso de Sotomayor sailed,[6] and the other with Captain Gutiere de Solis. The latter was taken to the House of Trade in Seville under arrest, because he had left the *nao* before it entered into the port.[7] Another *nao* entered Guelba,[8] with its captain Jodar Alferez.[9]

This incident and misfortune caused great pain and grief to all in the armada, and General Diego Florez felt it very much, because, besides the loss of so many people, provisions, artillery, and other munitions, many captains and [f. 5r] high-ranking dependants of his were drowned. He wrote at once to His Majesty at Lisbon, giving him an account of this very painful event, advising him that the other *navios* needed repair, and some needed careening because they were taking on much water, and that, given the days that were necessary to put them to rights, there would not be time for them to be far enough along for the armada to leave until the winter passed, so that His Majesty should

---

[1] *Sancti Espíritu*; the Río del Oro (Spanish for the Arabic *Río Guadiaro*) empties into the Atlantic at the Bay of Algeciras, south-east of Cádiz and just west of the Strait of Gibraltar. El Picacho is a peak more than 800 m tall, inland from that bay and visible at sea.

[2] Juanes de Villaviciosa Lizarza; Rada uses the word *socorro* (succor), in this context meaning a subsidy or payment.

[3] All of the captains who drowned were experienced mariners. Like Martín de Quirós, Pedro Estebáñez de las Alas, also known as Pedro Esteban de las Alas, belonged to a distinguished naval family from Asturias, related by marriage to the Menéndez clan. He had served Captain General Flores as a sergeant. The ship he captained had arrived in Spain with Pedro Sarmiento in 1580, after traversing the Strait from west to east. Héctor Abarca had served in the Indies fleets at least since 1573. Captain General Flores sent him to recruit men in Málaga for the Armada of the Strait. AGI, Contratación, leg. 713; Navarrete, *Colección de documentos*, vol. 20, f. 154r. There is no further information on Captain Álvaro Romo.

[4] The *San Juan Bautista*. Rada often refers to the vessel simply as the *almiranta* (variant *almirancta*), rather than by its name.

[5] The *Arenas Gordas* (lit., Big Sands) are a long stretch of coastal dunes running north-west from the mouth of the Guadalquivir River at Sanlúcar de Barrameda. They were notorious among mariners nearing Cádiz, especially in bad weather, because of the danger of running aground.

[6] Probably the *nao Santa Catalina*; Navarrete, *Colección de documentos*, vol. 20, f. 164r.

[7] Gutiérrez Suárez de Solís, a native of Burgos, was rated highly as a captain by the Council of the Indies before the armada sailed, which makes his conduct during the storm surprising; see above, p. 16. The ship was the *María Jesús*, a *nao* of 450 *toneladas*; Chaunu, *Séville et l'Atlantique*, vol. 3, p. 295, citing AGI, Contratación, leg. 2933. In addition to Gutiérrez, the House of Trade charged other officers on the ship for abandoning the armada; AGI, Escribanía, leg. 1068B.

[8] Guelba is the port of Huelva, north-west of Cádiz at the confluence of the Tinto and Odiel rivers.

[9] The man whom Rada called Jodar Alferez signed his name as Luís de Jodar Alférez; see below, p. 146 and Appendix 1. It is possible that he was the same Jodar Alférez, identified in 1556 as a licenciado with an official position in Seville and experience in the Indies trade; AGI, Indiferente, leg. 13, ff. 171v–172r. Jodar was captain of the *Santa María de Buen Pasaje*, presumably the *nao* that entered Huelva after the storm.

send him orders of how best he should be served.[1] [The king] responded to this letter that the armada and *navios* that remained should be repaired and readied with all brevity, and that he should depart again with it in continuance of its voyage, because this would best correspond to his service.

The work was begun promptly, and to help carry it out quickly, Don Francisco Tello came to Cadiz, and Dom Pedro de Tarsis. And because the preparations and the illness of General Diego Florez[2] had delayed the work for some days, His Majesty wrote to the general that he should go to winter with the armada in the Rio de Jenero, or in the most convenient port in Brasil, and that he should remain there until October of the year 1582, which was a good time to depart for the Strait. And that he would send the provisions and other munitions lacking as relief supplies with the two *navios* from the armada that remained being repaired,[3] and in others that would be readied, and that in the month of August they would be with him in the Rio de Jenero.[4]

And with this resolution, and the armada being ready, General Diego Florez embarked, as did the [f. 5v] Governors Don Alonso and Pedro Sarmiento, on the first of December of 1581, in order to set sail. And the next day, the 2nd of the aforesaid, as they were intending to leave, a strong *levante*[5] came up that lasted four days with such force that the armada was in grave danger. The *fregatta Guadalupe*[6] was lost next to the bulwark of San Felipe[7] on the cables that were holding her, and although great diligence was done to aid her with boats and launches,[8] the situation could not be remedied, though the people and part of the provisions and munitions were saved.[9] Some of the other *naos* lost some cables and anchors with this weather.

[*margin:* The armada under sail] The *galeaza capitana* made sail from the Baya de Cadiz Saturday morning, the 9th of December of the same year of 1581, and anchored

---

[1] Rada does not mention that Captain General Flores told Don Francisco de Tello to ask the king to replace him as commander of the armada; AMN, MS 496, f. 98r, Philip II to Medina Sidonia, 22 Oct. 1581. See above, p. 31.

[2] Flores suffered a serious attack of kidney stones. See above, pp. 30–31.

[3] Here, the word *navío* denotes armed military vessels of the king, but it is not clear which vessels Rada means.

[4] In fact, the relief supplies would not reach Rio de Janeiro until 21 Dec. 1582, almost two months after Flores and the armada had departed for the Strait. See above, pp. 44–5.

[5] A *levante* is a strong east wind, very common along the coast near Cádiz in certain seasons.

[6] *Fragata* (frigate), a small armed warship with both sail and oars. Elsewhere Rada uses the variants ,*fragatta*, *fregata*. Here as elsewhere Rada refers to a specific vessel by its type rather than its given proper name. The name of the *fragata* in question here was *Nuestra Señora de Guadalupe*. It had been part of the guard squadron that Captain General Flores commanded in 1580. Chaunu, *Séville et l'Atlantique*, vol. 3, pp. 276–83, lists all the ships in that year's fleets. With the loss of the *Guadalupe*, three *fragatas* remained in the Armada of the Strait: *Santa Isabel, Santa Catalina*, and *La Magdalena/María Magdalena*. See above, pp. 36–7, 43–4, and below, Appendix 1.

[7] The *baluarte* (bulwark) was a two-sided fortification jutting out into the water. The bulwark of San Felipe was at the north-east edge of the city proper of Cádiz, on the south side of the bay, opposite the town of Puerto de Santa María on the other side of the bay.

[8] *Lanchas* (launches). In the 16th-century Spanish context, the word denoted a small vessel with oars and/or sails that could be carried on a larger sailing ship.

[9] The *Guadalupe* was commanded by Captain Álvaro del Busto (variant de Busto), a son-in-law of Captain General Flores. Sarmiento mentioned the relationship, but nonetheless claimed that nothing would have been done to help the stricken vessel without his own exhortations. Sarmiento, *Viajes al Estrecho*, vol. 1, pp. 211–12 and *Narratives of the Voyages*, p. 237.

outside the bay, waiting until all the armada should leave, until the 9th at night when it again set sail with sixteen *navios* in continuance of its voyage. We sailed with the wind north-east and east-north-east until Monday, the 11th of the aforesaid, when we had calm. Tuesday the 12th we had contrary weather and downpours, the wind west-north-west and variable; to avoid prolixity, I am not going to go on indicating [the winds]. We sailed until Monday, the 18th of the aforesaid, when at midnight, with the south-west wind blowing with force, the *galeaza* fired a piece and changed course, which is the signal that the other *navios* do the same. And at dawn [f. 6r] the next day, Tuesday the 19th, the *nao almiranta* did not appear, which the general and everyone else felt keenly. This weather lasted with much force until Thursday the 21st in the afternoon. The following Friday and Saturday, the armada was hove to, with the wind southerly. Sunday, Monday and Tuesday the 26th, it sailed with the wind north-west. This day in the morning the Ysla de Fuerte Bentura[1] was sighted. We passed by the south-south-east side of it, and in the afternoon we saw the Ysla de Canaria,[2] and we passed it on the south-south-east.[3] We passed by at a distance, our course straight toward Cabo Berde, sailing with contrary weather and calms, until Sunday the 31st of the aforesaid. This day, the sun was taken at barely 25 degrees,[4] and there was bottom at 75 *brazas*,[5] and we saw the land of Berveria,[6] the Vayya de Caballos,[7] at about eight leagues. In the afternoon, we saw two caravels[8] very far upwind.[9] Although the *fragatas* went in pursuit of them, they could not catch up with them.

Tuesday, the 2nd of January of the year of 1582, the general ordered Captain Gregorio de las Alas to raise the flag of the *almiranta,* as the almirante had not reappeared.[10] From this day until Monday the 8th we had good weather, winds north-west and north-east. This day at four in the afternoon, from the *capitana* we saw the island that they call Buena Vista, which is one of those of Cavo Verde. We passed at some distance from it on the

[1] The Isla de Fuerteventura, coordinates 28°20′N, 14°1′W, is one of the 7 Canary Islands, claimed by Castile in the late 15th century.

[2] Isla de Gran Canaria, coordinates 27°58′ N, 15°36′W.

[3] Given the course followed by the armada, Rada is referring to the part of the islands that the ships passed.

[4] By '*grados escasos*'(scant degrees), Rada seems to mean barely or just under a given latitude.

[5] For *braza* here and below, see 'Weights, Measures, and Currency', p. xiv above.

[6] Berbería (Barbary), the coast of North Africa.

[7] Bahía de Caballos (Bay of Horses). Rada's reference is not clear. It is possible that he was referring to Dahkla in Western Sahara, coordinates 23°43′ N, 15°57′W, which has a prominent bay. Spain claimed the area that is now Western Sahara from 1502 to 1975.

[8] A *caravela* or *carabela* was a sailing ship generally smaller than a merchant *nao*, although some Portuguese caravels in the late 16th century were 150 *toneladas* or more. A caravel generally had one full deck and a half deck, and from 2 to 4 masts. The sail plan might include both square and lateen sails or only lateen sails. Caravels were prized for their agility and versatility from the mid-15th century on, as they could manoeuvre in waters and winds that thwarted other types of vessels. See Phillips, *Six Galleons*, pp. 37–8.

[9] *Barlovento* means upwind, or the direction from which the wind blows.

[10] According to Chaunu, *Séville et l'Atlantique*, vol. 3, p. 298, n. 15, Gregorio de las Alas was a brother of Almirante Rivera. Captain General Flores had sailed with Alas at least since 1571, when he praised his service in a letter to the king. See Flores to Phillip II, 15 March 1571, in Navarrete, *Colección de documentos*, vol. 22, ff. 498v–501r. In February of 1581, Alas was the second name on the list of captains that Flores proposed for the Armada of the Strait, an indication of his merit; AMN, Sanz Barutell, MS 388, f. 143r–v, Flores to Philip II, 26 Feb. 1581. With Almirante Rivera and his vessel out of contact, Flores designated Alas as the almirante and his vessel, the *nao La Concepción*, as the *almiranta*. See below, pp. 90, 94–5, 97, 106–7, 135, 147, 154, 179, for the subsequent role of Alas in the armada.

south-east side. Tuesday, the 9th of the aforesaid, we saw the Ysla de Mayo[1] and the Ysla de Sanctiago, which is ten leagues one from the other east to west. Thursday the 11th in the afternoon, we entered [f. 6v] into the port of the island and city of Sanctiago de Cavo Verde. The governor and the bishop,[2] with all those of the land, showed themselves to be very pleased[3] at our arrival.

The general wrote to the governor and the city,[4] sending them the letters that he carried from His Majesty, and told them to bring the necessary meat, salt, firewood, and water for the armada, because the island had been ordered to provide them right away, and they would be paid in cash; and that, if they needed some things for the defence of the land, they would be provided with them from those that the armada carried. They responded that what was requested would all be provided as time permitted, because the meats would have to be slaughtered and salted, which had not yet been done. Saturday, on the 13th of the aforesaid, after the general had made sure all the *navios* were moored very well, and having given orders that repairs be made to those that needed them, he disembarked in the city to hear mass. The governor and all the principal people[5] of the land came to the *galeaza capitana* to accompany him, and at their departure, the armada fired a very good salvo with artillery and harquebuses,[6] which gave great satisfaction to all the island. They hosted him and he ate in the house of the governor, and in the afternoon, he came to embark, and the city fired a good salute for him with the artillery that they have in the fort. Thursday, the 18th of the aforesaid, the *nao almiranta* arrived at this port, which gave great contentment to all, because, given its delay, we feared lest some [f. 7r] disaster had occurred. It arrived in good shape, with all its men. They said it had separated from the armada the night that the *capitana* changed course,[7] not having heard the piece fired, and that it had encountered contrary weather, and that it went in pursuit of two French *navios*, and that it did not catch up with them.[8]

[*margin:* The standard was blessed] Sunday, the 21st of the aforesaid, we blessed the royal standard that was made in Seville for this armada. The bishop blessed it in the principal church, with great ceremony. We put ashore from the *galeaza capitana* General Diego Florez, Don Alonso de Sotomayor, Pedro Sarmiento, Almirante Diego de la Rivera and the royal officials, with all the captains and alferezes[9] and the principal persons of the armada, in all 150 men, very resplendent and in formation with their rifles. Waiting for us on the beach were the governor and all the principal persons of the city, with its

---

[1] Ilha da Boa Vista, located at 16°05′N, 22°50′W, is the easternmost of the Cape Verde Islands; Ihla do Maio is located at 15°3′N, 23°10′ W.

[2] The obispo (bishop) was the highest ecclesiastical official on the island.

[3] Rada uses the verb *holgarse*, which can mean to be relieved or satisfied, as well as pleased.

[4] Presumably, the officials of the city of Santiago.

[5] *Principales*; the leading members of the island community.

[6] An *arcabuz* (harquebus) was an early type of portable gun with a long barrel, varying in size but generally larger than an *escopeta* (rifle) and smaller than a *mosquete* (musket). The long barrel was supported on a tripod, trestle or forked 'rest' for use.

[7] The *almiranta* of a fleet brought up the rear. At midnight on 18 Dec. 1581, the wind was blowing strongly from the south-west, so it is logical that the *almiranta* did not hear the shot fired to indicate a change of course.

[8] These were perhaps the same vessels that Rada reported seeing from the *capitana* on 31 Dec. 1581.

[9] An alférez (pl. alféreces) was a minor official in the context of civil administration on land. In a military context on land or sea, an alférez could be subordinate to a ship's captain or to the head of an infantry unit. The rank is often translated as 'ensign', but it will be left in Spanish to avoid confusion with the modern rank of ensign in various military contexts. The ensign, in this instance was presumably serving as standard-bearer.

standard, which they struck against ours. And together, the ones and the others, arranged in very good order by the almirante and by Pero Martinez de Loaissa, chief sergeant[1] of the armada, we went marching through all the streets firing the rifles and harquebuses until arriving at the main church, where the bishop with all the clergy waited. Once blessed, and the mass finished, we returned to embark on the *capitana* in the same order. The whole city celebrated, and in the [f. 7v] afternoon there was a *sortija*[2] and they ran bulls.

The general wrote from there to His Majesty at Lisbon about what had happened up to this time, in duplicate, by two caravels that were going to Canaria and to Lisbon, on the 26th of this said month. And by another caravel that was going to Brasil, he wrote to the governor of the Baya who resided there, ordering him to provide advice about the state of the whole coast, and whether some corsairs were roaming along it, and whatever he could offer touching upon the pacification of the land;[3] and that this news he should send right away to the Rio de Jenero, where he [the general] would go on a direct course with all the armada as His Majesty ordered, giving him sufficient time for it;[4] and he sent him a sealed document that he carried from His Majesty. And this same order he sent to the captain who governed Pernambuco, which is on the same coast of Brassil at the upper end of it.

[*margin:* Departure from Cavo Berde] The armada departed with the same 16 *navios* from the port of Sanctiago de Cavo Berde Friday afternoon, the 2nd of February of the year 1582, on a direct course to the Rio de Jenero, with light breezes, steering to the south-south-west,[5] and the wind north. The next day, Saturday the 3rd in the morning, the *nao Maria de San Vicente*, in which Captain Hernando Ortega Morejon[6] sailed, discovered a leak at the prow. We made little progress this day for attending to her and until Thursday, the 8th of the aforesaid, when [f. 8r] the latitude was taken at six degrees and a half. Sailed well with the same course and wind from this day until Saturday, the 10th of the aforesaid, steered to the south-south-west with a light north wind, and the latitude was taken at five degrees. And until the following Saturday, the 17th of the aforesaid, we had many calms and heavy showers, with changeable winds. This day, the latitude was taken at 2 degrees, and until Wednesday, the 21st of the aforesaid, when the latitude was taken at barely one degree in the part north of the line,[7] sailed with calms and contrary winds; and until Saturday, the 24th of the aforesaid, steered toward the south-south-west, the wind south-east, with some heavy showers, and the latitude was taken at one degree in the part south of the line.[8]

---

[1] The sargento mayor (chief sergeant), Pedro Martínez de Loaísa (variants Loaisa, Loaysa), sailed on the *capitana* because he was an officer of the armada as a whole.

[2] A *sortija* was a game on horseback in which each rider attempted to thread a lance through a suspended ring.

[3] See above, pp. 33–4.

[4] i.e. sufficient time for the governor to collect the information Captain General Flores wanted.

[5] Rada uses the word *susueste*, which in this context must mean south-south-west. The modern word would be *susudoeste*.

[6] Hernando Ortega Morejón is listed as Hernán Ortega Morejón in some documents. He later served as captain of one of the 5 ships that succeeded in landing Governor Sarmiento and his remaining settlers at the Strait. See below, p. 106.

[7] i.e. north of the Equator.

[8] From this point, all of the latitudes recorded were in the Southern Hemisphere, though Rada rarely indicates it.

And until Thursday, the first of March, when the latitude was taken at five degrees, we had good weather, winds south-east, course toward the south-south-west until Wednesday, the 7th of the aforesaid, when the latitude was taken at 12 degrees and two-thirds. With the same course and wind, Friday the 9th of the aforesaid, the latitude was taken at 15 degrees and a half; and the next day Saturday the 10th it was taken at 17 degrees; and the following Sunday we had many heavy showers. Monday the 12th of the aforesaid, the latitude was taken at 19 degrees and a half, and we steered toward the south-west with the wind north-east. This day the pilots reckoned that they were 28 leagues away from the Ysla de la Asencion,[1] which is 20 degrees in the southern part,[2] north-east to south-west, a quarter [f. 8v] from east-west.[3] Until Wednesday, the 14th of the aforesaid, when the latitude was taken at 20 degrees and one-quarter, and we were eight leagues to the west-north-west of the said Ysla de la Asencion, we steered to the west-south-west[4] with the wind north-east, until Friday the 16th of the aforesaid, when the latitude was taken at 21 degrees.

The next day, Saturday the 17th, the wind from the north-west freshened and we sailed to the south-west, quarter to the west until Monday the 19th, when the latitude was taken at 22 degrees and one-third. And until the following Wednesday, the 21st of the aforesaid, when the latitude was taken at 22 degrees and one-quarter, we made little headway, because we had calms and heavy showers. This day the pilots reckoned themselves to be 72 leagues from Cabo Frio,[5] east to west. And with the wind from the south, we sailed toward the west-south-west. The next day, Thursday the 22nd, the latitude was taken at 22 degrees and three-quarters, and at midnight a sounding was taken and found bottom at 50 *brazas*.[6] And the next day, Friday the 23rd, at 10 in the morning we saw the land at Cabo Frio, which made us go more slowly toward the west-south-west, and there was bottom at 55 *brazas*, and the latitude was taken at 23 degrees.

[*margin:* Arrival of the armada at the Rio de Jenero] And the next day the 24th, at night the armada arrived at the entrance of the Rio de Jenero, about six leagues from the city of San Sevastian,[7] which it is also called, and anchored for the night in 60 *brazas*. And the next day, Sunday the 25th of March, as the armada was entering straight into the port, many canoes came out [f. 9r] with people from the land to reconnoitre it; they already had news that we were coming to spend the winter there. All the land had given its obedience to His Majesty a few days before, and it was very peaceful. We arrived to anchor about a league from the city, and from the two forts they have they fired a salvo with all the artillery. And the governor, who is called Salvador Corea,[8] came out to the *galeaza capitana* with many people from the city, in 22 canoes with many Indian bowmen in them, naked except for some animal skins. And all the Indian women went about thusly

---

[1] What Rada called the Ysla de la Asención was probably the modern Ilha da Trinidade (Trinity Island), discovered by the Portuguese in 1502 and located at 20°31′12″S, 29°19′12″W.

[2] South of the Equator.

[3] i.e. they were 28 leagues east-north-east of the island.

[4] Rada's text says *essudueste* (east-south-west), but he surely meant west-south-west.

[5] Cabo Frio, Brazil, is located at 22°52′44″S, 42°01′08″W.

[6] See above, p. xiv.

[7] São Sebastião (San Sebastián in Spanish) was the name of the town at the mouth of the Rio de Janeiro, located at 22°54′S, 43°14′W. Through most of his *Relación*, Rada indicates the location as the river, rather than the town.

[8] Salvador Correa de Sáa.

within the city and in all the land, as is customary; and there are many slaves among them, captured in just wars, who are sold like Negroes.[1] They are of a very good disposition, well formed and good workers.

The reception concluded, the general got into a shallop[2] with two pilots and went around taking soundings in the port, which is very good, large and sheltered, in order to see where the armada would be best situated and most secure and where the shipworm would do the least damage.[3] And ascertaining this, the next day, Monday the 26th in the morning, the armada approached and anchored next to the city and moored the *navios* well. And the *navios* had their rigging taken down, in order to store the sails, cables and other munitions. And we carried out a review of all the men of war and sea, and it was found that more than 150 persons had died between Cavo Berde and this port, and many more arrived ill. These we [f. 9v] promptly brought on land in order to cure them.

[*margin:* Disembarkation of the general and all those on board the armada] And having done this, the general, Don Alonso de Sotomayor, Pedro Sarmiento, and the almirante and captains and all of the most important people disembarked, and they took lodgings in the city. And then the general and royal officials of the armada met with the said governor of the city, and they discussed what provisions there were in the surrounding region to sustain the armada – meats, flour, *caçabe*[4] and other provisions.[5] And with the tally finished, they discovered that there was little meat, but with what they had brought, plus other provisions, and by reducing the rations as needed, the armada could be sustained for the time it had to be in this port. For the provisions that would be necessary before departure for the Strait, it was absolutely necessary to collect and bring them from elsewhere. The port of San Vicente and its captaincy, which is 48 leagues farther on from here, would be able to provide them.

And this being understood, the general wrote a letter to Geronimo Leiton,[6] who governs that captaincy, advising him of his arrival and of other things touching on the service of His Majesty; and that for the sustenance of the men of the armada, there was a need for many provisions; and that in Jenero there was not what was necessary; and that right away he should notify those in that captaincy who could provide [f. 10r] salted meats, salt pork, flours, rice and other things to do so, paying them at once in cash. To this,

---

[1] In medieval Christian doctrine, non-Christians captured in a just war could be enslaved; the doctrine was debated and redefined in the process of overseas conquest and colonization. King Sebastião I of Portugal issued a law in 1570 that prohibited the enslavement of Brazilian Indians, but with numerous exceptions, including capture in a just war and other circumstances. King Philip would confirm the law and its exceptions in 1587. Laws notwithstanding, Portuguese colonists and their allies, both Indian and European, continued to carry out slaving raids into the Brazilian interior. See Hemming, *Red Gold*, pp. 149–52, 245–51, and *passim*.

[2] A *chalupa* (shallop) was a small, light, open vessel, larger than a *batel* and pointed at both ends. It could carry 1 or 2 sails, but more often was propelled by 6 or 8 oars.

[3] The word *broma* (shipworm) referred to the various marine molluscs of the genus *Teredo* that bore into wooden vessels in tropical waters.

[4] *Caçabe* (Cassava) was a staple prepared from the roots of the manioc plant (*Manihot esculenta*). A kind of flat bread could be made from the flour. Rada later refers to *caçabe de guerra* and *harina de guerra*, but it is not clear if the latter was an alternative designation for cassava flour or something different.

[5] Because Rio de Janeiro had a maximum of 400 households, the sojourn of the Armada of the Strait overwhelmed the usual channels of supply in the region.

[6] See above, p. 61.

Geronimo Leiton responded that they would provide all that they could procure; and he sent a memorandum of the items that could be provided and saying that the householders of that captaincy were ready and very obedient in the service of His Majesty. The general, having seen this, at once sent his own representative to San Vicente, with orders to begin to collect the said provisions, and that for the payment and transport thereof, he would go in person to the said captaincy, and he would carry out a review and would provide whatever they needed, and he would examine the samples from certain mines of silver and gold that the said Geronimo Leiton wrote him had been discovered.

Thereafter, it seemed to the said general not to be advisable for him to be absent from the Rio de Jenero, for the quietude of the men of the armada and the local population, and in order that items being prepared to take to the Estrecho de Magallanes were made with the greatest diligence and care. These included a large wooden house with planking, to store all the arms, supplies and munitions that were carried for the said strait, and earthen bricks, wooden containers, stakes, tools and other things for the forts, in order to provide everything necessary.[1] Thus, he did not go to the said town and captaincy of San Vicente, and decided that [f. 10v] in his place the Almirante Diego de la Rivera would go to inspect the area and bring the provisions, to whom he gave orders and his power of attorney for what he had to do, charging him to do all with diligence and brevity.

[*margin:* The departure of the almirante and officials to San Vicente] And to go with him, he sent the purveyor Esteban de las Alas[2] and Pedro Desquibel, who held the office of treasurer, so that they could receive and pay for the provisions.[3] And they carried monies and other things for the payment thereof. And they departed from the port of Jenero to that of San Vicente on the 25th of June of 1582 in trading vessels[4] in which they carried salt to preserve the meat and empty barrels in which to send the provisions as they were prepared. And the said almirante and royal officials returned on the 17th of October with the remainder, when the armada was readied and on the point of departure, with the general waiting, anxious at their tardiness. They said that, because of bad weather, they had not been able to arrive before.

During the time that the almirante was in San Vicente, the general had all the *naos* in the armada careened and their carpentry repaired and refitted, and they were repaired very well, because there was a good supply of wood. And he built the *bergantin*, the parts

---

[1] For Sarmiento's description of these preparations, and Captain General Flores's interventions therein, see above, pp. 34–40.

[2] Esteban de las Alas was proveedor (purveyor) of the armada as a whole and captain of the *nao* named *San Esteban* of Soroa. His father of the same name had served for decades as a trusted lieutenant of Pedro Menéndez de Avilés in La Florida and elsewhere and as purveyor of the guard squadron of the Indies fleets in 1573–6. Esteban de las Alas the younger helped to sort out and file his father's accounts when the squadron returned to Spain and thereafter was assigned to the Armada of the Strait. It is likely that he was related to Gregorio de las Alas, captain of the *nao La Concepción*, who had served with Diego Flores, and to Alonso de las Alas, captain of the *almiranta San Juan Bautista*. They were all related to Almirante Diego de la Rivera as well. Esteban de las Alas the elder was Rivera's uncle and Alonso de las Alas was Rivera's brother; AGI, Contaduría, leg. 466; Chaunu, *Séville et l'Atlantique*, vol. 3, pp. 292–3, citing AGI, Contratación, leg. 2899, lib. 1.

[3] Pedro de Esquivel sailed on the *capitana* as tesorero (treasurer) of the armada as a whole, the second financial officer after the contador (accountant), Andrés de Eguino. The treasurer was the officer entrusted with the keeping and dispersal of money or goods. In all, Esteban de las Alas and Esquivel arranged for the purchase and preparation of 21 large barrels (*pipas*) of salted beef; Navarrete, *Colección de documentos,* vol. 20, f. 357v.

[4] The phrase used is '*navíos del trato*'.

for which had been carried from Spain, and they launched it into the water.[1] And he ordered to be gathered in the city and the farmsteads[2] surrounding it, and in the village of the Indians,[3] all the flour, salted meat, and rice that could be had so that there would be no lack of provisions, because he feared [f. 11r] that the *navios* that were to come from Spain with relief supplies would not arrive in time, and he was determined that the armada should not delay going to the Strait and carrying out what it had to do for lack of them. On the 8th of August of this said year, a small sailing vessel[4] arrived in this port of Jenero that the governor of Baya sent with a packet of letters from His Majesty for General Diego Florez, in which he had news that he had been granted the *Encomienda de Oreja* in his Order,[5] at which he rejoiced greatly, along with all those in the armada. And His Majesty wrote him that he was dispatching the *navios* that were to come with the provisions. With this same *navio*, which returned to the Baya, the general wrote to His Majesty about what had happened to that point.

On the 24th of October, he prepared to leave with the armada in two or three days for the round-trip to the Strait; at that point, he was not waiting for the *navios* that were to come from Spain with the relief provisions, because this day a trading bark[6] entered this port with the Franciscan commissary, Juan de Rivadeneira, who had left Spain in the month of May of this year. And he said that four or five *navios* that were ready to come to this port with provisions and other things for the armada had been ordered by His Majesty to go to La Tercera with the armed warships[7] and galleys that were going there.[8] And thus was lost the hope that we had. The general wrote to the governor of the Bayya, because the packet that he had written to His Majesty was already en route with the first *navio*, [f. 11v] that he would depart, and that he would return with the greatest possible brevity, so that he could reconnoitre all the coast of Brasil and cleanse it of the corsairs who were there. And thus he left orders in Jenero and San Vicente that they have supplies ready for when the armada returned, so as not to stay more time in the port of Rio de Jenero than was necessary to receive them.

The men had been well disciplined and drilled with their weapons, and they were skilled in their use. And great care had been taken so there would be no disorder, and that they would have good relations with the people of the land, and not give them any offence.

---

[1] A *bergantín* (lit., brigantine) in late 16th-century Spanish usage was a small, light launch with a single lateen sail and an open deck. Such vessels were often built from a kit with numbered pieces, for fitting together after an ocean crossing, and were used for coastal reconnaissance and transport. In the later 18th and 19th centuries ships called brigantines were transoceanic vessels in their own right, quite different from the early *bergantín*.

[2] Rada uses the word *estancias*, which could mean anything from small cattle ranches or farms to large landed estates.

[3] Presumably, there was a village (*aldeia* in Portuguese, *pueblo* in Spanish) of pacified Indians near Rio de Janeiro.

[4] The word used is *navichuelo*.

[5] i.e. an income-bearing title in the Order of Santiago; see AHN, OM, Carpeta 247, N. 7. As the comendador of Oreja, Flores would collect an annual sum of 2,000 ducats, generated by income from a government bond (*juro*). The actual conveyance of the *encomienda* is dated 1584, after Flores's return to Spain. The ducats mentioned in Rada's *Relación* were Castilian ducats, each valued at 11 silver *reales*, or 375 *maravedís*.

[6] The phrase used is *barco de trato*, denoting a small sailing vessel or bark used for coastal trade.

[7] The phrase used is *navíos de armada*.

[8] For the struggle over Terceira in the Azores, see above, pp. 7, n. 3, 37.

And those who did give offence the general punished rigorously, and that is why he punished some soldiers who had deserted the armada. And with this fear of punishment, there was no disorder.[1] And having paid for all the provisions that had been supplied in this port, the general embarked to set sail on the 26th of October of this year of 1582. And he had barely left when, on the 28th of the aforesaid, an abundant leak of unknown source was discovered on the *nao Maria de San Vicente*, whose captain was Hernando Ortega Morejon. The general, with some pilots, went to inspect it, and they agreed that it made sense to leave the vessel behind and break it up, because it was very old and not fit to sail and all the people and munitions that it carried would be at risk. And thus, with great speed all the [f. 12r] people on it, and all the provisions, artillery, arms and munitions that it carried were taken off and distributed among the other *naos*, with the cables, rigging and other things duly accounted for, and the *nao* was left behind.

[*margin:* The armada departs from Jenero on course to the Strait] The armada set sail from this port of the Rio de Jenero on Friday morning, the second of November of the said year of 1582, because until this day there was not weather fit to leave with the 15 *naos* that remained and the *bergantin*, which made a total of 16 sails. With the wind north-east, we went on a southerly course until midnight, when the *capitana* anchored in 40 *brazas*,[2] waiting to collect the armada that trailed behind. And the next day, Saturday at dawn, we set sail on a south-south-west course, with the wind east-north-east, until Monday, the fifth of the aforesaid, when the latitude was taken at 25 degrees. The next day, Tuesday, the armada lowered sails,[3] with a strong south-west wind. The next day, Wednesday, the latitude was taken at 26 degrees. Thursday the 8th, the sails were lowered, because of having a contrary wind. Friday the 9th little progress was made, with the wind south-east, and the latitude was taken as 26 long degrees.[4] Saturday the 10th we had good following winds,[5] and the latitude was taken at 26 degrees and two-thirds. Sunday the 11th the latitude was taken at 27 degrees and one-quarter. Monday the 12th the latitude was taken at 27 degrees and a half, with good following winds. Tuesday the 13th, with the wind east-south-east, the latitude was taken at 28 degrees. Wednesday the 14th in the morning, the north wind freshened; steered to the south, and the latitude was taken at 29 degrees and one-quarter. Thursday the 15th, with the wind north, the latitude was taken at 31 degrees minus one-third; steered toward the south, quarter south-west.

Friday the 16th we had contrary wind south-west, and the armada lowered sails. Saturday the 17th the wind was west-south-west; steered toward the south and this day took [f. 12v] the latitude at 33 degrees. Sunday the 18th the latitude was taken at 33 degrees and one-third. Monday the 19th the northeast wind freshened; steered to the south-west. This day the latitude was not taken because the sun was not visible, nor the next day, Tuesday the 20th. This day in the afternoon and all night there was such heavy

---

[1] By contrast, Sarmiento's narrative criticized the behaviour of the men and what he perceived to be Captain General Flores's laxity in punishing wrongdoers. See above, pp. 36–7.

[2] See above, p. xiv.

[3] The Spanish verb is *amainar*.

[4] By the phrase *grados largos* (long degrees), Rada seems to mean more than an even degree of latitude, but less than one-quarter more. The latitudes he records nearly always involve whole numbers, or a whole number and the phrase one-quarter, one-third, one-half, two-thirds, or three-quarters more or less than a whole number.

[5] The Spanish word is *bonanza*.

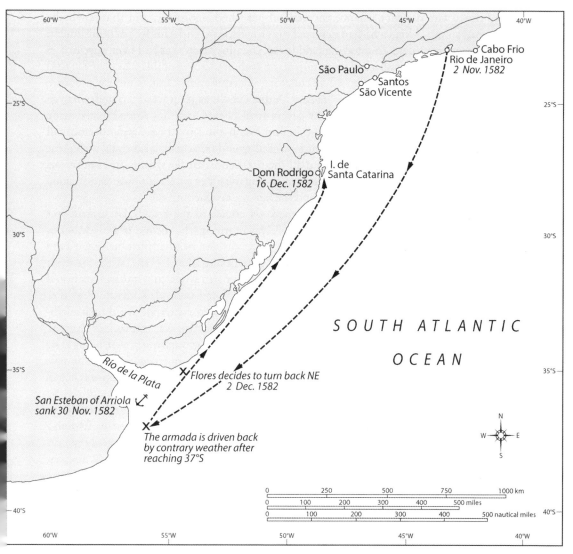

Map 2.   The first attempt to reach the Strait.

weather north-east that the *naos* ran with only the topsail set very low on the foremast[1] on a course south-west. And the *capitana* lost the launch that it towed behind, because the hawser[2] broke with which it was tied; and with great luck the *bergantin* saved two sailors who were on [the launch].

Wednesday the 21st the latitude was taken at 36 degrees and a half. Thursday the 22nd there was such weather [from the] south-west that the *naos* were forced to take down their top-masts and to run on an east-north-east course. The latitude was taken this day at 36 degrees and one-third, less than the day before. Friday the 23rd the latitude was taken at 36 degrees and one-quarter, and this day in the afternoon the *galeaza capitana* untied the *bergantin*[3] that it towed behind, saving the men on it, because the strong southwest wind that had blown the day before had raised such high seas that it had run into the *capitana* itself and was badly damaged.[4] Saturday the 24th the latitude was not taken because there was no sun, and the wind came from the south-west. Sunday the 25th the latitude was taken at 36 degrees and one-quarter, because the southwest wind drove us back. Monday the 26th the sun was not taken, and with the wind north-north-west that blew with such force, the course was steered to the south-east,[5] quarter east. Tuesday the 27th the latitude was not taken because the sun was not visible, and we had so much wind from the west and south-west that the armada did not set sail until the next day, Wednesday the 28th, when the latitude was taken at 37 long degrees. This day in the afternoon, so much south-west wind blew, [f. 13r] with such heavy seas, that we were all at great risk and very fearful. And the general saw that the *naos* would not be able to withstand the weather, being hove to and buffeted by the wind, and the *capitana* was carrying only the topsail of the foremast set very low, until 10 at night when the wind calmed; and suddenly the north wind began to blow again, and we sailed on course south-west quarter west.

Thursday the 29th the latitude was not taken, and the afternoon brought so much south-west wind that the armada struggled against it, and the *nao* named *Sanctiestevan* of Ariola,[6] whose captain was Jhoan Gutierez de Palomar,[7] fired a shot about midnight and lit many flares and lanterns, because it was taking on much water. [*margin:* The *nao* of Riolas that was lost] Friday the 30th at dawn the *galeaza capitana* approached her, with much wind and sea, and we asked what had happened, and the captain responded that they were sinking, that the *nao* was open at the prow, and they could not remove the water with the pumps as fast as it was rising. The general told him to follow behind the *capitana*, that he would not

---

[1] *Papahigo* is the fore-topsail; *trinquete* is the foremast.

[2] By hawser Rada refers here to a *guindaleza* a heavy rope or cable used for towing or for mooring a vessel.

[3] See above, pp. 76–7.

[4] Rada's phrase is '*se hizo pedazos*' (was broken into pieces), but it was obviously able to stay afloat until it was deemed necessary to save the two men and cut it loose.

[5] Rada initially wrote south-south-east, but crossed out the first word.

[6] *San Esteban*. Rada writes the names as one word, elsewhere *Sanctiestevan*, *Sanestevan*. There were two *naos* named *San Esteban* in the armada. To distinguish between them, each was identified with its owner – in this case, Martín de Arriola. See Chaunu, *Séville et l'Atlantique*, vol. 3, p. 294.

[7] Juan Gutiérrez de Palomar (variants in Rada's *Relación* and other documents, Gutierez de Palomar, Gutiérrez de Palomares) was one of the most senior and experienced captains in the armada, having served in La Florida with Pedro Menéndez de Avilés and Diego Flores. He sued the House of Trade in Seville in 1571 for back pay for his service in La Florida. See, AGI, Justicia, leg. 906, N. 6. When Captain General Flores fell ill in October of 1581, Gutiérrez wrote to the king's secretary, offering to serve in his place; AMN, Sanz Barutell, MS 388, ff. 207v–208r, Gutiérrez to Antonio de Eraso, 23 Oct. 1581.

abandon him, although the wind and sea were an unrestrained tempest. And all day long the said *nao* came following close behind the *capitana*, firing shots from time to time so that they might be given assistance. But the wind and sea were so strong that none of the *naos* could come near enough to help, although they tried to do so. And thus with effort it stayed in the body of the armada until one hour after nightfall, when we lost sight of her, without the tempest ceasing for an hour. And the next day, some *naos* that sailed near her said that she must have gone to the bottom around midnight, because they already saw her without a mainmast, lagging behind [f. 13v] and unmanoeuvrable.[1] And according to this, we took it as very certain that she went to the bottom, without being able to save a man from her, which was a great pity, because she was one of the largest and best *naos* in all the armada, and the captain one of the best and oldest[2] in it. More than 220 men and some women were in this *nao*, and the majority of the supplies that were going to the Estrecho de Magallanes.[3]

The next day, Saturday the first of December, the latitude was taken at 36 degrees and a half, with the same contrary wind, although gentler. Sunday the 2nd the latitude was not taken, and the armada was hove to with a strong storm. The *capitana* set sail and turned on a north-east course. This day Don Alonso de Sotomayor came near the *capitana* with his *nao*. And he said to the general that he knew that two *naos* that carried his men, which were *Sancta Marcta del Pasage*[4] and *San Niculas*,[5] were taking on much water, and the same in the one where he sailed,[6] and that they would not be able to withstand more weather; and that if it seemed [acceptable to the general], he would wish to go with his *naos* and men to the Rio de la Platta, and that there they would disembark and go by land to Chile. In this way His Majesty would be served better than if they were all lost and drowned going by way of the Strait. Moreover, he carried few provisions, and that, as a gentleman and a Christian, if it were necessary to die he would accept it and was ready for it, but His Majesty would not wish, nor would God be served, for him to die fighting the elements. The general responded that this plan would be carried out, but that he should not go nor withdraw without his orders.

The next day, Monday the 3rd of the aforesaid, the latitude was taken at 36 degrees, going on a north-east course, with much [f. 14r] south-west wind, which lasted with excessive force until the next day, Tuesday the 4th, when it abated a little, although it had raised heavy seas. This day the latitude was taken at 35 degrees and a half, and with this wind, we sailed on course for the Rio de la Platta, and the weather did not give occasion for anything else.[7] The next day, Wednesday the 5th, the latitude was taken at 35 degrees. This day, the *capitana* hove to, with a light wind, in order to gather the armada together, because the *naos* were very worn; and some were complaining that they were taking on

[1] Rada's phrase is '*atravesada que no governaba*'.

[2] Here again, Rada seems to be referring to the captain's long experience at sea, rather than to his age.

[3] Sarmiento later claimed that he and the *Begoña*'s crew did everything possible to save the stricken ship and spread the story that Flores callously chose to do nothing; Sarmiento, *Viajes*, vol. 1, p. 257 and *Narratives of the Voyages*, pp. 250–51. Navarrete, *Colección de documentos*, vol. 20, f. 201r–v, lists the settlers who drowned. Friar Rivadeneira heard the story of Flores's supposed callousness when he next encountered the armada, ibid., vol. 26, ff. 83r–84r; also in *CODOIN*, vol. 94, pp. 549–52.

[4] *Santa María de Buen Pasaje* was one of the *naos* carrying Don Alonso's men. *Santa Marta* was another *nao* in the armada, carrying mostly settlers. Presumably, Rada confused the two ships here.

[5] *San Nicolás*; elsewhere Rada uses the variants *San Miculas, Sant Miculas*.

[6] Don Alonso sailed on the *nao* named *Santa Catalina*.

[7] In other words, the armada had turned north, abandoning the attempt to reach the Strait.

much water and could not hang on, saying that if they were to wait to make further effort at sea, they would be lost with another tempest like those in the past. Seeing this, the general convened a *junta*[1] on the *galeaza*, to which Don Alonso de Sotomayor and his brother, Don Luis, and Governor Pedro Sarmiento, and Almirante Diego de la Rivera, and some captains and pilots of the armada came. And having proposed to them what seemed to him, and the necessity that the *naos* had, it seemed to all that it would serve His Majesty that they head for the Rio de la Platta, or the first port that the weather brought them to, so that they could repair the *naos* that needed it, and that there they would decide what was best to do. And all signed with their names; and the proposal with the opinions of all will be found on leaves 65 to 69.

[*margin:* The armada comes to port] This done, we made sail on course to the Rio de la Plata. The next day, Thursday the 6th, we did not take the sun. Friday the 7th the latitude was taken at 33 degrees and a half. The next day, Saturday the 8th, the latitude was taken at 33 degrees. The next day, Sunday the 9th, the latitude was taken at 32 degrees and a half. Monday the 10th, it was taken at 32 degrees, and at midnight the *capitana* threw out the sounding line and found bottom at 70 *brazas*,[2] coming along the coast of Brasil [f. 14v] from the Rio de la Platta toward the north. Thus we ran along that coast, and although we were gaining distance sailing against the wind, the *bendavales*[3] did not allow us to reach the Rio de la Platta. Tuesday the 11th the latitude was taken at 30 degrees and a half, and we saw land on the same coast to the west-north-west. This day we had *brisas*[4] and we changed course and headed out to sea until the next day, Wednesday the 12th, when the latitude was taken from one side and the other at 30 degrees and one-quarter, because the wind was contrary.[5] Thursday the 13th the latitude was taken at 29 degrees and a half, with the wind south, steering to the north and to the north-west in order to reach land. The next day, Friday the 14th, the latitude was taken at 29 degrees, with the wind north-north-east, the course east, and we tacked from one course to another until night, when the armada was with lowered sails until the next day, Saturday the 15th, when at dawn we discovered a sail about four leagues from land.

The *nao almiranta* launched its shallop and went to reconnoitre her, and brought her to the *capitana*. She was a single-decked trading bark, carrying Don Francisco de Vera and the commissary Friar Juan de Rivadeneira, with another five friars who were going to the Rio de la Platta.[6] [*margin:* The bark of the friars that the armada encountered] This bark

---

[1] *Junta* (committee), often convened for a limited time to consider a specific issue. It was common practice for *juntas* to be formed within the various councils of state.

[2] See above, p. xiv.

[3] A *vendaval* is a strong south wind with a westerly tendency; elsewhere Rada uses the variants *bendal* and *bendaval*. At that point, the vessels were north of the Río de la Plata, and the *vendaval* would not allow them to make enough progress against the wind to reach the entrance.

[4] A *brisa* is a light wind or breeze from the north-east.

[5] Rada seems to mean that the latitude had to be taken twice, from one side of the ship and the other, because the shifting wind made it difficult to sight the horizon long enough to take a reading.

[6] The English reckoned the bark to be of 46 tons; see Donno, *Diary of Richard Madox*, p. 248, n. 2. According to English reports, there were 21 persons on board: 7 Franciscans, Don Francisco de Vera, and 13 others, including 2 women and 2 infants; see Taylor, *Troublesome Voyage*, p. 211. Rada seems to have missed counting 1 Franciscan. Don Francisco de Vera had left Spain with the soldiers going to Chile. In Rio de Janeiro, Don Alonso de Sotomayor gave Vera permission to sail to the Río de la Plata on the small bark carrying Rivadeneira and his friars, so that he could carry news of the armada's arrival overland to the viceroy of Peru; see Donno, *Diary of Richard Madox*, p. 249.

had left with the aforesaid from the Rio de Jenero the same day that our armada left, the 2nd of November of this year of 1582. And the said Don Francisco told the general that they departed the previous day, Friday the 14th, from the port of Don Rodrigo,[1] 10 leagues away. Eight days earlier, they had left the port of Sancta Catalina[2] on the way to the Rio de la Platta, sailing close to the coast, when an English *patache*[3] and two launches came out, chased them for four or five leagues, overtook them, and brought them to the said port of Don Rodrigo, where there were two large English *naos*, *capitana* and *almiranta*, very well gunned and outfitted.[4] And they held them there for six days, informing themselves [f. 15r] about the officers of the *navio* and the friars who travelled in it. And they knew of our armada and of its aims, and they satisfied themselves well in detail about what it was like; and this will be seen in the report I wrote about all this, from the mouth of the said Don Francisco, which is from leaves 84 to 90.[5]

And he also told the general that this day makes three days since the said English *naos* had left from the said port of Don Rodrigo, and that, from what he could understand from them, they were going back toward the Rio de la Platta,[6] because they took two mariners with them who were familiar with the said river and its sailing directions.[7] And

---

[1] The English called the port of Dom Rodrigo (today's Garopaba Bay) the 'Bay of Good Comfort', due to the water, varieties of fish, and other supplies that they were able to gather there. Richard Madox, the clergyman who was the official chaplain of the English expedition, made a careful sketch of the port; see Taylor, *Troublesome Voyage*, pp. 117–18 and pl. XIII, facing p. 190. The other clergyman in the expedition, John Walker, explicitly equated Dom Rodrigo with the Bay of Good Comfort; see Donno, *Diary of Richard Madox*, app. II, p. 330.

[2] The island of Santa Catarina near Dom Rodrigo also has numerous bays, lagoons, beaches, and other places where ships might anchor.

[3] *Patache*; Rada uses the variants *pataj, pataje*. In Spanish usage, the word generally referred to a small dispatch boat that accompanied a larger vessel. However, it could sometimes refer to a vessel that separated from a larger fleet to sail toward a different destination. For example, the '*patache de Margarita*' was the ship – often a galleon – that sailed from Spain with the Tierra Firme fleet but separated from it to approach the island of Margarita off the coast of Venezuela. In the case of Fenton's fleet, Rada means a small dispatch boat or pinnace.

[4] This was the expedition under Edward Fenton, planned as a trading mission to the Moluccas. See above, pp. 39–43, and Andrews, *Elizabethan Privateering*, pp. 203–5. Fenton's official instructions appear in Taylor, *Troublesome Voyage*, pp. 50–59. At that point, Fenton's expedition consisted of the flagship *Galleon Leicester*, formerly the *Bear Gallion* (400–500 tons); the *Edward Bonaventure* (250–300 tons), commanded by Luke Ward; and the bark *Francis* (40 tons), commanded by John Drake, first cousin of Sir Francis Drake, who had provided the bark to the expedition. See Donno, *Diary of Richard Madox*, pp. 20–21, and Wagner, *Drake's Voyage*, p. 215. Among the notables in the expedition were William Hawkins, a nephew of John Hawkins, and representatives of several prominent English commercial houses. Various English accounts of the capture, detention, and interrogation of the bark and its passengers appear in Taylor, *Troublesome Voyage*, pp. 190–92, 211–16, 228–38; Donno, *Diary of Richard Madox*, pp. 248–59.

[5] In his testimony, Don Francisco de Vera confirmed that there were six friars with Commisary Juan de Rivadeneira.

[6] See above, p. 40. By the time Fenton captured the friars' bark, disagreements about the course and aims of the expedition had reached a crisis. After releasing their captives, the English headed south to a latitude of 33°15'S. On 20 Dec., Fenton called a council and decided to head north again, after which John Drake abandoned the expedition.

[7] One of the men the English took from the friars' boat was a hispanicized Englishman, Richard Carter, who lived in Asunción under the name Juan Pérez and later gave testimony to Spanish authorities. The other was a Portuguese named Juan Pinto (also known as Juan Pino or del Pino). Although Pinto would later claim that the English had held him as well as Carter under duress, he seems to have remained willingly, leaving his wife with the friars. See Donno, *Diary of Richard Madox*, pp. 257–8. The full testimony of Pérez (Carter), dated 24 Jan. 1583, appears in Navarrete, *Colección de documentos*, vol. 25, ff. 184r–187r.

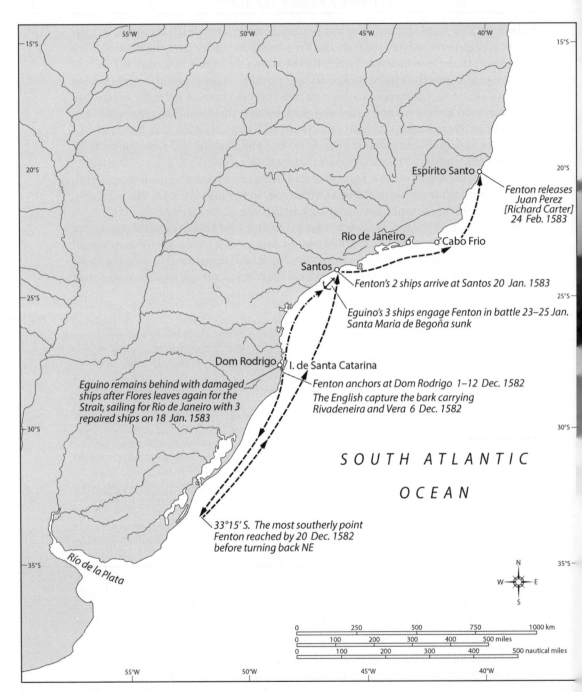

Espírito Santo

Fenton releases
Juan Perez
[Richard Carter]
24 Feb. 1583

Rio de Janeiro   Cabo Frio

Santos

Fenton's 2 ships arrive at Santos 20 Jan. 1583

Eguino's 3 ships engage Fenton in battle 23–25 Jan.
Santa Maria de Begoña sunk

Dom Rodrigo   I. de Santa Catarina

Eguino remains behind with damaged
ships after Flores leaves again for the
Strait, sailing for Rio de Janeiro with 3
repaired ships on 18 Jan. 1583

Fenton anchors at Dom Rodrigo 1–12 Dec. 1582
The English capture the bark carrying
Rivadeneira and Vera 6 Dec. 1582

SOUTH ATLANTIC

OCEAN

33°15′ S. The most southerly point
Fenton reached by 20 Dec. 1582
before turning back NE

Rio de la Plata

N
W   E
S

0		250		500		750		1000 km
0	100	200	300	400	500 miles
0	100	200	300	400	500 nautical miles

Map 3.   Encounters with Edward Fenton's ships.

he believed they would remain there until such time as this armada left the Strait, in order for them to go there and pass through into the Mar del Sur and to go to the Malucas. This considered, the general ordered the almirante to bring the bark in tow from the stern of his *nao*; and because the wind was a *bendal* [*sic*], we came straight toward the port of Don Rodrigo and to that of Sancta Catalina to refit the *naos*, both to see if the corsair had turned around and come back to the said port, because there had been *vendavales* after they left, and because the said Don Francisco said that the English *naos* had reached a latitude of 33 degrees, being near the Rio de la Plata, and that they had done repairs in the said port of Don Rodrigo in the ten days that they were there.[1]

[*margin:* The loss of the *nao Santa Marta* in El Biaza[2]] The next day, Sunday the 16th at dawn, coming rapidly along the coast with a following wind close to El Biaza, heading for the port of Don Rodrigo and about six leagues from it, the *capitana* heard two shots fired by the *nao almiranta*, which was upwind with the other *naos* about three leagues away. And we turned around and sailed toward them, and from the *nao Maria de Buen Pasaje* we knew that one of our *naos* from the armada had run aground. And as it was not [f. 15v] possible for the *capitana* to reach where the stricken *nao* was located, and because the *almiranta* and another four *naos* were near her with sails lowered, they were sufficient to aid her, with advice from the pilots. We turned around in order to anchor in the port of Don Rodrigo, as it was nearby, there to await the *almiranta* and the other *naos* that remained with her.

And thus the *galeaza* came with seven *naos* to the port of Don Rodrigo, and we anchored at two in the afternoon. [*margin:* The arrival of the armada at the port of Don Rodrigo and Sancta Catalina] And two hours after nightfall the almirante arrived with the four *naos* that had remained with him, and he said that the *nao* that had run aground was the *nao Sancta Marcta*,[3] whose captain was Gonçalo Melendez,[4] and that he had left the bark of the friars and a ship's boat[5] and a shallop, with its master, Martin de Goiçueta[6] and other sailors, in which they could bring the people from the said *nao*, which would be about ninety persons, as they would be sufficient to transport them to this port. As the weather looked bad, he did not dare wait to bring the people in the *naos*, because the weather might worsen, in which case more *naos* might be lost. And thus, it seemed best to him to come to this port. We remained there on the next day, Monday the 17th, and the next day, Tuesday the 18th at dawn, the armada set sail, and we came to the port of

---

[1] Vera was either mistaken about how far south the English had sailed before their encounter, or his informants on the English ships may have exaggerated their progress. According to Fenton's journal, they had reached 27°46′S on 29 Nov. before being blown back north; Taylor, *Troublesome Voyage*, p. 116. Richard Madox as well as John Walker estimated that they reached about 30°S on 1 Dec.; Donno, *Diary of Richard Madox*, pp. 244, 323.

[2] Elsewhere Rada uses the variant el Byaza.

[3] *Santa Marta*; elsewhere Rada uses the variant *Sancta Marctta*.

[4] Gonzalo Meléndez de Valdés was captain of the *nao Santa Marta* as well as captain of the military contingent that it carried – in other words, a capitán de mar y guerra (captain of sea and war). See Phillips, *Six Galleons*, pp. 123, 125, 128, 146–7. His name suggests that he was related to Captain General Flores and the Meléndez and Valdés clans. A man with the same name served as a receiver of the *alcabalas* tax for México 1579–84; AGI, México, leg. 215, N. 5. Moreover, a Captain Gonzalo Meléndez de Valdés, identified as a nobleman from Asturias, served as governor of Soconusco (México) in the late 16th century; see Lokken, 'Angolans in Amatitlán', p. 45.

[5] The word used is *batel,* a ship's boat propelled by oars.

[6] Goizueta.

Sancta Catalina, which is at 28 degrees, six leagues farther on than Don Rodrigo, and we anchored at two in the afternoon.[1]

The next day, Wednesday the 19th, the general convoked the pilots and masters of the armada, and they declared before me on oath about the needs of some of the *naos* and the time that was required to repair and refurbish them so that they could again [f. 16r] leave and continue their voyage. And he looked over the *naos* in person and ordered the *almirante* and Anton Pablos,[2] and Captain Juan Ramos, adviser,[3] to inspect them. And giving their opinions, they agreed that the *naos San Juan Bauptista* (the *almiranta*), and *La Concepcion*[4] and *La Vegoña*[5] could not continue the voyage with the necessary brevity, because they would need more than forty days to refit, and that the *nao San Niculas* had opened up so much that it was not of use nor was it fit to sail; and that all the other *naos* would be able to make the voyage and go in pursuit of the corsair by outfitting them with some absolutely necessary items. [*margin:* The *nao Sant Miculas* discarded] Work began right away, and we discarded the *nao San Niculas*, and the equipment and other things carried on her were distributed among the others.

[*margin:* The three *naos* remain in Sancta Catalina] And the general resolved that the three *naos* – *San Juan Bauptista, La Comcepcion*, and *La Begoña* – would remain in this port, so that they could go to the Rio de Jenero or San Vicente to be refitted more slowly; and that the other *naos* would carry to the Strait the equipment from them that was most indispensable and necessary; and that the settlers, with their wives and children, and the sick men who were not fit to serve, would remain in these three *naos*, which would carry them to the said Rio de Jenero or San Vicente, because there were not sufficient *navios* nor provisions to carry so many people;[6] and thus it was done. And he ordered the accountant and overseer Andres de Eguino[7] to take charge of these three *naos* so that the captains and all the men of war and sea who sailed in them would be under his orders, and to whom he gave an *instruccion* about how he had to exercise command on the coast of Brasil and to attend to all the situations that were offered, because they had sufficient *naos* and men to attack and defend themselves from the corsair in case they met him or any others that were there; and that the large pieces of artillery that they carried, and other [f. 16v] supplies for the Strait that they could not carry should be stored in the Rio de Jenero or in the port where they arrived. And he wrote to the governors on the coast that they

---

[1] Other accounts estimate that Santa Catarina was only 4 leagues from Dom Rodrigo. Santa Catarina is a long, narrow island with various ports, which may explain some of the discrepancy. See above, p. 58, n. 2.

[2] Antón Pablos was *piloto mayor* (chief pilot) of the armada, appointed because he had sailed with Sarmiento on the eastward voyage through the Strait. Elsewhere Rada uses the variants Antom Pablos, Antom Pablo, Anton Pablo. In other documents, he is sometimes referred to as Antón Pablos Corzo, which may indicate a Corsican origin. See above, pp. 24–5.

[3] *Consejero* (adviser). Captain Ramos had been Flores's choice for chief pilot of the armada. When the king named Pablos to that post at Sarmiento's urging, Flores made sure that Ramos was appointed as senior adviser to Pablos. See above, pp. 24–5.

[4] *La Concepción*; elsewhere Rada uses the variants *Comcepcion, Concecion*.

[5] *Santa María de Begoña*; elsewhere Rada uses the variants *Begoña, La Begoña, Vegoña*.

[6] i.e. to transport them to the Strait.

[7] Andrés de Eguino was *contador* (accountant) and *veedor* (overseer) of the Armada of the Strait – bureaucratic offices – but he also had ample experience as a naval officer, which explains why Captain General Flores gave him such wide responsibilities for the ships and people left behind at Santa Catarina. At various points in the manuscript, Eguino is identified as the accountant, at other times as the accountant and overseer. There is no reason to suspect that his appointment changed, however.

cooperate with the said Andres de Eguino and that they advise him of what they had need for the service of His Majesty and the protection of the coast, so that he could take the *naos* that he brought to where they were needed; and that they give to the settlers a distribution of supplies and monetary allowances so that they could sustain themselves for as long as necessary to carry them to the Strait. And because the general was determined, if he did not encounter the corsair, to continue his pursuit into the Mar del Sur, he ordered the said Andres de Eguino to wait for him in the Rio de Jenero until the end of the month of May of the year 1583; and that if, during this time, he had not returned from the said strait, that [Eguino] should sail with the three *naos* to Spain, not having a clear need of them for the protection and defence of the coast.[1] This *orden y instruccion* was issued at the time, and is on leaves 58 to 60.

[*margin:* Captain Gonzalo Melendez arrives with the men of his company] And the nine *naos* that remained being ready for us to go in pursuit of the corsair and the voyage, on the last day of this said month of December there arrived at this port Captain Gonçalo Melendez, who had remained with the *nao Sancta Marctta*, the one that ran aground twelve leagues from this port, with up to thirty men whom he brought overland with much travail, because they had nothing more to eat than what shellfish and fish they could catch along the way. [*margin:* Soldiers who mutinied] He said that 64 soldiers of his company had mutinied and did not want to come with him and remained with their weapons, [f. 17r] well provided with powder and munitions that they took from the lost *nao*; and from the bark of the commissary Friar Juan de Rivadeneira, which was also lost on the coast going to the aid of the *nao*, the mutineers took the religious ornaments and all the other things that the friars carried, and they went together to a settlement of Indians that was seven leagues from there. And they said to the captain that they wanted to die among those Indians, rather than returning to serve in the armada. Since God had liberated them from so many tempests, they did not want to see any more of them, but to finish their lives in that land unpeopled by Spaniards. And thus they remained, and the pleas that their captain made that they come with him were insufficient.

And being ready to leave with the nine *naos*,[2] the general resolved not to go on the *galeaza capitana*, and he left her and went aboard the *fragatta Sancta Ysavel*,[3] because it was a light and small *navio*, so as not to miss reconnoitring any port on the coast down to the Strait, one after another, so that this corsair could not hide. And he ordered Almirante Diego de la Rivera and Governor Pedro Sarmiento to move to the *galeaza*.[4] [*margin:* Departure of the armada from the port of Santa Catalina for the Strait] And with all embarked, we waited three days for weather to depart until Monday, the 7th of January

---

[1] In other words, the settlers were to be left in Rio de Janeiro and remain there until they could obtain transport to the Strait, presumably supplied by Governor-designate Sarmiento. Captain General Flores did not intend that the three armada ships under Eguino's command would transport them.

[2] Antón Pablos, the chief pilot, later named the nine ships as the *galeaza capitana San Cristóbal*; the *fragatas Santa Isabel, Santa Catalina, María Magdalena*; and the *naos Santa Cruz, Trinidad, María de Villaviciosa, María del Buen Pasaje*, and *Sanestevan* of Soroa; Navarrete, *Colección de documentos*, vol. 20, f. 347v. Pablos's memory was faulty. The *Santa Cruz* was part of the relief fleet of Don Diego de Alcega, which had recently arrived in Rio de Janeiro. The ninth ship was the *nao Santa Catalina*, which carried Don Alonso de Sotomayor and many of his soldiers.

[3] *Santa Isabel*; elsewhere Rada uses the variant *Santa Ysavel*.

[4] Rada's narrative during the second attempt at the Strait would record the position and activities on the *galeaza capitana*, where he remained after Captain General Flores moved to the *fragata Santa Isabel*.

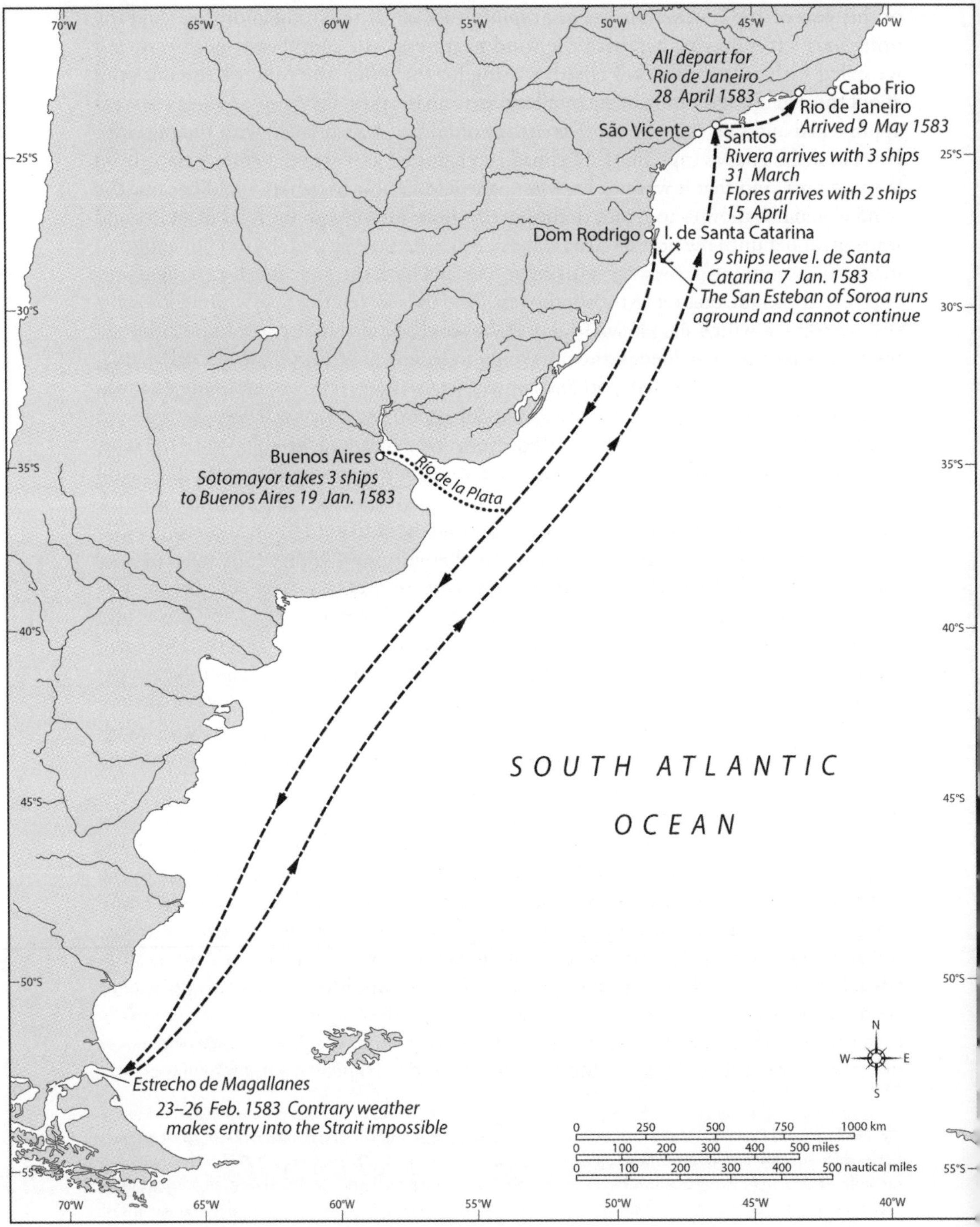
All depart for Rio de Janeiro 28 April 1583
Cabo Frio
Rio de Janeiro
Arrived 9 May 1583
São Vicente
Santos
Rivera arrives with 3 ships 31 March
Flores arrives with 2 ships 15 April
Dom Rodrigo
I. de Santa Catarina
9 ships leave I. de Santa Catarina 7 Jan. 1583
The San Esteban of Soroa runs aground and cannot continue
Buenos Aires
Sotomayor takes 3 ships to Buenos Aires 19 Jan. 1583
Río de la Plata
SOUTH ATLANTIC OCEAN
Estrecho de Magallanes
23–26 Feb. 1583 Contrary weather makes entry into the Strait impossible
N
W
E
S
0 250 500 750 1000 km
0 100 200 300 400 500 miles
0 100 200 300 400 500 nautical miles
70°W
65°W
60°W
55°W
50°W
45°W
40°W
25°S
30°S
35°S
40°S
45°S
50°S
55°S

Map 4. The second attempt to reach the Strait.

of this year of 1583, when the *galeaza capitana* set sail at ten in the morning. And the other *naos* left following her, with the wind north-east, the course east-south-east, and we sailed with only the foresail raised, waiting for the other *naos* to finish leaving. And about three in the afternoon, being four leagues from the port, the *fragata Sancta Catalina* approached and said that the *nao Sanestevan* of Soroa,[1] which sailed with the purveyor Estevan de las Alas as captain, [f. 17v] had run aground as it set sail before leaving from the said port, and that it was not known if it would be able to depart.[2] And because the wind would not allow us to return to the port, we were sailing with the foresail set low and waiting for her until the next day Tuesday the 8th, when seeing that she did not come, we made sail continuing our voyage with eight *naos* and with the same north-east wind on a course to the south, quarter to the south-west. And thus we left this *nao*, without knowing the necessity in which she remained, nor if she would be able to depart or not, although the three *naos* that remained in the port to go to Jenero, as aforesaid, would help refloat her and she would be able to depart and come after us; if not, they would decide what was most suitable to do. God save her and give us all a good and successful voyage.

This day the latitude was taken at 29 degrees and a half, and we sailed with the same wind and course until the next day, Wednesday the 9th, when the latitude was taken at 31 degrees and a half, and the wind shifted to the south-west, which was a contrary wind, so the armada lowered sails at four in the afternoon and hove to until the next day, Thursday the 10th, when at eight in the morning we set sail with the wind south-south-east; and then it shifted to east-south-east, and we set a course south, quarter south-west. The latitude was not taken this day, because it rained. In the afternoon the wind was south-south-east, and we sailed on a course east, quarter to the north-east, with the lower sails set; and on this course we sailed until the next day, Friday the 11th, when at two in the afternoon the wind was east, and we sailed on a course [f. 18r] to the south, quarter south-west. The latitude was taken this day at 31 degrees, and thus we sailed until the next day, Saturday the 12th, when at three in the morning the wind shifted to the north-east and freshened well. We sailed on the same course until midday, when we steered to the south-west to approach land. The latitude was taken this day at 32 degrees and two-thirds.

And with this weather we sailed until the next day, Sunday the 13th, when at seven in the morning the wind decreased. With a heavy shower, we tacked from one course to another until two in the afternoon when, making no progress, the armada lowered sails and hove to, the south wind blowing with much force. The latitude was not taken this day, for the sun was not visible, and thus we remained until the next day, Monday the 14th, when in the morning we set the lower sails in order to steady ourselves, because the sea had risen much;[3] and at ten in the morning, a leak was discovered on the *galeaza capitana* in the heavy timbers at the starboard poop,[4] and a good quantity of flour was wetted that was in a store room. And with much diligence, we dismantled it and we found where the water

---

[1] *San Esteban*, the second ship of that name in the armada, was further identified by the name of its owner, Juan López de Soroa. See below, Appendix 1, p. 180.

[2] Because the ship was commanded by the proveedor mayor (chief purveyor) of the armada, any ship he sailed on might be called the *proveedora*. Sarmiento noted that the engineer Battista Antonelli was aboard, along with many of the fort-builders for the Strait. Sarmiento, *Viajes al Estrecho*, vol. 1, p. 268. The mishap was therefore a major setback for Sarmiento's plans.

[3] Rada's phrase is '*dimos las uelas mayores para nos reparar porque auia lebantada mucha mar*'.

[4] Rada's phrase is '*aleta de popa de la banda destribor*'.

entered, and they took two divers outside to do the best they could to repair us in this weather, until the next day, Tuesday the 15th, when at two at night[1] the wind was south-east, and then came shifting toward the north-west, and we steered to the west-south-west in order to reach the Rio de la Platta. The latitude was taken this day at barely 34 degrees, [f. 18v] and thus we sailed until the next day, Wednesday the 16th, which had wind from the north-north-west. We steered to the west, quarter to the south-west, and the latitude was taken at 34 degrees and a half, and in the afternoon we threw out the sounding line and we found the bottom at 80 *brazas*, and at nightfall it was thrown out again and there was bottom at 48 *brazas*. We took down the topsails,[2] and with the lower sails we sailed all night until the next day, Thursday the 17th, when at dawn we raised all the sails with a brisk wind from the north-north-east and steered to the west to reach land. This day the latitude was taken at 34 and a half long degrees, and about four in the afternoon, the *fragata Sancta Ysavel*, where the general travelled, lowered its sails and the *galeaza* approached her, and he ordered that it proceed with little sail, because they had seen the land of the Rio de la Platta, and we were 14 leagues from the mouth of it. And thus we sailed with fair winds until 10 at night, when the wind jumped to the south-east, which was a *travesia*[3] off the coast. And it blew with much force, and we had to turn around with great difficulty toward the open sea, for being so close to land. We sailed along avoiding grounding on land until Saturday the 19th, when at 9 in the morning the armada lowered sails in 38 *brazas*.[4]

[*margin*: Arrival of the armada near the Rio de la Platta] The general sent word to summon Don Alonsso de Sotomayor and Governor Pedro Sarmiento and Almirante Diego de la Rivera and Captain Gregorio de las Alas, and Antom Pablo, chief pilot, and Captain Jhoan Ramos, and they all met together on the *fregata Sancta Ysavel*, where the general was. They agreed – seeing that the weather [f. 19r] was very extreme, and that if the armada entered into the Rio de la Platta the *navios* that had to leave for the Strait would not be able to arrive when they should, and that the *galeaza* would run a risk by entering into the Rio de la Platta, which had little water where they had to anchor and there was no shelter – that the said Don Alonsso would go with his men in the three *naos* that carried them, which were *Sancta Catalina*, *La Trenidad*[5] and *Maria del Pasajé*[6] to the Rio de la Platta, and would disembark there in order to take them by land to Chile. [*margin*: The departure of Don Alonso with three *naos* for the Rio de la Plata] And [General Flores] gave him instructions about how he had to command and that some of the munitions carried in those *naos* be sent to the Rio de Jenero in the *nao Trenidad*, which was the newest, in which Martin de Çubietta[7] sailed as captain, because we would not be able to unload [the munitions] for the Strait [at sea] from those that we carried;

[1] i.e. at 2 a.m.
[2] *Velas de gavia.*
[3] A *travesía* is a traverse wind that blows perpendicular to and toward the coast.
[4] For *braza* here and below, see above, p. xiv.
[5] *La Trinidad.*
[6] *María del Buen Pasaje.*
[7] Martín de Zubieta was the owner of the *nao La Trinidad* as well as its captain. An experienced mariner and shipowner, he was one of the 7 men, including Flores and Sarmiento, asked to give their written opinions of the galleons being built for the crown in Vizcaya in February of 1581. All of their reports appear in Navarrete, *Colección de documentos*, vol. 22, ff. 286r–329r.

and that the other two *naos* could be cut down to carry the men upriver if necessary. This *acuerdo* and *instruccion* will be found on leaves 60 to 62.

[*margin:* From the mouth of the Rio de la Plata to the Strait] And the aforesaid being concluded, each one returned to his *nao*, and the said Don Alonso set sail with the three *naos* and went on course to the Rio de la Platta. And the general, with the five *naos* that remained to us,[1] at four in the afternoon set sail with a mild east wind on a course toward the Estrecho de Magallanes – south, quarter south-east – sailing close to the wind[2] in order to stay clear of the land. And the next day, Sunday the 20th, the latitude was not taken for lack of sun, and with this weather we sailed until the next day, Monday the 21st, when the wind was east-south-east; we steered [f. 19v] to the south, with fair wind and sea. The latitude was not taken this day for not being able to see the sun. At four in the afternoon the sounding line was thrown out, and there was bottom at 45 *brazas*; and thus we sailed until the next day, Tuesday the 22nd, and with a fair east wind we sailed to the south, quarter south-west. This day the latitude was taken at 35 degrees and two-thirds, and this day the fore-mast of the *galeaza* split one *braza* above the first deck on the poop side;[3] and for lack of anything with which to strengthen it, it was necessary to take down the top-mast of the same fore-mast and to yoke the two pieces together, and we bound them with many strong braided cords.[4]

And thus we sailed with the same wind and course until the next day, Wednesday the 23rd, when the latitude was taken at barely 37 degrees, as we were steering toward the south-west with the same fair east wind. And thus we sailed with this weather until the next day, Thursday the 24th, which had north-east wind, and we sailed on course to the south-west. And at eight in the morning we discovered a sand flat that would hold an anchor, where the water was very clear and seemed to come from a river about four leagues away, and there was bottom at 55 *brazas*, though we could not see land;[5] and we sailed along it until eleven and a half in the morning, when we left it. And with this same wind and course we sailed until the next day, Friday the 25th, when at dawn we discovered another sand flat like the last one, with the water even clearer, which lasted until nightfall and had more than twelve leagues of width and a depth of 52 *brazas*, without seeing land. The latitude was taken this day at 39 degrees, and with the same north-east wind and a calm sea we sailed on a course to the south-west until the next day, Saturday the 26th, [f. 20r] when at seven in the morning there was a north wind; we steered south-west, quarter to the west, in order to approach land. This day the latitude was taken at 40 degrees.

In the afternoon we had a north-east wind, and on the same course we sailed until the next day, Sunday the 27th, when at five in the morning we had a north-west wind that blew briskly; we sailed on a course to the south-west. This day the latitude was taken at 41 long degrees, and in the afternoon a fair southwest wind arose. We threw out the sounding line and found bottom at 40 *brazas*. The next day, Monday in the morning, there was a north-east wind until two in the afternoon, which then shifted to the south-east; we steered to

---

[1] The remaining 5 ships were the *galeaza capitana*, the *nao María de Villaviciosa*, and the 3 *fragatas* owned by the crown.

[2] See above, p. 68.

[3] Presumably, the mast split on the side facing aft.

[4] Rada uses the word *reatas*, which refers to cords, made of multiple braided fibres that grow stronger when pulled.

[5] In a *plazel* (sand flat) such as the one Rada describes, fresh water can surface at sea, miles from land.

the south-west, quarter to the south, heading out to sea, because the pilots estimated themselves 12 leagues from land. The latitude was not taken this day, because the sun could not be seen; there was bottom at 45 *brazas*. At nightfall this wind diminished; we continued with little sail to the south-east, until the next day, the 29th, when the wind was east; we sailed on a course to the south-west, quarter to the south. This day the latitude was taken at 42 degrees and one-third, and there was bottom at 50 *brazas*. At 12 at night this wind diminished and shifted to the north-west until the next day, Wednesday the 30th, when in the morning there was a north-east wind. And at 10 in the morning, it shifted to a contrary wind from the west-north-west, and the armada lowered sails until nightfall, when the wind came from the north-east. The latitude was taken this day at 43 degrees and a half. At midnight we had a very heavy downpour and much thunder and lightening, and the wind was from the west-north-west, which blew with great force.

[f. 20v] The next day, Thursday the 31st of January, the latitude was taken at 43 degrees and two-thirds, and because the weather continued to be very turbulent we made little progress, and at midnight, the armada lowered sails and hove to until the next day, Friday the first of February, when the wind was from the west-north-west, and we sailed on a course to the south-west. This day the latitude was taken at 44 degrees and one-third. And the next day, Saturday the 2nd, the wind was north-west with high seas at the prow; we sailed on a course toward the south-west. This day the latitude was taken at 45 long degrees, and thus we sailed until the next day, Sunday the 3rd, when in the morning the wind shifted to the south-west, which blew with excessive force, and the *naos* ran before it with their mainsails secured. It lasted with this fury until five in the afternoon, when it calmed. The latitude was not taken this day, because there was no sun. The next day, Monday the 4th, the wind was west; we steered a course toward the south, quarter to the south-west. The latitude was taken at 45 degrees and two-thirds, and this wind diminished and the armada lowered sails because it was not making any headway. And at nightfall the wind was north-west, and we sailed with it on the same course until the next day, Tuesday the 5th, with a fair wind from the west-south-west we steered toward the south. The latitude was taken this day at 46 long degrees.

[*margin:* Sight of land] Thus we sailed until the next day, Wednesday the 6th, when at nine in the morning we saw a very high piece of land off the prow. The wind was fresh from the north, and we went on [f. 21r] a course toward the west-south-west. And to keep far enough away from this land, it was necessary to steer to the south-east, because the land juts far out. They say it is named for a sand flat at the end of it; it makes some white gorges that bore north-east of us, and here the water was very clear, and there was bottom at 45 *brazas*. This day the latitude was taken at 47 degrees, and thus we sailed until the next day, Thursday the 7th, when we had wind from the north-north-east, and we sailed on a course to the south. [*margin:* Sighting of the Islas del Asencion] And at nine in the morning we saw some islands that are named for the Ascension.[1] The latitude was taken this day at 48 long degrees, and thus we sailed until the next day, Friday the 8th, which had a fresh wind from the north-north-west, and we sailed on a course to the south-west, quarter to the west, in order to approach land. The latitude was taken this day at 49 degrees and a half, and at three in the afternoon, the wind was south-west; the armada

---

[1] This is a group of several rocky islands off the coast of Argentina just south of Cabo Blanco. The largest, Isla Pingüino, is located at 47°54′S, 65°43′W.

lowered sails and hove to until the next day, the 9th, which was Saturday, the *Dia de Carnastoliendas*.[1] At dawn we set sail, with the wind west-north-west, on course toward the south-west. And at 9 in the morning the southwest wind began to blow again with such force that the armada hove to. And the latitude was taken this day at 50 degrees, and we threw out the sounding line and there was bottom at 57 *brazas*. And thus we remained without making sail until the next day, Sunday the 10th, when we set sail in the morning with the wind north, the course to the west-south-west, in order to approach land. The sun was measured this day at 50 degrees minus one-quarter, less than the day before, because of not knowing [f. 21v] how the time declined.[2] And there was bottom at 64 *brazas*.

And thus we sailed the next day, Monday the 11th, when the wind was south-east. The latitude was taken this day at 50 degrees and one-third, and we found bottom at 54 *brazas*. And thus we sailed until the next day, Tuesday the 21st, when the wind was north-east. We sailed on a course west-south-west, and the latitude was taken this day at 51 degrees. And because it was very misty and the pilots carefully calculated that we were very close to land, so as not to touch it we threw out the sounding line and there was bottom at 17 *brazas*. [*margin:* Sight of land] And then we saw land off the prow at about four leagues. We steered to the south, quarter to the south-east, in order to pull ourselves away from it; the land was not very high. And thus we sailed on this course and wind until the next day, Wednesday the 13th of the said month, when at 10 in the morning it began to blow from the west-south-west with such force that the armada took down all the sails, and the pilots calculated the location of the mouth of the Strait at 12 sea leagues.[3] The latitude was not taken this day, as it was very cloudy. We found bottom at 34 *brazas*, and Antom Pablo said that the tip of high land that was visible came skirting more or less north-west from where the mouth of the Strait commenced. And the wind blowing like a furious gale made us lose sight of the land, and for this reason we remained with sails lowered until the next day, Thursday the 14th, when at dawn we set sail with a fair north wind. At 10 in the morning we saw the same land that we had seen the day before, and at midday the latitude was taken on the *galeaza* at 52 degrees, 12 minutes.[4]

[f. 22r] [*margin:* Error recognizing the Strait] And being straight out from land at the said point, Governor Pedro Sarmiento and Antom Pablos, the chief pilot, said that it was the mouth of the Strait that bore away from us to the west, quarter to the north-west. And being about four leagues from this land and point, we threw out the sounding line and there was bottom at 12 *brazas*, the water very clear. And going farther, within the time of turning two watch-glasses[5] we came to be in eight *brazas*. The bottom was covered with small pebbles and did not indicate if this was the Strait or not, because there was a

---

[1] The *Dia de Carnestolendas* (Carnival Day) is the last Saturday before Ash Wednesday, which begins the penitential season of Lent, the 40 days before Easter.

[2] Rada's phrase is '*por no saber descaído el tiempo*'. He is referring to the rate of declination of the sun. Navigation manuals with tables for the declination of the sun for every day of the year did not yet include figures for latitudes so far south of the Equator.

[3] Rada's phrase is '*leguas de la mar*', presumably nautical leagues. This is the only mention of nautical leagues in Rada's *Relación*.

[4] This is the first time in the *Relación* that Rada includes a figure for minutes, though the logs of the pilots may habitually have used both degrees and minutes.

[5] Watch glasses, or sand clocks, on Spanish ships were turned every 30 minutes to keep track of the time.

very large cove, and to the south of this land there was another low piece of land with some not very tall flat-crowned rocks.[1] And veering a bit toward the sea at two in the afternoon we found bottom at 11 *brazas*. And sending inquiries from this *galeaza* to the other pilots who sailed in the other *navios* about the latitude that they had taken, some said 52 long degrees, and others 52 minus one-third, and others 52 minus one-quarter – this last from Juan Ramos and the general, who sailed in the *fragata Santa Ysavel*. And because Anton Pablo and Pedro Sarmiento were not certain if this was the Strait, the general ordered Antom Pablo to get into the *fragata Sancta Catalina*, whose captain was Gregorio de las Alas, and he told him to go with it to reconnoitre this cove so that they should know if it was the Strait or not; and thus they went, the rest of us remaining in waiting.[2] And they returned the next day, Friday the 15th at midday, and they said that they had reached the end of the cove, and that it was not the Strait, nor did it even have indications of it.

This day, being anchored, the latitude was taken at 52 degrees. Here the sea rose about [f. 22v] four *brazas*, because we were anchored in 11 *brazas* at low tide, and at high tide in almost 15. This sandy cove, according to the report of the Englishmen that will be found at leaves 91/93, is what they called Rio Fresco.[3] From here to the Estrecho de Magallanes it is 14 leagues, and at about three in the afternoon we raised anchor and sailed toward the Strait. With a fair north wind, we steered to the south-east, quarter to the south, because we now knew the way, and thus we came in sight of land about two leagues away, until nightfall when the wind calmed. And we found bottom at 34 *brazas*, and we were anchored until the next day, Saturday the 16th, when in the morning we made sail with little wind. And at 10 in the morning, we again took a sounding, because there were high seas and the currents pushed us toward land, from which we were about a league away. The land is not very high, with white sands, and inland it is very flat as far as can be seen, which gave us much contentment. There was much smoke in the distance, which the Indians must have made, and who must have seen us, although from the *naos* we saw no one. This day the latitude was taken at 52 degrees and one-quarter. The day did not look good. We again made sail at one in the afternoon with the wind north, on course to the east-south-east pulling away from the land, and at nightfall we again anchored in 30 *brazas*, because the wind calmed. And we were there until the next day, Sunday the 17th, when at three in the morning the north wind freshened and we sailed toward the mouth of the Strait, and we saw it at 8 in the morning.

[*margin:* The mouth of the Strait] And entering into it on the north side, [f. 23r] about one league from the point of land, the sounding line was thrown out and there was bottom at 12 *brazas*. We continued entering the Strait and steering ourselves toward the channel, and within an hour we were inside it with 40 *brazas* of bottom. And sailing inside the channel at 11 in the morning we found a sandy bottom at 50 *brazas*. The land at the point

---

[1] Rada's word is '*mogotes*', which denotes a series of isolated conical rocks with flat tops, visible at sea.

[2] Pablos later claimed that he knew this was the mouth of the Río de Gallegos, located 12 leagues from the mouth of the Strait, and that he obtained Captain General Flores's permission to explore it on the *fragata Catalina* to see if it might be a suitable refuge for future armadas that encountered bad weather; Navarrete, *Colección de documentos*, vol. 20, f. 348v. Although Pablos is not named as the author of the document, his identity is clear from his narrative.

[3] The unnamed deponent whose testimony appears on ff. 91v–93v accompanied Francis Drake's expedition on the *Elizabeth* with Captain John Wynter. It is not clear when or where Rada obtained this document.

on the north side is high and very recognizable, and that on the south side is very low. The mouth from the one point to the other at the entrance is more than 10 leagues in my opinion, and at midday we were about four leagues inside the channel of the Strait. The latitude was taken at 52 degrees and two-thirds. And having finished taking it, so much wind began to blow from the west and west-south-west that we were forced to lower the sails and heave to, tossed from one course to another.[1]

This weather lasted with excessive force until Tuesday the 19th and blew us out to sea about 20 leagues from the mouth. In the morning we again made sail with a fair north-west wind, the course west-south-west, directly toward the mouth of the Strait in order to enter it on the south side. The chief pilot Anton Pablo returned to this *galeaza* yesterday, Monday in the afternoon, from the *fragata Sancta Catalina* where he had spent Friday, and on her he had continued forward with Captain Gregorio de las Alas. On entering into the Strait, this day in the afternoon we had a heavy downpour with much wind. We lowered sails and within two hours we again set sail with the wind north, and at midnight it was west-north-west, and with lowered sails we remained hove to until the next day, Wednesday the 20th, when the wind was west, contrary and at the prow. The latitude was taken at 52 degrees and two-thirds, and we were not able to set sail until the next day, Thursday the 21st, when at three in the morning we set sail with a north wind. [f. 23v] And at eleven in the morning, we saw the land of the cape of the Strait on this south side; we could not see the point on the north side, from which the wind had edged us far away. And thus we sailed toward it until three in the afternoon, when the wind diminished, and we turned on a course toward the north-east, quarter to the north. This day the latitude was not taken, because the sun was not visible.

And at 11 at night, the armada with lowered sails and hove to because the wind had diminished more, the wind began to blow from the west-south-west with such force that the *naos* could not withstand it. And at dawn the *fregatas* were very far from this *galeaza*, and with so much wind they sailed with one lower sail, steering as well as they could on a course toward the north-east. And in order to reach them the *galeaza* raised the foresail and the spritsail and followed them, and about three in the afternoon this day, Friday the 22nd, we reached them. And the almirante and Pedro Sarmiento and Anton Pablo said to the general that it could be done. He responded that it would have to be done soon, as the wind was so forceful and contrary and the *vendaval* was very well established, and that we had few provisions to wait so long, since each day would only be worse, but with all this we would continue on course toward land, sheltering along the coast as well as possible. And thus we sailed with the foresail set low, on the alert for the return of weather to enter the Strait, and thus it was done. And at sunset we lowered sails and hove to until the next day, Saturday the 23rd, when at seven in the morning we again set sail with the wind north-north-west, on course west toward the Strait. And at midday the latitude was taken at 52 degrees, 12 minutes, and thus we sailed until [f. 24r] four in the afternoon when the wind began to diminish, and we continued along from one tack to another until sunset, when the *fragata Sancta Ysavel* where the general sailed, fired a shot and the *galeaza* approached her.

And the general said that [although we had intended to go forward into the Strait], the weather did not give us opportunity to do so and continued to look very bad. From the

---

[1] The phrase used is '*echados de una buelta y otra*'.

galeaza we said to wait until the waning moon to see what the weather would do. He responded that was very well and good, although the *fragatas* could not defend themselves[1] like the *galeaza*. And thus we sailed keeping hope until nightfall, when the armada lowered sails and hove to, because the wind began to blow from the west-south-west in an unrestrained tempest. And at 10 at night, not being able to ride it out because of the high wind and seas, we set sail with the foresail set very low and steered as well as possible on a course toward the north-east, quarter to the north. And thus we sailed until dawn, when we could not see the *nao Maria de Villa Viciosa*,[2] whose captain was Alvaro del Busto.[3] And the storm and high seas continued to increase, and thus it was this day the 24th all day and night without ceasing one bit. And at 10 at night, a leak was discovered on this *galeaza* in the heavy curved timbers at the poop,[4] which caused us great concern, because much water was coming in. And with the good diligence that we applied, we remedied it on the inside, so that it [leaked] only a little.

And the next day, Monday the 25th at dawn, this tempest began to slacken, and the wind was south-west, and we sailed on a course to the north-east with few sails raised all day and night, hoping to see the *nao Maria*. [f. 24v] [*margin:* Turn from the Strait][5] And after another day, Tuesday the 26th, when it did not arrive, we set all the sails, sailing and tacking with the west wind on a course toward the north-east, quarter to the north. This day the latitude was taken at 48 degrees, and with the fresh wind lasting until midnight we sailed on this course, and the wind returned from the north-north-west and north, which lasted the next day Wednesday the 27th all day, and we sailed on a course toward the east, quarter to the north-east. This day the latitude was taken at 46 degrees, and at 10 at night the wind shifted to the south-east, and we turned to the north-east, quarter to the north. This day, the latitude was taken at 45 degrees and a half. And thus we sailed with this wind until the next day, Thursday the 28th, the last day of this month, until 10 at night when the wind was west-north-west, and we turned toward the north.

[*margin:* March] The next day, Friday the first of March at dawn, with a light wind from the north-west, we sailed toward the north quarter to the north-east. This day the latitude was taken at 44 degrees and one-third, and at midnight the light wind was north, and we sailed on a course toward the north-east quarter to the east, until the next day, Saturday the 2nd, when the latitude was taken at 44 degrees. And with the same wind and course we sailed until the next day, Sunday the 3rd, when at dawn the wind again

---

[1] Rada repeatedly uses the verb '*repararse*', when the ships were trying to withstand heavy winds and seas. In other contexts, the verb means to shelter a vessel along a coast, but in this context it seems to have the more general meaning of the ships defending themselves or withstanding the elements.

[2] *María de Villaviciosa*. This was likely the 400 *tonelada nao* earlier called *María* or *La María*. The revised designation presumably related to the town of Villaviciosa in Asturias. See Chaunu, *Séville et l'Atlantique*, vol. 3, pp. 292–3, for the ships that formed the armada, and Appendix 1, below, for their fates.

[3] See above, pp. 32, 70, n. 9.

[4] *aleta de popa*.

[5] Rada uses the word '*arribada*', which generally means to turn the prow away from the direction of the wind. After the consultation on 23 Feb., another storm forced the armada away from the mouth of the Strait toward the north. Sarmiento would later write that Flores decided to abandon the attempt to reach the Strait during the consultation on the 23rd. He did not mention the new storm but complained that the bureaucrats on board the *galeaza* wanted to head north and that Antón Pablos told him that he would never have signed on had he known what the Strait was capable of in terms of wind, sea, and weather. Sarmiento, *Viajes al Estrecho*, vol. 1, pp. 276–80.

returned to the west-north-west, and at midday it shifted to the west-south-west, and we sailed on a course toward the north-east. The latitude was taken this day at 43 degrees and a half, and with this wind and on this course we sailed along until the next day, Monday the 4th, when with the wind south-south-west and then fresh from the south we sailed on the same course toward the north-north-east all day. The latitude was not taken this day because [f. 25r] the sun was not visible, and at 10 at night the wind slackened and shifted to east-south-east. We sailed on a course toward the north-east until the next day, Tuesday the 5th, when the wind was east-north-east and we sailed on a course toward the north. The latitude was taken this day at 41 long degrees, and the wind returned from the north-east. We sailed on a course toward the north-north-west until the next day, Wednesday the 6th, when at dawn the wind was north-north-east and then north. We lowered sails and hove to, and this wind blew with much force and lasted until the next day, Thursday the 7th, when at dawn it calmed down and until four in the afternoon we did not make sail.

[*margin:* The distress of the *fragata Santa Ysavel*, and the general's staying behind] And the *fragata Sancta Ysavel* on which the general sailed fired three shots from where it was, upwind of the *galeaza* by about one league, which was the signal that it was in some distress. We changed course to approach her because she was not under sail; and the other two *fragatas* arrived near her. And from the *fragata Santa Catalina* where Captain Gregorio de las Alas was, they launched the shallop and they came to *La Madalena* and took from her a diver, and they brought him to the *fragata Sancta Ysavel*. And then the shallop returned to its *fragata Sancta Catalina*. And from there an hour later the *fragata Madalena* came to this *galeaza* and said that the large iron hinges of the rudder on the *fragata Sancta Ysavel* had come unnailed, and that the general was [now] on the *fragata Sancta Catalina*, and that he ordered this *galeaza* not to set sail until he sent word. And thus we remained with sails lowered all night with two signal lanterns lit. And at dawn we could not see the two *fragatas* [f. 25v] *Sancta Ysavel* and *Sancta Catalina*. And the pilots said that at midnight they saw them to windward of this *galeaza*, and that they had signalled with a lantern the one to the other, and that then they must have made sail, because they had wind from the west-north-west, and they were going on course to the north-north-east. And as there was no other sign, nor did those on guard see them, this *galeaza* and the *fragata Madalena* stayed where they were, without going after them.

We consulted this day, Friday the 8th in the morning, and most were of the opinion that we should follow them on a course to the north-east, sailing close to the wind, because the wind was north-north-west. And thus we sailed all day with the mainsail and the foresail, and there were heavy seas and little progress was made, and we did not see the two *fragatas*. This day the latitude was taken at 43 degrees and a half, and thus we sailed until the next day, Saturday the 9th, when in the morning the wind was south-west and then south. We steered a course toward the north until midday when it was east-south-east; we sailed on course toward the north, quarter to the north-east, making little progress, because there were heavy seas at the prow. The latitude was not taken this day, because the day was very dark, and it rained during the night and well into the next day, Sunday the 10th, when at nine in the morning, the wind south-west, we sailed with this following wind on course toward the north-east. The latitude was not taken this day for not being able to see the sun. And thus we sailed with this brisk weather until the afternoon, when the [wind] was west-south-west, on the same course until the next day, Monday the 11th, when the wind was west-north-west, and we sailed on a course toward the north-north-east. The latitude was taken this day [f. 26r] at barely 42 degrees, and with this weather we sailed until the next day, Tuesday the 12th, when at dawn the wind was fresh from the south-west, and we sailed on the same course. This day the latitude was taken at 40 degrees and one-third. And with this wind and course we continued until the next day, Wednesday the 13th, when at dawn we had wind from the east-south-east, and we sailed on the same course toward the north-north-east. The latitude was not taken this day, because there was no sun. And thus we sailed until the next day, Thursday the 14th, when at dawn we had an east wind and we steered toward the north, quarter to the north-east, and it was rounding to the north-north-east and we sailed on a course toward the north-west, quarter to the north. The latitude was not taken this day because the day was dark, and thus we sailed until 8 at night when the robust wind was from the north. We hove to until the next day, Friday the 15th in the afternoon, when we set sail with the wind south-west which freshened well, and with only the foresail we sailed along all night on a course toward the north-north-east because there were heavy seas at the prow.

The next day, Saturday the 16th at dawn, we hoisted all the sails with the same wind and course. The latitude was taken this day at 37 degrees, and with the same weather and direction we sailed along until the next day, Sunday the 17th, when at dawn we steered to the north with the wind west-south-west. The latitude was taken this day at 35 degrees and one-quarter, and the wind shifted fully to the west and we sailed on the same course toward the north until the next day, Monday the 18th, when the latitude was taken at 34 degrees minus one-quarter, and with the same wind and course we sailed until night [f. 26v] when the wind turned again to the west-south-west. And it was calm until the next day, Tuesday the 19th, when in the afternoon the wind was north-east and we sailed on a course toward the north, quarter to the north-west, until the next day, Wednesday the 20th, when the latitude was taken at 32 degrees and one-third. And we sailed on the same course until the next day, Thursday the 21st, when the wind was north-north-east and we sailed on a course toward the north-west. The latitude was taken this day at 31 degrees and one-quarter. And thus we sailed until the next day, Friday the 22nd, when in the morning we had a heavy shower with wind from the east until 10 in the morning when it was south-east; we steered a course to the north. The latitude was not taken this day and at night the wind was south, and on the same course we sailed until the next day, Saturday the 23rd, when with this wind we sailed on a course toward the north-north-west until the afternoon, when it slackened. The latitude was taken this day at 28 degrees and one-quarter, and thus we sailed until the next day, Palm Sunday the 24th, when in the morning the wind was west-north-west with a heavy shower, and we sailed on a course toward the north-north-east. The latitude was taken this day at 27 degrees and one-third, and in the afternoon the wind was west and we sailed on a course toward the north-north-west until the next day, Monday the 25th, when in the morning the wind was west-south-west and we sailed on a course to the north-west, quarter to the north.

[*margin:* The *nao Maria de Villaviciosa* appeared] This day at dawn we discovered the *nao Maria de Villaviciosa* about three leagues away, which on the 25th of February past had separated from us near the Strait, and at midday we reached her. The latitude was taken this day at 27 degrees minus one-third. And with this same wind and course we sailed [f. 27r] until the next day, Tuesday the 26th, when we threw out the sounding line and there was bottom at 53 *brazas*, and we steered a course toward the east-north-east in order to veer away from the land. And at 10 in the morning we steered a course toward the north-north-east with the wind south-east. The latitude was taken this day at 26 degrees minus one-quarter, and thus we sailed on this course until midnight, when we threw out the sounding line and found bottom at 48 *brazas*. And the next day, Wednesday the 27th, with the same wind south-east we sailed on a course north-north-east. This day the latitude was taken at 25 degrees and we steered toward the north, and at four in the afternoon we saw land that bore north-north-east of us; it was very high. We steered toward the north, quarter to the north-east and the wind was east-south-east. And thus we sailed until the next day, Thursday the 28th, when at dawn the sounding line was thrown out and we found bottom at 48 *brazas* at most.

[*margin:* Sighting of Isla Quemada] And we saw an island they call Quemada[1] that is 8 leagues from the port of Sanctos y San Vicente and runs north-east to south-west; it is one league long and half a league wide. We sailed straight toward it with a fair wind from the east-south-east on course north-north-east. The latitude was taken this day at 24 degrees and one-third. We had fair winds and calms until the next day, Friday the 29th, when in the afternoon we had a *viraçon*.[2] We sailed along near the coast in order to enter the port, and we anchored at midnight in 12 *brazas*, four leagues from the port of Sanctos. And the next day, Saturday the 30th in the morning, we set sail with a *terral*[3] on a course toward the north-north-east and entered into this port, and at nightfall we cast anchor at the entrance to the port.

[f. 27v] [*margin:* Arrival at the port of Sanctos y San Vicente] And the next day, Easter Sunday the 31st of the said month of March, we entered inside and found in this port the accountant and overseer Andres de Eguino, in whose charge the three *naos* from the armada had remained in the port of Sancta Catalina with orders to bring them to this port or to Rio de Jenero to protect this coast, as aforesaid. He said that the *nao San Estevan* of Soroa with the purveyor Estevan de las Alas as captain, which had run aground when we left Sancta Catalina for the Strait, was wrecked and could not leave. The people aboard and part of the provisions, artillery and munitions were saved, and he distributed them among the three *naos* in his charge.[4] And he also took in the 64 soldiers of Captain Gonçalo Melendez who had mutinied from the *nao Sancta Marta* that was lost in El Byaza; they had come overland along the coast to the said port of Sancta Catalina, because the Indians would not take them in and they had quarrelled with them.

Having accepted these men, the said Andres de Eguino set sail and left the port of Sancta Catalina with the three *naos San Juan Bautista*, *La Concepcion* and *La Begoña* on the 18th of the month of January of 1583. And on the 24th of it he arrived at this port of Sanctos y San Vicente, where it seems that he found two English galleons with the flags of *capitana* and *almiranta*, the *capitana* of 450 *toneladas* and the *almiranta* of 350, which

---

[1] Ihla Queimada. See above, p. 42.

[2] A *virazón* is a coastal wind blowing toward the land, usually at night.

[3] A *terral* is a wind blowing from the land, usually during the day; typically, it alternates with a *virazón*, as in this instance.

[4] The engineer Battista Antonelli sailed on the *San Esteban* of Soroa and remained at Santa Catarina with the ships and people left behind under Eguino's leadership. Gasparini, *Los Antonelli*, pp. 38–9, is mistaken in stating that Antonelli sailed on *La Concepción*, which ran aground upon leaving Rio de Janeiro. See above, p. 43, n. 4. Instead, *La Concepción* made the first attempt at the Strait and was left for repairs at Santa Catarina. Antonelli presumably shifted to *La Concepción* after the *San Esteban* of Soroa was wrecked.

had arrived three days earlier at this port well-crewed with men of war and sea and with much artillery and munitions.[1] [f. 28r] [*margin:* The English galleons] And the accountant, having seen and recognized them, had his three *naos* drop anchor at the mouth of this port at four in the afternoon, and he held a meeting to reach agreement with the purveyor Estevan de las Alas, and with the other captains of his *naos* about what they ought to do. And they said – and it seems they were in accord – that they would attack the enemies that night so that they not get away, and that the *nao Concepcion* whose captain was Francisco de Cuellar, in which the purveyor Estevan de las Alas sailed, would attack and take the *nao almiranta* of the enemy; and that the *nao San Juan Bautista* whose captain was Alonso de las Alas,[2] which flew the flag of our *capitana*, on which the accountant Andres de Eguino sailed, would attack the *nao capitana*[3] of the enemy on the larboard side, and that the *nao Nuestra Señora de Vegoña* whose captain was Rodrigo de Rada,[4] and which flew the flag of our *almiranta*, would attack the same enemy *capitana* on the starboard side or would go where it was needed most.

And with the three *naos* being well in order as decided, they moved toward the enemies about 9 at night with their boats towing them, because it was calm without any sort of wind. Our *capitana* arrived alongside that of the enemy and dropped anchor, firing all the artillery and harquebuses, and the enemy *capitana* did the same toward ours and was lengthening its cable and pulling away from our *capitana*. And Captain Rodrigo de Rada with his *nao Begoña* together with its tow, came up side by side with the enemy *capitana*, and they commenced to [f. 28v] fight between them and fire artillery the one against the other. And being fighting thus, the *nao almiranta* of the enemy arrived and, perpendicular to the stern of the *nao Begoña*, fired all its artillery. And by this assistance, they killed, on the said *nao Begoña* Captain Jodar Alferez[5] who had sailed on her, and with him another thirty men not counting others wounded. And there were so many pieces of artillery that the two enemy *naos* fired at the *nao Begoña* that they opened her up in many places; and without the power to remedy the damage she went to the bottom in eight *brazas*, and nothing at all could be saved from her, and most of the people who were saved were clinging to the rigging and the topmasts and others were swimming.[6] Six men drowned.

And the next day in the morning the enemy galleons exchanged cannon fire with the two of our *naos* that remained, and in good order they sailed away, and releasing[7] some

---

[1] The larger vessel was Edward Fenton's *Galleon Leicester*, the smaller was the *Edward Bonaventure* with Captain Luke Ward. John Drake and the crew of the pinnace *Francis* had deserted the expedition after the council at the Río de la Plata on 21 Dec. 1582. See above, p. 40.

[2] See above, p. 76, n. 2.

[3] Rada's phrase is *nao capitana*, which means the flagship of a squadron or fleet. In this case, the word *nao* is used as a generic, as he further describes Fenton's flagship as a galleon.

[4] Rodrigo de Rada had helped to recruit men for the armada in the summer of 1581. Pedro de Ledesma to the Council of the Indies, 7 July 1581, in Navarrete, *Colección de documentos*, vol. 20, f. 153r. He began the voyage as captain of the *galeaza capitana*, and was later reassigned to various other ships as circumstances changed. It is not clear if he was related to Pedro de Rada, the chief scribe.

[5] See above, p. 69.

[6] The *Begoña* carried mostly settlers and their families as well as sailors and soldiers. See above, pp. 38, 41, 101. Fenton picked up one sailor who described the 3 Spanish ships and the reason they came upon Fenton at Santos. Nonetheless, Donno, *Diary of Richard Madox*, notes that Eguino's arrival at Santos with the 3 ships 'is puzzling', and accepts Sarmiento's claim that they 'were the best of the fleet though Don Diego, with dissembling intent, declared them unseaworthy', p. 37.

[7] Rada's word is '*largando*', which means loosening or releasing.

cables they fled the port. Our two *naos* did not pursue them because they say the *nao San Juan Bauptista* had many holes at the waterline from artillery shots, and that without patching them she could not go to sea. It was understood that the enemy *capitana* was very damaged and taking on water, because having left the port it was firing pieces toward its *almiranta*, which went ahead.[1] And they said that the next day from the watchtowers on land they did not see more than one [ship]. And on the coast they found a large spar from the mainmast and a dead man in a box, and by these signs it was [f. 29r] understood that the enemy *capitana* had been lost or that these galleons sustained much damage.[2] They were the ones that captured the bark in the port of Don Rodrigo in which Friar Juan de Rivadeneira and Don Francisco de Vera travelled, about which they gave a report to General Diego Florez, as stated.[3] They say the *patache* that these enemy *naos* brought with them was blown off course by a storm.[4]

The general of these galleons is called Eduardus Fenton, who having arrived at this port of Sanctos wrote a letter to Geronimo Leiton, who governs the captaincy of San Vicente, and another to an Englishman who is a married householder in this town of Sanctos,[5] the *traslados*[6] of which were sent to me and will be found on leaves [sic] 91. [margin: Departure of the English *naos*] That these corsairs left without having captured our *naos*, although they had great strength and could have achieved a better result, according to the reports and papers that have been written about this, and about who was to blame and was the cause of their leaving, I submit that I do not write more extensively

---

[1] Captain Luke Ward later accused Fenton of withdrawing from the fight the next morning and sailing away in the *Leicester*. According to Donno, *Diary of Richard Madox*, pp. 36–7, 'The defection of the Galleon, strongly taken amiss by those on the *Edward*, was later laid to the insobriety of the crew who had drunk a hogshead of wine during the heat of the fight.'

[2] Rada is recording no more than rumours, as he was not an eye-witness.

[3] See above, pp. 39–40.

[4] What Rada calls a patache was John Drake's pinnace, *Francis*. Drake abandoned Fenton and planned to resupply at the Río de la Plata and continue on to the Strait; Taylor, *Troublesome Voyage*, pp. 248–50, 280–81. Instead, the pinnace ran onto the rocks on the north shore of the Río de la Plata. Trekking inland, the men fought local Indians, who killed 5 of their party and took the other 13 captive. After an enslavement of 15 months, Drake, Richard Faireweather and another young man escaped in a small canoe. Naked and hungry they rowed for three days across a river, presumably the Paraná, to seek a Christian settlement. On land following a road they came upon some local Indians, whom Drake later described as 'servants of the Spaniards'. The Indians fed and clothed them and sent word to the nearest town. Spanish authorities treated them well and took a statement from John Drake in Santa Fe on 24 March 1584, mostly about Francis Drake's 1577–80 voyage. Juan Pérez (Richard Carter) translated Drake's testimony for the notary. Drake and his two companions remained in the area for several years. The captain in charge of the district planned to send them to Spain, but the viceroy of Peru summoned them instead. John Drake travelled overland to Lima; his companions remained near Santa Fe, having married and settled there. Drake's lengthy testimony in Lima on 9 Jan. 1587 appears in Navarrete, *Colección de documentos*, vol. 26, ff. 112r–126r. He seems to have remained there for the rest of his life. A very brief translated excerpt from Drake's testimony appears in Taylor, *Troublesome Voyage*, pp. 291–2.

[5] The Englishman was John Whithall, son-in law of the Italian Giuseppe Adorno, one of the most important landowners in the district. See Andrews, 'Drake and South America,' p. 55; and Donno, *Diary of Richard Madox*, pp. 34–5. Richard Hakluyt published correspondence between Whithall and English merchants interested in reviving the Brazil trade in *PN*1 (1589), pp. 638–40; reprinted in *PN*2, III (1600), pp. 701–3. Governor Leitão responded to Fenton the day after receiving his letter, saying that the captaincy had given its loyalty to the king of Spain and that Captain General Flores of the Armada of the Strait had told him not to trade or deal with the English or the French. Taylor, *Troublesome Voyage*, p. 126; Donno, *Diary of Richard Madox*, pp. 34–6.

[6] A *traslado* is an official copy of a document. It is not clear if the copies that Rada received were in Spanish or in the original English.

because I was not present and I do not wish to comment about those who fought or ceased to fight, except that the enemies had good fortune and ours had misfortune.[1]

This [encounter] being finished, the said Geronimo Leiton and the official overseers of this captaincy of San Vicente, in the name of His Majesty and for all the land,[2] required that the accountant Andres de Eguino should make a fort in this port for the security of this captaincy, mindful that it has no [f. 29v] defences despite being of such importance. And from it His Majesty would be well served, because it is not fitting that enemies should take this port, since it is already known that there are mines of gold and silver and copper in this captaincy, as we have seen by experience and made an assay of it, as His Majesty will see. And Accountant Eguino, having considered that this would be fitting, and having consulted and conferred with his captains and with Bauptista Antoneli, the engineer whom we carried for the Strait and whom he brought with him, commenced to make a fort in the best and most suitable place that there was in this port. And thus we found all of the men from the *naos* working on it with much speed. And inspected by Almirante Diego de la Rivera, because the general had not arrived, the fort seemed very well made, and he urged them to hurry to advance the work. And he made all of us work on it who had arrived in the *galeaza* and the *nao Maria* and the *fragata Madalena*.

And because the said almirante learned here that Don Diego de Alzega, who had arrived from Spain with four *naos* carrying provisions, was in the Rio de Jenero and that he brought packets of letters[3] from His Majesty for General Diego Florez, he hurried so as to leave this port and go with the *naos* that were here to the Rio de Jenero. And thus he agreed with the royal officials[4] and captains to leave in this fort 50 soldiers with a trusted sergeant and some artillery and other munitions for its defence. And with an order that the work move forward until the general arrived or was informed about it and gave fuller instructions, [f. 30r] he left Governor Geronimo Leiton in charge, to whom he gave the title of alcaide of the said fort. And in his hands,[5] he made the customary pledge of homage that he would defend it and sustain it for His Majesty the king Dom Phelipe, our sovereign lord. And having left all in order we set sail with all the *naos* that were here on course to the Rio de Jenero, Sunday the 14th of April in the afternoon. We anchored outside the entrance to the port that night, and the next day, Monday the 15th in the morning, intending to leave we saw two sails that were coming straight toward this port, which was General Diego Florez with the two *fragatas Sancta Ysavel* and *Sancta Catalina*, who on the past eighth of March had been separated as aforesaid.

[*margin:* Arrival of the general at the port of Sanctos] He came into port with great difficulty, because the *fregatas* were taking on much water, and *Sancta Ysabel* could barely sail, because the rudder had come off. He arrived in great need of food and drink and carried sick men, because he had not stopped in any port from the day that he separated from us until this day, 17 days later, when we fortunately met him here. As soon as he arrived, he ordered us to return to port with the *naos* and made us diligently refit the

---

[1] Rada uses the word '*desgracia*', which can mean anything from misfortune to disgrace, which may have been deliberately ambiguous. See above, pp. 101–2.

[2] Governor Leitão was presumably referring to the captaincy of São Vicente, but he may have meant all of Brazil.

[3] The word used is '*pliegos*', which can mean packets.

[4] i.e. the bureaucrats present on the various ships.

[5] In other words, Leitão placed his hands within those of the *almirante*, as a gesture of homage.

fragatas that he brought. And he inspected the said fort named Sancta Elena and it seemed well to him, and he hurried the work to move it along. And he also inspected this port and the river, which is very good, and that of San Vicente. And being that it is of great importance, as much for the security of this captaincy as [f. 30v] for the offence and defence of this coast, he resolved that there needed to remain at the fort more soldiers and officers, artillery, powder and other munitions, both for defence and so that the work could be finished more quickly. And he made provisions for this and newly named Tomas Gari as alcaide of the fort, who held that title from His Majesty for one of the two forts that were to be built at the Estrecho de Magallanes, as a person worthy of merit with experience both in the militia and in similar construction projects and [labour] forces;[1] and [he named] Hernando de Miranda, a gentleman of this armada, as its captain,[2] with one hundred soldiers who were to remain in it as a permanent garrison. And from the *nao Begoña* that the English had sunk he ordered the salvage of three pieces of bronze artillery from beneath the water by two very good divers whom he brought with him. [*right margin:* As will be found on leaves 63 to 65] And this being done and all things left suitably in order, we set sail Sunday afternoon the 28th of April with seven *navios* of the armada and anchored at the mouth until the next day, Monday the 29th, when at dawn we again set sail with the wind west-north-west on course for the Rio de Jenero.

[*margin:* Departure of the armada from San Vicente for the Rio de Jenero] And thus we were sailing with fair winds until midnight, when a sudden strong wind from the south-west caught us with our sails aloft and the *naos* were in great danger. This weather [f. 31r] lasted for two hours. The next day, Tuesday the 30th, with the same south-west wind we came to the Isla de San Sevastian,[3] which is 16 leagues from the port of Sanctos, and at five in the afternoon the *galeaza capitana* dropped anchor, because the sky looked bad. And the *nao Concepcion*, whose captain was Rodrigo de Rada, which sailed somewhat behind, threw out an anchor at nightfall and while trying to get the anchor to grip against the strong current and wind, broke three cables and touched ground next to the island. And they exercised such good skill that they were able to get out to sea again without receiving any damage. [*margin:* May] The next day, Wednesday the first of May in the morning, we set sail with a south-west wind toward the entrance of this island on the north-east side, and we dropped anchor for lack of wind to make way and because the sky looked bad. [*margin:* Here the armada anchored] And thus we were tied up until Sunday the 5th, when we set sail with the same south-west wind until two in the afternoon, when it was east at the prow, which forced us to anchor again in the same place where we had departed this day. The next day in the morning, Monday the 6th, we again made sail with the wind west and the coast at hand, and at midday the wind was south-west, and with it we sailed until the next day, Tuesday the 7th, when at nightfall we were about 9 leagues from the Rio de Jenero. And the next day, Wednesday the 8th, the day dawned with us 6 leagues from the port, because there was little wind and that was east,

---

[1] See above, p. 60. Although Santos y São Vicente undoubtedly needed proper defences, Tomás Garri had originally been named to command one of the forts planned for the Strait. By re-assigning him to the new fort at Santos, Captain-General Flores undercut those plans.

[2] Hernando de Miranda had served with Pedro Menéndez de Avilés and Diego Flores de Valdés in La Florida. He was married to Catalina Menéndez de Avilés, daughter and heiress of Pedro Menéndez; AGI, Escribanía, leg. 153A.

[3] The Ilha de São Sebastião is located at 23°50′46″S, 46°37′47″W.

and we meandered all day tacking from one course to another to reach the port until night, when we dropped anchor 4 leagues from the port.

And the next day, Thursday the 9th, we [f. 31v] set sail with the wind north-west until midday, when it shifted to the south, and with it we entered into this port of the Rio de Jenero at 5 in the afternoon. From the port of Sanctos to this, there are 48 leagues and the coast runs east to west. [*margin:* Arrival at the Rio de Jenero, where Don Diego de Alcega waited] And in this Rio de Jenero we found Don Diego de Alcega, who had been within days of ceasing to wait for us with the four *naos* in his command that he brought from Spain with provisions for the armada. He took great pleasure in our arrival. And having met with General Diego Florez, he gave him the letters and dispatches that he brought from His Majesty for him. And having read them, [General Flores] ordered that the *galeaza* and the other *naos* be refitted quickly with the carpentry work and the other things that they needed.

Monday the 13th of this said month, the *nao* named *La Trenidad*, whose captain was Martin de Çubietta, entered into this port coming from the Rio de la Palata. This is one of the three *naos* that carried Don Alonso de Sotomayor with his men to the said Rio de la Plata. He said that the *nao corça Santa Catalina*[1] had been lost in the said river near Buenos Ayres, and that the *nao Maria de Buen Pasaje* had been broken up after the said Don Alonso and his men were disembarked, and this *nao Trenidad* was all that remained to carry the men upriver. And the said Don Alonso went expeditiously to Chile and left his men to get there little by little. Some munitions for the Estrecho de Magallanes that could not be removed from these three *naos* when the said Don Alonso left, he gave instruction to the said Captain Çubietta to return them in his *nao Trenidad* to this port, [f. 32r] where the said Don Alonso said he should sell or barter them in order to provide rations for his men. This day, the said day Monday the 13th, General Diego Florez, after having heard the provisions that Don Diego de Alcega brought and the supplies and munitions that he had, and what remained of those that were carried for the Strait, and having estimated the one and the other and having ascertained the necessity for rigging and other things for the *naos*, considered all that had been offered to him and that had been collected after he left until now at his return. And he met and consulted with the said Don Diego de Alcega and Pedro Sarmiento and with the almirantes Diego de la Rivera and Juan de Medina and with the royal officials of the armada.

[*margin:* Almirante Diego de la Rivera remains with the five *navios*, in order to return to the Strait] And having met and conferred with them, as will all be seen in detail in the said proposal and resolution that was written and signed, which will be found on leaves 69 to 73, which I remit, General Diego Florez resolved that the Almirante Diego de la Rivera would remain in this port with the five *navios* of the armada that were the best and most suitable, in order to return with them to the said Estrecho de Magallanes and to do there what could be done, as his Majesty commanded;[2] and as his almirante for these

---

[1] The phrase *nao corça* (*corza*) identifies this ship as the *nao* owned by Juan Antonio Corço Vicentelo, just as Columbus's *Niña* was the nickname of a ship owned by Juan Niño; Chaunu, *Séville et l'Atlantique,* vol. 3, p. 294, citing AGI, Contratación, leg. 2933. Both Corço's *nao* and one of the *fragatas* in the armada were named *Santa Catalina,* as was the island and the port that the armada frequented. Presumably to avoid confusion, Rada often calls the *nao Santa Catalina* the *nao corza.*

[2] Rivera would lead the third attempt at the Strait as captain general, a distinction he held from 2 June 1583 to 24 Sept. 1584. When he arrived back in Spain, he petitioned for extra pay for his temporary commission and was granted 400 ducats; AGI, Patronato, leg. 33, N. 3, R. 65.

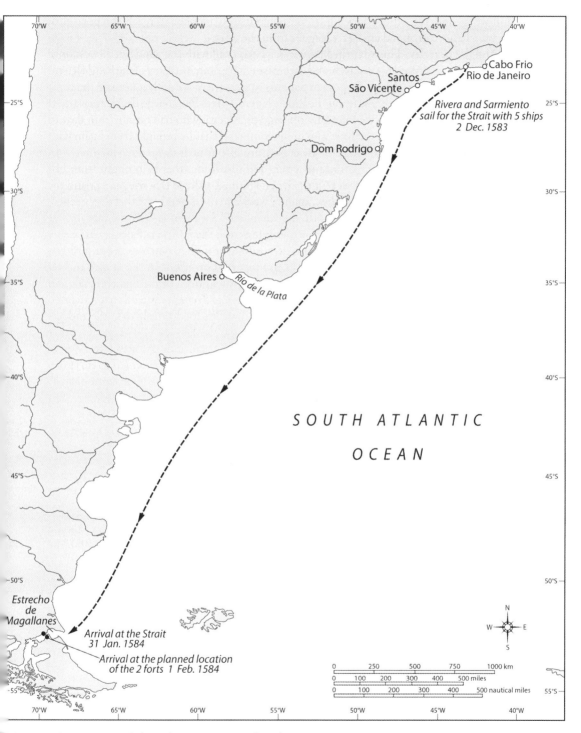

Map 5.   Sarmiento and the colonists conveyed to the Strait.

navios and men [General Flores named] Captain Gregorio de las Alas,[1] who had been to the said strait; and for royal officials Marcos de Aramburu,[2] who came with Don Diego de Alcega, as accountant; and Pedro Desquibel, who would exercise the office of treasurer; and as captains, Domingo Martinez de Avendano,[3] Hernando Ortega Morejon, Martin de Çubietta, Alonso de las Alas, and Gonçalo Melendez, for the five *navios* named *La Trenidad, La Maria, Santa Maria de Castro,*[4] [f. 32v] and the *fragatas Sancta Catalina* and *La Madalena*, as these [were] the most fit for returning to the said strait; and Antom Pablo, chief pilot, with the other pilots and men of war and sea and the settlers who have to go in them. As there [were] five hundred and fifty men for whom an estimate was made, we left them provisions for the time that they [would] have to remain in this port and until arriving at the said strait and for the three hundred men of war to remain there for about a year, not counting the governor and the officials and settlers.[5]

And an order was left for them to depart from this port at the end of the month of November of 1583, and they were left thirty thousand *reales*[6] for fresh meat and other things and four thousand *alqueres*[7] of flour from here and from San Vicente, which are paid for, and some salted meat. As subsidy to meet their needs, eight thousand and six hundred *reales* were given to Governor Pedro Sarmiento and to the captains, officials and

---

[1] Gregorio de las Alas served as captain of the *nao La Concepción* when the armada left Spain. When that ship was left behind for repairs at Santa Catarina, Captain General Flores shifted him to one of the 8 vessels that made a second attempt to reach the Strait. He was serving as captain of the *fragata Santa Catalina* when Flores named him as Rivera's almirante for the third attempt at the Strait.

[2] Marcos de Aramburu served as the veedor y contador (overseer and accountant) of Alcega's armada. He also owned the four *naos* that sailed to Brazil under Alcega's command; Navarrete, *Colección de documentos*, vol. 20, f. 177r.

[3] Domingo Martínez de Avendaño helped to recruit men for the armada in the summer of 1581, as he had done earlier in his career. Pedro de Ledesma to the Council of the Indies, 7 July 1581, in Navarrete, *Colección de documentos*, vol. 20, f. 153r. In the Armada of the Strait, he sailed as captain of the king's *fragata María Magdalena*.

[4] This is the first time that the *nao Santa María de Castro* appears in Rada's manuscript, and it is not on earlier lists of ships in the armada; see below, Appendix 1. It is likely that the ship was one of the 4 that Don Diego de Alcega brought to Brazil. Its relatively small size, over 200 *toneladas*, made it a likely choice for the third attempt at the Strait; Navarrete, *Colección de documentos*, vol. 20, f. 442v.

[5] Governor Sarmiento remained responsible for the provisions and supplies for the colony and strongly objected to Flores's decision to split the fleet. An anonymous pilot on the expedition also criticized Flores for separating the contingent for the Strait from the remnant of the armada. The critique was written after 9 May 1583, and its author may have been Gaspar Conquero; see Navarrete, *Colección de documentos*, vol. 20, ff. 345r–355v. Conquero originally served as pilot of the *nao San Nicolás*, which Captain General Flores declared unseaworthy at Santa Catarina and distributed its supplies, men and equipment among the remaining ships; see above, p. 81. Thereafter, Conquero was reassigned to various vessels. He sailed to the Strait with Rivera and Sarmiento, returned to Rio de Janeiro with Rivera, then carried more supplies to the Strait on Rivera's order; see Navarrete, *Colección de documentos*, vol. 20, f. 442v. Originally from the Triana district of Seville, Conquero was about 25 years old in 1583. He would continue to serve as a pilot for the Río de la Plata region, where he gave testimony in 1623 at the age of about 65. I thank Kara Danielle Schultz of Vanderbilt University for information about Conquero's 1623 testimony.

[6] Spanish silver coins, each worth 34 *maravedís* in money of account; 10 *reales* was worth 1 *escudo* and 11 *reales* equalled 1 ducat. A silver coin worth 8 *reales* was called a *peso de a ocho*, or piece of eight. For *maravedís*, see below, p. xiv.

[7] By *alquer(es)* Rada refers to an *alqueire*, an ancient Portuguese dry measure, varying considerably from place to place. In Rio de Janeiro, it seems to have been equal to about 35–40 litres. However, according to Sarmiento, *Viajes al Estrecho*, vol. 1, p. 190, an *alquer* equalled about one-third of a Castilian *fanega*. As the *fanega* was 55.5 litres, the *alquer/alqueire* would have been only 18.5 litres in Sarmiento's reckoning.

pilots who remain[ed]; and with this, all the money that the armada had was used up. And [General Flores] left particular instructions regarding what the said Diego de la Rivera and Captain Gregorio de las Alas, his almirante, had to do until arriving at the Strait and therein. And the original *instruccion* of His Majesty, with other important papers that Diego Florez had touching upon the said strait, will be found on leaves 73 to 75, which I remit. And in order to refit these five *navios* and the others that remained, it was necessary to break up the *nao* of Pablos Buzomo, one of the four [vessels] that [f. 33r] Don Diego de Alcega brought from Spain, for the cables, anchors, rigging and sails and other things that the others lacked, which were distributed to each one in conformity with what they had and what they needed.

And having refitted four *naos* that remained of the armada, and two of those commanded by the said Don Diego de Alcega, and having left the said five *navios* in suitable order with the men that were to return to Magallanes and the equipment and munitions, provisions and other things, the general embarked and Don Diego de Alcega and all the others, in order to leave this port to sail along the coast of Brasil with the design of cleansing it of corsairs that might be there and expelling them, and to go to la Paraiba, where the French had fortified themselves. And then we went on course toward the Baya del Salvador, both to learn what has been done by them as well as to send from there tar, oakum, rigging, sets of sails and other things to this port to refit and prepare the said five *navios*, so that they can be given a careening before departing to the said Estrecho de Magallanes. And to fetch these things, we brought along Captain Alonso de las Alas, who sailed in a small trading vessel.[1]

[*margin:* The departure from Jenero on course for the Baya] And thus the said armada departed from this port of the Rio de Jenero Sunday in the morning, the second of June, with the said six *naos* of the armada, and the small trading vessel that came as aforesaid. And having gone outside the port we dropped anchor, because it was calm, and we were moored until the next day, Monday the 3rd, when at dawn we set sail with the wind north-north-east on course toward the east, quarter to the south-east. And with this weather [f. 33v] we sailed this day and the next day, Tuesday the 4th and Wednesday the 5th until midday, when the latitude was taken at 24 degrees, and the wind was north-north-east, which blew with force. We sailed on course toward the east until the next day, Thursday the 6th, when the *nao* of Don Diego de Alcega broke the spar of the mainmast. And at midnight, there being much wind and high seas, the *galeaza capitana* fired a shot and lowered sail, so that the other *naos* would do the same. We were hove to until the next day, Friday the 7th, when at dawn the *nao Sancta Cruz*, whose captain was Francisco de Castrejon, did not appear. [*margin:* The *nao Santa Cruz* did not appear] And about 8 in the morning, Captain Alonso de las Alas approached to speak to us on the small sailing vessel in which he was going to the Baya for the tar and other things, as aforesaid. And they said that the same *navio*[2] was taking on much water from the seas that broke on top of it, and it came seeking the shelter downwind of our *galeaza*. By accident it approached so close that it rammed the side of the *galeaza*, and the sailors and men who travelled in it leaped aloft into the rigging in fear. And with the rush to see who could climb up first, a woman and an Indian and a man fell into the sea. The man immediately drowned, and the

---

[1] The phrase used is *navichuelo del trato*, presumably a small sailing vessel used for coastal trade.
[2] Here Rada uses *navío* as a generic to describe the small trading vessel.

woman and the Indian remained swimming in the water, without our being able help them, and we left them on the surface of the water as lost and drowned.

And the *navio* [f. 34r] detached from us and drifted away from the *galeaza*, and ten persons remained inside of it, incapable of doing anything.[1] The general ordered the *fragata Sancta Ysavel*, whose captain was Suero Queipo,[2] to go to her aid and take her in tow one way or another. And although there was much wind and sea, they exhibited such good skill on the *fragata* that they were able to launch the shallop into the water, and they went to the small sailing vessel and repaired it, and because the sails had been ripped to pieces they towed it behind the *fragata*. And at five in the afternoon we set sail with the foresail set low, and with the wind west-north-west we sailed on a course toward the north-east until the next day, Saturday the 8th, when in the morning the general ordered that all the people from the small sailing vessel who were aboard this *galeaza* be returned to it, and they were given sails to refit her, and thus they all transferred over.

And we ran with the wind from the west-south-west on course to the north-east until the afternoon, when the *nao* of Don Diego de Alcega approached to speak to us. And he said that the woman who had fallen into the water from the small sailing vessel had been rescued, and he brought her in his *nao*. And the *nao Concepcion*, with Captain Rodrigo de Rada, had rescued the Indian. And this was taken as a miracle, because when they fell into the sea these two *naos* were a long league upwind from us and the wind and sea at that time were stormy. [*margin:* The *nao Santa Cruz* appeared] This day in the afternoon, the *nao Sancta Cruz* reappeared that yesterday had gone off course from us. We remained with lowered sails until the next day, Sunday the 9th, because we had wind from the north-east at the prow. [f. 34v] The latitude was taken this day at 26 long degrees, because all this weather had beaten us back. And this night the wind blew from the north with much force and a storm. The next day, Monday the 10th, we had many downpours and the wind was from the west. We sailed on course toward the north-north-east, because of high seas and wind.

[*margin:* Distress of the *nao almiranta*] The small sailing vessel separated from us and was not seen any longer, and in the afternoon the *nao San Juan Bauptista*, the *almiranta*, fired three artillery pieces and this *galeaza* approached her, and they said that there was much water coming in at the prow, and they were repairing it. We again set sail with the same wind, the course toward the north-north-east, until the next day, Tuesday the 11th, when with a south-west wind we sailed on course toward the north-north-east until midnight, when the wind was from the north-east. And the armada lowered sails until the next day, Wednesday the 12th, when we set sail with the same wind on a course toward the north-north-west; and on this course we sailed until 4 in the afternoon, when we tacked to a course toward the east-south-east. This day the latitude was taken at 24 degrees and a half. The next day, Thursday the 13th, the *nao* that carried Don Diego de Alciega did not appear, and the general ordered the *fragata Sancta Ysavel* to sail for two hours on

---

[1] Rada describes them as '*inútiles*' (useless). Presumably, all the sailors had escaped onto the *galeaza*.

[2] Captain Suero Queipo de Llano served throughout the Armada of the Strait as captain of the royal *fragata Santa Isabel*, which had been part of the Armada de la Guardia (see above, pp. 12–13) under Captain General Flores. Queipo de Llano appears to have been a native of Asturias, as the name is identified with that region. A man with the same name was involved in a lawsuit in 1588 over properties in Asturias; ARCV, Registro de Ejecutorias, caja 1612, 54.

the course that we had followed yesterday afternoon, in case Don Diego had not tacked from that course when the *capitana* and the other *naos* had done so. We remained waiting until the *fregata* returned and said it had not seen it. And thus we sailed with the wind north-east [f. 35r] on a course toward the north-north-west until five in the afternoon, when the wind was west-south-west.

This day the latitude was taken at 24 degrees, and thus we sailed on course toward the north-north-east until midnight, when [the wind] shifted to the south-east. We followed the same path until the next day, Friday the 14th, when in the afternoon the wind was north-east. The armada lowered sails and hove to, because the wind was contrary, until the next day, Saturday the 15th, when in the morning we set sail to go where the wind was pleased to blow us,[1] because it was the same contrary wind. The latitude was taken this day at 23 degrees and a half. And in the afternoon, with the wind from the north-north-west, we sailed on a course just barely toward the north-east until midnight, when the wind came from the north-north-east. The armada lowered sails until the next day, Sunday the 16th, when in the morning the wind was east-north-east and we sailed on a course toward the north. This day the latitude was taken at 23 degrees and the wind was east, and we sailed on a course toward the north, quarter to the north-east, until the next day, Monday the 17th, when the latitude was taken at 22 degrees.

And with this wind and course we sailed until midnight, when the wind was east-north-east and we sailed toward the north until the next day, the 18th, when the latitude was taken at 21 degrees and one-quarter. And with this weather we sailed until the next day, Wednesday the 19th, when the latitude was taken at 20 degrees and one-third. And at five in the afternoon we came about, because the wind was light and we [f. 35v] were being pushed toward land, and on this course toward the east-south-east we sailed all night. And the next day, Thursday the 20th, the latitude was taken at 20 degrees and two-thirds, and with the wind north-north-east we sailed until the next day, Friday the 21st, when the latitude was taken at 21 degrees and one-third, until the afternoon, when the wind was north and we sailed toward the east-north-east, until the next day, Saturday the 22nd, when the latitude was taken at 21 degrees and a half, and the wind was north-west. We sailed toward the east-north-east until 10 at night, when a great downpour came, and the wind was rotating around the whole compass, and then it stopped at the south-west and we sailed on a course toward the north-north-east until the next day, Sunday the 23rd, when the latitude was taken at 21 degrees. And at midnight the wind was south-east and we sailed on the same course until the next day, Monday the 24th, the day of San Juan, when the latitude was taken at 20 degrees minus one-third.

And thus we sailed until the next day, Tuesday the 25th, when the latitude was taken at 17 degrees and two-thirds. [*margin:* Bottom was found] Here we threw out the sounding line and there was bottom at 40 *brazas* on a sand flat that continued for five leagues. In the afternoon the wind was east and we sailed on a course toward the north until the next day, Wednesday the 26th, when the latitude was taken at 15 degrees and two-thirds, and we steered toward the north-north-west until nightfall, when the wind was north-east. And thus we sailed until the next day, Thursday the 27th, when the latitude was taken at 14 degrees and a half. And [f. 36r] we sighted a sail downwind that was following our course, and it was recognized as the *nao* in which Don Diego de Alcega

---

[1] The phrase is '*para irnos entreteniendo*'.

sailed. And at midnight the wind was north and we sailed on a course toward the west-north-west. And the next day, Friday the 28th, at eight in the morning the wind calmed and we lowered sails, and we saw off our stern the sail that came in sight behind us yesterday. This day the latitude was taken at 13 degrees and a half, and we did not set sail until 10 at night, when the wind was east-south-east and we sailed on a course toward the west-north-west until the next day, Saturday the 29th, the day of San Pedro, when the latitude was not taken for not being able to see the sun. And at nightfall sail was lowered in a downpour, and the wind calmed until two at night when, with the wind from the east we set sail on a course toward the north-north-west.

[*margin:* The *nao Concepcion* did not appear] And the next day, Sunday the 30th, the *nao Concepcion*, whose captain was Rodrigo de Rada, was not visible, and land was sighted 15 leagues from the Baya. And going straight toward it at 10 in the morning, the general decided to enter and reconnoitre a port bearing west from us that is called Tinahe,[1] which is 12 leagues from the Baya. And thus we sailed astern toward it, and the *nao Concepcion* was sighted and seemed to be following us. [*margin:* The armada entered the port of Tinahe, Moro de Sant Pablo] And the wind was running toward the south and with it we entered into this port of Tinahe at 4 in the afternoon, and we anchored at the entrance at the west-south-west in 8 *brazas*, and the *nao Concepcion* did not enter, because it must have gone to the Baya, for not having seen us. [*margin:* July] The next day, Monday the first of July, [f. 36v] with the general wanting to depart for the Baya the sky looked bad and remained so. And in the afternoon it began to rain and blow strongly, which lasted all night without ever ceasing. The wind was from south-east and south with much force, and the *nao San Johan Bauptista*, the *almiranta*, lost two cables. And the *nao Sancta Cruz*, with Captain Francisco de Castrejon, was almost stuck on a sand bank; it was fortunate not to be wrecked, and it lost a cable.

[*margin:* He wrote to the governor of the Baya] Saturday in the morning, the 6th of this month, the general wrote to the governor of the Baya de Todos Sanctos, who is said to be Manuel Tellez Bareto,[2] and sent it with Captain Alonso de las Alas, who left from this port in a bark that was found there, asking to know if the *nao* in which Don Diego sailed and *La Concepcion* had entered there, and that he advise him about what was there,[3] and that he immediately send him a skilled coastal pilot. And the governor complied and sent him the pilot and told him what was there, and that the *nao* of Don Diego and La *Concepcion* were anchored in the Baya, although the *nao* of Don Diego was pushed by a *travesia* wind coming into port and had been in danger of wrecking, because it lost three cables and also lost the rudder and had entered port without it.

[*margin:* Departure from this port to the Baya] The general set sail from this port on Saturday, the 13th of this said month of July, two hours before dawn, with the wind south-south-east. And there are 12 leagues from this port to the Baya, north-east to south-west,[4] and we entered into this Baya at 4 in the afternoon. [*margin:* The arrival

---

[1] The island of Tinharé, is located at 13°22′54″S, 38°54′50″W, south-west of Salvador da Bahia. A point of land on the island, called Morro de São Paulo is visible at sea.

[2] See above, pp. 47, 60.

[3] Rada's phrase is '*de lo que havia*', which literally means 'what was there' or 'what there was'. He could have been referring to supplies or to the general state of affairs in the area. Captain General Flores was concerned with both.

[4] i.e. the bay lay 12 leagues north-west of the port of Tinharé.

at the Baya del Salvador] Having arrived here, the judicial officials and other principal persons of this city of [f. 37r] Salvador de Todos os Sanctos came to this *galeaza capitana* to visit the general, and they received us well, showing themselves to be very pleased with our arrival. And Monday the 15th, the governor with a great entourage came to the *galeaza* to confer with the general and took him with him to the city. And at their departure, the armada fired a very good salvo of artillery and harquebuses, and once they disembarked on land, the city fired another with artillery, and they went to their lodgings. Then the general informed himself from the governor and from the bishop and from the other persons of account about the status and degree of peacefulness regarding things on this coast.[1]

They met and conferred, taking into consideration the quietude of this city and the somewhat unquiet state of the hinterland and the restiveness of some personages.[2] If the marquess of Sancta Cruz were to be victorious with the second armada that those in Baya heard had departed for La Tercera,[3] and if some *navios* of the enemies from the defeated side were to come to this coast, they would be able to arrive during the month of October or November of this year of 1583. If this armada remained here until that time it would bolster the hopes of the disheartened people on this coast, and the *navios* that might come would find forces able to confront them and thwart their bad intentions. And thus it seemed to the general suitable to the service of His Majesty to remain in this Baya until that time and for all the month of November, and then to leave from this port on course to Pernambuco and la Paraiba to expel the French who are fortified there [f. 37v] and who have done and continue to do much harm on this coast. Fructuoso Barbosso had already routed them and killed many people, and it had no effect.[4] Having [expelled the French from Paraiba, General Flores] would go from there to Spain.

And having resolved on remaining to carry out the said tasks and whatever others presented themselves, he decided to write thus to His Majesty about everything else that had happened since the day that he left with the armada from the Rio de Jenero on course toward the Estrecho de Magallanes and other things touching upon [the king's] royal service.[5] And it seemed suitable to him that this packet of letters should be carried by Don Diego de Alcega, who would sail to Spain in the *nao Sancta Cruz* to give it to His Majesty. And because the things of the sea are uncertain, he sent a duplicate of this packet to the Royal Council of the Indies in another *navio* that was accompanying [Alcega] as far as Lisbon. This he entrusted to Pedro de Rocas, alférez real of Don Diego, to carry and

---

[1] Captain General Flores was concerned about corsairs and French interlopers, about the quantity of supplies available in Bahia to send to Rio de Janeiro, and about the loyalty of the city of Salvador and the captaincy of Bahia and the rest of northern Brazil to King Philip.

[2] The word *personaje* (personage) connotes a person of distinction.

[3] The marquess of Santa Cruz, Don Álvaro de Bazán, would win the Battle of Terceira on 2 Aug. 1583 against the supporters of Dom António, the Prior of Crato. His victory consolidated Philip II's hold on the Portuguese throne.

[4] Fructuoso Barbosa; elsewhere Rada uses the variants Fructuoso Barbozo, Frutuoso Barbosa, Frutuoso Barboso. Barbosa was a rich landowner in Pernambuco who obtained permission from King Philip to found a colony in Paraíba. In 1582 he organized a force to oust the French from the area and establish the colony, but after initial success they were forced to withdraw by the Potiguares, who were allied with the French. See Hemming, *Red Gold*, pp. 162–3.

[5] See above, pp. 47–8, for Captain General Flores's letter.

deliver it to the said council.[1] And the almirante Jhoan de Medina wished to go with Don Diego to Spain. [*margin:* Departure of Don Diego de Alcega to Spain] And with these dispatches completed, they embarked and set sail in continuation of their voyage on Tuesday morning, the 13th of August of the year of 1583. The said Don Diego took with him eight small sailing vessels that were going to Lisbon loaded with sugar. God give them a good voyage. The captains Francisco de Castrejon and Don Juan de Paços,[2] who had come [from Spain] with him, remained in the armada with their companies.

[*margin:* The departure of Captain Alonso de las Alas from this Baya to the Rio de Jenero] With this done, the general hurried to dispatch Captain Alonsso de las Alas to return to the Rio de Jenero with the tar, rigging, [f. 38r] sail canvas and other things for which he had come for the five *navios* and the people who remained to return to the Strait. And thus all that could be collected here was provided. And with it he departed on the 14th of September of this year of 1583 in the small sailing vessel in which he had come.

The general wrote to Almirante Diego de la Rivera and to Governor Pedro Sarmiento about what he was sending them, commending them very earnestly to complete the expedition to the Strait as he hoped.[3] And to better assure this he sent them a chart on which was painted all the coast from the Rio de la Platta to the mouth of the Strait, with all the ports and places where Francisco Draque had been, painted by a pilot who was called Duarcte Clifes, an Englishman who was on one of the three *navios* that came out the mouth of the Strait with El Drac. And the *navio* on which this pilot sailed, having come out the mouth and being in the Mar del Sur, was blown off course with a gale and turned around to traverse the same strait and was in many ports therein, and thus he paints them better and names them more precisely than any others who have passed through.[4] This pilot came to this Baya del Salvador and here he became a Theatine in the Company of the Name of Jesus on the second of May of the past year of 1582.[5] And he died on the

---

[1] The king had been in Portugal since the autumn of 1581, while the Council of the Indies remained in Madrid. It is not clear if Flores and Alcega knew that the king had left Portugal in March of 1583. Nonetheless, it made sense to send a separate dispatch to the council.

[2] After returning to Spain, Don Juan de Paços would file numerous petitions with the Council of the Indies asking for payment of the back wages owed to him and other members of the armada; AGI, Patronato, leg. 33, R. 65, Memo dated 17 May 1586.

[3] Nonetheless, by then Captain General Flores thought the plans for the Strait would be impossible to accomplish; see above, pp. 47–8.

[4] Edward Cliffe, who identified himself as a mariner, not a pilot, was on Francis Drake's voyage through the Strait, sailing with Captain John Wynter on the *Elizabeth*. On the way back to England, Wynter and the crew of the *Elizabeth* spent 4 months on the Brazilian coast, mostly in Santos; Andrews, 'Drake and South America', p. 55. In England, Cliffe claimed that Wynter had turned back after traversing the Strait against the wishes of his men; Cliffe, 'Voyage', p. 281.

[5] The Theatines were a male religious order founded in southern Italy in 1524, dedicated to moral reform through preaching and evangelization. The Society of Jesus, commonly known as the Jesuits, was an order founded in Spain in 1539–40 with very similar aims. It was fairly common for lay-people to confuse the Theatines and the Jesuits, either by mistake or to suggest that the Jesuits had no claim to originality; see, for example, Lach and Van Kley, *Asia in the Making of Europe*, p. 208. Rada seems to have confused the two orders by mistake, as it is most likely that he was referring to the Jesuit house in Bahia, which was flourishing by the late 1570s. Jesuits had arrived in Bahia with the first governor, Tomé de Sousa, in 1549 and continued to play a major role in the Christian evangelization of Brazil. See Alden, *Making of an Enterprise*, pp. 71–5; Hemming, *Red Gold*, pp. 97–118; Metcalf, *Go-betweens*, pp. 90–91; and Vasconcelos, *Chronica da Companhia de Jesu* (1663), *passim*.

20th of April of this year of 1583 before the armada arrived here.[1] And this [chart] was found amongst his papers and none other, nor a rutter, although such was solicited in the monastery, which is the best on all the coast.[2] And General Diego Florez carries a *traslado* of this paper.

With this dispatched[3] he made haste to careen the *naos* of the armada that [f. 38v] remained. And he gave an order for this city of the Baya and the *estancias*[4] and *lugares*[5] of its territory to prepare all the flour for *caçabe de guerra*,[6] and salted meat that they could get, and other provisions of fava beans[7] and rice, and some wine and oil which would be bought, although of this there was little because they did not have it. And the men of war and sea suffered much want all the time in which they were in this Baya, as much because of the few provisions, as for not having money from His Majesty to procure them. And with what the general sought out by all means that he could, and what they gave him on credit, a quantity of flour and other provisions was gathered.

And because the general was not confident regarding some disturbances and malcontents that there are in this land,[8] he did not want to leave until he had news from Spain or Lisbon. And then a *navio* arrived here on the 12th of January of 1584 that had left Viana[9] in the month of October of the year 1583. It brought news that La Tercera and the other islands were won by the marquess of Sancta Cruz, and that the French who had been there had been sent back to France. This news was of the greatest satisfaction for those who had hoped for it, and caused much fear and disquiet for those who had hoped otherwise. With this known, which was what the general had hoped for, he [f. 39r] made much haste to get the armada with spars aloft[10] to go to Pernambuco and la Paraiba. And thus he ordered Governor Manuel Tellez Bareto to finish refitting the two *navios* with which he had come here. It had been agreed that he would take them with the armada, as they were small *navios* and would be suitable to enter into la Paraiba, and that in them would go Diego Baez de Vega, son of the former governor, Lorenço de Vega, who died here, whom His Majesty had ordered to sail in them to

---

[1] Despite Rada's unequivocal description, Edward Cliffe cannot have been the man who joined the 'Company of the Name of Jesus' in Bahia in 1582. Cliffe returned to England with Wynter in 1579 and wrote about his pleasure to be home. Cliffe, 'Voyage', pp. 283–4. If he made the chart that Captain General Flores acquired, it had presumably passed into the hands of someone who either claimed to be Cliffe or was mistaken to be so by his religious brethren in Bahia. Besides the men on Wynter's ship, Drake's expedition lost three pinnaces before traversing the Strait. Any survivors may have made their way to Brazil. See Kelsey, *Sir Francis Drake*, pp. 123–4.

[2] Presumably, Captain General Flores asked the company whether their deceased brother had left other nautical papers.

[3] i.e. having sent the dispatches to Rivera and Sarmiento.

[4] An *estancia* was a rural estate of indeterminate size. The Portuguese *fazenda* has the same meaning of rural estate but is more or less equivalent to the larger Spanish *hacienda*.

[5] A *lugar* (lit. place). In Brazil the word denoted a place inhabited by Indians, although Europeans might also be found there.

[6] See above, p. 75.

[7] *Habas*. There are several varieties of fava beans.

[8] Presumably, the disturbances and malcontents related to continued resistance to Philip Habsburg as king of Portugal, but local settlers may also have resented the attempts by government officials, reinforced by the presence of the armada, to eliminate contraband trade with the French or English.

[9] Viana is in northern Portugal.

[10] Hoisting the spars and sails up the masts was the last major task before a ship set sail.

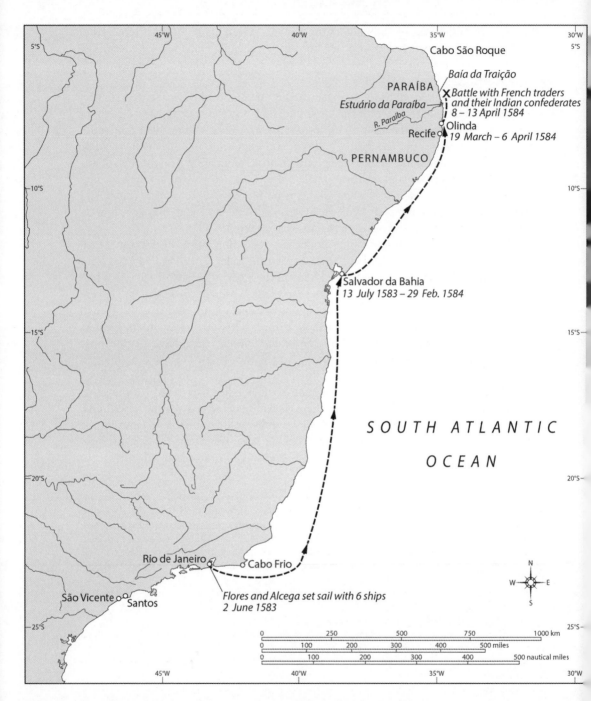

Map 6. Movements of General Flores from June 1583 to 30 April 1584.

Lisbon.[1] And the *requerimientos* and *acuerdos* that there were about this matter between the general and the governor will be found on leaves 75 to 77.[2]

And the armada being ready, the general and all the others embarked on the 20th of February of this year of 1584. And they waited until the 29th of this said month of February for the *navios* of the governor to finish being readied and to embark the bishop and the oidor general[3] of this Baya and the purveyor Martin Carballo, who were going to Pernambuco and its district on a tour of inspection. [*margin:* March. The departure of the armada from the Baya de Todos Sanctos on course to Pernambuco] And thus Thursday, the first of March of this year of [15]84, we set sail and left from this Baya with the five *naos* of our armada[4] and one caravel and the two Portuguese *naos*, and another two small *navios* loaded with sugar that were sailing under the protection of the armada, which in all were ten sails. And to all the *navios* was given the *instruccion* that will be found on leaves 77 to 79.

And having left from the port, we sailed with the north wind toward the [f. 39v] east-south-east all day and night. This day the latitude was taken at 14 degrees. And the next day, Friday the 2nd, we sailed with the same wind and course. This day we had wind from the north-north-east and sailed on a course toward the east until the next day, Saturday the 3rd, when the latitude was taken at 14 long degrees. And with the same wind and course we sailed until the next day, Sunday the 4th, when the latitude was taken at 14 degrees and three-quarters. And with the same weather we sailed until the next day, Monday the 5th, when the latitude was taken at barely 15 degrees. And with the same weather we sailed along until the next day, Tuesday the 6th, when the latitude was taken at 15 long degrees. And with this same north-east wind, we sailed until the next day, Wednesday the 7th, when the latitude was taken at 15 degrees and one-third. And in the afternoon the wind was east-north-east, and we tacked to another course toward the north-north-west. And on this course we sailed until the next day, the 8th, when at dawn Thursday we tacked to another course, because the wind returned from the north-north-east and we sailed toward the east. And at night there was a light wind from the north-east, and we tacked to another course toward the north-north-west until the next day, Friday the 9th, when we again tacked to another course, because the wind was north-north-east and we sailed toward the east. This day the latitude was taken at 15 degrees. And the next day, Saturday the 10th in the morning, we tacked to another course toward the north-west with the wind north-east until the next day, Sunday the 11th, when the wind was east-north-east and we sailed toward the north. The latitude was taken this day at 14 degrees and three-quarters. And with this weather we sailed [f. 40r] until the next day, Monday the 12th, when the latitude was taken at 14 degrees and one-quarter.

---

[1] King Philip had summoned the governor of Brazil, Lourenzo da Veiga, to Lisbon, but before the armada sailed in 1581 the king learned that Veiga had died and been replaced by Manoel Tellez Bareto; AMN, Sanz Barutell, MS 388, f. 212r–v, Report of the Junta, 27 Oct. 1581. Dom Lourenzo's son, Diogo Báez da Veiga, was travelling to Iberia in his father's place to pay his respects to the king.

[2] Governor Barreto was evidently slow to provide Captain General Flores with the supplies needed by the armada, leading to the *requerimiento* from Flores to demand them.

[3] An *oidor general* was the chief judge of a district high court authorized to hear pleadings and decide lawsuits.

[4] The 4 ships remaining from the armada were the *San Cristóbal* (*galeaza capitana*), *San Juan Bautista* (*almiranta*), the *nao La Concepción*, and the *fragata Santa Isabel*. Another unnamed *nao* had arrived in Brazil with Don Diego Alcega and was incorporated into the Armada of the Strait.

And with this same weather we sailed until the next day, Tuesday the 13th, when the wind returned to the north-east and we sailed on course toward the north-west. The latitude was taken this day at 13 degrees and three-quarters. And in the afternoon we sailed toward the north, because the wind was east-north-east, until the next day, Wednesday the 14th, when the latitude was taken at 13 long degrees. And with the same wind and course we sailed until the next day, Thursday the 15th, when the latitude was taken at 12 degrees and a bit more than one-quarter. And we sailed toward due north until the next day, Friday the 16th, when the latitude was taken at 11 long degrees. And following this course we sailed until the next day, Saturday the 17th, when the latitude was taken at 10 long degrees. And with the wind east we sailed on a course toward the north until midnight, when we sailed toward the north-west until the next day, Sunday the 18th, when at dawn we sighted land when we were 12 leagues from the Cabo de Sanct Agustin,[1] and we sailed toward the north, quarter to the north-east. The latitude was taken this day at 8 degrees and two-thirds, and the wind slackened and came from the south and we sailed on a course toward the north. And the next day, Monday the 19th at dawn, we were next to the cape and we saw a *navio* anchored there. [*margin:* Arrival at the Cabo de Sant Agustin] And thinking it to be an enemy we sailed toward it, but it was a *navio* that had just arrived with merchandise from Lisbon, whence it had departed three months before. And from it we learned that Don Diego de Alcega had arrived safely in Lisbon, although after enduring severe weather.

This *navio* came with us to Pernambuco, [*margin:* Arrival at the town of Olinda] which is seven leagues farther along from the Cabo de Sant Agustin, and we anchored at two in the afternoon [f. 40v] in sight of the town of Olinda about two leagues away, because it[2] does not have a port where *navios* can enter except those that are smaller than two hundred *toneladas*, and thus it was necessary to be anchored off the coast. There the bishop disembarked and the oidor general and the purveyor Martin Carvallo, whom as stated above we had brought from the Baya. The next day, Tuesday the 20th, the general wrote to the town and *camara*[3] of Pernanbuco about his arrival, and that it was necessary to dispatch all the things necessary for the expedition to la Paraiba quickly. They responded to him that it would thus be done and that it was necessary that he meet with them.

The next day, Wednesday the 21st, the general disembarked on land; and in a house that is on the seashore a league from the town, those from the *camara* and the principal men of the town and the bishop and oidor general met. And all of them being together, the general gave a *parlamento*[4] about what had happened, proposing to them how important and suitable this enterprise was for the well-being and tranquillity of all of them and the other householders and those who dwelled in the town and the countryside, to expel the French from la Paraiba once and for all and to populate and sustain that port and its hinterland, subduing the Pitiguares[5] for being so bellicose, because it was not fitting for the reputation of His Majesty that the French should any longer control that port and hold these Indians

---

[1] Elsewhere Rada uses the variant Cabo de Sant Agustin. The Cabo de São Agostinho (Cape St Augustine) is located at 8°17′23″S, 35°14′8″W.

[2] i.e. Pernambuco; elsewhere Rada uses the variant Pernanbuco.

[3] The *cámara* (chamber) was the town council.

[4] Rada's use of the word '*parlamento*' here has the meaning of public speech or consultation.

[5] For the Potiguar Indians, see Hemming, *Red Gold*, ch. 8; Wright and da Cunha, 'Destruction, Resistance, and Transformation', pp. 336–7.

under their will and subjection, with whose help they had done and each day were doing so much harm.[1] And since now that he had the armada and sufficient men here, he assured them that they would pacify the land and expel [f. 41r] the French from the port. This accomplished, he would aid them and would make a fort in the most suitable part and he would leave the men for the garrison; and that it was necessary that they should stir themselves and help very earnestly, going on this expedition overland with their persons, Indians and slaves,[2] pacifying and making war on those Indian enemies, and in this manner the situation would be resolved that for so many years had resisted a solution. This seemed good to all, and they were much heartened by what the general proposed to them. And they all offered to go at their own expense on this conquest and expedition with their persons and slaves, and that he should wait for them while they made preparations. The general promised them that he would wait for them as long as the weather permitted and that they should make great haste, because the armada was anchored on a dangerous coast and at great risk. And this agreed upon, he embarked once again.

And the next day, Thursday the 22nd, he gave licence to the small sailing vessels loaded with sugar, which had come from the Baya under our protection, to go to Lisbon as they requested, because they did not have enough provisions to wait. And thus they left. The general informed himself from the experienced pilots who had entered the port of la Paraiba about the [depth of] water it had, and they certified to him that the four large *naos* in the armada [f. 41v] could not enter inside the port, because it did not have more than three *brazas* at high tide. This ascertained, he ordered the chief purveyor[3] Martin Carvallo to commandeer two *navios* from those now in port that had come from the kingdom[4] and that were suitable to enter into la Paraiba, and thus it was done; and they were readied with much diligence, and provisions and other things that were necessary for this expedition were purchased and loaded on them, the accountant Andres de Eguino taking them in his charge; and he took them from the port and joined them with the armada.[5] [*margin:* April] And because the men of the town who had to go overland were already assembled, the general wrote to Martin Leiton,[6] oidor general, that he should help in

---

[1] By blaming the French for the bellicosity of the Potiguares, Captain General Flores simplified the intricate and shifting political alliances and enmities in the region. Whether or not he was aware of the complexities involved, it made strategic sense to define his aims in a manner most likely to enlist the aid of the colonists. See Introduction, p. 48.

[2] The separate mention of Indians and slaves suggests that the colonists had free as well as enslaved Indians under their orders. It is also likely that other Indians had their own reasons to attack the Potiguares in alliance with the Portuguese.

[3] Elsewhere Rada identifies Carballo simply as the proveedor (purveyor).

[4] Presumably the kingdom (*reino*) of Portugal.

[5] Eguino resented being assigned to take charge of the small *navíos* and supplies for the Paraíba expedition, arguing that it should have been the job of Captain Esteban de las Alas, the proveedor y tenedor de municiones (purveyor and keeper of munitions). Perhaps to vent his resentment, Eguino wrote that it was he who had persuaded a reluctant Captain General Flores to carry out the attack on Paraíba. Navarrete, *Colección de documentos*, vol. 20, ff. 359r–363r, Eguino, early April 1584. Rada's *Relación* provides no support for Eguino's claim, which is further belied by the elaborate preparations that Flores made to organize men, ships, and supplies in Bahia and Pernambuco.

[6] Oidor Martím Leitão became a brilliant military commander. The fort built by Captain General Flores at Paraíba in 1584 came under assault in 1585 by the returning French and their Potiguar allies, forcing the garrison to withdraw. In response, Leitão assembled a force that reconquered the area and re-established the fort and settlement at Paraíba. See Hemming, *Red Gold*, pp. 163–8.

readying these men with much diligence, and that he should have them leave and march out right away this day, Thursday the 5th of April of this year of eighty-four. And he wrote to Dom Phelipe de Mora, who was going as chief captain,[1] that he not stop on the road more than absolutely necessary and that he wait for them in la Paraiba, which is 20 leagues from here.[2]

[*margin:* The course to la Paraiba] And with this resolution and all embarked, the armada set sail on course to la Paraiba on Friday the 6th of April, one hour before dawn, with the wind east-south-east, direction north-north-east, with few sails, waiting for all the *naos* [f. 42r] to catch up with us. We were ten sails: five from the armada; and the two Portuguese of Diego;[3] and the two that had been commandeered; and one caravel in which Tome de Roche,[4] a nobleman from Pernambuco, travelled, which also carried Fructuoso Barbosa, who transferred this day to the *galeaza capitana*. And from an island that is called Tamaraca,[5] which is five leagues beyond Pernambuco, the captain, who is said to be Pero Lopez,[6] came out to join us with a well-manned galliot[7] and three barks of Indians, as was agreed beforehand.[8] This day and night we continued with few sails set, because the pilots said that the waters run very swiftly on this coast and that otherwise we would arrive too soon.

And at dawn the next day, Saturday the 7th, more than ten leagues before arriving at la Paraiba, we raised all sails going toward the north, and at three in the afternoon we anchored in nine *brazas* a bit beyond Cavo Blanco,[9] three leagues from la Paraiba, because the other *naos* lagged very far behind, and it seemed to the pilots that they would not be able to reach the mouth of the port of la Paraiba to anchor by daylight and the coast was not clear[10] where it was necessary to anchor. And thus the armada remained anchored here. And that afternoon, because the *naos* that had to enter inside the port were in order and prepared, the general ordered Captains Francisco de Castrejon and Don Juan de Paços, each one with his company that they brought in the *nao almiranta*, to embark onto the two *naos* that we brought from Pernambuco, and they did so right away. And the next day, Sunday the 8th in the morning, as we continued [f. 42v] under sail they saw, from the

[1] Capitão-mor (chief captain), in this case the head officer in charge of the soldiers. The title could also be used to denote the head of one of the Portuguese captaincies in Brazil.

[2] i.e. from Pernambuco.

[3] i.e. Diogo Báez da Veiga.

[4] From 1591 to 1594 or 1595, Thome da Rocha would serve as chief captain of the new captaincy of Sergipe, after distinguishing himself in warfare against French and Indian forces for control of the region. He again served as the captain of Sergipe in 1603–6, as the area grew and prospered from the trade in brazil wood. Freire, *História de Sergipe*, pp. 23, 26, 29, 40.

[5] Tamaracá or Itamaracá is a long, narrow island located at 7°44′52″S, 34°49′33″W.

[6] The original *donatário* (donatary) and captain of the island of Tamaracá in the 1530s was Pedro Lopes de Sousa, the brother of Martim Afonso de Sousa. In 1584, the captain of Tamaracá was Pedro Lopes Lobo. He participated in both the Battle of Paraíba in 1584 and in the later retaking of the area with Martim de Leitão. See *ABNRJ*, vols 13–14, pp. 145–6.

[7] A *galeota,* variant *galiota* (galliot) in the late 16th century was a small galley with up to 20 oarsmen and a single mast and sail.

[8] Presumably, the contingent from Tamaracá had arranged to join the expedition as it made its way up the coast toward Paraíba.

[9] Cabo Branco, Brazil, is the easternmost point of land in the Americas, located at 7°9′S, 34°47′W.

[10] Presumably, Rada meant that there were obstructions on the coast where the ships would have to anchor and they could best be seen in daylight.

fore-top of the *galeaza*, a *navio* that had left from the port of la Paraiba, sailing very close to the coast, and we all much regretted not being able to capture it.

And at 10 in the morning we arrived near the port and anchored in 9 *brazas*, and we saw inside la Paraiba French *navios* that they had beached on the shore, at which all the armada greatly rejoiced.[1] The general immediately moved to the *fragata Sancta Ysavel* with the officers and men of war that he had considered and selected from the *galeaza* to go with his person. And having given orders to Diego Baez de Vega to embark on one of the two *naos*, and to Captains Castrejon and Don Juan de Paços to go in the other two *naos* from Pernambuco, he ordered Captain Alvaro de Busto to come as almirante, and Captains Rodrigo de Rada and Juan de Salas[2] to come in the boats from their *naos* which – being large – could not enter inside the port, and to man them very well with soldiers and come with them alongside the *fregata*.

And with this order the general entered the port in front with this *fragata*, [*margin*: Entry of the port of la Paraiba] and the said captains with the boats and the other three *navios* following them.[3] And we anchored at nightfall about half a league from where the four French *navios* were, three of them together and one apart and a bit farther on. And from the bulwark that they had constructed on land they fired five pieces of artillery at us. And the next day, Monday the 9th in the morning, we proceeded carefully and entered inside the channel. And as we were entering they were firing shots at us from many pieces of artillery, [f. 43r] without the general allowing anyone to return fire until we were within range of their shot. He also ordered a white flag raised to see if they wanted peace, but all this was not sufficient and they were firing shot at us very frequently from many pieces. This considered, the general had the prow of the *fragata* turned toward the bulwark from where the enemies were firing, and he ordered Espinosa, captain of the artillery, to fire at them with the two culverins at the prow, each one of thirty-two *quintales*.[4] And thus he began to fire at them very well, and the *nao* of Diego Baez de Vega, who followed behind us, did the same. And as our artillery had to be doing them much damage and the French had few resources to defend themselves, they set fire to their three *navios* and to the houses in which they dwelled, and they ceased firing their artillery from the bulwark and continued burning and made a good and thorough job of it.

Seeing this, the general ordered Captains Rodrigo de Rada and Juan de Salas, with the boats in which they had brought fifty musketeers and harquebusiers, to go and reconnoitre and defend the other *nao* that was a cannon-shot farther along, so that they could not burn it, and to capture it if they could. And as they went to do this, two pieces of artillery were fired at them from land, next to where the *nao* was. And with this they attacked, skirmishing in very good order straight toward the *nao*. And although the Pitiguares shot many arrows at them from land, they arrived at the *nao*, and Captain Juan

---

[1] Because the vessels were beached in the estuary of Paraíba, they could not be used quickly by the French to escape.

[2] Captain Juan de Salas would continue to serve on Spain's Atlantic fleets for several decades, eventually as almirante of the New Spain fleet of 1597; AGI, Indiferente, leg. 1952, lib. 4, f. 111r–v, royal provision dated 12 Jan. 1596.

[3] Pedro de Rada appears to have been part of the assault forces at Paraíba.

[4] Each gun weighed about 3,247 *libras*, given the weight of a *quintal* (cwt). See above, p. xiv. A *culebrina* (culverin) fired shot of 20–50 *libras*, depending on the weight and bore of the gun; a half culverin fired a shot of 10–18 *libras*.

de Salas with his men got inside it; and Captain Rodrigo de Rada was skirmishing with the Indians until [f. 43v] he got to land, and he got out with his men and made the Indians withdraw inland a great distance. And then so many of them came against him that he was forced to withdraw and embark on his boat. Captain Alvaro del Busto came to his aid after six soldiers had been wounded, and with his arrival the Indians fled and eight of them were killed, among them a principal,[1] as later became known.

The next day, Tuesday the 10th, the general ordered the soldiers to disembark in order to find out what defences the French and Indians had there and to learn if they had prepared some ambush amidst the woods, because this land next to the shore is very wooded. And thus they were divided up in twelve barks and a *galiota* to disembark. And in good order we disembarked a little below the bulwark and three hundred harquebusiers and musketeers went on land, and among them all the principal men of the armada. And a squadron was formed with all of them by Captain Pero Nuñez de Loaissa as chief sergeant.[2] And with an auxiliary arm of fifty Indian archers they went forward reconnoitring the area. We marched along until reaching the bulwark of the French without encountering any resistance, because all of them had fled. We found eight pieces of cast iron artillery and some *versos*[3] with which they had fired at us and the rigging from the *navios*[4] that they had burned, and up to nine hundred *quintales* of brazil wood and untapped butts of beer and other minor things of little value, and five dead men that we had killed with the artillery, whom they had buried.

[f. 44r] And from the place where the *nao* was that had not been burned, six Indians came with a white flag as a sign of peace. The general went to receive them and beckoned to an Indian who was in the water who said that all the Indians of the land wanted peace. Seeing this, he ordered that the squadron not proceed farther. And being thus, at four in the afternoon they surprised us with many Indians shooting arrows at Captain Juan de Salas and the twenty-five harquebusiers who were inside the *nao* that had been captured. And thus we put ourselves in battle order and remained alert. And the general got into a boat with harquebusiers and went to see what was happening and arrived near the *nao* where the arrow volley from the Indians was coming. And they shot the general in the breast with an arrow that hit a piece of doubled buckskin leather and passed through without doing him more harm. And with his arrival they withdrew, which suggested that the Indians understood that we wanted them to betray [the French], as we had not disembarked in the place where the Indian with the flag of peace had come.[5] The general, seeing that it was late, came presently to order us to embark, and thus we did.

---

[1] i.e. an important person or leader.

[2] i.e. head of the squadron.

[3] See above, p. 20.

[4] Once the French had beached their ships, they had removed the rigging to protect it from the elements. That would have made it impossible for them to escape by sea, so their best option was to burn the ships.

[5] Rada's language is not clear in this passage. He presumably thought the Indians were at first unsure whether the small force that captured the beached *nao* and the large squadron that disembarked later were on the same side. The men who captured the beached *nao* were clearly enemies of their French allies. They might have thought at first that the squadron that disembarked farther away and did not proceed when the Indian of peace appeared was allied with the French, and therefore was their ally as well. When Captain General Flores arrived to aid the besieged *nao*, it was finally clear to them that the two groups of outsiders were all enemies of the French and wanted them to betray their former allies.

The next day, Wednesday the 11th, he ordered an interpreter to say to the Indian with the flag of peace, whom we held hostage, that he should go to tell the *caciques*[1] and principal Indians that he would show them much friendship and would consider them brothers and would leave them secure and free in their houses with their wives and children, and that they should hand over the Frenchmen who were in the land, and that from this point on they should not permit any more, as they could not come here without licence from the king of Spain, Don Phelipe, our sovereign lord, [f. 44v] because this land was his. And with this, having regaled him and given him a pair of trousers and a doublet with fancy trimming, and a cap of velvet cut-work that the general took from his own head so that it be given to the most principal chief as a token of what he had told him and how all of them would be treated, we put him ashore. And he went away, saying that he would return with the response. And the next day, Thursday the 12th, another Indian came with the same embassy of peace and said that he whom we had sent yesterday had gone to speak to some principal Indians who were inland, who wanted this same gift – no more, no less. And the general told him what he had told the other one, and that the principal men should come soon and with them the peace agreements would be affirmed.

The next day, Friday the 13th, about twenty Indians arrived at the shore, and among them came one principal person. The general sent the shallop to bring them to the *fragata*, and they said that unless they were given one of our principal men as hostage they would not come. The general did not trust them, and he assured them that no harm would be done to them; they responded that they were awaiting the arrival of other principal Indians. And in these demands and responses they kept us in expectation for three days, seeing what they would agree to. And as they must have sensed that the men from Pernambuco whom we were awaiting had already come near, they fled inland. Because these Indians are so treacherous and have caused so many deaths and harm on this coast, one has to pardon them for not trusting them nor taking them as friends. [f. 45r] And this was said by the same ones who had brought the embassy of peace.[2]

And an Indian slave from Pernambuco who was captive among them, whom the French had seized as he was fishing and had sold in exchange for brazil wood, escaped from them fleeing and came swimming to this *fragata*.[3] He said that many Indians were gathered together three leagues from this port in a village that they were fortifying in order to defend themselves in it, and that some Frenchmen were among them and were advising them to abandon the area and go to the Rio de San Francisco, which is 70 leagues from this port at a latitude of 11 degrees. And the Indians said that they did not want to go away from their land until they could do no more and would be forced to leave. This Indian said that the day we arrived near this port a *navio* had left from it with the most principal men among the French who were here, and that he believed they would go to the Baya de la

---

[1] *Casiqui*, Spanish spelling *cacique*, denoted an Indian chief or war-leader. Although the word was of circum-Caribbean origin, Spaniards used it to refer to local leaders in many other parts of their American empire.

[2] Rada does not make clear which Indians were treacherous and which ones had to be pardoned for not trusting them. The Indians that Rada calls treacherous would seem to have been those coming with the Portuguese from Pernambuco, who may have been traditional enemies of the Indians around Paraíba. See above, pp. 5–6, 117.

[3] In other words, the French had captured him and sold him to their Indian allies in Paraíba; he was presumably from the Indians allied with the Portuguese in Pernambuco.

Traicion,[1] which is five leagues down from this port, where he believed there was another *navio*, and that the other Frenchmen had gone there overland. And this is taken as certain because we found three launches, one of them fitted with oars and sail and provisions and an astrolabe and sea chart,[2] and two in an arm of the sea that goes inland from this Baya de la Traicion, which they went up about two leagues until they got to dry land. In these they stored clothing and other things.

[*margin:* The arrival of the men from Pernambuco to this port of la Paraiba] The men from Pernambuco arrived at this port Thursday in the afternoon, the 19th of this month; they took up quarters right away and they armed their *real*[3] where we had disembarked. [f. 45v] One hundred and twenty men came on horseback, and more than two hundred on foot and one thousand and five hundred Indian archers, slaves and freemen. The next day, Friday the 20th in the morning, the general went ashore and he received them with much contentment, thanking them for their arrival. And having told them what had been done, as aforesaid, he proposed to them anew what would be most suitable to the service of His Majesty: to construct a fort for the defence of this port as well as for the security of the land. And to do this and to populate it quickly, it was necessary that they all help with their persons, Indians and slaves with as much dedication as they had shown by arriving. They responded that with very good will they would do all that they could and that he should direct and order them regarding what would be of service.

And because the general had understood in Pernambuco that the principal men among them were not well pleased with Frutouso Barbosa, in his presence and so that all would assist with more obligation in the service of His Majesty and the fortification and population of the land, he told them that, notwithstanding that His Majesty had favoured Fructuoso Barbozo with the government of the land, unless they were content with him they should elect a person with whom they were [content], and who had the quality and merits that were suitable for such a post. They talked amongst themselves about it, and they agreed to entrust the government and land to the same Frutuoso Barboso, and that he exercise the power and favour that he had from His Majesty until such time as He be served otherwise, and that they would help him in settling the area in order to serve His Majesty. [f. 46r] And with this resolution, the general again embarked.

[*margin:* The fort commenced to be made] The next day, Saturday the 21st, it rained all day. Sunday the 22nd, [General Flores] again disembarked and together with them the [outline of the] fort was traced out in the place that seemed the most suitable, and he gave it the name of San Phelipe y Sanctiago.[4] And he then took a spade in his hand and commenced to work on it, having assigned among the principal men what each one had to do on the fort. And thus all commenced to work and to make much haste. And because

---

[1] Baia da Traição (Bay of Treachery or Bay of Treason), now more commonly referred to as Baia de Paraíba, located at 6°42′S, 34°55′59″W. The name recalled an incident in 1556 when the first bishop of Brazil, Dom Pero Fernandes Sardinha, was shipwrecked near the bay. He and the other survivors were attacked, killed, and eaten by the Caeté Indians; Henderson et al., *Reference Guide to Latin American History*, p. 93.

[2] Rada uses the phrase '*carta de marear*', which means a sea-chart, but it is not clear how extensive it was. Presumably, the French would have needed a map of the coastal areas where they procured the brazil wood.

[3] A *real* (royal) in this context seems to have denoted a main encampment; in other contexts it would have denoted a royal encampment, hence the name.

[4] As Rada does not mention the engineer Battista Antonelli, it seems likely that he had already returned to Spain with Don Diego de Alcega.

they had brought few tools such as spades, wooden shovels, hatchets, sickles and other things for so many men, Indians and slaves, the general then dispatched a launch to Pernambuco to the oidor general and chief purveyor, that they should send them at once, even if they had to seek them from house to house; and he sent them a report about what had happened. The launch returned Saturday the 28th of this said month and brought the tools that it had been sent to acquire. And the construction of the fort moved forward in good order, without the work ceasing a bit, the general being present at it every day and having us work with some squadrons of soldiers who would be left for its defence.

Because the large *naos* were outside the port, they experienced great difficulties on the sandbar, each day breaking cables and anchors, being on such a rough coast, and they were not able to hold on much longer. This considered, it was necessary to put everything in order suitable for the fort and the defence of it. [*margin:* The appointment of Captain Francisco de Castrejon as alcaide] And thus [General Flores] assigned Francisco de Castrejon, captain of infantry, as alcaide [f. 46v] with one hundred and ten soldiers as a garrison with muskets and harquebuses, and he left them provisions for seven months and the artillery, powder and other munitions necessary at present, although it lacked two large pieces [of artillery] to cover the whole port. These could not be left, as to try to disembark them from the *galeaza* in the heavy seas ran the risk of losing them. And because the *naos* could not hold on, and the *nao San Juan Baptista* was under sail for lack of cables as all had been broken, the general brought together all the noblemen of Pernambuco. And he told them that they had already seen the distress and risks of the armada and that it was not possible to remain there any longer and he was forced to leave. And on behalf of His Majesty he ordered and entrusted them to stay there until the fort was finished, as they had promised to do before the work commenced. They offered their pledge anew, although they much regretted the departure of the general, and they promised him not to depart from there until they could leave it finished. And although later they would have to patrol inland to make war on the Indios Pitiguares and thus would not be taking care of the fort, they would leave seventy men from those that they had brought and a dozen horses, as they had promised beforehand, in addition to the men that remained as its garrison. And thus the general, in front of all of them on Sunday the 29th of the said month, handed over the fort to the alcaide Francisco de Castrejon, who made the customary vow and pledge of homage in his hands. And he gave him [f. 47r] the title and the *instruccion* for what he had to do, which will be found with all the things that were handed over for the said fort on leaves 79 to 82. And for his use, he left him the three French launches, which were very good, and the *navio* from which to make the platforms for the artillery and for doors and other things necessary for the fort.[1]

And he wrote to the oidor general and the chief purveyor of Pernambuco that they should assist with much diligence to supply the fort with provisions as well as the other things necessary, as the said alcaide Francisco de Castrejon, in whose charge it remained, would ask them, turning over to him all that might be sent. And to the oidor general he wrote in particular to send all the men that he could, both married and unmarried, as settlers, with those that were in Pernambuco that Fructuoso Barboso had brought from Spain for this settlement, and that he should write to the governor of the Baya to do the

[1] The word used for platforms is '*planchadas*'. In other words, they would break up the *navio* and use its materials for the fort.

same. And with this done, many others will come from all the coast of their own volition, because the land is very good and fertile, and it will return all that is planted in it. It has a very good and secure port, and *naos* of four hundred *toneladas* can enter inside it,[1] because at the entry where there is a sandbar, it has almost three *brazas* at low tide, and at high tide more than four. And inside the port, many *naos* can be anchored and well sheltered from all the winds and there are five *brazas* at low tide. This port is of much importance, [f. 47v] because there is not another on all this coast until the Baya. And by sustaining it, *navios* can enter it seeking port during the storms that come to these parts. Until now, for not having a secure port when they have a storm, they were forced to keep looking for a port as far as our Yndias, as Fructuoso Barboso did. Having come to expel the French from this port and finding himself on the sand bar of Pernambuco in a galleon, it seemed prudent to him to return to Spain.[2] And with this port being ours, as from now on it will be, the *navios* that arrive here will be able to enter securely as long as they are not larger than four hundred *toneladas*.

They say that it is six or seven leagues from this port to where the brazil wood is cut. And the Indians bring it on their backs for three or four leagues and they put it near the shore for the French. And the French go to get it via an arm of the sea that extends inland and bring it to their *naos* in launches. It is the best brazil wood that there is in all these parts, and what we obtained here from the French was embarked on one of the *navios* that we brought from Pernambuco, chartering it based on the value of the wood in order to bring it with us, as was done. And with all things left in order, and the general having given certifications to those from Pernambuco for the services that they have done and continue doing here for His Majesty, leaving them all very content and Fructuoso Barboso with the governance [f. 48r] of the land and its population, he took leave of them Monday, the last day of this month of April of this year of 1584.

And the next day, [*margin:* The departure from la Paraiba] Tuesday the first of May, the Day of San Phelipe y Sanctiago, we set sail on a course to Spain with the wind from the south-south-east our direction north, with eight sails: five from our armada, two of Diego Baez, and one that brings the brazil wood. This day at three in the afternoon we overtook the *nao San Juan*,[3] which was waiting for us, for not having hawsers with which to anchor. And at midnight the wind was east-south-east and we sailed toward the north, quarter to the north-east, until the next day, Wednesday the 2nd of May, when the latitude was taken at five degrees; la Paraiba is at barely seven degrees.[4] And with the same wind we sailed until the next day, Thursday the 3rd, when the latitude was taken at three degrees and one quarter; and with the wind south-east we came we came [*sic*] on course toward the north, quarter to the north-east, until the next day, Friday the 4th, when the latitude was taken at one degree, and the wind was north-east and we sailed

---

[1] Local pilots in Pernambuco had told General Flores that the port had no more than 3 *brazas* at high tide, but they were proven wrong; see above, p. 117.

[2] Rada's general point about the lack of a port for large ships north of Bahia is valid. His reference to Fructuoso Barbosa's difficulties is not accurate. In 1579, Barbosa had brought 4 ships from Recife in Pernambuco to combat the French in Paraíba. Unable to find a proper anchorage near Paraíba, he was blown to the Caribbean and then crossed the Atlantic to Iberia. He finally returned to Brazil in 1582 with the backing of King Philip. See Hemming, *Red Gold*, pp. 162–3.

[3] The *almiranta San Juan Bautista*.

[4] The coordinates of Paraíba are 7°0′49″S, 34°37′44″W.

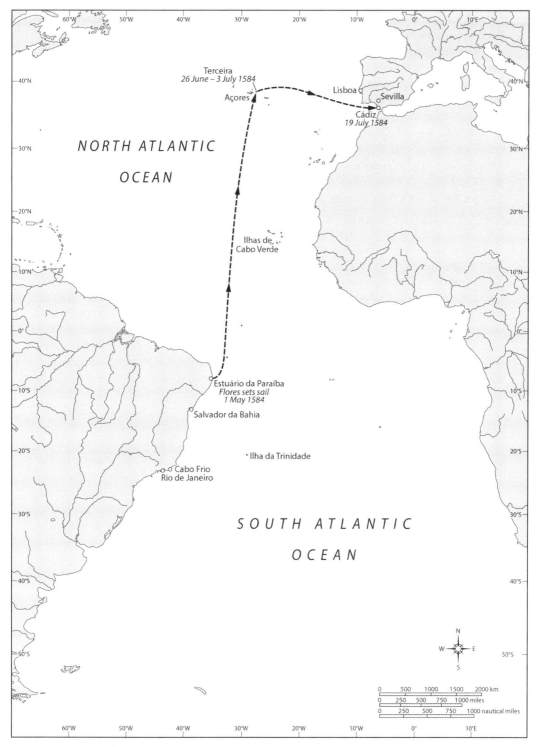

Map 7. Return of General Flores to Cádiz with five ships; three more arrive in September.

toward the north-west. And thus we sailed until the next day, Saturday the 5th, when the wind was north and we tacked to another course toward the east-north-east. This day the latitude was not taken. There were many downpours on Sunday, Monday, Tuesday and Wednesday the 9th. We tacked from one course to another with wind from the north and north-north-east, with many downpours and calms, without making any progress. This day the latitude was taken at one-third of a degree on this part north of the line.[1]

And with the wind north-north-east we sailed toward the north-west until the next day, Thursday the 10th, when [f. 48v] the latitude was taken at one degree. And at nightfall the wind was north-east and we sailed toward the north-north-west until the next day, Friday the 11th, when the latitude was taken at one degree and one-third. And thus we sailed until the next day, Saturday the 12th, when the latitude was taken at one degree and a half, with many downpours. And the next day, Monday the 14th in the morning,[2] the wind was north-north-east, and the direction was north-west, with many downpours until the next day, Tuesday the 15th, when the latitude was taken at barely three degrees. And at three in the afternoon the wind slackened, coming from the east-south-east and we sailed toward the north; and at midnight the wind was east-north-east, the course toward the north, quarter to the north-west, until the next day, Wednesday the 16th, when the latitude was taken at three and a half long degrees. And thus we sailed until the next day, Thursday the 17th, when the latitude was taken at four degrees and two-thirds. And with this wind we sailed until the next day, Friday the 18th, when the latitude was taken at five degrees and a half, and the wind was north-east and we sailed toward the north-north-west until the next day, Saturday the 19th, when the latitude was taken at 6 degrees.

And with this wind and course we continued until the next day, Sunday the 20th, the *Dia de Pascua*,[3] when the latitude was taken at 7 degrees. And the next day, Monday the 21st, the latitude was taken at 8 degrees and one quarter. And with the same wind and direction we sailed until the next day, Tuesday the 22nd, when the latitude was taken at 9 degrees and one-quarter. And thus we sailed until the next day, Wednesday the 23rd, when the latitude was taken at 10 degrees and one-third. And with this weather and direction we sailed until the next day, Thursday the 24th, when the latitude was taken at 11 degrees and three-quarters. [f. 49r] And with the same wind north-east, progress was made toward the north-north-west until the next day, Friday the 25th. The latitude was taken at 13 degrees, and with the same weather we sailed until the next day, Saturday the 26th, when the latitude was taken at 14 degrees and one-quarter. And at four in the afternoon the wind was east-north-east and we headed to the north, quarter to the north-west, until the next day, Sunday the 27th, when the latitude was taken at 15 degrees and one-third. And thus we sailed until the next day, Monday the 28th, when in the morning the wind was east and we sailed toward the north, quarter to the north-east. This day the latitude was taken at 17 degrees, and at three in the afternoon the wind was east-north-east and we sailed toward the north, quarter to the north-west until midnight, when the wind was east. We sailed along toward the north, quarter to the north-east, until the next

---

[1] i.e. north of the Equator.
[2] There is no entry for Sunday, 13 May 1584.
[3] The *Dia de Pascua* (Pentecost) is the 7th Sunday after Easter.

day, Tuesday the 29th, when the latitude was taken at 18 degrees and one-third. And with this weather and direction we sailed until the next day, Wednesday the 30th, when the latitude was taken at barely 20 degrees. And thus we sailed until the next day, Thursday the 31st, the *Dia de Corpus Xpti* [*Christi*],[1] when the latitude was taken at 21 degrees and three-quarters.

[*margin:* June] And thus we sailed until the next day, Friday the first of June, when the latitude was taken at 22 long degrees. And with this wind, which was east-north-east, we sailed until six in the afternoon toward the north, quarter to the north-west, until the next day, Saturday the 2nd, when in the morning the wind was north-east and we sailed toward the north-west. [f. 49v] The latitude was taken at 23 degrees and three-quarters, and at nightfall the wind was east-north-east and we sailed toward the north. And the next day, Sunday the 3rd, the latitude was taken at 24 degrees and one-third. And at nightfall the wind was east and we sailed toward the north-east until the next day, Monday the 4th, when in the morning it was east-south-east and we sailed toward the north-east. This day the latitude was taken at 25 degrees and a half. And the next day, Tuesday the 5th, the latitude was taken at 26 degrees and three-quarters, and at nightfall the wind was south-east. We sailed toward the north-east until the next day, Wednesday the 6th, when in the morning it rained heavily and the wind was south-west; we sailed toward the north-east. This day the latitude was taken at barely 28 degrees, and the wind shifted again to the south-east and we sailed toward the north-east until the next day, Thursday the 7th, when the latitude was taken at 29 degrees minus one-quarter. And with this fair weather we sailed until the next day, Friday the 8th, when the latitude was taken at 29 degrees and a half. And the next day, Saturday the 9th, the latitude was taken at 30 degrees and one-quarter, and the wind was south-west behind us, pushing us north-east until the next day, Sunday the 10th, when the latitude was taken at 31 degrees and a half. And at nightfall the armada lowered sails and hove to, because the sky was very overcast and looked bad. It rained all night and the wind came swirling from the north. And the next day, Monday the 11th, the latitude was taken at 32 degrees, and at nightfall the wind was south-east; we sailed toward the north-east until [f. 50r] the next day, Tuesday the 12th, when the latitude was taken at 32 degrees and three-quarters, and the wind was south. And thus we sailed until the next day, Wednesday the 13th, when the latitude was taken at 33 degrees and one-third.

And with this weather we sailed until the next day, Thursday the 14th, when the latitude was taken at 34 degrees, and thus we sailed until the next day, Friday the 15th, when the latitude was taken at 35 degrees, and the wind was swirling around from the north-north-west. And the next day, Saturday the 16th, the latitude was taken at 35 degrees and a half, and thus we sailed until the next day, Sunday the 17th, when the latitude was taken at 37 degrees minus one-quarter and the wind was north-east; we tacked to another course with the prow toward the north-north-west. And on this course we sailed until the next day, Monday the 18th, when the general moved to this *galeaza*, though until this point he had been on the *fragata Sancta Ysavel*, because the pilots judged that we were near Fayal.[2] This day the latitude was taken at 37 degrees and the wind came

---

[1] The *Día de Corpus Christi* (Feast of Corpus Christi) is a movable date in the Christian calendar, falling on the Thursday after Trinity Sunday. For the use of the *crismón,* see above, p. 65, n. 6.
[2] The Ihla do Faial is the westernmost island of the Portuguese Azores, located at 38°34′12″N, 28°42′36″W.

from the south-south-east, and we sailed toward the north-east until the next day, Tuesday the 19th, when the latitude was not taken, because the day was dark, and the wind was south-west. And thus we sailed until the next day, Wednesday the 20th, when the latitude was taken at 38 degrees and a half.

And because we found ourselves at the latitude of Fayal, we sailed toward it on course to the east. And on this course we sailed until the next day, Thursday the 21st, when the same latitude was taken. And in this direction we sailed until the next day, Friday, and Saturday the 23rd, when the latitude was taken at 38 [f. 50v] degrees and three-quarters. And the next day, Sunday the 24th, the *Dia de San Juan*,[1] at three in the afternoon the Isla de Florez[2] was sighted, which is at 39 degrees, and we sailed directly toward it. And the next day, Monday the 25th at dawn, the island of Cuervo[3] was sighted. We passed both of them at a distance with the wind south-west our direction east-south-east until the next day, Tuesday the 26th, when in the morning the islands of Graciosa and San Jorje[4] were sighted. We passed between them and the armada came to anchor at the port on the island of La Tercera, next to the city of Angla.[5] [*margin:* Arrival at La Tercera] At nightfall, when Jhoan de Urbina, the maestre de campo,[6] knew [the armada] was there, he immediately came to the *galeaza capitana* and conveyed to the general, whom he knew, the news that he had from Spain. And [General Flores] was very sorry not to find here letters or orders from His Majesty about what he should do. And because he had need of food and water and some special provisions[7] for the sick, the general was forced to wait for them to be provided, and we had north-east winds in the port.

[*margin:* July] We did not set sail until Tuesday, the 3rd of July, when in the morning we left port with the eight sails that we had entered with. And all day and night we had calms without being able to leave the island. We left Juan de Urbina some quantity of gunpowder, match-cord and lead that he needed. And the next day, Wednesday the 4th, the wind was north-north-east and we sailed toward the east-south-east; and then we had calm at eight leagues from the Isla de San Miguel[8] [f. 51r] until the next day, Friday the 6th, when the wind was south-east and then south-west. We came on course toward the north-east until the next day, Saturday the 7th, when the wind was west-north-west, the course east-north-east. And with this wind and direction we sailed Sunday and Monday the 9th. And the next day, Tuesday the 10th, it was north-west, our direction east, quarter to the north-east, until the next day, Wednesday the 11th, when the wind was west at the stern, the course east, until the next day, Thursday the 12th, when with the same wind we sailed toward the east-south-east. And this day the two Portuguese *naos* in which Diego

---

[1] St John's Day.

[2] The Ihla das Flores is located at 39°28′N, 31°13′19″W.

[3] The Ilha do Corvo, the northernmost of the western Azores, is located at 39°42′7″N, 31°6′6″W.

[4] The Ihla Graciosa is located at 39°3′5″N, 28°1′W, the Ihla de São Jorge at 38°39′N, 28°5′W.

[5] Angra is the principal city on the Ihla Terceira.

[6] A maestre de campo (campmaster) was a military position with administrative and judicial powers over infantry forces, usually on land. A governor or captain general named a maestre de campo as his second in command. In a largely civilian context, a maestre de campo could function as a chief of staff.

[7] Rada uses the word *regalos*, which generally means gifts. In this context, it means more delicate foods than the standard rations, which were considered too difficult for the sick to digest. The word *dietas* often referred to the food items carried on board Spanish ships for those who fell ill. See Sorapán, *Medicina española*, pp. 219–20, 404–28.

[8] The Ihla de São Miguel, at 37°48′35″N, 25°12′51″W, is the largest of the Azores.

Baez de Vega was travelling sailed toward Portugal, and the armada set a course straight toward San Lucar. And the next day, Friday the 13th, the wind was north-west and we saw six sails that were going on a course toward the north-east. And to find out if they were enemies the armada followed them in good order, and we overtook them at midday; they were six Flemish *urcas*[1] that were loaded with salt for Mostradama.[2] They said they had left from Setubar[3] eight days before. And with the wind south-south-west, we sailed until the next day, Saturday the 14th, when with a fresh wind west-north-west we sailed on a course east-south-east until the next day, Sunday the 15th, when at 9 in the morning we sighted land at Cavo de San Vicente.[4] And then we saw ten caravels that came straight toward the armada that were going to Portugal. And at five in the afternoon we overtook the galleon *San Matheo* that was going to Lisbon [f. 51v] and was coming from the Algarbes.[5] And at nightfall a caravel arrived alongside the *galeaza*, which came from the Cabo de San Vicente with an order from the president and judges of the House of Trade in Seville[6] to give a message to the fleets or *navios* coming from the Indies to warn them that *galiotas* were patrolling the coast.[7]

And with the wind west-north-west we sailed Monday and Tuesday the 17th, when at dawn we arrived at the bar of San Lucar and anchored the armada on it, firing some pieces of artillery so that the pilots of the port would come to guide us inside it. And two barks came and said to the general that they would not dare to bring the armada in until the next day, Wednesday the 18th, because the tide this day was at low water, and when the *galeaza* arrived at the sand bank the tide was going out. [*margin:* Arrival of the armada at Cadiz] And because the *naos* did not have good hawsers to anchor there until the next day, the general decided to set sail and take the armada directly to the Baya de Cadiz, where it arrived at four in the afternoon. As soon as it anchored, he wrote to His Majesty, giving him an account of the voyage and of what had happened to him since he left the Baya del Salvador de Todos Sanctos until entering into this port on the 19th of July, the date of this packet. And on the 21st of this month, Don Francisco Tello came to review the armada, and he praised the men of war and sea from it and dismissed them, so that from this day forward they would not earn any more wages.

[f. 52r] The general saw that the said Don Francisco had dismissed the men of war and sea without giving them any aid, and because all arrived in rags, he arranged to sell in Cadiz the brazil wood that was brought from la Paraiba, won in a just war with the French as stated. And the money that was made from it he divided among all the men of the armada. Although their shares were small, they had to travel with it to Seville, where they had to be paid what was owed them for almost three years in which they had not been given anything, for lack of money. They had already ceased to be given the daily ration that His Majesty orders, for lack of provisions to give them, from which they have suffered much want and hunger. And for the many risks and travails on the voyage – it being so

[1] Flemish *urcas* were cargo hulks with large capacity and shallow draft.
[2] Amsterdam.
[3] Setúbal in south-western Portugal was a major source of sea salt for various European fishing industries.
[4] Cabo de São Vicente (Cape St Vincent) is the south-western tip of the Iberian Peninsula, a landmark for ships sailing toward south-western Spain.
[5] The Algarve is a coastal region of south-western Portugal.
[6] See above, p. 22, n. 6.
[7] In other words, galliots carrying corsairs from North Africa who aimed to rob incoming ships.

long and with so many tempests – His Majesty has a great obligation to those who have made it and for their services. And the principal persons used up their funds for the men who had nothing to sustain themselves so they would not abandon his royal service, because six months have passed in which they were not given any other ration but flour and water. With this travail they have arrived in Spain. May it please God that He reward us well.[1] The general travelled to the court[2] and went to the Escurial[3] where His Majesty was, to give him an account of the expedition, on the 24th of August of this year of one thousand and five hundred and eighty-four.

[1] Rada's phrase is '*Plegue a Dios se nos gratifique bien*', which could mean that the deserved reward would come either from the king or from God.

[2] The city of Madrid was often referred to as 'the court' after Philip II established the royal court there. Except under extraordinary circumstances, the various councils of the royal government remained in Madrid even when the monarch travelled elsewhere.

[3] The Escorial Palace was the new summer residence of Philip II, located in the foothills of the Guadarrama Mountains north-west of Madrid. It was sufficiently complete by the summer of 1584 for the king to reside there.

[f. 52v] *Instruccion y orden* that must be maintained and complied with by the captains, pilots and masters of the Royal Armada of His Majesty, which at present is gathered in the port of San Lucar de Barameda in order to go to Las Indias and Estrecho de Magallanes, whose Captain General is Diego Florez de Baldes:[1]

1   Firstly, that all the captains, pilots, and masters take particular care of the things for the service of God, Our Lord, making sure that no one swears nor blasphemes, and whoever should do so the captain should seize and make a report with the scribe of rations[2] of his *navio* and notify me, in order that he be punished in conformity with justice.

2   That no *navio* nor *fragata* of this said armada, nor any other that is joined to it after departure from this said port, shall stop at night nor leave at dawn before the *capitana*; and if able to do so it will come twice to salute it, once in the morning and the other time in the afternoon, and it will get the name.[3] And the *navio* that is nearest the *capitana* will pull away and make way for the one that is approaching.

3   And if it happens that the *capitana* wants to tack to another course from the one that it followed at sunset, it will fire a piece and display a lantern in addition to the poop lantern. Then all the *navios* in the armada will display another [lantern] and tack to the same course. And if by chance some *navio* of the said armada be lagging behind so that it cannot hear the piece that the *capitana* will fire, the *navio* that is closest to it will fire a piece and hang a lighted lantern so that the lagging *navio* will understand.

[f. 53r] 4   If the *capitana* should lower its sails at night for any distress or occasion that arises, it will display two lighted lanterns besides the poop lantern. All the *navios* in the armada will display another two lanterns.

5   That no *navio* nor *fragata*, nor any other that may go with the said armada, shall separate from it without my licence, on pain of life and loss of his goods. And if by chance, because of the weather, some *navio* or *navios* be forced to separate from the armada, it will continue to follow the course that I set, so that once arrived at the port and region where I am going, it will find me, and if not, my order of what has to be done, which you will guard and carry out, on pain of the said penalty.

6   And the said *navio* or *navios* of the said armada, as aforesaid, that with violent weather should separate, will follow a course directly to Gran Canaria, and from there to Cabo Berde, where they will find me, or the said order for what they have to do, because from then on orders will be given to each *navio* about the course and voyage that it has to follow. And if such *navio* or *navios* should arrive at Cabo Berde before me, they will wait for me and not leave the said port without my order.

7   That no *navio* of the armada, nor any that travel under its authority, shall enter into any port nor anchor without the *capitana*'s having entered first, or without my order and licence, on pain of fifty ducats for the expenses of the said armada, and legal procedures will be taken against such captain.

---

[1] Unless otherwise noted, these *instrucciones y órdenes* were dictated personally by Captain General Flores. Rada records them in the captain general's voice.

[2] The escribano de raciones (scribe of rations), often called the maestre de raciones (master of rations), or simply the maestre (master), was responsible for keeping track of everything and everyone on board.

[3] i.e. the password name for the day, used to distinguish friends from foes.

[f. 53v] 8   The almirante, with his *nao*, shall sail to windward or leeward, according to where seems best to him, and all the *navios* of the armada shall first fire three times to salute him, and he to them twice.

9   The pilot of each *navio* will take care that at daybreak and at sunset he will have a man atop the main topmast[1] to see if there is any sail or [something that] looks like land. And this shall be done each day, else pay a fine of ten ducats for the expenses of the said armada. And if in case some sail or sails be seen, the captain will fire a piece and raise and lower the topsail as many times as there are sails seen, and then hoist sail and follow it. And if there be many *navios*, he should go after them, engaging with them as best he can until the *capitana* and the rest of the armada arrives. And it being a single *navio* and it seems that he has more force than the corsair, he should board and capture it. And if perchance two or three *navios* or *fragatas* arrive together to board him, they have to take care not to impede one another so that the said *navio* escape from them, because the captain who is culpable in this will be punished in conformity with justice. And if the *capitana* wishes that it not be pursued, it will fire a piece and approach, so that it advise him about what was sighted, and he can give it orders about what it has to do.

10   All the captains and officials of war and sea of the said armada should freely give over authority for navigation to the pilot [f. 54r] so that they do not impede him, and they should follow his instructions, unless the pilot does not want to follow the course that the *capitana* set, on pain of fifty ducats for the expenses of the said armada; and legal measures will be pursued against the captain or other person.[2]

11   The whole armada should travel in good order in convoy and friendship, and the *navio* that has an emergency should fire a piece, and the other *navios* should approach it to help and tell the *capitana* what the trouble is.

12   As aforesaid, each *navio* of the armada will get the name from the *capitana* each day. And on a day in which they cannot get it, they will use the following as the name for each day. And a *nao* that cannot approach will get it from one that got it from the *capitana*:

Sunday, La Sanctisima Trenidad
Monday, SSam [*sic*] Pedro
Tuesday, SSam [*sic*] Pablo
Wednesday, San Jhoan
Thursday, El Espiritu Sancto
Friday, Sanctiago
Saturday, Nuestra Señora de la Comcepcion

Order of War[3]

[f. 54v] 13   The captain of battle order, such as the alferez and sergeant, should take very particular care that the soldiers have their firearms clean and ready for the time of need, and instruct and drill the soldiers so that they become very good harquebusiers, making them fire at targets whenever there is a place for it, so that they are skilled when the occasion is offered.

---

[1] *Mastil de gavia*.
[2] i.e. against any person who disobeys this order.
[3] i.e. the order of battle.

14   Take care to order that the said alferez and sergeant have shot made and ready at hand so that it is not lacking when needed; and that the master of cord, lead shot and powder have them ready, counted and measured, according to the orders that the captain will issue, and have the scribe of rations of the said *navio* or *fragata* keep accounts of its discharge in accordance with the royal instruction; and review the men each Saturday.

15   When the occasion to fight is offered, the captain will divide the soldiers into four parties in this manner: one in the stern area and another around the mainmast, and another in the area of the prow and another to help with the artillery and in the areas where they are needed most, according to the situation and to what seems most effective to the captain. And the leaders of these four squadrons should be competent and trustworthy men whom the soldiers respect, [f. 55r] especially he who has to expose himself to danger in order to help the gunners and to do the other things that are most needed.

16   See that all the artillery is loaded and ready, even when it is inside,[1] so that if it were necessary to have use of it quickly, they have to do no more than aim it outside its portholes. And next to the artillery, there should be with each gun a box where they keep the shot for that same piece, without mixing some shots with others.

17   See that they always have two *pipas*[2] sawn in half to make four tubs, which they will keep above and below, filled with water for the time of fighting, so that if there were a fire to defend themselves from it by having the tubs ready with old clothes in them to put out the fire[3] and jugs [of water] to throw from the topmast.

18   If by chance there should be many *navios* of corsairs so that it is necessary to arrange the armada in order, as will be said below, the *navios* will approach the *capitana*, which will give them orders about what has to be done.

19   For the *navio* of the armada that boards some corsair, the first officer, soldier or sailor who leaps inside, in addition to what he gains from its pillage, will be given thirty ducats of bonus; and the second, twenty; and the third, ten; and the next fifteen will be given five ducats each; in addition to which, [f. 55v] particular care will be accorded their persons to give them honourable offices in the armada, and I will write to His Majesty that he grant them a *merced*.[4]

20   That the captain, pilot and master take care with lights, so that no candle goes below deck unless the master or dispensero[5] carries it in his hand. And having a fire in the *fogon*,[6] that there be posted a guard of soldiers there. And that the dispensero going below with a candle take another man with him and carry the candle inside a lantern.

---

[1] i.e. drawn back from the portholes.

[2] A *pipa* was a large barrel, used for transporting and storing various liquids and comestibles, equal to about 27.5 *arrobas* in the late 16th century. An *arroba* (Rada's variant *aroba*) was a Castilian weight equal to 11.5 kg, slightly more than 25 lb.

[3] i.e. with old clothes and rags soaking and ready to throw on a fire.

[4] A *merced* (lit. mercy) in this context was a favour or reward.

[5] A dispensero, variant despensero, was the person responsible for the maintenance and distribution of rations. The word is often translated as steward, which implies that the dispensero prepared the rations as well as dispensing them. On Spanish ships at this time, however, the crew and soldiers seem to have been responsible for preparing their own food, usually in groups related to their assigned times on duty.

[6] A *fogón* (cookstove) was usually a large rectangular metal firebox, about 3 feet tall and open on most of one side, with sand in the bottom on which to build the cooking fire. It was generally kept on the main deck, sheltered as much as possible from the wind and sea but situated to minimize the danger of fire.

21   That the captains, pilots and masters treat the men of war and sea well and see that they are given their full rations, as His Majesty orders in his *instruccion*. And if anyone should commit some serious crime, the captain should not punish him without his legal process before the said scribe of rations, and that I be notified of it, in order to provide justice.

22   The captain on his *navio* should not permit any men of war and sea to play prohibited games,[1] and the contrary occurring I will consider them guilty, on penalty of fifty ducats; and the players will be proceeded against with justice.[2]

23   That the pilots, each one in his *navio*, should chart his course for the whole voyage, and write down the latitudes taken and the signs of lands, and take soundings in the ports and places where they shall be and enter into, and that they include sufficient *racion*,[3] as they are obliged to do, and that they maintain the original in their power, so that I can review it [f. 56r] and order what is to be done, on penalty of fifty ducats to those that do not do thus and comply.

The aforesaid *instruccion* will be complied with and maintained, without exceeding it in anything, subject to the said penalties.

Dated on the *galeaza capitana* on the 24th day of September of one thousand, five hundred and eighty-one years. By order of His Lordship Diego Florez. Pedro de Rada, chief scribe.

This *instruccion* was given to the captains, pilots, and masters of the said armada in the port of San Fanejos[4] on the 25th of September of the year 1581, when the armada set sail for the Strait.

———

— 1582 —[5]

Instrucciones y ordenes to be maintained and complied with by the captains, pilots and masters of the Royal Armada of His Majesty of the Guard of the Indies and the Strait of Magellan,[6] of which I am captain general, is the following:

1   That the said captains, pilots and masters maintain and carry out my *instruccion* and see that it is maintained and carried out, which has my signature and is countersigned by Pedro de Rada, chief scribe, which they were given before leaving from Spain, its date the

[1] Games of chance – gambling – were prohibited on board as an offence to God and to avoid the occasion for disputes. Of course, such games occurred, but they had to be organized discreetly to avoid punishment.

[2] i.e. the captain would automatically be held responsible and fined if gambling occurred on his ship; the players would face legal proceedings to determine their guilt or innocence.

[3] In this context, Rada's use of the word *ración* seems to mean the *horizonte racional*, referring to the mathematical calculations required to transform the viewed angle between the horizon and the sun at midday into a figure for latitude.

[4] San Fanejos was a traditional anchorage at Sanlúcar de Barrameda.

[5] Rada's insertion of the heading 1582 suggests that he intended to copy the documents into his *Relación* in chronological order. However, he inserts no other such heading and seems to group the remaining documents related to incidents during the voyage. His Table of Contents indicates where each document occurs in the manuscript.

[6] This was the official designation of Flores's armada. In many contemporary documents, it is called simply the *Armada del Estrecho* (Armada of the Strait). In the early 17th century, a different armada with the latter name patrolled the strait between Spain and North Africa.

twenty-fourth of September of the year 1581, in matters of navigation as well as in all the other matters that are therein declared.

2   And if by chance it happens that after the armada departs from this port of Sanctiago de Cavo Berde, some *navio* [f. 56v] or *navios* from it with violent weather cannot follow the poop lantern, it should continue its voyage and course straight to the Rio de Jeneiro, where it will find the armada. And if it should arrive at the port beforehand, it should remain in it until the armada arrives, on penalty of one thousand ducats, besides being punished for carelessness and excess.

3   And if the occasion arises and it should become necessary for the whole armada to be put into battle order to fight, it will maintain the following order, taking the places that will be declared:

Vanguard

4   The *galeaza capitana* will go in the vanguard, and with the captains Estevan de las Alas, Juan Gutierez de Palomar, Domingo Martinez de Avendano, Rodrigo de Rada, and Suero Queipo, with their *navios*.

Battle Centre

5   The lord Don Alonso de Sotomayor will be in the battle centre and the captains Martin de Çubietta, Hernando Ortega Morejon, Jodar Alferez,[1] and Pedro de Eguino.[2]

Rear Guard

6   In the rear guard will go the Almirante Diego de la Rivera, and the captains Gregorio de las Alas, Francisco de Nebares,[3] Gonçalo Menendez, and Francisco de Cuellar.

The said captains, pilots and masters will maintain and carry this out, each one according to what pertains to him without exceeding it in anything, on the penalties contained in the said *instruccion*.

[f. 57r] Dated on the galeaza capitana, anchored in the port of Sanctiago de Cavo Berde on the 26th of January 1582. By order of His Lordship Diego Florez de Baldes. Pedro de Rada, chief scribe.

This *instruccion* was given to the captains of the armada in Sanctiago de Cavo Berde on the 28th day of the month of January of 1582. And the armada departed from this port in continuation of its voyage toward the Rio de Jenero on Friday after midday on the 2nd of February of the said year.

———

The *instruccion y orden* that must be maintained and carried out by the captains, pilots and masters of the Royal Armada of His Majesty of the Guard of the Indies and the Strait of Magellan, of which I am captain general, is the following:

[1] See above, p. 69, n. 9.

[2] Pedro de Eguino began the voyage as captain of the *nao Santa María de Begoña*. Sarmiento, *Narratives of the Voyages*, p. 220, gives his name as Aquino and indicates that he was replaced by Rodrigo de Rada when the armada reached the Cape Verde Islands. Assuming that his surname was Eguino, he may have been related to Andrés de Eguino, the accountant and overseer of the armada who was in command of the three Spanish ships at the Battle of Santos.

[3] Captain Francisco de Nevares had served for many years in Spain's transatlantic fleets and was described as a sound man and a good and noble soldier; AGI, Indiferente, leg. 739, N. 22, Report of the Council of the Indies to Philip II, 8 May 1581.

1 That the said captains, pilots and masters in their *navios* maintain and carry out my *instruccion*, and see that it is maintained and carried out, which was given to them in Spain, its date the 24th of September of the past year of 1581, as well as that in Cavo Berde, dated on the 26th of January of this year of 1582, in matters of navigation and the good order of war, as in all of the other things that are declared therein.

2 This Royal Armada, having left from this port of the Rio de Jenero, will go on a direct course toward the Estrecho de Magallanes to do in it what His Majesty orders; all the *navios* of it will follow the *capitana*, and none shall pass ahead [f. 57v] of her by day nor by night, going with much care and diligence so that they not lose [sight of] the poop lantern. And if it should happen – may God not wish it – that before arriving at the said strait the armada encounters a storm whose force blows some *navio* or *navios* off course, those *navios* shall continue the said voyage directly to the said strait, until reaching a latitude of 52 degrees and a half, where it is located. And the one that arrives first at the entrance of the said strait, which is flat land, will go ashore and leave a marker by which to recognize that it has entered. And if the armada should arrive first, it will do the same. And once entered into the said strait, the said *navio* or *navios* will wait, anchored in what seems the best and most comfortable place, so that the armada will find it. And if in the said strait there be enemies or some fort that they have made, the said *navio* or *navios* will leave and wait at the mouth of the said strait, tacking back and forth until the armada arrives. This shall be maintained and complied with, on penalty of deprivation of their offices, and for which they will be punished with rigor in conformity with their offences.

Dated in the port of the Rio de Jenero on the 3rd day of the month of October of the year 1582. By order of His Lordship Diego Florez. Pedro de Rada.

This *instruccion* was given to each one of the captains of the said armada in the city of San Sebastian of the Rio de Jenero on the 4th day of the month of October of this year of 1582.

————

[f. 58r] *Instruccion y orden* that must be maintained and complied with by the accountant Andres de Eguino, in whose charge remain the three *naos* of the Armada of His Majesty of the Strait of Magellan, of which I am captain general.[1]

1 Firstly, once I have left from this port[2] with the *naos* that go in my company, the said accountant has to gather the *naos* that remain here and ready them with their artillery, so that they can leave from this port and bay on course for the Rio de Jenero as soon as possible. And with the said *naos* he will collect all the married householders, women and children, and transport them to the said Rio de Jenero, or the port of San Vicente, and there he will disembark them on land and turn them over to the governor and justicia mayor[3] who are in the said places, so that they give them provisions and a place to stay, in conformity with the other *vecinos*.[4] The said governor or justicia mayor will not give them

---

[1] Throughout this *instrucción y ordén* for Eguino, Captain General Flores alternates between addressing him directly and referring to him in the third person, which is reflected in Rada's text. Eguino was not present when Flores dictated the *instrucción y ordén*, which may explain the linguistic confusion.

[2] The port on Santa Catarina Island.

[3] The justicia mayor was the chief judicial official.

[4] i.e. like those of the resident householders. See above, p. 58, n. 1.

licence to go to any other parts unless they are provided for, until Pedro Sarmiento or the person [he designates] comes or sends for them to populate the Strait, so that they can fulfil the intent with which they left from Spain. And once they have arrived on land in whatever port of Brasil, [Eguino] does not have to give them any more rations than for the time that they remain on this island until arriving at any of the said ports, as there are no funds to provide for them, and because the said governors will do so for having a lack of people in the said lands.

[f. 58v] 2   You must give rations to the men of war and sea in conformity with the distribution that has been done, and to provide for them, until the armada returns to the said Rio de Jenero, and for this you are to give all the necessary orders so that the said men of war and sea show good discipline so that they do not have differences with the peoples of the land, as this corresponds to the service of His Majesty, with which there should be all conformity.

3   Having left this port, the said three *naos* will go in convoy so that none among them is separated, so that if they come across some corsair they can defend themselves and attack, having collected all the men that remain, who will proceed in a very orderly manner with their arms, as they have done until now.

4   That once arrived at the said Rio de Jenero or in any other port, if the governor who is there should ask for some men to help with things touching on the service of His Majesty during the time that you are in the port, you should provide them to him to fulfil his royal duty; also, anything that serves His Majesty should be done with the greatest possible diligence and care.

5   That if having arrived at any of the said ports, any of the said *naos* is not fit to sail, [Eguino] must notify the master or the person who has the authorization of its owner, so that releasing it from service he can do [f. 59r] what he wishes with it. And the said accountant will receive the artillery and munitions and other things that belong to His Majesty, putting them in His storage facilities in a place where they be secured and guarded.

6   That if the said governors ask [Eguino] for some artillery for the defence of the said land, he should give it to them, taking sufficient recompense, which, if they do not have enough money, they and the *vezinos* of the land will pay for it from their goods.

7   Item,[1] to the extent that I carry out the design and intention of arriving at the Strait, and from there passing into the Mar del Sur in pursuit of the English corsair that is understood to have the same design as the other time,[2] and that the weather needed for that permits it, I will not be able to return very soon to the coast of Brasil. If this were to happen, having the *naos* outfitted and ready you will wait for my order for all the month of May upcoming of this year of 1583. And if in this time neither I nor an order of mine arrives, you can leave, making your voyage to the Kingdoms of Spain, not having need of the said men and *navios* for other things in the service of His Majesty that are more pressing. That this be remitted, in conformity with the weather and the opportunity, communicating it to the governor of the Rio de Jenero, or of the port where I will arrive,

---

[1] In Spanish documents, items on a list are often preceded by the word *yten/ytem* or *iten/item*, or by a stylized 'i' or 'y', in place of numbering. This list begins with a simple numbering of the items but finishes with both numbers and the word *item*. Presumably, Rada faithfully recorded Captain General Flores's dictation.

[2] The other time being Francis Drake's voyage.

that in this particular [f. 59v] you must follow the orders that the said governor will issue, these being in His Majesty's service; and being contrary to it, you will try to hinder it with all the forces you can muster, so that you follow and fulfil the service of His Majesty.[1]

8   Item, insofar as I left orders in the captaincy of San Vicente that provisions be prepared for the return of the armada, these are not to be touched nor any of them used up at any time until the end of the said month of May, when, having waited for me as is stated, you will depart from the said Rio de Jenero and go to San Vicente, and you will collect from the captain and officials of that captaincy the quantity of [provisions] that you need to go to Spain.

9   Item, because much heavy artillery remains in the said *naos* that cannot be taken to the Strait in the armada, and because carrying them to Spain would run great risk, as much from the sea as from corsairs, those that the said *naos* are not able to carry you will leave, and also the rest of the heavy bronze artillery, stored in the *almacen* of His Majesty,[2] if that is possible, or in the forts and fortified places of His Majesty, until something else be ordered. And thus you will take them from the said *navios* and leave them. And in the said *navios* you will be able to carry the cast-iron artillery that they have, as it is [f. 60r] sufficient [for *navios*] to defend themselves and to attack. In addition, you will leave in the said *almacenes* the munitions and other things that are destined for the said strait, with an official accounting for the governor and officials of the land.

10   Item, that if by chance it be known that some men from the company of Captain Gonçalo Melendez are staying in the said ports where you should arrive, you will take measures to have them punished in an exemplary manner for having risen up and mutinied from the said company, and having done things in disservice to God Our Lord and to His Majesty. You are charged to do this with much diligence and care during the time that you are in this port, as well as in the others where you will touch and will be. What you are principally charged to do is the service of Our Lord, shunning and punishing those who did these things in his disservice, as is confided to your person, giving this and the service of His Majesty your constant attention. For all of which you are given full authorized powers, which I have from His Majesty and I have given you in the title and nomination that you carry. Signed with my name, and dated in the port and island of Sancta Catalina, on the first of January of this year of 1583.

11   Item, because in the said *navios* there are men of war and sea who have not received provisions for two months, and in order to provide for the said men it is requisite that they be given their ordinary ration, you will arrange and communicate with the governors [f. 60v] of the land regarding the best way that it seems to them to provide for the said men, as well as to refit the *navios*. It is suitable and necessary that you carry some money from what there is in the *caja real*,[3] and from it should be taken seven thousand *reales* for the said effect, at the rate of two thousand and three hundred *reales* each month, which are

---

[1] Presumably, Captain General Flores was referring to orders issued by any local governor who did not support King Philip.

[2] Rada's variant is *almazen* for *almacén* (plural *almacenes*), meaning warehouse. Presumably, these were simple covered and secured buildings to protect items from the weather and from pilferage. Such structures may already have existed before the arrival of the armada, or they may have been built thereafter. Sarmiento had storehouses built during the first layover in Rio de Janeiro to store provisions and equipment for the settlement at the Strait. See above, pp. 35–6.

[3] Royal strongbox.

necessary for the rations of the men, more or less, and which the purveyor and the treasurer will hand over to you, taking it from them with the necessary care, and the chief scribe Pedro de Rada making an accounting of it, who will exercise the said office of accountant and overseer until such time as the said armada comes back together,[1] because this is suitable to the service of His Majesty. By order of His Lordship Diego Florez. Pedro de Rada, chief scribe.

This *instruccion* was given to the accountant Andres de Eguino at the island and port of Sancta Catalina on the 5th day of the month of January of 1583.

———

What was agreed about the departure of Don Alonso de Sotomayor to the Rio de la Platta at a latitude of thirty-three degrees and one-third, and the *instruccion* that was given him, which is as follows:

On the *fragata Sancta Ysavel* at a latitude of thirty-three degrees and one-third near the Rio de la Platta on the nineteenth day of the month of January of 1583 years, the very illustrious lord General Diego Florez de Valdes; [f. 61r] Don Alonso de Sotomayor, governor and captain general of the provinces of Chile; Pedro Sarmiento de Gamboa; and Diego de la Rivera, almirante of the said armada, met together. And the said lord general proposed that, since on the 17th past off the Rio de la Platta at its latitude, the weather produced a *travesia*, and it was necessary to change course and go back out to sea in order not to be wrecked on this coast; and they well knew the plan by which the *galeaza*, and the *nao corça*,[2] and the *nao Sancta Maria del Pasaje*, and the *nao Maria de Villaviciosa* and three *fragatas* left from Sancta Catalina in order to enter into the said river[3] and to leave the said lord Don Alonso there with his men to continue their journey from there, leaving the *nao corça* and *Sancta Maria de Buen Pasaje* with the said lord Don Alonso, and taking the *nao Trenidad* with them to continue the voyage. And now the time is so advanced that if all the armada were to enter into the said river, it would risk being lost, especially the *galeaza*, there not being enough water for it to go upriver. And if the *galeaza capitana* were to be lost it would be a great misfortune, because this is the season ruled by winds from the south-south-east, which are *travesias* in the said river and have already begun to blow.[4] We are near the coast, and they should consider whether we should enter into the said river with the *galeaza* and *fragatas* and wait until the *nao Trenidad* unloads in order to bring her with us, or if the said lord Don Alonso should go from here [f. 61v] with the *nao corça* and the *nao Sancta Maria del Pasaje* and the *Trenidad*, which carry all of his men, because it is not possible to unload the *nao Trenidad* here, though it is [possible] in the said river.

After having considered the one possibility and the other, they were in accord that the said lord Don Alonso, without losing time, should go to the said Rio de la Platta and continue his journey by land to Chile, and that he should take the three *naos* that carried his men, and that after they arrived at Buenos Ayres, or at the place where it was most

---

[1] In other words, Rada took over Eguino's titles and functions for the armada's second attempt at the Strait.

[2] i.e. the *nao Santa Catalina*. See above, p. 104.

[3] i.e. the Río de la Plata.

[4] In other words, with winds from the south-south-east prevailing, the ships might not be able to sail back out of the Río de la Plata.

convenient to do so, he should send the said *nao Trenidad* with all the rigging and munitions that were going to the Estrecho de Magallanes to the Rio de Jenero in the said *nao*, so that with them the other [ships] that remain there can be outfitted. The said *nao corça* and the *Sancta Maria del Pasaje* need to be cut down in order to ascend upriver, and they have no need of more than one cable and anchor each to do so, and only what rigging is needed for the foremast and mizzen. And with the said *galeaza* and three *fragatas* and the *nao Maria de Villaviciosa*, the voyage to the Strait will proceed; and that the lord general should give Pero Diaz de Lagos,[1] the pilot who came in the *almiranta* whom he brings with him, mindful that he is the most skilled in this armada for the said river, to the said lord Don Alonso de Sotomayor to bring him upriver and place him there.

And they agreed upon this *parecer*[2] and they signed it with their names: Diego Florez, Don Alonso de SSotomayor [*sic*], Pedro Sarmiento de Gamboa.[3]

[f. 62r] The *instruccion y orden* that the lord Don Alonso de Sotomayor has to maintain and carry out with the three *naos* that he brings in his company in which he carries his men who are going to the provinces of Chile, is the following:

1   That he enter into the Rio de la Platta with the *nao corça*, *Sancta Maria de Buen Pasaje*, and the *nao Trenidad* in the part and place where with the greatest convenience the artillery can be unloaded that travels in the *nao corça* and *Sancta Maria de Buen Pasaje* and all the munitions that were going for the Estrecho de Magallanes; and that he load it and the rest that came for this purpose onto the *nao Trenidad* to take to the Rio de Jenero.

2   Item, that if it be necessary to make *chatas* and *rasas*[4] from the *nao corça* and the *Sancta Maria de Buen Pasaje* to go from Buenos Ayres to Sancta Fee up the river, it can be done to accommodate his men, as the *navios* that remain would draw less water and can pass through the shallows; and doing thus, they have no need to carry more than one cable and anchor each, so that the others on the said *naos* he should load on the said *Trenidad* and send them to the Rio de Jenero to serve the other *naos* that have urgent need of them. And this the said lord Don Alonso de Sotomayor will do, taking into consideration that

---

[1] Pedro Díaz (variant Pero Diez), a Portuguese pilot with experience of Brazil, the Río de la Plata, and points south. He was often identified with Lagos, presumably his town of origin on Portugal's southern coast, to distinguish him from other men with the common name Pero or Pedro Díaz.

[2] In this document, Rada records the unanimous *parecer* (opinion) of the men present at the meeting. Elsewhere in another consultation (see below, pp. 145–9) he records statements by individuals more or less in their own words. This form of record was standard practice for official consultations. For example, the same form appears in the minutes of the various royal councils whenever the king asked its members to comment on a proposal or a range of alternative actions.

[3] Unless Rada is in error, Almirante Rivera did not sign the accord, possibly because the transfer of Pedro Díaz de Lagos would deprive him and his vessel of the pilot most experienced with that part of the coast. Sarmiento took part in the consultations and signed the *parecer*, but he would later write that Sotomayor had abandoned the expedition against the king's orders and that none of the actions should have happened without his consent, continuing the delusion that he shared command of the armada. He also claimed that he held firm against various efforts to persuade him to abort the plantation of the colony, and there is no reason to doubt that claim; Sarmiento, *Viajes al Estrecho*, vol. 1, pp. 269–73.

[4] The words *chatas* (Rada's variant *chattas*) and *rasa* refer to flat-bottomed lighters and rafts, used in shallow waters. They were to be made from the cut-down *naos*.

if he can accommodate his men without cutting down the said *nao*, in particular the said *nao corça*, that he will do so, because *Sancta Maria de Buen Pasaje* is not destined to return and would be useful only for this. It would not be ideal to take apart the other unless all else fails, because the present enterprise has need of it.

[f. 62v] 3   Item, that the iron that is carried in the said *nao Trenidad* he should send in it, as it is among the things that came consigned for the Strait and it would not be justifiable to use it for anything else.

4   Item, that he will send the masters of the *naos* that he brings with him to give an accounting to His Majesty regarding the things that they have received, and an official account and reckoning of what he will transfer to the said *nao Trenidad*, sending a duplicate account of what he will transfer.

5   And having transferred the aforesaid to the said *nao*, he should hand it over to her master, and Pero Diaz[1] will return in it to go to the said Rio de Jenero, where he will find my order. And if when there he does not find it, he will go on the return voyage to Spain.

All of what is said and contained in this *instruccion*, I order Captain Çubietta[2] to carry out and follow, and I order him to hand it over to the lord Don Alonso, so that it be thus complied with. I order all the men of sea and war who sail in the said *navio* to obey [Zubieta] and hold him as their captain, and in his absence, the person that the said lord Don Alonso will name. Dated on the *fragata Sancta Ysavel* on the 19th of January of the year 1583. Diego Florez.

I, Don Alonso de Sotomayor, state that I received the copy of this *instruccion* and it is carried with me. Don Alonso de Sotomayor.

———

Instruccion y orden that the alcaide Tomas Gari must maintain and carry out in the fort named Sancta Maria Madalena that is being built for His Majesty in the port of the town of Sanctos, captaincy of San Vicente, of which he is the alcaide by my nomination, and by virtue of the title that he holds from His Majesty as alcaide of one of the forts that have to be made in Magallanes,[3] which is as follows:

Alcaide Tomas Gari

[f. 63r] 1   That the said alcaide Tomas Gari make haste with the fabrication of the said fort, so that it be finished with suitable dispatch, having the officers as well as the soldiers that are to remain in it work; and see that the Indians and other persons from the land[4] come and work on the said fort, doing everything with all diligence that he can, attending with his own person without neglecting a single point, as thus is fitting.

---

[1] i.e. Pero Díaz de Lagos, the Portuguese pilot.

[2] Don Alonso de Sotomayor evidently returned to the *nao corza Santa Catalina* after the meeting on 19 Jan. 1583 to prepare for departure. After Captain General Flores wrote the *instruccion y orden* for the contingent going to the Río de la Plata, Captain Martín de Zubieta, owner and captain of *La Trinidad*, came to the *fragata Santa Isabel* to collect it.

[3] With authority from the king, the duke of Medina Sidonia had appointed Garri as alcaide (see above, p. 60) for one of the forts to be built in the Strait; AMN, MS 496, f. 104v, Philip II to Medina Sidonia, 29 Oct. 1581.

[4] Presumably, the land close to the future fort.

2   That he not allow the soldiers to leave the said fort, nor to be absent, nor consent for them to go to the *estancias* or grazing lands, for the harm that they will do in them. And that he have them and all the other men and officials well disciplined and instructed, and see that they comport themselves well with the people of the land. And that he punish with rigour anyone who is rebellious and gives cause, and render justice by virtue of the said title that he holds from His Majesty, without giving occasion for revolts or other scandals with the said people settled on the land, because their friendship and confederation has such importance.

3   That the soldiers and sailors and any other men of the armada who may have fled from it and absented themselves, and are named on a list like the others,[1] he should capture and hold in the said fort, to work on it and serve in the garrison like the others who are being left there. And who seem guilty of having fled [royal service] he should condemn for the time that seems appropriate to him as *gastadores*[2] of the said fort; and likewise, that he should gather the sick who remain from the said armada in this captaincy, and that they serve like the others in the said fort.[3]

[f. 63v] 4   That with the soldiers who now remain in the said fort, and those who fled and the sick who are in this captaincy, there will be one hundred soldiers, who must serve continuously as the garrison in the said fort without absenting themselves, unless there is need for some of them to make an expedition inland against *Indios de paz* who might rise up,[4] or for anything else in the service of His Majesty. The said alcaide Tomas Gari can supply a squadron of the said soldiers for that said purpose or those that seem appropriate to him, retaining in the said fort those for its defence.

5   For what touches upon the work of the said fort and other things that have to be done and to provide for them, he should communicate and deal with the governor Geronimo Leiton, in whose charge remain the things that have to be provided for the said fort; and between them they should maintain good friendship and confederation, since all that has to be expended and done has to be accounted for and certified by both of them. And His Majesty will be well served by good correspondence between them, and very ill-served by the contrary, since from their friendship redounds that of the said fort with all the people of this captaincy.

6   That the rations that are to be given to the soldiers, officials and workers in the said fort remain under the *instruccion* of Melchior de Acosta, almojarife,[5] who has to distribute the provisions that are required for this armada, which he will view and ensure they are given as ordered, so that they lack nothing; and he must [f. 64 r] receive into account all that shall be given by certification of the said alcaide Tomas Gari and of Geronimo Leiton, until such time as His Majesty provides what is most suitable for the the [*sic*] said fort.

---

[1] The phrasing seems to refer not only to the mutineers from the company of Captain Gonzalo Meléndez, but also to any other soldiers or sailors who subsequently failed to appear at musters.

[2] *Gastadores* is a term that can be applied to forced labourers, working without pay.

[3] Rada presumably means the sick from the armada who were sent ashore to be cured.

[4] Based on European legal precedent, *Indios de paz* (Indians of peace) were defined as those that had been conquered or had otherwise made peace with European invaders. If they subsequently rebelled, it was considered a just war to proceed against them. See Zavala, *Instituciones jurídicas*, pp. 97, 441, 445.

[5] An almojarife was a collector of royal taxes but the person appointed could act in other capacities dealing with wages, rations, or other items that required enumeration and accounting. In this instance, he served as the official middleman to ensure that the rations were given to the men.

7   That if the *casados*[1] left in this captaincy who are going to the Estrecho de Magallanes as settlers be needed to work on the said fort, he will meet with the said Geronimo Leiton and they will have them come to work on the said fort. And those who work thus will be given their rations like the other men of the said fort on the days that they work.

The said *instruccion* will be maintained and complied with as stated. Dated on the *galeaza San Xptobal* on the twenty-sixth day of the month of April of the year 1583. On order of His Lordship Diego Florez. Pedro de Rada.

I, Tomas Gari, alcaide for His Majesty in the fort named Santa Maria Madalena, received the original of this *instruccion* from the hand of Pedro de Rada, chief scribe, signed by the lord General Diego Florez, and I affirm I signed my name the said day. Tomas Gari. Pedro de Rada

By *instruccion* to Melchior de Acosta, almojarife, the ration that he has to give to the soldiers of this fort and those who work on it is one *alquer* of flour to each one per month, and three days of meat in the week, recorded in the account book for each one, until something else be provided. This order is left to the same alcaide Tomas Garri.

[64v] Report of the artillery, arms and munitions from the armada of His Majesty that went to the Estrecho de Magallanes that were sent to the alcaide Tomas Gari in the port of Sanctos for the fort named La Magadalena that is being made, which is the following:

Artillery:

1   Firstly, one bronze half saker,[2] round,[3] of a weight of up to nine *quintales*, which has a shield with the royal arms and the *tuson*[4] as a border and two serpents as handles, with its gun carriage.[5]

1   One bronze assault cannon,[6] round, which has the royal arms of His Majesty with the imperial crown[7] and as a border the tuson and two dolphins as handles, which weighs from 45 to 50 *quintales*, with its boxes for shot and wheels rimmed in iron.

---

[1] *Casados* were settled householders. In Portuguese colonies, the term was generally applied to Portuguese men married to indigenous wives. In this instance, the word seems to apply to the married householders who came from Spain, but it may have included male settlers who married indigenous wives while awaiting transport to the Strait.

[2] A *medio sacre* (half saker) was a gun firing balls of 5–7 *libras*. See 'Weights, Measures, and Currency'.

[3] With a round barrel.

[4] A *tusón* (*toisón de oro*) was the emblem of the Order of the Golden Fleece, represented by a golden chain and a pendant of the head and fleece of a merino ram. The kings of Spain were members of this order as descendants of the dukes of Burgundy. The emblem identified an item, often a piece of artillery, as the property of the crown.

[5] The word for gun carriage was *encabalgamiento*.

[6] An assault cannon for battering walls (*cañón de batir*) generally fired balls of about 32 *libras*. The armada presumably carried it in case it had to attack fortifications made by the French or English in Brazil or the Strait.

[7] The imperial crown suggests that this gun was made in the time of Philip II's father, Charles V of the Holy Roman Empire (King Charles I of Spain).

1   One bronze half saker, round, which has some serpents as handles and a stamp of 15 *quintales*, 2 *arrobas*, and 8 *libras* weight, and a plaque that says Francisco Duarte and some lettering that says 1578, with its gun carriage without rims [on the wheels].

1   Another bronze half saker, round, which has a shield without arms[1] and which seems to weigh as much as the one above; and it has a *balazo*[2] in the rear and one handle, with its gun carriage.

2   Another two bronze half sakers, octagonal,[3] each weighing from eleven to twelve *quintales*; and one has a shield in relief without arms, and the other a shield without arms and not in relief, and both have their gun carriages.

1   One half saker of wrought iron[4] which weighs 730 *libras*, and some lettering in figures that says 1578.[5]

2   Two sakers[6] of wrought iron, with their gun carriages.

9 pieces

[f. 65r] ~ Three loaders or scoops[7] of copper for the said three pieces;
    ~ One loader of copper on a shaft;
    ~ Five blocks and four shafts, for gun rammers;[8]
    ~ One shot extractor[9] on a shaft;
    ~ One hundred balls of wrought iron, forty for sakers, and sixty for half sakers;
    ~ Twenty balls of wrought iron for a falcon;[10]
    ~ Twenty balls of iron of twenty-six *libras* each;
    ~ Forty balls of iron for half sakers;
    ~ Thirteen *quintales* and one *aroba* of gunpowder, contained in thirteen wooden barrels;
    ~ Two hundred and eighty-eight *libras* of lead in chunks;
    ~ Three hundred and sixty-five *libras* of match-cord for harquebuses;
    ~ One barrel of saltpeter;
    ~ Forty campaign pikes[11] with their iron fittings;

---

[1] i.e. without a coat of arms.

[2] i.e. a mark left on an object hit with a cannon ball. The single handle also suggests that the gun had been damaged in battle, as it would have been very difficult to manoeuvre without a second handle.

[3] i.e. with an octagonal barrel.

[4] *Hierro colado* (wrought iron) is an alloy of iron ore and slag with a lower carbon content than cast iron. It is more ductile and more suitable for weaponry than cast iron and cheaper but less durable than bronze.

[5] Rada's phrase is *en guarismo*, presumably meaning the Arabic figures for 1578, rather than the words or Roman numerals.

[6] A *sacre* (saker) was a gun that fired shot of 7–10 *libras*.

[7] A *cargador* (loader) or *cuchara* (spoon or ladle) in this context was a metal scoop affixed to a shaft and used to scrape the residue from inside a gun's barrel between shots and to measure and place the powder in the bore. The scoop had to fit properly inside the barrel of the gun, and its fabrication was one of the most important skills that a gunner had to learn.

[8] An *atacador* (rammer) was a *zoquete* (cylindrical block) affixed to an *asta* (shaft), used to ram the powder, wad, and shot firmly into the bore. The diameter of the rammer had to fit properly inside the bore.

[9] *Saca pelota* (shot extractor).

[10] A *falcón* (falcon), was a small gun that fired shot weighing 3–4 *libras*.

[11] A *pica de campaña* (campaign pike) was a long pole with an iron spear on the end, used by infantrymen for thrusting, not throwing, at an enemy.

~ Fifty-seven large mattocks and adzes,[1] fifty with their irons, and seven with open mouth;

~ Fifty iron shovels;

~ Nine long iron bars,[2] three of them small;

~ Six iron wedges to break up large rocks;

~ Four sledgehammers;[3]

~ Twenty-three metal plates[4] for the said effect;

[f. 65v] ~ Two picks[5] for the said effect;

~ Twenty-one iron picks for stone workers;

~ Six hatchets for cutting;

~ Five *arrobas* and two *libras* of unworked iron in three bars;

~ Twenty-seven *arrobas* and twenty-two *libras* of unworked iron in plates and chunks;

~ Plus eight *arrobas* of steel;

~ Twenty buckets for water, each one with two iron bands;

~ Two linen flags of the sort that serve on the topmasts of the *capitana* and *almiranta*, with the royal arms of His Majesty on one side and the other;

~ Six large barrels, each one with ten iron bands.

All of the things named and declared above, I the said alcaide, Tomas Gari, received from the royal officials of the armada of His Majesty, and all the aforesaid were listed in its royal books. And as I am satisfied and have received the aforesaid, I signed my name, being present as witnesses Pedro Dessquibel and Bartolome de Bracamonte. Tomas Gari. Before me, Pedro de Rada.

———

What was agreed upon on the *galeaza capitana* on the fifth of December of the year 1582, the armada being hove to at a latitude of 35 degrees, with the *pareceres* of the governors Don Alonso[6] and Pedro Sarmiento and the captains and pilots of the said armada, that it would seek port, which is as follows:[7]

[*margin:* Arrived at the latitude of 35 degrees] On the *galeaza Sam Xptoval, capitana* of the armada of His Majesty that is going to the Estrecho de Magallanes, being hove to with all sails lowered, at a latitude of 35 degrees. Having come to the said *galeaza*, the lords Don Alonso [f. 66r] de Sotomayor and Governor Pedro Sarmiento; and Diego de

---

[1] An *azadón* was a large mattock or adze, used mainly for shaping wood. The mattock typically had two sides to the head, one that came to a spike, and the other that formed a curved blade, which Rada refers to as *sus yeros/hierros* (their irons). The adze typically had only the curved blade, which Rada refers to as *con boca abierta* (with open mouth).

[2] A *palanca* was a long iron bar for levering out rocks and other tasks.

[3] An *almádena* was a sledgehammer.

[4] *Hojas* (lit., leaves or plates); presumably, these were replacement fittings for the tools designed to break up rocks.

[5] A *camartillo* was a pick with two sharp points at the end of a shaft. Each tool weighed 10–12 *libras* and was used for stonework in construction.

[6] Don Alonso de Sotomayor, governor-designate of Chile.

[7] In this document, Rada records the *pareceres* (opinions) of the men present at the meeting, more or less in their own words; this was standard practice for official consultations. For example, the same form appears in the minutes of the various royal councils whenever the king asked its members to comment on a proposal or a range of alternative actions.

la Rivera, almirante; and some captains and pilots of the said armada, General Diego Florez de Baldes said to them and proposed that the violent weather and storms that the armada had experienced for more than twenty days had not diminished until this day, Wednesday the fifth of December, when the weather slackened a bit, although always contrary; and that already they knew that the *nao Sanestevan* had been lost, without being able to aid her with the heavy storm; and that some of the *naos* of the armada had been complaining that they would go to the bottom because of the quantity of water that they had taken on, and that if they had to do much more against the sea, they would be lost without remedy; and that in order to determine how best to fulfil the service of His Majesty, it seems to me that those who find themselves here should say what seems to them should be done to execute what is important to His royal service and for the security of this armada. And they said the following:

[*margin:* Gaspar Madera; Captain Jodar; Escobar] The pilot Gaspar Madera[1] of the *nao Santa Maria del Pasaje* said that his *nao* was not fit to sail, because it is opened up at the prow, and that for many days it had been held together with turnbuckles,[2] and they had lightened up the *nao* of many things, and that the majority of the provisions had gotten wet, and that it is impossible to be able to continue the voyage; and that if the *nao* does not reach the first available port it will be lost. The same [f. 66v] say Captain Jodar and the pilot Escobar, who came on the same *nao*. And they signed it with their names: Luis de Jodar Alferez,[3] Gaspar Madera, Juan Escobar, before me, Pedro de Rada, chief scribe.

[*margin:* Diego de Olavari;[4] Antonio Rodriguez] The pilot Antonio Rodriguez and the captain and master Diego de Olabari of the *nao corça Sancta Catalina* say that the said *nao* sails very laboriously[5] and was taking on much water below decks, and is not in a condition to be able to continue the voyage, nor to continue at all if first it does not enter a port and be repaired; and thus it makes sense that the said *nao* enter the nearest port and be repaired. And if it must sail thus, it seems to them that the said *nao* cannot continue the voyage; and also because the *nao* is very old, in continuing the voyage it will be lost, and this is how it seems to them. And they signed their names: Antonio Rodriguez, Diego de Olavari, before me, Pedro de Rada.

[*margin:* Captain Çubietta] Captain Martin de Çubietta of the *nao Trenidad* said that the aforesaid, his galleon, with respect to being a new *nao* and on its first voyage, until now has been able to withstand all the storms, although with much travail, because it has always been aided by the continual use of the pumps to remove the large amount of water that collects in the hull. And in order to remedy this totally, they lack tar and oakum and are without a skilled calafate.[6] And regarding the rigging, they lack much, [f. 67r] especially sails, because some of them have been ripped apart and ruined with

---

[1] At the start of the voyage, Gaspar Madera was alférez on the *Santa María de Buen Pasaje*; he then replaced Juan de Sagasti as pilot of that ship; see Appendix 1.

[2] In extreme situations at sea, the crew would attach cables to each side of the hull, twisting and tightening them like a turnbuckle (*tortor*) and literally holding the ship together against the forces of nature.

[3] See above, p. 69, n. 9.

[4] Diego de Olabarri. The surname is common in Vizcaya.

[5] The phrase used was '*b/va muy trabajada*'.

[6] A calafate (caulker) was responsible for hammering twists of tow or oakum in the seams between the planks of the hull. Anyone can do the job but it takes a skilled calafate to do it properly.

the adverse events that have occurred; and despite all this, the *nao* is fit to withstand its travails, as the water that it is collecting can be dealt with; and that most of the flour has gotten wet, so that it cannot be eaten nor used; and that there are few provisions that it has been assigned for the voyage to Chile; and he considers it impossible to remedy the water taken on without arriving at a port where it can be done. And this is what seems to him. And he signed it with his name, Martin de Çubietta, before me, Pedro de Rada.

[*margin:* Rodrigo de Rada] Captain Rodrigo de Rada of the said *nao Begoña*[1] says that the aforesaid, his *nao*, where he sails as captain, is taking on much water through all the decks and joints and seams, which are all loose. And the wales[2] on the outside of the hull are coming apart at the joins, and the same at the *amuras*.[3] And for this reason, given the storms that it has passed through, it is not fit to sail nor to continue onward without taking port, for being so opened up; and it cannot be repaired at sea, and it would mean risking it and losing the men with some storm if it were forced to go onward. And thus it seems to him suitable to take port in order to be able to repair her, having to complete the voyage. And this is what seems to him, and that if there were to be other weather like what they have had, the *nao* and men would be lost. And he signed it with his name, Rodrigo de Rada, before me, Pedro de Rada.

[*margin:* Pedro Diaz] The pilot Pero Diez[4] of the *nao almiranta* says that it is taking on water through all its upper works, and that having heavy weather it cannot be steered, and that is what he has [to say] and nothing else. And he signed it with his name, Pero Diaz, before me, Pedro de Rada.

[*margin:* the captain Gregorio de las Alas; Rodrigo de Mora] The pilot Rodrigo de Mora, who sails on the *nao La Concepcion*, whose captain is Gregorio de las Alas, says that the said *nao* is opened up at the prow and has spit out all the oakum from beneath the wales; and the *madre del espolon*[5] is broken, and one joint behind the mainmast has broken because of the rolling, and all the planks on the poop deck near the rudder have lost their nails with the force that the rudder has made. And every time it rolls, the whole *nao* from the prow to the mainmast opens up a finger's width on both sides to about half a *braza* below the water line. At the aft quarter of the hull, about half a *braza* of the seam has spit out its oakum, and with violent weather it cannot be steered, and that with more of the least of the weather that we have had in the past, the *nao* and men will be lost. And thus it makes sense to reach the first available port to repair it. The same was said by the said captain Gregorio de las Alas, and they signed it with their names: Gregorio de las Alas, Rodrigo de Mora, before me, Pedro de Rada.

[*margin:* The lord Don Alonso de Sotomayor] The lord Don Alonso de Sotomayor says that seeing what the pilots and captains of the *naos* say, and particularly of the four *naos* that carry the men in his charge, and the lack of victuals that there is, and the scant confidence regarding the weather, and the large [storms] that they have had,

---

[1] *Santa María de Begoña.*

[2] Wales (*cintas*), were strips of thick wood affixed to the outside of the planking to reinforce the hull.

[3] On Spanish ships, the *amuras* denoted the point at each side of the hull where the planking began to narrow toward the prow, generally about one-eighth the length of the ship, measured from the prow.

[4] Pedro Díaz de Lagos, see above, pp. 27, 140–41.

[5] The *madre del espolón* was the principal supporting timber of the beak-head, the forward projection of the hull at the prow of the ship.

and what the [f. 68r] lord Captain General Diego Florez proposes to him, this is his opinion:

That the said lord captain general and all the armada ought to gather and enter the first port that they can. And there his lordship will be able to see and confer more particularly about the damage to the said *naos* and to compare the timetable with the victuals and munitions; and according to what he will find about the one and the other, he will be able to decide what he ought to do. And the *naos* that seem to him able to proceed to the Strait should be refitted and reinforced from the others that will be left [behind], as they have to undergo much travail in going and coming. And the others that remain can return to the port of Brasil that seems to his lordship most suitable for them to be of service to guard that coast, in conformity with the dispatches from His Majesty. And for the Strait, lacking the things that were lost with the equipment on the *nao* of Ariola,[1] and the others that have been jettisoned, and the shortage of victuals, it will be appropriate to transport only the people who can be sustained with the provisions that remain. And regarding what concerns him and the men in his charge, the lord general will see what is most suitable to accomplish the service of His Majesty, and between the two of them they will decide upon what is most suitable to the service of His Majesty. And thus he asked and required of the said lord general, and he signed his name, Don Alonso de Sotomayor, before me, Pedro de Rada.

[*margin*: Pedro Sarmiento] The lord governor Pedro Sarmiento, responding to what the lord general Diego Florez [f. 68v] de Baldes has proposed about the necessity and deficiencies of this armada to carry out the voyage to the Strait, or to take other more expedient means to save the armada and serve His Majesty, says that he has seen what this armada has suffered since it left from the Rio de Jenero on course to the said strait, and has seen that from 35 degrees and a half until 38 degrees it has always run into violent storms and weather contrary to what is needed to carry it to the Strait, in such a manner that, although his lordship the lord general has done all that has been humanly possible, repairing it and making sail strongly like a good mariner, for which reason and for the damage that the *naos* have received in losing their rigging as well as discovering leaks and lacking all the rigging necessary to sail, without which it is impossible to navigate, it has not been possible to go onward. And in order to remedy these needs, it was necessary to turn around to reach a lesser latitude, in order to find milder weather and to be able to make repairs. And at present, being in fair and calm weather, some *naos* are in danger of going to the bottom because of the amount of water they have taken on, and each day more leaks are discovered; and for the common good and the service of His Majesty, it seems to him that, his lordship being served, that he should order that this armada try to reach the nearest port between the Cavo de Sancta Maria, which is the Rio [f. 69r] de la Plata, to San Vicente and the Rio de Jenero. And among these, the closest would be to take the Rio de la Platta; and having arrived there, the said lord general will be able to decide what is most suitable to the service of His Majesty in the matter of the Strait, as well as that of Chile; and that in all this he is ready to do the service of His Majesty and that which the said lord general will order him. And this is his opinion, and he signed it with his name, Pedro Sarmiento, before me, Pedro de Rada, chief scribe.

---

[1] i.e. the *San Esteban* of Arriola.

148

[*margin:* Don Luis de Sotomayor] The lord Don Luis de Sotomayor,[1] jointly with the said lord general and Don Alonso de Sotomayor and Pedro Sarmiento, says that he defers in everything to what they have said and what seems to the lords Diego Florez de Valdes and Don Alonso de Sotomayor and Pedro Sarmiento, because it is the most certain and suitable to the service of His Majesty; and he signed it with his name, Don Luis de Sotomayor, before me, Pedro de Rada.

[*margin:* Diego de la Rivera] The lord almirante Diego de la Rivera says that the opinions of the lords Don Alonso de Sotomayor and P[ed]ro Sarmiento are suitable to carry out to achieve the service of His Majesty, and that he says the same. And he signed it with his name, Diego de la Rivera, before me, Pedro de Rada.

[*margin:* Andres de Eguino; Pedro Desquibel] The lord accountant and overseer, Andres de Eguino, and Pedro Desquibel, treasurer, say the same as the said lords Don Alonso de Sotomayor and Pedro [f. 69v] Sarmiento, because it is what conforms to the service of His Majesty and the security of the said armada; and they signed it with their names, Andres de Eguino, Pedro Desquibel. Pedro de Rada.

[*margin:* Auto[2] with resolution of going to port] And the said lord general, having considered the said *pareceres* and declarations, and Antom Pablo, chief pilot, and Juan Ramos, captain adviser,[3] being of the same *acuerdo* and *parecer*, they resolved to go sailing on course toward the Rio de la Platta or the port that could be reached. And they signed it with their names: Diego Florez, Antom Pablo, Juan Ramos, before me, Pedro de Rada, chief scribe, which I certify that the aforesaid was in concordance with the original, which is in my authority.[4]

The proposal by General Diego Florez in the Rio de Jenero on the 13th of May [1583] about the five *navios* that remained there in order to return to the Strait of Magallanes, and the *paraceres* of Governor Pedro Sarmiento and Don Diego de Alzega and the almirantes and royal officials of the armada are as follows:

Diego Florez de Baldes, comendador of Oreja and captain general of the Royal Armada of His Majesty of the Guard of the Indies, the Coasts of Brasill and the Strait of Magallanes, etc., I state that inasmuch as I left from this port of the Rio de Jenero on the 2nd day of the month of November of the past year of 1582 with fifteen *naos* of the armada and one *bergantin*[5] on course toward the Strait of Magallanes; and sailing from a latitude of 25 degrees [f. 70r] to 38, I always had contrary weather; and being in

---

[1] Don Luis was the brother of Don Alonso de Sotomayor. He would later accompany the latter's contingent to the Río de la Plata and be responsible for conducting the troops upriver and then overland to Chile. He would return to Spain as a maestre de campo (campmaster) in 1589 to recruit additional troops for the ongoing wars in Chile, Navarrete, *Colección de documentos,* vol. 20, ff. 184v–185r; AGI, Indiferente, leg. 541, lib. 1, f. 75v.

[2] An *auto* was an official statement of an act, often recording the outcome of a consultation; in this case a statement of the agreement to seek port.

[3] Rada's phrase is 'capitán consejero', indicating Ramos's rank and his role as adviser or councillor to the chief pilot.

[4] After the others had signed their individual statements, Rada certified, on his authority as chief scribe of the armada, that Captain General Flores and the two principal pilots of the armada agreed to head for a port.

[5] See above, pp. 8, n. 1, 77, n. 1.

that place[1] on the 29th of this said month, the wind began to blow so strongly from the south-west with a destructive storm that the *nao* of Arriola,[2] in which Jhoan Gutierez de Palomar sailed as captain, went to the bottom the next day Friday at night, without being able to assist her, and more than 250 persons who had travelled in her drowned. And with the force of the wind and sea, it was necessary to turn back until reaching a latitude of 35 degrees, where in this place, Wednesday the fifth of December, I took an *acuerdo y parecer* with Don Alonso de Sotomayor and Governor Pedro Sarmiento and the Almirante Diego de la Rivera, and some captains and pilots about what ought to be done. And all shared the *acuerdo y parecer* that [the armada] should make for the first port that it could reach, in order to repair the *naos*, some of which were taking on so much water that they were not able to be repaired more at sea. And thus I was forced to come to the port of Sancta Catalina.

And before arriving there I encountered a trading bark that was going to the Rio de la Platta with some friars, and in it sailed Don Francisco de Vera, and they gave me a report that three English *navios* had seized them in the port of Don Rodrigo, and that they were going on course toward the said Rio de la Platta. And this being known, [the armada] arrived at the said port of Sancta Catalina; and I repaired the armada with all [f. 70v] the brevity that I could, and I left from [that port] on a course toward the Strait and the Rio de la Platta on the seventh of January of this year, with eight *navios de armada*; and I left in the said port[3] the accountant Andres de Eguino with three *naos*, so that with them he should come to this port[4] and to that of San Vicente and secure this coast, in case the said corsair should return to these parts. And sailing to a latitude of 34 degrees and a half, near the mouth of the Rio de la Platta, Saturday the 19th of the said month of January, I held a consultation about what should be done. And it was agreed that the said Don Alonso de Sotomayor should go to the Rio de la Plata with three *naos* from the armada in which he carried all of his men, thus to disembark them and to go overland to Chile; and if the enemy should be in the said Rio to attack them and defend themselves from them, as he brought sufficient men and *navios* for it. And thus I sent him off, giving him orders about what he had to do.

And with the five *navios* that remained to me I sailed on course toward the Estrecho de Magallanes, and I arrived on Sunday the 17th of February of this year, in the morning. And entering into it more than four or five leagues, at midday, having just taken the latitude at 52 degrees and two-thirds, the wind began to blow so hard from the west and east-south-west [*sic*][5] that with all sails down and hove to, this weather blew us more than 50 or 60 leagues back out to sea from the said strait. [f. 71r] And I returned to attempt it another two times, and being at its latitude and seeing it, I braved the same storms, exerting all the forces that were possible to me in order to be able to enter it, until Sunday the 24th of February, when, at dawn the *nao Maria*[6] did not appear. And with the unleashed force of the storm and the wind west-south-west, the armada was forced to

---

[1] i.e. at 38°S.

[2] The *San Esteban* owned by Arriola.

[3] i.e. Santa Catarina.

[4] i.e. Rio de Janeiro.

[5] The text says *essudueste* (east-south-west), which is surely an error. Rada's *Relación* (f. 23r) says west-south-west.

[6] i.e. *María de Villaviciosa*.

turn around seeking port, because it could not hold out any longer,[1] and the weather was very extreme and kept worsening, and the provisions were running out. And thus I came with contrary weather to a latitude of 41 degrees, Thursday the 7th of March, when the *fragata Sancta Ysavel* lost the large iron fittings of the rudder. And that night, the *galeaza* and the *fragata Magdalena* separated from me, and they came to the port of San Vicente, and I remained with the two *fragatas Sancta Ysavel* and *Sancta Catalina*, refitting the rudder.[2] And with much travail and lack of food and drink, I arrived at the port of San Vicente on the 17th of April, where I found the other *naos* from the armada. And having done what was appropriate there, and leaving the fort that is being made in the port of Sanctos in order with the men necessary, which the accountant Andres de Eguino began after defeating and routing the two English galleons that were there,[3] I left from the said port with seven *navios* on Monday the 29th of April. [f. 71v] And I entered into this port Thursday, the 9th of this month of May, where I found the lord Don Diego de Alcega, who with orders from His Majesty has arrived in this port with four *naos de armada* with provisions and other things for this armada, who for days has been waiting for me.[4]

And having seen the packets that were brought to me from His Majesty, and the provisions that are here, and the equipment and other things that have remained from what was carried for the said strait, which is very little for the sustenance of all this armada, it has seemed to me that from the seven *navios de armada* with which I entered into this port; and with the *nao Trenidad*, which is one of the three *naos* that carried the said Don Alonso de Sotomayor, which came from the Rio de la Platta and entered this day, Monday the 13th of this month, and the four *naos* that are here under the charge of the said lord Don Diego de Alcega, that five *navios* should be selected that are the best and most fit and appropriate to return to the said Strecho de Magallanes with the men for the garrison, officials, settlers, and supplies that are to remain in the said strait. These *navios* will be sufficient to carry [everything], given the accounting made of the munitions and men that have to travel in them, and considering the provisions that they will be eating for all the time they will be here and until arriving at the said strait, and to leave provisions for a year for the people that will remain there, and to repair and refit these *navios*. And from those that are not fit [f. 72r] to go on the said journey, the oldest *nao* should be broken up, so that from the cables, anchors, rigging, and other things, and sending to the Baya for tar and other things, careening can be done to the said five *navios* that remain. And that for the said journey the almirante Diego de la Rivera be assigned with the said five *navios* and with the captains and men that I will designate to go to the said Strait, which has already been reconnoitred,[5] and to do in it what His Majesty orders, so that I will not find fault with his person.

And the other remaining *navios* that remain [*sic*] that are not fit to make the journey and are very deteriorated and deficient in rigging, I will take them to run along all this

---

[1] Flores uses the phrase '*ya no estaba para reparar*'.

[2] See above, p. 97, for the account of the separation as seen from the *galeaza*.

[3] Captain General Flores misrepresents the Battle of Santos. The English clearly had the advantage over the Spaniards during the battle, though they sailed away unexpectedly thereafter. See above, pp. 100–102.

[4] Here again, Captain General Flores misrepresents the facts. Alcega had been waiting for him for more than 4 months, having arrived in Rio de Janeiro near the end of December of 1582. At the point that Flores arrived, he was within days of departing for Spain.

[5] Rada, uses the verb *descubrir*, which in this context means to reconnoitre.

coast of Brasill, driving off the corsairs that are here. And having done this, I will go with [the *navios*] to Spain to give an account to His Majesty of the things that have happened after I left it, which there is need to give, and of many other things to attend to and remedy that are suitable to His royal service. And so that what is proposed be done in conformity and most appropriately, the said lord Don Diego de Alcega and Governor Pedro Sarmiento, and the almirantes Diego de la Rivera and Juan de Medina,[1] and the royal officials were brought together on the said *galeaza San Xptoval*.

And having read the aforesaid, the said General Diego Florez stated that they should give their *paraceres* about what would be most suitable to the service of His Majesty and the greatest benefit [f. 72v] to His royal finances. Dated on the 13th of May of this year of eighty-three. Diego Florez, before me, Pedro de Rada.

The said lord governor Pedro Sarmiento said that he had conferred with the lord general about these things in writing, as Pedro de Rada, chief scribe, certifies. But seeing the calculations and balance of the provisions that are here and those that can be had from the fruits of the land, they are not sufficient to sustain more people in relation to the said provisions than absolutely necessary to go to the Strait and return with the *naos* that have to return, and to do the most that can be done in the said Strait in conformity with the men and provisions available to remain, until such time as His Majesty is served to provide more. In accordance with this, it seems to him to conform to His royal service, and supposing this and that more people cannot go, that the lord general or the lord almirante, or one of the two, have to go for that effect. It seems to him that it is very well agreed and provided to order that the lord almirante go to the Strait, since the lord general says that it conforms to the service of His Majesty that he go to give an account of the things that touch upon His royal service. And this is his opinion, and he signed it with his name, Pedro Sarmiento de Gamboa, before me, Pedro de Rada.

And considering what was proposed by the said lord general, the lord Don Diego de Alcega, and the almirantes Diego de la [f. 73r] Rivera and Juan Gomez de Medina, and the royal officials said that regarding what is proposed and resolved by the said lord general Diego Florez, having conferred and consulted with them, they are of the same opinion, and that it conforms to the service of His Majesty. Having done the accounting of the provisions that there are, and of the hardship of the *naos*, and that the five selected from all the armada are sufficient and capable to again make the said voyage to the Strait, and that the armada be divided to this effect between this coast and in the said Strait, there is nothing lacking for those that have to go, as they remain with sufficient men and the rest to be able to do what is suitable.

And they signed it with their names: Don Diego de Alcega, Diego de la Rivera, Juan Gomez de Medina, Andres de Eguino, Estevan de las Alas, Pedro Desquivel, before me, Pedro de Rada.

---

[1] Juan Gómez de Medina served as almirante on Alcega's fleet.

Instruccion y orden that the lord almirante Diego de la Rivera has to obey on his journey to the Strait is as follows:

1 Firstly, that he take much care and diligence with the service of God Our Lord, so that He not be offended, but that everything in His service and that of His Majesty be obeyed and complied with.

2 That once I have left from this port, he issue a public order that all the men of the sea as well as of war, those absent as well as those present, come together and sign up like the others who remain on the *naos* [f. 73v] under his charge; and with the ones and the others, that he take care and diligence so that there be no conflicts with the people of the land, but that they be disciplined and kept busy as they have been until now so that there be good agreement [among them].

3 That he take much diligence and care in the refitting of the *navios* that remain here in his charge, and that they be ready and with spars aloft in order to leave from this port with the blessing of Our Lord on the 15th or 20th of November and not before, as he already has experience during the past navigation. And at the said time that he make his navigation directly to the said Strait, and entering into it that he obey and carry out the *instruccion* that I have from His Majesty in all that is possible, which is confided to the diligence and care of his person so that he discover and see if the said Strait has more than one mouth. And if it should not have more than one, that he try to fortify it as best he can, in conformity with the weather and the condition of the materials and people that he carries.

4 And having arrived at the said Strait that he try with all diligence and care to see if the said Strait has more than one mouth, or if they have what is said in the reports that His Majesty sent me, which he carries in his possession, from the dispatches that the ambassador to England has provided;[1] and if there be, that with the said Pedro Sarmiento he establish the settlement in the most comfortable and appropriate place, [f. 74r] so that it is left in the best order possible; and that he make a true report of it to give to His Majesty.[2]

5 That he carry in the *navios* of the said armada five hundred men of sea and war, besides the settlers and *casados* that Pedro Sarmiento brings for his settlement. And if at the time of departure it seems to them consistent with the provisions that he carries, he can bring another fifty persons from among those that remain in San Vicente; and this remains at his disposition in conformity with the weather and the provisions that there be.

6 That he should leave in the said Strait three hundred men, and more if he can, in conformity with the means of sustenance. And that he, as the person who has charge of

---

[1] The Spanish ambassador in England, Bernardino de Mendoza, sent dispatches to Philip II dated 16 and 26 April 1582. Copies were carried by Diego de Alcega's relief mission, which left Spain in the summer of 1582 and arrived in Brazil in December. Captain General Flores saw Mendoza's dispatches when he returned to Rio de Janeiro on 9 May 1583. Based on information Mendoza acquired in England, he wrote that the Strait of Magellan had more than one entrance and exit; see above, pp. 14–15. According to Kelsey, Mendoza was repeating a story that the English government wished to circulate. Though there was no corroboration for it at the time, later mapmakers and commentators accepted its validity; Kelsey, *Sir Francis Drake*, pp. 124–9.

[2] Regarding the feasibility of fortifying the Strait of Magellan, Rivera would report that he and the majority of those who saw the narrowest point estimated its width as more than 1 league – twice as wide as the highest estimate of Sarmiento and Antón Pablos; see Sarmiento, *Viajes al Estrecho*, vol. 2, p. 333. Nonetheless, Sarmiento later argued that Flores and Rivera simply made up false information so as to 'flee from the work of fortifying [the Strait] that Your Majesty ordered and return to their merchandising and pretensions'. Sarmiento to Philip II, 18 Sept. 1584, in Pastells and Bayle, *Descubrimiento del Estrecho de Magallanes*, pp. 701–2. See also p. 735 for Pablos's reiteration that the narrowest point was 'little more than a half league' wide.

the present business, see that the disposition of the land and the other things conform to what is most suitable to the service of His Majesty; in this he will do as he sees fit and seems best to him.

7   He has to leave for the governor Pedro Sarmiento one *fragata* or *navio*, whichever seems best and most appropriate, suitable to the disposition of the land and bay, with a warning that it not be a cause for the people to revolt by leaving in the said *navio*. And this he should see to very well, and the said almirante and Governor Pedro Sarmiento should consult with the other persons that seem best. And having done in person everything possible in the said Strait, he will return to this coast with two or three *navios* in the way that seems best to him and come directly to the port of San Vicente [f. 74v] or the Rio de Jenero, because there he will find orders from His Majesty about what he has to do.

8   He has to collect the two thousand *alqueres*[1] of flour that the captaincy of San Vicente must provide, which are paid for; and in the Rio de Jenero, he has to try to get as much as he can and pay for it from the money that remains, at the prices for which they have provided the rest, so that he can leave provisions in the Strait for one year for the people who remain there, and more if more there can be.

And so that the said almirante has authority in my absence for all the aforesaid, and all the other things that be necessary and have to be provided for the said journey, I give him all the full power[2] that I have from His Majesty. And I give the same to Captain Gregoro de las Alas who goes as his almirante, so that in case – may God not wish it – the said Diego de la Rivera should die or be missing, that he can carry out and maintain this *instruccion*. Dated in the port of the Rio de Jenero on the last day of May of 1583 years. By order of His Lordship Diego Florez. Pedro de Rada, chief scribe.

9   I, Diego de la Rivera, almirante of the Royal Armada of His Majesty of the Guard of the Indies and the Strait of Magellan, received the original of the *instruccion* here contained, signed by the lord General Diego Florez, and truly I signed it with my name on the said day, month, and year said. Diego de la Rivera, before me, Pedro de Rada, chief scribe.

10   I, Diego de la Rivera, almirante of the Royal Armada of His Majesty of the Guard of the Indies and the Strait of Magellan, received from His Lordship Diego Florez de Valdes, Captain General of it, an original *instruccion* from His Majesty, [f. 75r] signed with His royal name, dated in Tomar on the first of May of the year 1581, about what has to be done on the said journey and Estrecho de Magallanes, and an original decree[3] from His Majesty for the governors and judicial officials of this coast of Brasil, so that they give provisions, favour and aid to the said armada, dated in Lisbon on the 12th of September of the said year; and a letter from Don Bernaldino de Mendoça that he wrote to His Majesty on the 16th of April of the year of 1582, with dispatches and news of corsairs and of things touching upon the said Strait; and another letter from the said Don Bernaldino de Mendoça that he wrote to His Majesty on the 26th of April of the said

---

[1] See above, pp. xiv, 106.
[2] Rada's phrase is '*poder cumplido tan bastante*', which is a legal phrase meaning a full and complete power of attorney, sufficient for all actions required.
[3] The word used is *provisión*, which in this context means a royal decree.

year of 1582 to the same effect, all of which I carry in my possession for what will touch upon the service of His Majesty on this voyage on which I have to go, with God's intervention, on a course to the said Strait.

And he signed it in his name on the *galeaza capitana* on the 2nd of June of 1583, before me, Pedro de Rada, chief scribe.

———

Requerimiento that General Diego Florez made to Manuel Tellez Bareto, governor of the Baya del Salvador de Todos Sanctos:

I, Diego Florez de Baldes, comendador of Oreja and captain general of the Royal Armada of His Majesty of the Guard of the Indies, the Coasts of Brasil and the Estrecho de Magallanes, etc., say that I arrived at this Baya de Todos Sanctos with six *naos* of the armada on the 14th of July past.[1] And having arrived here, I discussed and communicated with your lordship things regarding the service of His Majesty and the security of this coast. And in order [to assure that security] and remedy the harms that have been done and could be done on [this coast], it seemed to your lordship, and we were in [f. 75v] accord, that it would be very suitable that I personally remain in this city with the *navios* of the armada that I brought for the security of [this city], and to go from here to Pernambuco and to la Paraiba to expel the French who have fortified themselves there and who do so much harm on this coast. And our having resolved on this, I gave an account of it and of my remaining and about other things touching upon His royal service to His Majesty. And with these dispatches, I sent Don Diego de Alcega on a *navio* from among those of the armada that left from here on the 13th of the month of August past, as your lordship knows. And thus I wrote to His Majesty that the principal cause of my remaining was to go to la Paraiba and to expel the French from there and to leave that port with defence and security. And in order to go suitably prepared, I have refitted the *naos* of my armada and careened them. And I have treated with your lordship many times to give me the provisions that are necessary, so that for the lack of them I will not be prevented from doing what is so important to the service of His Majesty and the pacification of this coast.

And now the procurador general[2] of Pernambuco has come to discuss with your lordship matters of that city and its land and the harm that the French from la Paraiba are doing there, and to ask that your lordship go there in person to remedy it. And having seen, discussed and communicated about this, your lordship has resolved that, since I am here with this armada for the security of this coast and [to remedy the harm from the French], there is no need for your person to be absent from this city to conform to the service of His Majesty; and for things [f. 76r] related to judicature and other matters that present themselves in that city of Pernambuco, that the oidor general should go in my company to remedy them. And from the persons who have come from and who have been in la Paraiba, I have been informed that none of the four *naos* from my armada that I have here can enter la Paraiba because it has too little water for them, except for the *fragata Sancta Ysavel*.

---

[1] i.e. 14 July 1583.

[2] The procurador general was the chief solicitor or attorney in a district acting for the interests of the crown.

And because the two armed *naos* that your lordship brought are smaller *navios*, and these they say can enter and are ready to go to the kingdoms of Spain, it is suitable to the service of His Majesty and to be able to expel the French from there that your lordship give and hand over these two *navios* to me with the men and artillery that they have and will carry to the kingdoms of Spain, because, this done,[1] I have to go from la Paraiba straight to the said kingdom to give an account to His Majesty about what I have done and what will be done; and thus these two *navios* can serve on this urgent occasion of such importance, and the *navios* will go to Spain with more security in company and convoy with this armada. And if they have to carry heavy timber[2] and other things from here, these can be distributed among the *navios* of my armada, because they are large, so they do not have to carry anything; and all can go in a very battle-ready fashion for every occurrence that might present itself; and being alone and heavily laden, they would be at great risk and would cease to be of service to His Majesty. And thusly, all can be done without risk and delay.

On behalf of His Majesty, [f. 76v] I ask and require your lordship to order that the said two *naos* be given and handed over to me, with the men and artillery and other things that they have to carry to Spain, because this suits His royal service and the security of these coasts and of the said *naos*. And also that it be ordered to give me the provisions that I have asked for, and that all be provided quickly, because the season is very advanced and it is suitable to leave from here for the said purpose in this coming month of December. And if your lordship should not thus comply with the one request and the other, I protest the inconvenient damages and expenses to His Majesty and to His royal finances that will ensue and increase for not having thus complied, and all will be the responsibility and fault of your lordship. I am here ready with the *navios* of my armada and the men from it to put into execution all to which I have referred, and to depart as soon as the provisions that are necessary and urgent have been conveyed to me. And because this conforms to the service of His Majesty, on his behalf I again ask and require your lordship, before the scribe, that it be given to me by testimony for my discharge, and so that His Majesty understands what is done about this matter in His service.

In addition, I say that if by chance His Majesty gave your lordship some order that the said two *naos* be handed over to some person so that they convey them to the kingdom, this would be in case they would not be needed for another purpose of more importance to His service, and which this is. I say that if the person to whom His Majesty ordered that you convey them is thus not to achieve any other purpose, he should wish to sail in them [f. 77r] or in others of this armada that will be given him, as he will travel better and more securely than in the said two *naos*, which are small and do not carry men of war, which they need to have in order to defend themselves from any corsair that they should encounter. And this would detract much from the service of His Majesty, and the artillery and munitions and much reputation would be lost, as the corsairs are now moving about together and with much force. And all of these eventualities are remedied by travelling together, and the purposes that His Majesty desires will be achieved. For what concerns me in His royal name, I ask for what I have asked and testified to.

---

[1] i.e. once the French are expelled from Paraíba.
[2] Presumably logs of brazil wood.

Diego Florez, before me, Pedro de Rada. Dated in the Baya del Salvador, on the 28th day of the month of November of the year 1583.

———

The *instruccion y orden* that has to be obeyed and complied with by the captains, pilots and masters of the *navios* of the Royal Armada of His Majesty that went to the Estrecho de Magallanes, which is in the Baya de los Sanctos, of which I am captain general, is the following:

1   That the said captains, pilots and masters obey and carry out my *instruccion*, and see that it is obeyed and carried out, which was given to them in Spain, dated on the 24th of September of the year of 1581, regarding navigation and the good order of war and more things that are declared therein, to which I refer.

2   Having left from this Baya de Todos Sanctos, the armada will go on a course straight to Pernambuco, the *navios* of this armada following the poop lantern[1] with much [f. 77v] vigilance and care, so as not to go off-course and be lost. And if perchance – may God forbid it – before arriving at the port of Pernambuco there is some violent weather such that a *navio* or *navios* should separate from the *capitana*, such *navio* or *navios* that have been separated will anchor at Pernambuco, where they will find me or my order about what they have to do. And if such *navio* or *navios* that thus went off course, having done everything possible to enter the port of Pernambuco, the weather not permitting it to take place, they will in such a case continue their voyage to the kingdoms of Spain, each one governing his *navio* in very good order on whatever occasion arises. And thus they shall obey and fulfil, on pain of being punished rigorously. Dated in the Baya de Todos Sanctos on the 27th of February of 1584 years.[2] By order of His Lordship Diego Florez. Pedro de Rada.

   This *instruccion* was given to each one of the captains of the armada in the Baya de Todos Sanctos on the last day of February of 1584 years. And the armada set sail for Pernambuco on the first of March of this said year.

———

The *instruccion y orden* to be obeyed and complied with by Lord Diego Baez de Vega and Captain Pedro Corea de la Cerda on their *naos* that go with the Royal Armada of His Majesty, of which I am captain general, is the following:

[f. 78r] 1   The *capitana* having set sail to depart from this Baya, you will depart following it and neither stop at night nor depart at dawn before the *capitana*. And being able to do so, you will approach to salute two times each day, once in the morning and the other in the evening, and you will get the name. And the *navio* that is near the *capitana* will pull away and give place to the one that is approaching.

2   And if in case the *capitana* wants to change to another course from that which it followed at sunset, it will fire a piece and display a lantern in addition to the poop lantern. The other *navios* of the armada and those that travel in its convoy will display another

[1] i.e. the poop lantern of the *capitana*.
[2] The phrasing implies '1584 years since the birth of our Savior Jesus Christ'.

and shift to the same course. And if in case some *navio* should be left behind so that it cannot hear the piece that the *capitana* will fire, the *navio* that is nearest to it will fire a piece and put up a lighted lantern so that it understands.

3 If the *capitana* lowers sails at night for some necessity that arises, it will display two lighted lanterns in addition to the poop lantern. All the *navios* of the armada will display another two lanterns.

4 No *navio* that goes with the said armada and in its convoy shall separate from it without my licence, on pain of life and loss of goods. And if in case of violent weather some *navio* or *navios* separates, it will continue the voyage that I laid out, which is to go to Pernambuco, where they will find me, and if not they will find there [f. 78v] my order of what they have to do, which they will follow and obey, on the said penalty.

5 And if perchance some *navio* discovers a leak or whatever other necessity it should have, it will fire a piece and display two lanterns, and if it be in daytime it will lower sails. And if perchance it should see some sail or sails, it will lower and raise its topsail as many times as there are *navios* seen, and it will approach the *capitana*, where orders will be given about what they have to do, if they have to fight.

6 That no *navio* with the said armada shall enter into any port nor anchor without the *capitana* having entered first, or without my order and licence, on the said penalty.

7 All the aforesaid they will do and fulfil, and and make sure are obeyed and fulfiled, and that the pilot and master of their *naos* take much account of the things contained in this *instruccion*. And when they are not able to come and take the name for each day, as aforesaid, they will use the following:

Sunday, La Sanctisima Trenidad
Monday, Sam Pedro
Tuesday, Sam Pablo
Wednesday, San Jhoan
Thursday, Yspiritu Sancto
Friday, Sanctiago
Saturday, Nuestra Señora de la Concepcion

[f. 79r] Which should be obeyed and complied with, as is stated. Dated in the Baya del Salvador, on the twenty-ninth of February of 1584. By order of His Lordship Diego Florez. Pedro de Rada, chief scribe.

I, Diego Baez de Vega, state that I received the original *instruccion* of the tenor of this, signed by the lord general Diego Florez, by the hand of Pedro de Rada, chief scribe, in the Baya, on the 29th of February of the year 1584. Diego Vaez de Beiga.

I, Captain Pedro Corea, state that I received the original *instruccion* in this tenor, signed by the lord general Diego Florez, by the hand of Pedro de Rada, chief scribe, in the Baya, on the 29th of February of 1584. Pedro Corea de la Cerda.

———

The vow and pledge of homage that Captain Francisco de Castrejon made as the alcaide of the fort named Sam Phelipe y Sanctiago, which was built in la Paraiba:

In the fort named Sam Phelipe y Sanctiago, which is being completed for His Majesty the King Dom Phelipe, our Sovereign Lord, in this port of la Paraiba, on the 29th day of the month of April of the year 1584, before me, Pedro de Rada, chief scribe.

The very illustrious lord Comendador Diego Florez de Valdes conveys the said fort and men of the garrison, with the artillery, gunpowder and other munitions that he left in it, to the alcaide Francisco de Castrejon; [*margin:* Pledge of homage] and in the said lord [f. 79v] general's hands, the said alcaide made the solemn vow and pledge[1] that is customary that he will sustain and guard the said fort for the royal majesty of the King Dom Phelipe, our sovereign lord, and will defend it from enemies; and he will not hand it over to any king nor prince nor to another person who does not have a power of attorney from His Majesty or is related to Him by direct lineage. And he will do and carry out what he ought and is obligated as a faithful servant, or incur the penalties that fall upon and are incurred by the alcaides and captains that for His Majesty and in his royal name have and have been entrusted similar forts. And thus the said alcaide Francisco de Castrejon made the said vow and promise, and that thus he will hold and guard it.

And he signed with his name, being present Fructuoso Barboso and Accountant Andres de Eguino and Chief Sergeant Pedro Nuñez de Loaissa, and many others. Francisco de Castrejon, before me, Pedro de Rada, chief scribe.

Instruccion y orden that has to be obeyed and carried out by Captain Francisco de Castrejon, alcaide of the fort named Sam Phelipe y Sanctiago, which is being built and finished for His Royal Majesty the King Dom Phelipe, our sovereign lord, in the port of Sancto Domingo de la Paraiba:

1   The men of the garrison that remain in the said fort are to be given the provisions that I left for them, in the following ration: To thirty soldiers one *alquer* of flour each day, which comes to one *alquer* of flour per month to each man; and one *quartillo* of pure wine[2] to each man each day; and half an *azumbre*[3] of oil per month to each one.
[f. 80r] 2   And when it is possible, give to each man a *libreta* of fresh meat,[4] or a half of salted meat, each day – I mean, each Sunday. And on Monday a *libra* of salted fish among three, and a half *almud*[5] of a mixture of fava beans or chick peas among twelve; Tuesday, a half *libreta* of salt pork to each one and a *libra* of rice among ten; Wednesday, the ration as on Monday; Thursday, the ration as on Sunday; Friday and Saturday, the ration as on Monday and Wednesday; vinegar, one *arroba* among five for one month.
3   The gunpowder, match-cord, shot and other munitions shall be used in conformity with the necessity that there be, taking much account and care in the custody and guarding and distribution of them, seeing that they are not put in a place where there is a flame, because of the inconveniences that this can offer.
4   To make haste in the building of the said fort, so that it be finished with suitable brevity, making the men of the garrison who will remain there work on it, following all the orders that I have given, and attending in person with the diligence and care that I entrust to you.

---

[1] *Voto y solemnidad*; vow and solemn pledge.
[2] *Quartillo* refers to a liquid measure equal to 504 ml. The reference to pure wine presumably meant undiluted.
[3] A liquid measure equal to about 2 litres; see 'Weights, Measures, and Currency', p. xiv.
[4] *Libreta* (Rada's variant *libretta*), often referred to as *libreta carnicera* or 'flesh pound', weighing 32 oz.
[5] See 'Weights, Measures, and Currency', p. xiv.

5   Do not allow the soldiers to leave the said fort nor to be absent from it, because of the harm that could result. And that the officers have them well disciplined and instructed and that there be no disorder. And that the settlers are to be well treated by them and assisted. And anyone who is rebellious and gives cause, you are to punish with rigour and render justice by virtue of your title, condemning them to [f. 80v] forced labour or to the most severe penalties that are merited, without allowing the opportunity or occasion for quarrels or other scandals with the said settlers and residents, as their friendship and confederation matters so much for furthering the settlement and the service of His Majesty.

6   That the soldiers, gunners, gunsmith and other officers now designated have to remain with the garrison continually until His Majesty orders otherwise, without being absent from the fort, unless there is a clear need for some of them to go out against Indian enemies who come to the area to do some harm in the towns of the settlers or for other things that are in the service of His Majesty. And for the defence of the port and land, you can send a squadron of soldiers, or as many more or less as it seems to you for the said purpose, retaining in the fort those that are necessary for its defence.

7   With regard to the provisions and munitions that I have left in the fort for its needs and those of the men of the garrison, you will write to Pernambuco for what is lacking and is needed, asking Martin Leiton, oidor general, and Martin Carvallo, chief purveyor, to send it, to whom I have written that they give orders to provide it; and with a *carta de pago*[1] of how you received what was sent for the sustenance and defence of the said fort, it will be well given, and you will receive [the supplies] and send your account to the said oidor and purveyor.

8   You will maintain all friendship and good relations with the lord Fructuoso Barbosa, to whom His Majesty has granted the favour of the government [f. 81r] and settlement of the land, helping him in all that you can, so that it may be populated with speed and security, always taking into consideration that your person not be absent from the fort with the men necessary for its defence, and that you always be in agreement, since from his friendship redounds the service of His Majesty and the growth of the settlements and the wellbeing of the land and of this coast.

9   And also I give you power to name a lieutenant so that he help you attend to and be present in the said fort as suitable for the things necessary, and that he be a worthy person.

10   Besides the said provisions that remain, take care to send to Pernambuco for what is lacking, in conformity with the *libranza* that remains for it with Martin Carballo; and this has to be with due consideration to not asking for anything that is not urgent and necessary.

This is charged to you, all of which you will obey and carry out with much diligence and care.

Dated in the port of la Paraiba, on the 29th of April of the year 1584. Diego Florez, before me, Pedro de Rada, chief scribe.

Copy of a *libranza* that Diego Florez issued for Martin Carvallo, chief purveyor in Pernambuco, so that he provide supplies and munitions to Captain Francisco de Castrejon, alcaide of the fort named San Felipe y Sanctiago in the port of la Paraiba:

[1] A *carta de pago* (letter of payment) was a receipt or proof that payment had been received.

[f. 81v] Lord Martin Carvallo, purveyor of His Majesty in the captaincy of Pernambuco: Your Grace already knows about the fort and the settlement being made in this port of la Paraiba, and how for the security of the said fort and land up to one hundred and ten men of war remain, at the expense of His Majesty, and with them as alcaide of the said fort Captain Francisco de Castrejon, in whose charge remains the said fort [margin: *Libranza*] and the men and artillery and other munitions and provisions. Your Grace will order that they be provided with victuals for the sustenance of the said men of war and the other things pertaining to and necessary for the said fort, as Your Grace knows, in conformity with which a *carta de pago* of what will be sent and received has to be given to Your Grace, or to whoever will have your power of attorney, taking note of it in the account books of His Majesty, until such time as His Majesty orders otherwise. With which and this my *libranza*, there will be received and paid out on the account of Your Grace the provisions and other things that will be given or sent to the said alcaide, Francisco de Castrejon, for the said purpose.

Dated in the port of la Paraiba, on the 29th day of the month of April of the year 1584. And this *libranza* or its *traslado* will be sufficient in the manner that I certify. By order of His Lordship Diego Florez. Pedro de Rada, chief scribe.

————

Report of the provisions, artillery, arms and munitions and other supplies [f. 82r] that were received by Captain Francisco de Castrejon, alcaide of the fort named Sam Phelipe y Sanctiago, which is being made and finished for His Royal Majesty the King Dom Phelipe, our sovereign lord, in the port of la Paraiba, for the sustenance of the men of the garrison that remain in it and the defence of the fort:

~ Twenty pipas of commmercial-grade wine;
~ Eight hundred and eighty *alqueres* of *harina de guera*, which is made from cassava;
~ Fifty large jugs of sweet oil for cooking, each of one half *arroba*;
~ Fourteen barrels of tunny, *quintalenos*;[1]
~ One *chinchorro*[2] of local design, for fishing;
~ Two bronze swivel-guns;[3]
~ Four bronze falcons, with seven iron firing chambers;
~ Two iron gun carriages;
~ Eight pieces of wrought-iron artillery with their gun carriages – half sakers, which are the guns that were used by the French corsairs in this port, from which we expelled them;
~ Twelve barrels of gunpowder, each holding a *quintal* or half a *quintal*;
~ Forty-one units of firearms;
~ Eighty-six carpenters' hatchets to cut wood and kindling;
[f. 82v] ~ Fifty-one iron bars;
~ Eleven iron picks for rock work;
~ Fifty spades;
~ Fifty sickles or reaping hooks;

[1] *Quintaleños*, i.e. each barrel holding 1 *quintal*.
[2] Elsewhere Rada uses the variant *chinchoro*; a small boat with oars, used for fishing with a large thrown net or *chinchorro*.
[3] A swivel gun (*pedrero*) which fired stone shot.

~ Fifty pikes for military campaigns;

~ Twenty-five *arrobas* of match-cord for harquebus;

~ Six chunks of lead for making shot;

~ Two hundred lead cannon balls: one hundred of one *libra* each, and one hundred for sakers and half sakers;

~ Twenty-four stone cannon balls;

———

Report on the money that was provided in Spain for the expenses of the armada, and what has been sought as loans for the sustenance of it, and what has been provided on His Majesty's account on the coast of the Brassil, in this manner:

~ Conveyed to the general and royal officials in the city of Cadiz at the end of November of 1581: fifteen thousand ducats, in *reales*, for the expenses of the armada, which amount to   Vq.s dc xxv U[1]

~ In the town of Sanctos, forty leagues farther than the Rio de Jeneiro, two hundred and forty *milreis*[2] were received, which were in the keeping of Melchior de Acosta for His Majesty, from the permits and fees from the English *nao* that came there   cc xl U

[f. 83r] ~ In the said town of Sanctos, another five hundred and eighty *milreis* were taken from the goods of the deceased, which were in the keeping of Juan Nunez. For these, a letter due from His Majesty was sent to Lisbon on 23 of October of 1582, payable in 60 days, to the attention of the treasurer of the goods of the deceased.[3] These and the sums above were to pay for the provisions that were supplied there;   d lxxx U

~ Another one hundred and seventy *millres* were taken in the Rio de Jenero from the goods of the deceased, which were in the keeping of Crispin de Acuña, in order to help pay for the provisions that were supplied there. For these, a letter due from His Majesty was sent on 23 of October of 1582, so that he order them paid in Lisbon to the treasurer for the said deceased.   c lxx U

[1] In Spanish accounting, q.s stood for *quentos*, or millions, and U stood for thousands. The Roman numerals represent 5,625,000 *maravedís*, the equivalent of 165,000 *reales* at 34 *maravedís* per *real*. In the 16th century, a *maravedí* was the smallest monetary unit of account: 1 *real* = 34 maravedís; 1 *escudo* = 340 *maravedís*; 1 ducat = 375 *maravedís*. Thus, 15,000 ducats = 165,000 *reales* = 5,625,000 *maravedís*.

[2] Rada's variant *millres*. In Portuguese accounting, 1 *milréi* was worth 1,000 *réis*, which seem to have been worth slightly more than 1,000 Spanish *reales*.

[3] The tesorero de bienes de difuntos (treasurer of goods of the deceased) took charge of the belongings of those who died, usually making an inventory and evaluation thereof and holding the profits from their sale or auction until they could be transferred to the heirs, if any.

~ In the Baya de Todos Sanctos for the month of August of the year of 1583, the almirante Juan de Medina loaned to the general and officials five thousand and two hundred and eighty *reales* in order to buy provisions and other things, for which he gave him a letter due from His Majesty, so that he pay them in Spain. They total	c lxx ix U d xx
~ In the said Vaya de Todos Sanctos, Pablo Buzomo also loaned to the said general and officials three thousand *reales* for the said purpose, which amount to	c ii U
~ In the said Vaya de Todos Sanctos, to pay for provisions and other things, Pedro de Arze gave [f. 83v] one *quento*, eight hundred and four thousand, and one hundred and fifty-one *maravedís*,[1] for which a letter due from His Majesty was issued, so that Juan Bauptista Rovelasca be ordered to pay them in Lisbon.	i q dccc iiii U c li
~ In the said Vaya, Governor Manuel Tellez Bareto gave on His Majesty's account to pay for provisions for the said armada two *quentos*, seven hundred and forty-nine thousand, one hundred and eighty-eight *reales*	ii q.s dcc xl ix U c lxxx viii
~ In the city of Angla of the Isla de La Terçera, Vibiam Perez, native of the town of Castropol, loaned to the general and royal officials one thousand and eight hundred and seventy-five *reales*, which amount to [64,430 *maravedís*],[2] to buy provisions for the armada, which arrived in great need. He was given a letter due from His Majesty	lx iiii U cccc xxx
~ Which totals, including what was carried from Spain and what was loaned, as stated,	xi q.s cccc xiiii U cc lxxx ix[3]

In addition to the aforesaid, Martin Carvallo, the chief purveyor in the town of Pernambuco, on order of the said governor, Manuel Tellez Bareto, gave the provisions and other things that are declared below for the journey from la Paraiba, on His Majesty's account; the cost of it is not known:

~ Forty-five *pipas* of wine;
~ One hundred small jars of sweet oil for cooking;
[f. 84r] ~ Thirty barrels of tunny-fish;

---

[1] See above, p. xiv.

[2] The total in Castilian *reales* would have been 63,750 *maravedís*. If the money was in Portuguese *reales,* that could explain the discrepancy.

[3] i.e. 11,414,289 *maravedís*. The total of the numbers stated in the right column is 17,752,847 *maravedís*. It is not clear what accounts for the discrepancy.

~ Two stream-cables of hemp, which weighed 16 quintales ½, 40 *libras*;[1]
~ Three towing cables of hemp, which weighed 9 *quintales*, 3 @, 14 *libras*;
~ Five small ropes for rigging, which weighed 2 *quintales*, [0] @,[2] 14 *libras*;
~ Nine *quintales* of minor rigging elements, 9 *quintales* , [0] @;
~ Sixty-four *baras*[3] of coarse linen cloth,[4] 37 *quintales*, 1 @, 68 *libras*, weight of Portugal;[5]
~ Four hundred scupper-nails;
~ Two thousand and four hundred tacks for the pumps;
~ Six tanned half-cowhides for the pumps;
~ One hundred needles for sewing sails;
~ Two hundred small rolls of thread for the sails, which weighed 22 *libras*;
~ Three *quintales* and a half of tar, weight of Castile;
~ Another twenty-two *arrobas* of tar from the Canary Islands, weight of Portugal;
~ One hundred heavy square nails;
~ Eight pieces of net to make a *chinchoro* in la Paraiba;

On the twenty-ninth day[6] of the month of June of 1584, the armada having arrived in the city of Angla on the Isla de La Tercera, on order of the general the gunpowder, lead and match-cord that will be declared below were given and handed over to Juan de Urbina and to the royal officials of his *tercio*,[7] of which they had much need:

Gunpowder   ~ twenty-five *arrobas* and a half of gunpowder;
Lead   ~ Twenty-six *arrobas* of lead;
Match-Cord   ~ Twenty-three *quintales* and one *arroba* of match-cord for harquebuses

---

[f. 84v] The report given by Don Francisco de Vera, who came from Spain on the Royal Armada of the Strait of Magellan with the men that were going to Chile, whom Don Alonso de Sotomayor gave licence to go to the Rio de la Platta in a trading bark that came to the Rio de Jenero from Spain with the commissary Friar Juan de Riva Deneira and other Franciscan friars who were going to the said Rio de la Platta, who left for the said Rio de la Platta in the same bark the same day as the said armada left from Jenero

---

[1] Weights of Castile in Spain are given in *qls* (*quintales* of 100 lb), @ (*arrobas* of slightly more than 25 lb) and *libras*, so that 4 *arrobas* equals 1 *quintal*. Following that standard, this item should have been listed as 16 *quintales*, 3@, 15 *libras*.

[2] In the entries for the weights for small ropes and minor rigging, the @ symbol is included, although the *libras* fall short of 1 *arroba*. When the symbol for *arroba* is used thus, with no number before it, this signifies 0 *arrobas*, or that there were insufficient *libras* to amount to an *arroba*. The [0] has been supplied here to avoid confusion.

[3] *Varas* (yards), each one equal to about 0.84 m.

[4] *Angeo*, coarse linen cloth or canvas.

[5] In general, the Portuguese *quintal* was worth 128 Portuguese *libras* about 129.54 lb or 58.75 kg; the Portuguese *arroba* was worth 32 *libras*. As in Castile, therefore, 4 *arrobas* equalled 1 *quintal*. By the generally accepted equivalents, this item should be listed as 37 *quintales*, 3 *arrobas*, 4 *libras*.

[6] Rada lists the day as *veinte* (20), with ix (9) written above the line.

[7] A *tercio* was a Spanish infantry unit, consisting of harquebusiers, musketeers, swordsmen, and pikemen; theoretically composed of 3,000 men, in reality the numbers varied considerably.

for the Strait – the second day of November of this year of 1582 – which is the following:[1]

The said Don Francisco, departing from the port of Sancta Catalina Thursday the 6th of December of the said year of [15]82, one hour before dawn discovered two *naos* and a *patache* that were anchored in the port of Don Rodrigo,[2] which is about four leagues to the south of the said Isla de Sancta Catalina. And then they saw the *patache* set sail, and it chased them for more than four leagues. And having seen that it was gaining on them, they headed for land at a sandy place. And the *patache*, having seen their course and gaining on them, fired a gun so that they would strike their sails. And two launches came with the said *patache*, which being very close to the bark lowered sails, and the said two launches arrived; and the almirante[3] and another English gentleman came aboard with twenty harquebusiers who did not maltreat us, reassuring the men of the said bark and saying that they would not do them any harm; from the said Don Francisco they took the keys for the coffers and opened them to see the dispatches that they carried. And to the *capitana* they brought the said Don Francisco and six friars who sailed in the said bark, but not their commissary.

And upon arriving there, their general[4] sent a courteous note to Don Francisco that he would not see him, being indisposed. [f. 85r] And he was entertained for an hour by some principal English gentlemen whom the almirante ordered to keep him company. And then the almirante left and took him by the hand and brought him to the poop cabin where the general was. He was seated in a chair, and with him a son of Francisco Draque[5] and another two English gentlemen, and a clergyman and a Portuguese pilot who was uncovered.[6] And the said Don Francisco entering the cabin, the general rose and went to him and embraced him and made him sit down and had wine and biscuits brought. And he toasted him, drinking first, and then begged forgiveness for not having gone out to speak with him outside. And he asked him if he came from Spain or from whence he came with the bark. And with this, the almirante went outside again with Don Francisco, saying that they were going to see where they were to be [lodged]. And then he ordered the friars called and toasted them and asked them from whence they were coming, and they left again. And the next day, Friday in the morning, a cleric-cosmographer[7] and the

---

[1] Donno, *Diary of Richard Madox,* pp. 249–59, contains a full account of the interaction of Vera and Commisary Juan de Rivadeneira with their English captors. Taylor, *Troublesome Voyage, passim,* includes excerpts from the diaries of Madox and several other men on Fenton's expedition.

[2] See above, p. 39, n. 5.

[3] Here and above, p. 40, this refers to Fenton's vice-admiral, Luke Ward of the *Edward Bonaventure.*

[4] Here used in the sense of captain general referring to Edward Fenton.

[5] John Drake, a young cousin of Francis Drake. See above, pp. 40, 50, 100.

[6] See above, pp. 39–40. The clergyman at the meeting was Richard Madox; Donno, *Diary of Richard Madox,* p. 249. The Portuguese pilot was Simão Fernandes, a pirate captured by the English who saved himself by offering to serve them against Spain. A veteran of several English voyages, he was Fenton's pilot on the *Leicester* and an outspoken proponent of plundering Spanish and Portuguese targets. Madox held him in very low esteem. See Kupperman, 'A Continent Revealed', pp. 368–9. Rada describes Fernandes as *descubierto* (uncovered) at the meeting, which in context means without a hat. Presumably the others in the cabin were wearing hats, a mark of distinction in Fenton's presence that Fernandes did not enjoy.

[7] i.e. Richard Madox. Another cleric with Fenton's expedition, John Walker, also wrote about the capture and release of the friars. Taylor, *Troublesome Voyage,* pp. 210–14.

Portuguese pilot called for the said Don Francisco, on orders from their general, and they interrogated him with the following written questions:

~ From whence he came with that very small bark. He responded from the Rio de Jenero, where those friars who came from Spain had arrived, the armada of His Majesty being there. And he had embarked in it in order to go to the Rio de la Plata.

~ They asked him if he brought a pilot and why they came in such a small *navio*. He responded that two sailors came with them [f. 85v] who knew the coast and the Rio de la Platta and said that it was better to come along the coast in such very small barks.

~ When the armada left from Spain, and how many *naos*. He responded that on the 9th of December of 1581 they left from Cadiz with 16 *naos*.

~ How many days it took from Spain to Cabo Verde and when they arrived. He responded that they took 32 days and arrived on the eleventh of January.

~ If all of the *naos* arrived at Cavo Verde together. He responded that all arrived, save the *almiranta*, which arrived eight days after.

~ If the armada prepared meat and water and other things there for provisions. He responded yes.

~ At what time they left Cavo Berde and what tempests they had on the route before arriving at the Rio de Jenero. He responded that their departure was on the second of February, and that they arrived on the 26th of March at Jenero, and that there was no notable storm, but some days of calms and heavy showers with whirlwinds.

~ They asked him how many people had died on the route from the three thousand men who left from Spain. He responded that three hundred men had died.

~ What provisions the armada brought of bread, wine, oil and vinegar, meat and other munitions, because they knew that it had departed from Spain very needy in everything. He responded that in general they would have enough [f. 86r] from what they brought from Spain until the end of December of this year of 1582.

~ What quantity of provisions they had taken from the Rio de Jenero. He responded that [they took] up to fifteen or sixteen thousand *alqueres*[1] of flour; and of meat he could not say how much there was, more than it came well provided with everything.

~ If the soldiers had been short of provisions in the Rio de Jenero. He responded that they had experienced some need, but not much.

~ Who the general was and what was his name. He responded that it was Diego Florez de Valdes, and that he was the nephew of the adelantado Pero Menendes.

~ What was the name of the general of Chile and how many men he brought. He responded that he was called Don Alonso de Sotomayor, and that he was an old soldier of Flandes[2] and that he brought 600 men.

~ What were the names of the captains of Chile and if they were old soldiers, and how many important men there were in this number of 600. He responded that all of the captains and officers were old soldiers, and that there were about 150 noblemen among them.

~ If the aforesaid men of Chile came well armed and what arms and munitions of war they carried. He responded that all of the men carry harquebuses, and some muskets, and that they brought six hundred harquebuses and muskets in reserve.

[1] See above, pp. xiv, 106, n. 7.
[2] Flanders; in other words, a veteran of the Spanish armies fighting the rebellion in the Netherlands.

~ What were the names of the almirante and the king's captains in the armada and in which *naos* they were distributed, and how many men sailed in each *nao*, and if they came [f. 86v] well provided with sailors, sails, cables, rigging, anchors, artillery, gunpowder and other munitions, and in particular, how much of these things each *nao* would carry. He responded and gave his opinion about what each *nao* would be able to carry and satisfied them.

~ What ration was given to the soldiers and if they had reduced it from what was given at the start of the voyage. He responded and said what was given.

~ How many large *naos* came among the 16, and one by one how many *toneladas* each *nao* had. He responded that there were four *naos*, that the least of them surpassed 700 *toneladas*, and that the *capitana* would have 900, and that the others would be from 300 to 400 *toneladas*.[1]

~ How much time they had wintered in the Rio de Jenero, and if the land was well supplied with provisions, and when the said armada departed. He responded, from the 26th of March until Friday the 2nd of November, when it left for the said Strait, and that the land was reasonably well provided.

~ How many *naos* left from the Rio de Jenero. He responded 15 *naos*, because the other one had remained because of leaking.

~ What quantity of foreign sailors there were in the armada and of what nations they were. He responded that there were up to 150 and that among them were some *levantiscos* and Flemings, and some English,[2] and that these would be very few.

~ How many gunners there were in the armada, and [f. 87r] particularly how many the *capitana* and *almiranta* and each *nao* would carry for itself, and if they carried the guns above or as ballast.[3] He responded that there were 150 gunners, and that the *capitana* and *almiranta* would carry 50 of them, and the other *naos* the rest, and that the *capitana* and *almiranta* would carry from ten to twelve pieces above and the others below, as the voyage was dangerous, and not fearing corsairs because the armada was powerful and because all of it could be brought above in an hour, if necessary.

~ If, in his opinion, the armada is in the Strait. He responded that it seemed to him that it would have been in the Strait for days, if they had good weather.

~ If he knew what the intent of the armada was, if to build a fort in the Strait or to plant a settlement in it or to pass through it into the Mar del Sur. He responded that it was going to plant a settlement at the Strait and to build two forts in the narrowest part, one on one side and the other on the other, and that it did not have to pass through into the Mar del Sur, except for the four *naos* for Chile.

~ How many men were to remain in the Strait in the forts and how many settlers there would be and the name of the governor of the Strait and of the alcaides and captains.

---

[1] This was either a mistaken estimate or a deliberate exaggeration. As noted above the *galeaza capitana San Cristóbal* was 700 *toneladas* in Spanish reckoning, the *almiranta San Juan Bautista* was 500 *toneladas*, and the other ships ranged downward from there; see Appendix 1.

[2] Rada uses the word *levantisco* as a generic term meaning anyone from the eastern Mediterranean, but not necessarily the Levant. *Flamencos* (Flemings) were from the Netherlands, but not necessarily from the province of Flanders. The few Englishmen, like other foreign sailors in Spanish fleets, would likely have been Roman Catholic, or would have claimed to be such; they would not have been captives.

[3] Artillery carried on the main deck or gun deck could quickly be deployed for battle. Guns carried further below, as ballast, would take much longer to move into position.

He responded that 400 soldiers were to remain, 200 in each fort, and about 60 settlers, in addition to the 400, and that the governor was called Pedro Sarmiento, and he told them the names of the other officers that he knew.

[f. 87v] ~ What provisions they would leave for those of the Strait and what artillery and if some *nao* would remain. He responded that they would leave provisions for one year, and that they would leave one *nao* and one *bergantin* with twelve rowing benches to serve the forts and to provide them with provisions, if they lack them, from Chile or from the Rio de la Platta. In the interim, the king would provide them from Spain; and that they carried wheat and barley and many other seeds to sow, and that they carried one dozen head of cattle for service and breeding, and that they would leave 100 pieces of large and medium artillery for both forts, among which there were some very good culverins and half culverins, and reinforced assault cannons, and half cannons and quarter cannons,[1] all of bronze.

~ If the gentleman who remained as governor in the Strait was he who had induced His Majesty [to send] this armada to close the Strait and had spent one million on it.[2] He responded that it was the same.

~ If upon arriving at the Strait the armada was to return right away, or if it had to wait until the forts were finished. He responded that the armada did not have to return until leaving the forts in a manner and state in which they could defend themselves from enemies, and that it would not leave the Strait until the end of February 1583.

~ If the general of Chile with his men had to remain at the [f. 88r] strait until the forts were finished, or if at the first opportunity they were to go to Chile. He responded that he did not have to remain in the Strait and that he would go to his government at the first [opportunity] he had.

~ If His Majesty had to send support to the Strait quickly and what *naos* could he send and if he knew something about this. He responded that there were four *naos* remaining to come with men and provisions.

~ All the aforesaid and many other things and details they questioned him about, which, for not being of substance, all that they wrote is not written here.[3]

The following day, Saturday the 8th of December, their general[4] invited the said Don Francisco and the commissary to dine. And before and during the meal he addressed them with very gracious words, without letting them discuss matters of faith, and he always treated the said Don Francisco with much respect and distinction, as he treated their general. And there he promised him that he would leave him free to go with the friars in their bark, except for two sailors whom he took with him because they knew the coast and between the two of them the local languages, and they were *casados* in the Rio de la Platta.[5] And he also saw the letter that was being sent from Pedro Sarmiento

---

[1] A half cannon fired shot of 24 *libras*; a quarter cannon fired shot of 9–12 *libras*.

[2] The question suggests that the English knew a great deal about the expedition and Sarmiento's role in its genesis and financing.

[3] According to Richard Madox, Vera also supplied detailed information about the Río de la Plata and Spanish settlements there; see Donno, *Diary of Richard Madox*, pp. 252–3.

[4] Edward Fenton.

[5] See above, p. 143, n. 1.

to the viceroy of Peru[1] and he took it with him, and all the other dispatches he returned opened, telling them that if they lacked something they should tell him and it would soon be returned.

This same day, being at table, and other days separately, he told him that the king Dom Phelipe had no conscience [f. 88v] for sending these people to the Strait to die, as the land was a thousand times colder than Flanders or England and settlements and forts would be of little advantage, because there is a league and a half in the narrowest part [of the Strait], and even if it were but one [league] it could be passed through, no matter how much artillery there be, because he knew it better than Pedro Sarmiento, as they had seen it and measured it.[2] And this day and others, speaking of these matters the general importuned the said Don Francisco to go with him, touching his hand in friendship and pointing out to him a place in the poop cabin where only the two of them would travel, saying to him that he was going to the Malucas because El Draque had left English traders there, and that he was not going there with the design of fighting but of trading. And he also asked him if the Indians of Chile knew how to extract gold without instruction from the Spaniards, and if by giving them barter they would become friends and extract gold for them; and what settlements and cities and men of war there were in Chile and how many. He responded that he knew no more about this than that there were Indian uprisings and people whom you could not trust, and that there were many cities of Spaniards and men of war on foot and on horseback.

Those whom the said Don Francisco understood to have passed through the Strait with Francisco Draque and now came on these *navios* are the following: The captain of the *capitana*, who is a very good pilot, and the grandson of Juan Aquines; and the cousin of Francisco Draque, a man of whom the general thinks very highly; and the owner of the said *nao capitana*; and a son of Francisco Draque, [f. 89r] a young man of 22 years who passed through the said Strait with his father. He was captain of the *patache* and is very respected by everyone; and an English pilot who sailed as pilot with the said Francisco Draque. And the said Don Francisco believes that all the mariners who sailed with Draq are there, because some are treated more graciously compared to sailors and go about very well dressed, and some told him that they were with El Draq, and more than 24 of them sailed on the *capitana*.[3]

The said Don Francisco says that he saw many gentlemen on the *capitana* and *almiranta* very well turned-out and who seemed in all things to be very important people. The *capitana* carried, as well as the aforesaid, five pilots and among them a Portuguese pilot from La Tercera who is a servant in England,[4] and a cleric-cosmographer who makes

---

[1] The viceroy at the time was Don Martín Enríquez de Almanza, who held office from 23 Sept. 1581 to 13 March 1583.

[2] Presumably, Fenton was referring to information from Francis Drake's voyage. Fenton's expedition had yet to attempt the Strait and would sail no farther south than about 33°S.

[3] Don Francisco was mistaken about several points. Taylor, *Troublesome Voyage*, p. xxxiv, says that only 'about a dozen' men from Francis Drake's voyage accompanied Fenton. William Hawkins, nephew of John Hawkins and Fenton's lieutenant on the *Leicester*, had sailed with Francis Drake. So had Thomas Blacoller, pilot on the *Edward Bonaventure*, and Thomas Hood, the second pilot on Fenton's *Leicester*. John Drake, Francis Drake's young cousin, was captain of the *Francis* and the elder Drake's only relative on Fenton's expedition; Taylor, *Troublesome Voyage*, pp. xxxiv, 157–60. Richard Madox referred to Hood, an ally of William Hawkins, as a 'boasting buffoon'; Donno, *Diary of Richard Madox*, p. 54.

[4] Simão Fernandes; see above, p. 165, n. 6.

maps and is painting the coast.[1] It carries as well twice as many officers, and on the *capitana* and *almiranta* there is much heavy artillery of wrought iron, and some very heavy swivel-guns and some pieces of bronze. The *capitana* is a *nao* of about 500 *toneladas*, very strong and also outfitted with everything necessary to attack and defend. And the *almiranta* is a *nao* of about 300 *toneladas*, very strong and also outfitted with everything, like the *capitana*.[2] And the said Don Francisco saw on the *capitana* and *almiranta* five or six merchants, men whom the general treated with favour, and who carried all sorts of goods that they said were necessary to barter in new lands.[3] He understood from their general and from [f. 89v] many others that they carried provisions for two years from this day, without having need for more than water. And although the said Don Francisco tried to know the name of their general, and he asked many, none would venture to tell him, and particularly one hispanized Englishman raised in Seville, whom they had brought by force and who is a Catholic. Upon asking him for the name of the general five or six times, he did not repond, and being alone, he told him, 'Do not question me except about my work, because I cannot tell you anything else, except that you not ask anyone, because they will not tell you.'

The said Don Francisco asked the captain and the English pilot who were with Francisco Draque when he entered into the Mar del Sur by which route and region they had returned to England, because in Spain he had understood that they had left toward the north for the codfish. To this they responded to him that those from Perú went to have a try at the codfish, but for the great cold in that region they could not,[4] and they returned to the Malucas to the Isla de Teranarte and they loaded up with spices. And they left English factors to trade, and from there they sailed to England via the Cavo de Buena Esperança and that on this voyage they discovered new lands that were not on the map, nor even now discovered, and they gave him to understand that they thought the queen of England would people them. They said also that they were travelling with letters of peace from the said queen, [f. 90r] and such they would have with our armada if they ran across it, but if our armada wanted to fight, they came prepared for everything. They said that another eight *navios* had separated from them at a certain place, and they were waiting for them, among whom *El Draque* was coming.[5] The said Don Francisco says that the English general is a small thin man, and he has a lean face with some wrinkles, a blond beard turning white and blue eyes, of an age of 42 to 44 years.

The said Don Francisco says that these *naos* left England in the month of June of this year of 1582 and that they were in Siera Leona, which is in Guinea, where they captured seven or eight slaves; and they had news from the Portuguese that this armada had been

[1] Richard Madox; see above, pp. 40, n. 1, 83, n. 1.

[2] The *capitana* was Fenton's flagship, the *Galleon Leicester*. The *almiranta* was the *Edward Bonaventure* under Luke Ward.

[3] These were merchants from the Muscovy Company. See the lists of names in Taylor, *Troublesome Voyage*, pp. 66–7.

[4] Drake's voyage reached somewhere between 43°N and 48°N on the north-west coast of North America. See Wallis, 'Cartography of Drake's Voyage', pp. 129–30.

[5] Drake was part of early discussions with the Earl of Leicester that led to Fenton's expedition but withdrew when the aim of the voyage shifted to the Moluccas. Drake was involved with planning the expedition of the elder William Hawkins that left for Brazil at the end of 1582; that, presumably, was the expedition that was expected to arrive. In fact, when Hawkins learned in the Cape Verdes that Captain General Flores's armada was in Brazil, he headed for the Caribbean instead. See Andrews, 'Drake and South America', p. 57.

in Cabo Berde and was going to winter at the Rio de Jenero.[1] He says also that in his life he has [not] seen[2] *navios* better outfitted and supplied with everything, nor men better treated, nor cleaner weapons, nor more artillery than these carry. And he learned from them that they had arrived at this port of Don Rodrigo, coming from 33 degrees at the said Rio de la Platta with the same storms that ought to have detained the armada. They also told the said Don Francisco that they well knew about the discontent with which all the men of this armada came, and that the soldiers had to be embarked with alguaciles[3] giving them blows, and the sailors [were embarked] by force; and that the master of this English *nao capitana*[4] was in Seville and San Lucar when this armada was dispatched.

To the commissary Friar Juan de Rivadeneira, the English general gave a safe conduct written in Latin, so that if other *navios* from England should encounter him they would do him no harm, which follows:[5]

[f. 90v] To the very faithful my lieutenant of General Captain Frobucer,[6] or to Captain Acles[7] or to any other; set down in this fleet under my jurisdiction, which sails destined for La China and Catayo,[8] greetings, etc.

I ordered that we seize this old friar, Juan de Rivadeneira, and scrutinized all things diligently, and we found that neither he nor his companions planned any ill against us. And thus it seemed to us an unworthy thing to do them ill, so we promised them that they could go freely wherever they wished. Thus, to you and to each one of you, we order that if perchance upon encountering them they should fall into your hands without causing any impediment or harm, it shall be licit for them to go on safely wherever they wish. Besides this, it was determined among us to go to the Rio de la Platta, and there to remain until the first day of January; and as now for other reasons we arrived at another closer port, and there we did everything necessary, we have determined to go by a direct route to the Cavo de Buena Esperança, and there in the port that you know to remain a little while until you arrive. That is why I ask and order each one of you that with all diligence you try to come to where I will be. May God give you health. From the port of Buena Consolacion[9] on the 9th of December of the year 1582.

This report, which was given by the said Don Francisco, whom the armada encountered with this bark on the coast of the Rio de la Platta at a latitude of 30 degrees, was written

---

[1] Fenton's expedition was in Sierra Leone from early August until early October of 1582; Taylor, *Troublesome Voyage*, p. 105.

[2] The text reads '*en su bida a bisto*' (in his life he has seen), but the context suggests that he meant he had not seen ships better outfitted in his life.

[3] An *alguacil* (pl. *alguaciles*) was a constable.

[4] Christopher Hall was the master of Fenton's *Leicester*, although the English presumably did not mention his name to Vera.

[5] Rada translates the letter from Latin into Spanish, and the phrasing is somewhat more stilted than the rest of his text.

[6] Martin Frobisher had originally been named to head the English expedition but had been replaced by Fenton, who had sailed with Frobisher on earlier voyages to the Arctic; Taylor, *Troublesome Voyage*, pp. xxxi–xxxii.

[7] George Acres; see Donno, *Diary of Richard Madox*, p. 257.

[8] China and Cathay, which Europeans of the time considered to be in the same general location in the vastness of Asia.

[9] Dom Rodrigo, which the English had dubbed the Bay of Good Comfort.

Saturday, the 15th of December 1582, by me, Pedro de Rada, chief scribe of the armada that was going to the Strait.

———

[f. 91r] *Traslado* of the letter written by the general of the two English galleons that came to the port of Sanctos, captaincy of San Vicente, to the governor:[1]
The overleaf says, To my good lord Geronimo Leiton.

My good governor: I wanted to write to your lordship in my own language, for having news that an Englishman named Master Ytall[2] lives in this land, and if this is seemly to your lordship, he can interpret my letter and the cause for having arrived here, which is also with respect to the favour that my countrymen have already received here from your lordship, principally having them trade truly, which ought to be, in the commerce of just and honest merchandise, bringing such as I have brought with this intent. And attempting in all faithfully and justly to deal truth with your lordship, for which I ask you greatly that you admit us and give us your favour in this district, giving orders to send us a pilot to bring my *naos* inside. I kiss the hands of your lordship, and in the rest all will be as you see fit, as I remain praying to God that he guide all your works. From this my *nao* on the 20th of January 1583.
A suitor of your lordship in all courtesy,
Eduarde Fenton

Another letter that the same general wrote to an Englishman who lives in this captaincy and is married therein:

To my very good friend Master Juan Uitall[3] in San Vicente

[f. 91v] Master Uithall: If my small and recent knowledge about you be worthy of such courtesy, I beg you that you interpret the letter that I send to the governor, by which you will understand the cause of being arrived here, which is solely to trade truly. And thus from the heart I send you great salutations, wishing you all the best, which for me I desire. And I would wish to see you as soon as you possibly can. For now, no more. I confide in your friendship that I remain prepared to satisfy you for all that you would do in this, and for whom, from the heart, I desire all health and prosperity. From this my *nao* on the 20th of January 1583.
Your beloved friend,
Eduarde Fenton

———

[1] Excerpts from a draft and a fair copy of this letter appear in Taylor, *Troublesome Voyage*, p. 251. Rada received official copies of this letter and the next from Portuguese officials in São Vicente. It is not clear whether the official copies were in the original English or already translated into Spanish.
[2] John Whithall. See above, p. 101, n. 5, and Donno, *Diary of Richard Madox*, pp. 34–6.
[3] Whithall became acquainted with Captain John Wynter of the *Elizabeth* in São Vicente in 1579 after the latter separated from Francis Drake. According to Wynter's later testimony in England, Whithall was keen to establish regular trade between São Vicente and England. He had corresponded with Richard Staper of the Levant Company in 1578 and with 'the adventurers for Brasil' in 1580. See the correspondence in Hakluyt, *PN1* (1589), pp. 638–40; reprinted in *PN2*, III (1600), pp. 701–3.

Traslado of the route taken by the English who sailed in company of he who passed into the Mar del Sur,[1] to where this Englishman arrived:[2]

Three *naos* departed from England, well armed and with heavy munitions and well-supplied men of arms, on the 14th of December, year of 1577,[3] making their route and course to the coast of Brasil – I mean from Berberia to Cavo Blanco, which they saw after a short time. And running along for three days in sight of land, they set their course straight to the Isla de Cavo Verde, and they saw the Isla de Sanctiago, where they stood off for three days, sailing back and forth between sea and land. And at the tip thereof they saw a Portuguese *nao* that had left from the port of Portugal, which was going toward the Baya loaded with merchandise. [f. 92r] And the Englishmen put their shallops into the water in order to go to her, and they saw men from the said *nao* going in a boat toward land, as they were very close to it.

And the said Englishmen arrived at the said *nao* and boarded it, without there being any resistance, nor were there any men aboard except the pilot, who was called Nuño de Silba,[4] and some sailors and one passenger, because the other men had fled toward land. And as they had boarded, they seized the said *nao*, and with the shallops at the prow towing her, they brought her alongside the English *capitana*. And the captain of it then ordered the men to be put ashore except for the pilot, whom he left with it and brought with him where he was going. And this finished, he ordered him to sail on course to the coast of Brasil on course to the Rio de la Platta, which they sighted without seeing any other land. And they entered into it at the end of the month of the following February, and they entered upriver for 40 leagues[5] until arriving at some islands that are inside the mouth of it on the north side, where they were until the end of March 1578.[6]

And from there they departed, making their voyage in sight of land. And being as far as about 150 leagues from the said Rio de la Platta on course to the Strait, they came to a river and port that Magallanes had given the name San Julian,[7] and it has as a landmark from the sea some tall rocks that look like towers at the point on the south shore, and inside this river there are many islands. And when they entered they did so by means of the bay, [f. 92v] coasting more toward the north shore and not toward that of the south. And inside they found some gallows made.[8] And they were with the said armada in this

---

[1] i.e. Francis Drake.

[2] In his Table of Contents, Rada notes that he obtained a copy of this testimony in São Vicente, and that the author was an Englishman who had sailed with Francis Drake through the Strait and then turned around – obviously on John Wynter's ship *Elizabeth*; see above, p. 61. At the end of the document, Rada adds that the deponent sailed on one of the 3 English *naos* that were in São Vicente. Although the phrasing is ambiguous, it suggests that the Englishman may have sailed on both the *Elizabeth* and on one of Fenton's 2 ships.

[3] Drake finally departed Plymouth on 13 Dec., after a month-long delay due to bad weather. See above, pp. 62–3, and Kelsey, *Sir Francis Drake,* p. 93.

[4] See above, p. 45, n. 4.

[5] Rada surely means 4 leagues, rather than 40.

[6] In fact, Drake did not reach the Río de la Plata until mid-April and departed again before the end of the month; Kelsey, *Sir Francis Drake*, p. 100.

[7] The Bay of San Julián is located at 49°15′S.

[8] Magellan had executed 2 men at San Julián after a failed mutiny in 1520. Decapitated and quartered, their body parts were displayed on poles, which presumably remained when Drake's expedition arrived in 1578. See Joyner, *Magellan*, pp. 137–43, for the mutiny and its aftermath.

river and port for three months,[1] not having weather,[2] where they suffered much cold, the land being very cold. And from there they departed on 15 of August, running along the coast in sight of land. And they went to see a river that they call Rio Fresco, which they did not enter, for finding themselves 7 or 8 leagues at sea and being shallow with seven or eight *brazas* of depth, and this seeming too shallow to them they left off entering into the said river.

And from there they sailed along always in sight of land on course to the Strait. And they saw a great mouth that would be about twelve leagues wide, and it has a tall white peak at the entrance on the north side, which is a good sign by which to recognize it, about two leagues from this mountain and high peak to the north shore. And entering inside, you will soon see it to be the Strait, and it runs toward the north-west. And being 20 leagues inside it you will find a good depth of ten *brazas* next to land, and you will anchor about a league from land, because it is all clean sand where one can anchor. And inside this strait, in the middle of it before you arrive at the high land, you will find some islands, which they claimed and gave the name San Jorje to one, and to another San Miguel and another remained without a name because they did not go to it.[3]

And these islands [f. 93r] have a great quantity of wild guanacos[4] in such quantity that they filled their boats with some that they had killed with cudgels. And it has a great number of sea wolves,[5] from which they prepared much salted meat.[6] And these islands have good woodlands and reed beds, and they have very good beaches on the south shore. On these islands they saw many fires night and day that were made inland, but they did not see any people, for the captain not wanting that they be seen nor spoken about.[7] And these islands are ten to twelve leagues from one shore and the other and are about half a league in size and the same distance from one another.[8] And this strait has many ports in the sandy places and good anchorages where many *naos* could be. And take warning that the sea always increases and decreases two *brazas*.[9]

Going from these islands sailing inside the Strait, you will see a high land that is always covered with snow, and you will find great depth where you can anchor directly to land with the proiz[10] if you wish, because you will find a depth of one hundred *brazas*, where it is suitable to anchor to the land with the *proiz*. And this strait has many islands and good anchorages and patches of woodlands. And whoever wishes to go into the high

[1] Drake arrived at San Julián on 20 June 1578 and departed again on 17 August; Kelsey, *Sir Francis Drake*, pp. 105–13.
[2] i.e. weather suitable to depart for the Strait.
[3] Accounts vary as to the names that Drake bestowed on the islands. All agree that one was named St George; another may have been called St Bartholomew and a third Elizabeth. See Kelsey, *Sir Francis Drake*, pp. 116–19.
[4] The wild guanaco (*Lama guanicoe*), which Rada called a *pacto bravo*, is a humpless camelid native to Patagonia.
[5] Rada called the animals *lobos marinos*, the English called them sea-wolves, both names referring to the South American sea lion (*Otaria flavescens*).
[6] *Salga*, presumably salted meat.
[7] Rada's phrase in modern Spanish is '*por el capitán no querer que obiesen vista ni habla dellos*'. Although the phrasing is ambiguous, Drake presumably did not want his diminished expedition to be noticed by the local inhabitants.
[8] In the present day, the largest island is called Isabel, located at 52°52′38″S, 70°42′46″W. The two much smaller islands are Magdalena and Marta; all host abundant penguins and other seabirds.
[9] i.e. there is considerable difference between the depth at high and low tide.
[10] A *prois* is a cable used for anchoring directly to the shoreline, if the water is deep enough close to shore.

places on land will find Indians dressed in the skins of deer and of other animals, and they carry bows and arrows placed in quivers. In this strait they remained two months, making repairs and salting fish and meat from [sea] wolves,[1] which are plentiful. And from there they sailed on to come out the mouth of the Strait, sailing [f. 93v] into the Mar del Sur. Coming out of the mouth,[2] they saw some islands, three of which are on the north side, and on the south side there are two tall rocks that seem to be islands, and there is nowhere around them to anchor because the bottom cannot be found. And the Strait on the south side is eight leagues wide at the mouth.[3] And after 17 days sailing in the Mar del Sur, a storm hit them that separated some *naos* from the others.[4] And because the captain of this *nao* was of a very delicate constitution,[5] he did not dare to continue onward, saying that he found himself ill at sea. He turned around on course to England to come out the mouth of the Strait again.

This rutter was given by one of the English who came on one of the three *naos* that were in San Vicente, 40 leagues from the Rio de Jenero, on the coast of Brasil.

Pedro de Rada [*signature and rubric*]

[ff. 94r–95r *blank*]
[ff. 95v–96r] I belong to Pedro Anton de Chopite, the year of 1742 years[6]

---

[1] Rada writes *lobos* rather than *lobos marinos*, but he clearly means sea-lions.

[2] The western mouth of the Strait of Magellan is located at 53°6′S, 73°54′W.

[3] i.e. the western mouth of the Strait.

[4] At that point Drake's expedition had only two ships, but the phrasing in the text is '*se apartaron unas naos de otras*'.

[5] The text uses the phrase '*muy regalado*', which could mean a very delicate constitution or a very timid disposition. The mention of illness suggests that the deponent was referring to Wynter's health rather than his state of mind. Edward Cliffe later wrote that the mariners were much against Wynter's decision to turn back, though this may have been a later fabrication to blame Wynter for deserting Drake. See Cliffe, 'Voyage', p. 281; Wilson, *World Encompassed*, p. 106; Kelsey, *Sir Francis Drake*, pp. 123–4.

[6] i.e. '1742 years from the birth of our Lord Jesus Christ'.

APPENDIX 1

Ships and Persons in the Armada of the Strait as of 7 December 1581[1]

The Year 1581

Listing of the men of sea and war and the settlers who are going to the Estrecho de Magallanes, in the armada composed of sixteen ships, in which Diego Flores de Valdés goes as general, which departed from the bay of the city of Cádiz on 9 December 1581; made on the 7th of the same month.

The *nao* named *San Cristóbal*[2] (700 *toneladas,* owned by the king), *capitana* of the armada
General Diego Flores de Valdés
Andrés de Eguino, accountant and overseer of the armada
Pedro de Esquivel, treasurer of the armada
Don Antonio de Quiñones, alférez real[3]
Rodrigo de Rada, captain[4]
Pedro Martínez de Loaísa, chief sergeant
Juan[5] de Salinas, alguacil real[6]
Pedro de Rada, chief scribe of the armada
Antonio Machado, alférez of the men of war

[1] A version of this list appears in several manuscript and printed sources, with variant spellings of the names of ships and persons; see Navarrete, *Colección de documentos*, vol. 20, ff. 161r–165r; AMN, *Sanz Barutell*, MS 388, ff. 220r–224r; Sarmiento, *Narratives of the Voyages*, pp. 219–25. Chaunu, *Séville et l'Atlantique*, vol. 3, pp. 292–9, identifies the ships, their masters, owners, types, and tonnages (AGI, CT, leg. 2899, lib. 1), plus additional information about several of the ships chosen and their officers (AGI, CT, leg. 2933). Sarmiento, *Viajes al Estrecho*, vol. 1, pp. 335–7, provides an abbreviated list of the ships and officers. This appendix is a composite of the various sources, all of which agree that, following the losses suffered in October, there were 16 ships and 2,408 persons in the armada in early December 1581. The names of persons are spelled according to standard modern usage, and most of the job titles have been translated into English. Otherwise, the translation follows the order and phrasing of the list as closely as possible. During the expedition, many officers and men were reassigned to different vessels as circumstances changed. The same ship might be called several different names. It is often, but not always, possible to make a firm identification by using the stated tonnage of the vessel or the name of the master, owner, or captain. When doubts arise, they are stated in a footnote. The names of the ships have been made consistent here and in Appendix 2 on the fate of each ship in the armada.

[2] The *San Cristóbal*, a galleass, is often identified in the documents as the *galeaza capitana* (flagship galleass). The word *nao* could refer generically to any large sailing ship, armed or unarmed, as it does here and in the rest of this appendix. See above, p. 30, n. 2.

[3] See above, p. 72, n. 9.

[4] Captain Rodrigo de Rada sailed as far as the Cape Verde Islands without an assignment. He then replaced Pedro de Eguino as captain of the *Santa María de Begoña*. Eguino shifted to the *San Nicolás* to replace Captain Vargas, who had died in the interim. See below, pp. 183–4, Sarmiento, *Narratives of the Voyages*, pp. 220–21.

[5] This proper name is sometimes rendered as Joán or Jhoan.

[6] The alguacil real was the chief constable in the armada, which explains why he travelled on the flagship.

Juan de Miranda, sergeant[1]
Eight gentlemen attending the general
One Franciscan friar
Pedro de la Rocha, chief surgeon[2]
170 men of war

Men of the Sea:
Juan de Garibay, captain[3]
Antón Pablos,[4] chief pilot
Captain Juan Ramos, adviser to the chief pilot
Pedro Jorge, Portuguese, assistant pilot
Master Juan de Arancibia[5]
Ninety-four men of the sea, among officers, seamen, apprentice seamen,
and ships' boys.
In addition, Pedro Sarmiento, governor and captain general of the strait,
goes on this *nao*, and with him twenty-four persons
Which are, counting all the persons carried by this *navío*,[6]
three hundred and thirteen —————————————————————— 313

The *nao* named *San Juan Bautista* (500 *toneladas*), *almiranta* of the armada
Almirante Diego de la Rivera
Captain of the *nao*, Alonso de las Alas[7]
The alférez Pedro Fernández
Sergeant Juan Martínez de Vargas[8]
140 soldiers
One Franciscan friar

Men of the Sea:
Master Martín de Goizueta[9]
Pilot Pedro Díaz de Lagos, Portuguese[10]

---

[1] Sarmiento, *Viajes al Estrecho*, vol. 1, p. 226, says that he was related to General Flores.

[2] Navarrete, *Colección de documentos*, vol. 20, f. 161r.

[3] Garibay, whom Sarmiento, *Viajes al estrecho*, vol. 1, p. 335, identifies as a Lombard, was one of the senior captains in the armada and captain of the flagship *San Cristóbal*. Several other qualified sea captains also sailed on the flagship at the start of the voyage.

[4] In various documents, the name of the chief pilot is given as Antón/Antonio Pablo/Pablos, and sometimes as Antón Pablos Corso, which may indicate a second last name, or it may identify him as a Corsican.

[5] Some lists spell his name Arancivia. Chaunu, *Séville et l'Atlantique*, vol. 3, p. 292, citing AGI, CT 2899, lib. 1, identifies him as a Vizcayan. He had previously served as master of the *fragata Santa Catalina*, in the guard squadron of the Indies fleets under Cristóbal de Eraso in 1575–7; AGI, CD, leg. 499.

[6] The word *navío* in the late 16th century often denoted a sailing ship smaller than a *nao*, though well armed; see above, p. 16, n. 3. In this list the word is used generically.

[7] Chaunu, *Séville et l'Atlantique*, vol. 3, pp. 292–3, citing AGI, CT, leg. 2899, lib. 1, identifies him as a brother of Almirante Rivera. See above, p. 76, n. 2.

[8] He is sometimes listed as Joán Martinez de Vergas.

[9] Some versions of this list identify him as from Vizcaya, though the surname Goizueta is more often associated with the province of Guipúzcoa. He appears as Güizueta in Sarmiento, *Viajes al Estrecho*, vol. 1, p. 335; Guirieta in Sarmiento, *Narratives of the Voyages*, p. 219; and Goçueta in AMN, *Sanz Barutell*, MS 388, f. 220v.

[10] Chaunu, *Séville et l'Atlantique*, vol. 3, p. 298, n. 14, identifies him as chief pilot of the Río de la Plata. See above, p. 140.

Luis Gómez, assistant pilot
Seventy-five men of the sea, among seamen, apprentice seamen, and ships' boys

People of the Strait:
The alcaide of one fort, Tomás Garri
Captain Juan de Íñiguez
Captain of artillery, Andrés de Biezma
Five gunners, among the married men[1]
Which are, counting all the persons that this *navío* carries,
two hundred and thirty-six persons ——————————————————— 236

The *fragata* named *María Magdalena*[2] (80 *toneladas*, owned by the king)
Captain Diego de Oballe, then Domingo Martínez de Avendaño[3]
Alférez Salvador Heredia
Sergeant Domingo Zorrilla
Forty soldiers

Men of the Sea:
Master Baltasar Domingo Moreno[4]
Pilot Fuente y Dueña[5]
Twenty-two men of the sea, among seamen, apprentice seamen, and ships' boys
In addition, the *fragata* carries four craftsmen as settlers of the strait, without wives
Which are, counting all the persons that this *navío* carries,
seventy-one persons ——————————————————————— 71

The *fragata* *Santa Catalina* (80 *toneladas*, owned by the king)
Captain Francisco de Cuéllar[6]
Forty-six soldiers

Men of the Sea:
Master Gaspar Alonso[7]

---

[1] When married men (*casados*) were listed, their wives were included in the count, whether or not the list mentioned wives. AMN, *Sanz Barutell*, MS 388, f. 220v, lists 5 gunners among the married men (*cinco artilleros de los casados*), or 5+5 = 10 persons, which leads to a correct total for the vessel. Other versions of the list misread the entry as 5 gunners, 2 of them married (*cinco artilleros, los dos casados*), or 5+2 = 7 persons, which leads to an incorrect total for the vessel.

[2] Also known as *Magdalena*.

[3] Before the first departure of the armada, Oballe was replaced on the *Magdalena* by Domingo Martínez de Avendaño, who arrived from his recruiting mission just in time to sail. Oballe shifted to the *Jesús María* (1,096 *toneladas*), often called the *nao francesa* (French ship). See Sarmiento, *Narratives of the Voyages*, p. 220. The *Jesús María* survived the storm in October 1581 but was not included among the 16 ships that departed in December for Brazil.

[4] Sarmiento, *Narratives of the Voyages*, p. 220, lists him as Salvador Moreno.

[5] Sometimes listed as Fontidueña.

[6] See above, pp. 36, 42, n. 1, 100, 135.

[7] Sarmiento, *Narratives of the Voyages*, p. 220, lists him as Gaspar Antonio.

Pilot Melchior París
Thirty men of the sea, among seamen, apprentice seamen, and ships' boys
Which are, counting all the persons that it carries,
seventy-nine ————————————————————————— 79

The *fragata Santa Isabel* (80 *toneladas*, owned by the king)
Captain Suero Queipo de Llano[1]
Alférez Juan de Salas[2]
Sergeant Antonio Juanez
Fifty-seven soldiers of war
One Franciscan friar

Men of the Sea:
Master Toribio de Santa María
Pilot Pedro Sánchez[3]
Thirty persons of the sea, among seamen, apprentice seamen, and ships' boys
Which are, counting all the persons that this *nao* carries,
ninety-three persons ————————————————————— 93

The *nao* named *San Esteban* of Arriola (500 *toneladas*)[4]
Captain Juan Gutiérrez de Palomar[5]
Alférez Luis García
Sergeant Juan de Entreberas
One hundred twenty-one soldiers in his company
Twenty-eight [soldiers] for Chile
Eighteen settlers for Magellanes, six of them married, and seven children
One Franciscan friar

Men of the Sea:
Master Juan de Villaviciosa Unzueta
Pilot Bartholomé Vázquez[6]
Seventy-three persons of the sea, among seamen, apprentice seamen, and ships' boys
Captain Andrés Salido goes on this *nao*
Captain Isidro de Figueroa
Which are, counting all the persons who go on this *navío*,
two hundred and sixty-one persons ———————————— 261

The *nao* named *La Concepción* (400 *toneladas*)
Captain Gregorio de las Alas

[1] See above, pp. 37, 108, 135, 179.
[2] See above, pp. 119–20, 179.
[3] Sometimes listed as Pero.
[4] There were 2 ships named *San Esteban* in the armada. The names of their owners differentiated them. See above, pp. 36, 80, 89, n. 1.
[5] See above, pp. 31, n. 3, 80, 135, 150, 179.
[6] Sometimes spelled Bázquez.

Alférez Martín de las Alas
103 soldiers

Men of the Sea:
Master Ortuño de Bilbao la Vieja[1]
Pilot Alonso Pérez, Portuguese
Seventy persons of the sea, among seamen, apprentice seamen, and ships' boys

Settlers of the strait:
Three married men with [wives and] eight children

Men for Chile:
Twenty soldiers under Don Alonso de Sotomayor[2]
Which are, counting all the persons that go in this *navío*,
two hundred and eleven persons ———————————————— 211

The *nao* named *La María de Villaviciosa* (400 *toneladas*)
Captain Francisco de Nevares[3]
Alférez Don Luis de Nevares
Sergeant Alonso Zis
Fifty soldiers

Men of the Sea:
Master Miguel de Sarasti
Pilot Francisco Jiménez
Thirty-seven persons of the sea, among seamen, apprentice seamen, and ships' boys

Settlers of the strait:
Fifteen settlers, three of them married, and one with two children
Which are, counting all the persons that go in this *navío*,
one hundred and twelve persons ———————————————— 112

The *nao* named *San Esteban* of Soroa (260 *toneladas*)
Esteban de las Alas, the purveyor of the armada, sails as captain of her[4]
Alférez Pedro de Avendaño
Sergeant Berinan Pérez
Fifty-six soldiers of war

Men of the Sea:
Master Juan de Esquivel

---

[1] Bilbao la Vieja is the oldest neighborhood in the city of Bilbao and sometimes is used as a patronymic. Sarmiento, *Narratives of the Voyages*, p. 219, lists his name as Ortiz of Bilbas, which presumably was an error of the editor and translator.

[2] See above, p. 17.

[3] On various versions of this list, the name is rendered as Nabares, Navares, Nebares, or Nivares.

[4] See above, pp. 76, 89, 99, 100, 117, n. 5, 135, 152.

Pilot Pedro Márquez
Thirty-four persons of the sea, among seamen, apprentice seamen, and ships' boys
Twenty settlers of Magellanes, all unmarried craftsmen
Which are, counting all the persons that go in this *navío*,
one hundred and fifteen persons ———————————————————— 115

The *nao* named *Santa María de Begoña* (230 *toneladas*)
Captain Pedro de Aquino[1]
Alférez Luis González de Paradiñas
Sergeant Alonso Gómez Negrete
Seventy-two soldiers

Men of the Sea:
Master Juan Rodríguez de Guillén[2]
Pilot Rodrigo de Mora
Thirty-five persons of the sea among seamen, apprentice seamen, and ships' boys

People of the Strait:
Ten married men with their wives, and eight children
Ten unmarried craftsmen
The accountant of the strait, with two servants
Two friars with two servants
Which are, counting all the persons who go in this *navío*,
one hundred and fifty-seven ———————————————————— 157

The *nao* named *Santa Marta* (400 *toneladas*)
Captain Gonzalo Meléndez de Valdés[3]
Alférez Juan de Valdés
Sixty soldiers[4]

Men of the Sea:
Master Pedro de Scarza[5]
Pilot Juan Quintero
Twenty-eight persons of the sea, among apprentice seamen, seamen, and ships' boys
Which are, counting all the persons that this *nao* carries,
ninety-two persons ———————————————————— 92

---

[1] Sarmiento, *Narratives of the Voyages*, p. 220, spells the name Aquino and indicates that he was replaced by Rodrigo de Rada when the armada reached the Cape Verde Islands.

[2] Navarrete, *Colección de documentos*, vol. 20, f. 163v. Other versions of the list give the name as Juan Rodríguez de Aguilera.

[3] See above, pp. 36, 85, 87, 99, 106, 135, 138.

[4] Given the total on board, 60 is the correct number. Navarrete, *Colección de documentos*, vol. 20, f. 164r, says 70. This may be a mistake in transcription, as *sesenta* (60) and *setenta* (70) can look very similar in manuscript.

[5] Navarrete, *Colección de documentos*, vol. 20, f. 164r, gives the name as Zarza.

The *nao* named *Santa Catalina,* the *nao corza* (300 *toneladas*)[1]
Don Alonso de Sotomayor, governor of Chile
Don Luis de Sotomayor, his brother[2]
Francisco del Campo, captain and chief sergeant[3]
Alférez Trebulcio de Heredia
Sergeant Peñaranda
115 soldiers
one friar

Men of the Sea:
Captain and Master Diego de Olabarri
Pilot Antonio Rodríguez, Portuguese
Forty-three persons of the sea, among seamen, apprentice seamen, and ships' boys
Which are, counting all the persons who go on this *nao,*
one hundred and sixty-six ——————————————————— 166[4]

The *nao* named *Santa María de Buen Pasaje* (400 *toneladas*)
Men of Chile:
Captain Miguel Fernández de Saravia
Captain Francisco de Palacios[5]
Captain Luis Troche de Heredia
Juan de Contreras, alférez
Pedro de Palacios, alférez
Francisco González, alférez
Jerónimo de Saavedra, sergeant
Luis Duque, sergeant
Orozco, sergeant
100 soldiers of all three companies; plus five married men with wives, and four children

Men of the Sea:
Captain of the ship, Luis Jodar[6]
Alférez Gaspar Madera

---

[1] This ship was often called the *nao corza* for its owner, Juan Antonio Corzo Vicentelo, to differentiate it from the other two vessels in the armada named *Santa Catalina.*

[2] See above, p. 149.

[3] Campo was known as a highly competent officer. He would be given command of the contingent of Don Alonso de Sotomayor's troops that remained in Santa Fe in the Río de la Plata. Navarrete, *Colección de documentos,* vol. 20, ff. 184v–185r.

[4] The persons on board total 166, though several versions of the list say 176. It is not clear if this is an error in transcription or an error in arithmetic in the original document.

[5] Palacios had previously served as a soldier in Italy and the Netherlands, where he was wounded and lost an eye. He went to Chile with Don Alonso de Sotomayor as a mounted soldier and chief among Sotomayor's captains and fought in numerous battles in Chile and Peru. By 1586 he had been a soldier for 22 years; AGI, Patronato, leg. 130, R. 13.

[6] Sarmiento, *Narratives of the Voyages,* p. 221, gives the captain's surname as Toder. This was the man whom Rada identified as Jodar Alférez and who signed his name Luis de Jodar. See above, pp. 69, 100, 135, 146.

Pilot and Master Juan de Sagasti; then Gaspar Madera[1]
Twenty persons of the sea, among seamen, apprentice seamen, and ships' boys
Which are, counting all the persons who go on this *navío*,
one hundred and forty six ———————————————————————— 146

The *nao* named *La Trinidad* (400 *toneladas*)
Men of Chile:
Captain Alonso García Ramón[2]
Alférez Don Alonso de Medina
Sergeant Juan de Cárdenas
Captain Francisco de Saavedra
Seventy soldiers in both companies, among them two married men with [wives, and] two children

Men of the Sea:
Owner and captain of the ship, Martín de Zubieta[3]
Alférez Tristán de Arana
Master Domingo de Celaya[4]
Pilot Gonzalo de Mesa[5]
Thirty persons of the sea, among seamen, apprentice seamen, and ships' boys
Which are, counting all the persons who go on this *navío*,
one hundred and twelve ————————————————————————— 112

The *nao* named *San Nicolás* (360 *toneladas*)
Men of Chile:
Captain Francisco de Cuevas
Captain Esteban Ydrogo
Captain Sancho de Vargas

---

[1] Chaunu, *Séville et l'Atlantique*, vol. 3, pp. 292, 299, n. 22, identifies the captain as Juan Álvarez, the master as Juan de Sagastín, and the pilot as Gaspar Madera. According to Sarmiento, *Narratives of the Voyages*, p. 220, Juan de Sagasti deserted at Sanlúcar de Barrameda before departure. Gaspar Madera, originally the alférez, was then appointed to the positions of both pilot and master.

[2] After Sotomayor's men arrived at the Río de la Plata, Captain Alonso García Ramón was assigned to oversee their provisioning in Córdoba; Navarrete, *Colección de documentos*, vol. 20, fol. 185r. He continued to serve in Chile at least until 1599; AGI, Chile, leg. 1, N. 38.

[3] See above, pp. 90, 104, 106, 135, 141, 146–7.

[4] Navarrete, *Colección de documentos*, vol. 20, f. 165r, gives the surname as Caleun, whereas the list of surviving ships on 14 October 1581 gives it as Leçayn; AMN, Sanz Barutell, MS 388, f. 204r–v. Sarmiento, *Narratives of the Voyages*, p. 221, and Sarmiento, *Viajes al Estrecho*, vol. 1, p. 336, list the name as Zeláin, whereas Chaunu, *Séville et l'Atlantique*, vol. 3, p. 292 renders the name Celaya, which would seem the most likely spelling

[5] Mesa, a native of Ayamonte near the Portuguese border, signed on as a pilot on 13 July 1581 in Seville. He had already served the crown for nearly 30 years. Mesa's salary was set at 35 ducats per month, and he received 300 ducats in advance, so that he could equip himself for the voyage and provide for his family during his absence. Mesa signed notarized documents guaranteeing his service and returned to Spain with the remnant of the armada in 1584. Had he survived but failed to fulfill the terms of his contract, he would have faced legal action and a fine of 1,000 ducats; AGI, Patronato, leg. 33, N. 3, R. 49. All of the ordinary pilots and other experienced officers would have signed on under similar circumstances.

Alonso de Ávila,[1] alférez
Juan de Campo, sergeant
Eighty soldiers, two of them married

Men of the Sea:
Captain Vargas; then Pedro de Eguino[2]
Master Miguel de Zabalaga
Pilot [Gaspar] Conquero[3]
Twenty-six persons of the sea, among seamen, apprentice seamen, and ships' boys
Which are, counting all the persons that this *navío* carries,
one hundred and sixteen ———————————————————————— 116

The *nao* named *Santa María de San Vicente* (260 *toneladas*)
Men of Chile:
Captain Leonardo Cortés[4]
Captain Diego Ruiz de Heredia
In these two companies go ninety-two officers and soldiers

Men of the Sea:
Captain of the *nao*, Hernando Ortega Morejón[5]
Alférez Diego de Albarracín
Sergeant Valentín Morejón
Master Juan de Arrieta[6]
Pilot García Bravo
Thirty-two persons of the sea, among seamen, apprentice seamen, and ships' boys
Which are, counting all the persons who go on this *navío*,
one hundred and thirty-one ———————————————————— 131

****

---

[1] This surname is sometimes rendered as Dávila.

[2] See above, p. 135.

[3] See above, p. 106, n. 5.

[4] A man named Leonardo Cortés was one of the original conquerors of Perú, having arrived there in about 1540. He later served in various official capacities in the imperial city of Cuzco. In the late 1570s, he filed proofs of his service in order to receive benefits promised him by the crown. Some of the documents are directed to the governor of Chile, the office to which Don Alonso de Sotomayor had been appointed. If indeed this was the same man, it is possible that he signed on with Sotomayor in order to collect his benefits in Peru; AGI, Patronato, leg. 115, N. 2, R. 2.

[5] See above, pp. 73, 78, 106, 135.

[6] Chaunu, *Séville et l'Atlantique*, vol. 3, p. 292, mistakenly identifies Arrieta as the ship's owner and the master as Juan de Villaviciosa, but on p. 295 he correctly lists Juan de Villaviciosa as the owner. The ship was left behind in Rio de Janeiro in November of 1582 due to its age and damages suffered on the first attempt at the Strait. Two months later, it was still in Rio and Don Diego de Alcega confirmed that its owner was Juan de Villaviciosa. Alcega to Philip II, Rio de Janeiro, 28 January 1583, in Navarrete, *Colección de documentos*, vol. 20, f. 181r.

All the men of war who go on the armada,
nine hundred and seventy-one soldiers —————————————————— 971
And of the sea, among officers and all the men of the sea,
seven hundred and twenty-two ———————————————————— 722
And settlers of the strait, among men, women, and children,
one hundred and seventy ——————————————————————— 170
And soldiers who are going to Chile with Don Alonso de Sotomayor,
five hundred and forty-five ————————————————————— 545

So that, counting all the men of the sea and war, settlers of Magellanes
and soldiers for Chile who travel on the sixteen ships that departed from
the Bay of Cádiz on 9 December 1581, there are in all two thousand and
four hundred and eight persons ——————————————————— 2,408

APPENDIX 2

The Fate of Ships in the Armada of the Strait

Name(s) of ship with carrying capacity in *toneladas*	Type	Last day in the armada	Circumstances
Nuestra Señora de Buena Esperanza (180)	*nao*	6 Oct. 1581	Wrecked off the coast of SW Spain, near Rota, during a storm after the first departure of the armada.
Nuestra Señora de Guía (400)	*nao*	6 Oct. 1581	Wrecked off the coast of SW Spain, in sight of Cádiz, during a storm after the first departure of the armada.
San Miguel (400)	*nao*	6 Oct. 1581	Wrecked off the coast of SW Spain, during a storm after the first departure of the armada.
Sancti Espíritu (400)	*nao*	6 Oct. 1581	Wrecked off the coast of SW Spain, near the Río de Oro, during a storm after the first departure of the armada.
Jesús María (1,096)	*nao*	10 Oct. 1581	Limped into port after the first departure of the armada; left behind.
María de Jesús (450)	*nao*	10 Oct. 1581	Limped into port after the first departure of the armada; left behind.
Nuestra Señora de Guadalupe (80)	*fragata*	2 Dec. 1581	Wrecked while anchored near the bulwark of San Felipe in Cádiz during a storm, before the second departure of the armada.
Santa María de San Vicente (260)	*nao*	26 Oct. 1582	Developed a leak while leaving Río de Janeiro for the first attempt at the Strait; left behind to be broken up.
San Esteban of Arriola (500)	*nao*	29 Nov. 1582	Sank during a storm at sea, just south of Río de la Plata, during the first attempt at the Strait.
Santa María (400)	*nao*	16 Dec. 1582	Wrecked at El Biaza, about 6 leagues south of Dom Rodrigo while returning from the first attempt at the Strait.
San Nicolás (360)	*nao*	19 Dec. 1582	Declared unseaworthy and left behind at Santa Catarina Island, while returning from the first attempt at the Strait.
San Esteban of Soroa (260)	*nao*	7 Jan. 1583	Sailed in the first attempt at the Strait; ran aground on leaving Santa Catarina Island for the second attempt at the Strait.
Santa María de Buen Pasaje (400)	*nao*	19 Jan. 1583	Sailed in the first attempt at the Strait; carried some of Sotomayor's men to the Río de la Plata during the second attempt; broken up thereafter.
Santa Catalina (*nao corza*) (300)	*nao*	19 Jan. 1583	Wrecked near Buenos Aires.

Ship	Type	Date	Notes
Santa María de Begoña (230)	*nao*	24 Jan. 1583	Sailed in the first attempt at the Strait; left for repairs at Santa Catarina; fought in Battle of Santos with Fenton's ships and sank.
Santa Cruz (not given)	*nao*	13 Aug. 1583	Arrived in Brazil with Don Diego de Alcega and was incorporated into Flores's armada; sailed to Bahia with the armada; left Bahia for Spain with Alcega; later arrived safely in Lisbon after a difficult voyage.
La Trinidad (400)	*nao*	18 Feb. 1584	Sailed in the first attempt at the Strait; carried some of Sotomayor's men to the Río de la Plata during the second attempt; returned to Rio de Janeiro with munitions; went to the Strait with Almirante Rivera and was then broken up.
Nao of Pablos Buzomo[1]	*nao*	late May 1584	Broken up in Rio de Janeiro; its equipment was distributed among the remaining 6 ships in the armada and the 5 ships going to the Strait.
La Concepción (400)	*nao*	19 July 1584	Sailed in the first attempt at the Strait; left for repairs at Santa Catarina; fought at Santos in Jan. 1583; sailed to Paraíba in April 1584; returned to Sanlúcar de Barrameda with Flores.
San Cristóbal (700)	*galeaza capitana*	19 July 1584	Sailed in the first two attempts at the Strait; then sailed to Bahia and Paraíba; returned to Sanlúcar de Barrameda with Flores.
San Juan Bautista (500–600)	*nao almiranta*	19 July 1584	Sailed in the first attempt at the Strait; left for repairs at Santa Catarina; fought at Santos in Jan. 1583; then sailed to Bahia and Paraíba; returned to Sanlúcar de Barrameda with Flores.
Santa Isabel (80)	*fragata*	19 July 1584	Sailed in the first two attempts at the Strait; then sailed to Bahia and Paraíba; returned to Sanlúcar de Barrameda with Flores.
Not identified (over 200)	*nao*	19 July 1584	Arrived in Brazil with Alcega; sailed from Rio de Janeiro to Bahia and Paraíba; returned to Sanlúcar de Barrameda with Flores.
La María de Villaviciosa (400)	*nao*	21 Sept. 1584	Sailed in all three attempts at the Strait; returned to Sanlúcar de Barrameda with Rivera the temporary captain general; served as his *capitana*.
María Magdalena (80)	*fragata*	21 Sept. 1584	Sailed in all three attempts at the Strait; returned to Sanlúcar de Barrameda with Rivera the temporary captain general.
Santa Catalina (80)	*fragata*	21 Sept. 1584	Sailed in all three attempts at the Strait; returned to Sanlúcar de Barrameda with Rivera the temporary captain general.
Santa María de Castro (over 200)	*nao*	late Sept. 1584	Arrived in Brazil with Alcega; incorporated into Flores's armada; made the third attempt at the Strait and remained there from Feb. to May of 1584; Carried Sarmiento back to Rio de Janeiro for supplies in May 1584; wrecked in a storm between Pernambuco and Bahia.

187

[1] One of the four ships brought from Spain by Don Diego de Alcega. Its size was not mentioned.

BIBLIOGRAPHY

MANUSCRIPTS

San Marino, Henry E. Huntington Library
MS HM 59416
Madrid, Archivo Histórico Nacional
OM, Car.247, N. 7
Madrid, Archivo del Museo Naval
Cartas de los reyes a los duques de Medina Sidonia, MSS 496, 497, 498, 499
Sanz Barutell, MS 388
Madrid, Biblioteca Nacional de España
MS 781
Seville, Archivo General de las Indias
Contaduría: leg. 466
Contratación: leg. 2899, lib. 1; 2933
Escribanía de Cámara de Justicia: leg. 227, 153A
Indiferente General: leg. 13, 541, 739, 1952
Justicia: leg. 906
México: leg. 215
Patronato: leg. 33, 261
Valladolid, Archivo General de Simancas
Cámara de Mercedes: leg. 227
Guerra y Marina: leg. 109, 264
Valladolid, Archivo de la Real Chancillería de Valladolid
Registro de Ejecutorias: caja 1612
Lisbon, Biblioteca de Ajuda
Cota 51-IV-38
London, British Library
Royal MS 20 E IX

PRINTED PRIMARY SOURCES

Amherst, W. A. T. [Lord], and Basil Thomson, eds and trans., *The Discovery of the Solomon Islands by Álvaro de Mendaña in 1568*, 2 vols, Hakluyt Society, 2nd ser., 7–8, London, 1901.

Andrews, Kenneth R., *The Last Voyage of Drake and Hawkins*, Hakluyt Society, 2nd ser., 142, Cambridge, 1972.

Brandão, Ambrósio Fernandes, *Dialogues of the Great Things of Brazil*, 'Dialogue III' excerp. and trans. in Stuart B. Schwartz, ed., *Early Brazil: A Documentary Collection to 1700*, New York, 2010.

Calvar Gross, Jorge et al., *Génesis de la Empresa de Inglaterra de 1588*, Madrid, 1988, vol. 1 of *La Batalla del Mar Océano: Corpus documental de las hostilidades entre España e Inglaterra (1568–1604)*, 5 vols, Madrid, 1988–2015.

Cliffe, Edward, 'Voyage of M. John Winter into the South Sea, by the Streight of Magellan, in consort with M. Francis Drake ...' in W. S. W. Vaux, ed., *The World Encompassed by Sir Francis Drake; Being His Next Voyage to That to Nombre de Dios*, Hakluyt Society, 1st ser.,16, London, 1854, pp. 269–84.

Colección de documentos inéditos para la historia de España, 113 vols, Madrid, 1842–95.

Collado, Luigi, *Practica manuale di arteglieria*,Venice, 1586.

—, *Practical Manual of Artillery (1586)*, trans. Oliver Lyman Spaulding, Washington, D.C., 1945.

Díaz de Guzmán, Ruy, *La Argentina*, ed. Enrique de Gandía, Madrid, 1986.

Donno, Elizabeth Story, ed., *An Elizabethan in 1582: The Diary of Richard Madox, Fellow of All Souls*, Hakluyt Society, 2nd ser., 147, London, 1976.

Drake, Sir Francis, *The World Encompassed by Sir Francis Drake, Being His Next Voyage to That to Nombre de Dios; Formerly Imprinted; Carefully Collected Out of the Notes of Master Francis Fletcher Preacher*, London, 1628.

Fernández Duro, Cesáreo, ed., *Disquisiciones náuticas* (1876), 6 vols, Madrid, 1996.

Fernández de Navarrete, Martín, see Navarrete, Martín Fernández de.

Greenlee, William Brooks, ed. and trans., *The Voyage of Pedro Alvares Cabral to Brazil and India from Contemporary Documents and Narratives*, Hakluyt Society, 2nd ser., 81, London, 1938.

Hakluyt, Richard, *The Principall Navigations, Voiages and Discoveries of the English Nation*, London, 1589.

—, *The Principal Navigations Voyages Traffiques and Discoveries of the English Nation*, 3 vols, London, 1598–1600.

—, *The Principal Navigations, Voyages, Traffiques & Discoveries of the English Nation*, 12 vols, Glasgow, 1903–5.

Léry, Jean de, *Histoire d'un voyage fait en la terre du Brésil autrement dite Amerique*, La Rochelle, 1578.

—, *History of a Voyage to the Land of Brazil, Otherwise Called America*, ed. and trans. Janet Whatley, Berkeley, 1990.

Menéndez de Avilés, Pedro, *Cartas sobre la Florida (1555–1574)*, ed. Juan Carlos Mercado, Madrid, 2002.

Navarrete, Martín Fernandez de, ed., *Colección de diarios y relaciones para la historia de los viajes y descubrimientos*, 7 vols, Madrid, 1943.

—, ed., *Colección de documentos y manuscriptos compilados*, 32 vols, Nendeln, Liechtenstein, 1971.

Parry, John H. and Robert G. Keith, eds, *The Conquerors and the Conquered*, New York, 1984, vol. 1 of *The New Iberian World: A Documentary History of the Discovery and Settlement of Latin America to the Early 17th Century*, 5 vols, London, 1984.

Pastells, Pablo, with Constantino Bayle, *El descubrimiento del Estrecho de Magallanes, en commemoración del IV Centenario*, Madrid, 1920.

Pedraza, Juan, '"The Battle of Paraíba": A Poetic Narrative Written in 1584', trans. Robert F. Estelle, Minneapolis, 1985.

—, 'Relación cierta y verdadera que trata de la victoria y toma de la Parayva ...' in Fernández Duro, ed., *Disquisiciones náuticas*, 6 vols, Madrid, 1996, vol. 6, pp. 465–74.

Robles, Diego, 'Discurso acerca en poblar a Estrecho de Magallanes, y de la demás guarda y defensa que sería necesario tener en la Mar del Sur ...' in Navarrete, ed., *Colección de documentos y manuscriptos compilados*, 32 vols, Nendeln, Liechtenstein, 1971, vol. 20, ff. 98r–108v.

Sarmiento de Gamboa, Pedro, *Narratives of the Voyages of Pedro Sarmiento de Gamboa to the Straits of Magellan*, ed. and trans. Clements R. Markham, Hakluyt Society, 1st ser., 91, London, 1895.

—, *Historia de los Incas*, Buenos Aires, 1943.

—, *Viajes al Estrecho de Magallanes (1579–1584)*, ed., Ángel Rosenblat, 2 vols, Buenos Aires, 1950.

—, *Derrotero al Estrecho de Magallanes: Relación y derrotero del viage y descubrimiento del Estrecho de la Madre de Dios antes llamado de Magallanes*, ed. Juan Batista, vol. 16 of *Crónicas de América*, 31 vols, Madrid, 1987.

—, *The History of the Incas*, ed. and trans. Brian S. Bauer and Vania Smith, Austin, 2007.

Schmidel, Ulrich, *Warhafftige und liebliche Beschreibung etlicher fürnemen Indianischen Landtschafften und Insulen*, Frankfurt, 1567.

Silva, Nuño da, 'Relación mui circunstanciada, deducida de la declaración que hizo ante el Virrey de Mexico en 20 de Mayo de 1579 el piloto Nuño de Silva natural de Porto de Portugal' in Navarrete, ed., *Colección de documentos y manuscriptos compilados*, 32 vols, Nendeln, Liechtenstein, 1971, vol. 26, ff. 47r–50v.

Socorro Ferraz Barbosa, Maria do et al., eds, *Documentos manuscritos avulsos da Capitania de Pernambuco: Fontes repatriadas. Anotações de história colonial referencias para pesquisa, ínice do catálogo da capitania de Pernambuco*, Pernambuco, 2006.

Sorapán de Rieros, Juan, *Medicina española contenida en proverbios vulgares de nuestra lengua* (1615), with introd. by Antonio Castillo de Lucas, Madrid, 1949.

Souza, Gabriel Soares de, *Derrotero de la costa del Brasil y memorial de las grandezas de Bahía* (1587), ed. Francisco Adolfo de Varnhagen, Madrid, 1958.

—, *Tratado descritivo do Brasil em 1587*, ed. Francisco Adolfo de Varnhagen, 4th edn, São Paulo, 1971.

Staden, Hans, *Warhäftig Historia und Beschreibung eyner Landtschafft der Wilden*, Marburg, 1557.

—, *Hans Staden's True History: An Account of Cannibal Captivity in Brazil*, ed. and trans. Neil L. Whitehead and Michael Harbsmeier, Durham, NC, 2008.

Taylor, E. G. R., ed., *The Troublesome Voyage of Captain Edward Fenton, 1582–1583: Narratives and Documents*, Hakluyt Society, 2nd ser., 113, Cambridge, 1959.

Thevet, André, *Singularitez de la France antarctique, autrement nommée Amérique*, Antwerp, 1558.

—, *Antarctike, Wherin is Contained Wo[n]derful and Strange Things*, London, 1568.

Vasconcelos, Simão de, *Chronica da Companhia de Jesu de Estado do Brasil* (1663), 2 vols, Lisbon, 1865.

Vaux, W. S. W., ed, *The World Encompassed by Sir Francis Drake; Being His Next Voyage to That to Nombre de Dios*, Hakluyt Society, 1st ser., 16, London, 1854.

Vaz, Lopez, 'A discourse of the West Indies and South sea written by Lopez Vaz a Portugall, conteining divers memorable matters not to be found in any other writers, and continued unto the yere 1587' in Richard Hakluyt, *The Principal Navigations*, London, 1598–1600, vol. 3, pp. 778–802; Glasgow, 1903–5, vol. 11, pp. 227–90.

—, 'An extract out of the discourse of one Lopez Vaz a Portugal, touching the fight of M. Fenton with the Spanish ships, with a report of the proceeding of M. Iohn Drake after his departing from him to the riuer of Plate' in Richard Hakluyt, *The Principal Navigations*, London, 1598–1600, vol. 3, pp. 728–30; Glasgow, 1903–5, vol. 11, pp. 92–5.

SECONDARY SOURCES

Alden, Dauril, *The Making of an Enterprise. The Society of Jesus in Portugal, Its Empire, and Beyond, 1540–1750*, Stanford, 1996.

Alegria, Maria Fernanda et al., 'Portuguese Cartography in the Renaissance' in David Woodward, ed., *History of Cartography*, Chicago, 2007, vol. 3, pp. 975–1068.

Andrews, Kenneth R., *Elizabethan Privateering: English Privateering during the Spanish War, 1585–1603*, Cambridge, 1964.

—, *Drake's Voyages: A Re-Assessment of Their Place in Elizabethan Maritime Expansion*, New York, 1967.

—, 'Latin America' in David B. Quinn, ed., *The Hakluyt Handbook*, 2 vols, Hakluyt Society, 2nd ser., 144–5, London, 1974, vol. 1, pp. 234–43.

—, 'Drake and South America' in Norman J. W. Thrower, ed., *Sir Francis Drake and the Famous Voyage, 1577–1580: Essays Commemorating the Quadricentennial of Drake's Circumnavigation of the Earth*, Berkeley and Los Angeles, 1984, pp. 49–59.

—, *Trade, Plunder and Settlement: Maritime Enterprise and the Genesis of the British Empire, 1480–1630*, Cambridge, 1984.

Ángelis, Pedro de, *Fundación de la ciudad de Buenos-Aires por D. Juan de Garay, con otros documentos de aquella epoca*, Buenos Aires, 1836.

Annaes da Bibliotheca Nacional do Rio de Janeiro, Rio de Janeiro, 1888, vols 13–14.

Arnold, J. Barto III et al., *The Nautical Archaeology of Padre Island: The Spanish Shipwrecks of 1554*, New York, 1978.

Bethell, Leslie, ed., *The Cambridge History of Latin America*, 2 vols, Cambridge, 1984.

Boucher, Philip P., *Les Nouvelles Frances: France in America, 1500–1815, An Imperial Perspective*, Providence, 1989.

Bradley, Peter T., *British Maritime Enterprise in the New World from the late Fifteenth to the mid-Eighteenth Century*, Lewiston, NY, 1999.

Briquet, Charles-Moïse, *Les filigranes. Dictionnaire historique des marques du papier dès leur apparition vers 1282 jusqu'en 1600*, facs. of the 1907 edn, ed. Allan Stevenson, Amsterdam, 1968.

Broussard, Ray F., 'Bautista Antonelli: Architect of Caribbean Defense', *The Historian*, 50, 1 August, 1988, pp. 507–20.

Brown, Jonathan C., 'Outpost to Entrepôt: Trade and Commerce at Colonial Buenos Aires' in Stanley R. Ross and Thomas F. McGann, eds, *Buenos Aires: 400 Years*, Austin, 1982, pp. 3–17.

Brunelle, Gayle K., 'Dieppe School' in David Buisseret, ed., *The Oxford Companion to World Exploration*, New York, 2007, pp. 237–8.

Buisseret, David, *Monarchs, Ministers, and Maps: The Emergence of Cartography as a Tool of Government in Early Modern Europe*, Chicago, 1992.

—, *The Mapmakers' Quest: Depicting New Worlds in Renaissance Europe*, Oxford, 2003.

—, 'Spanish Military Engineers in the New World before 1750' in Dennis Reinhartz and Gerald D. Saxon, eds, *Mapping and Empire: Soldier-Engineers on the Southwestern Frontier*, Austin, 2005, pp. 44–56.

Burkholder, Mark A., and Lyman L. Johnson, *Colonial Latin America*, 4th edn, New York and Oxford, 2001.

Cerezo Martínez, Ricardo, *Las armadas de Felipe II*, Madrid, 1989.

Chaunu, Pierre, and Huguette Chaunu, *Séville et l'Atlantique, 1504–1650*, 8 vols in 12, Paris, 1955–9.

Cintra, Jorge Pimentel, 'Reconstruindo o Mapa das Capitanias Hereditárias', *Anais do Museu Paulista*, São Paulo, n. sér., vol. 21, n. 2, jul.–dez. 2013, pp. 11–45.

Clissold, Stephen, *Conquistador: The Life of Don Pedro Sarmiento de Gamboa*, London, 1954.

Covarrubias, Sebastián, *Tesoro de la lengua castellana o española*, Madrid, 1611.

Dickason, Olive Patricia, *The Myth of the Savage and the Beginnings of French Colonialism in the Americas*, Edmonton, 1984.

Domínguez Ortiz, Antonio, *The Golden Age of Spain, 1516-1659*, trans. James Casey, New York, 1971.

—, *Las clases privilegiadas en la España del Antiguo Régimen*, Madrid, 1973.

—, Eve M. Duffy, and Alida C. Metcalf, *The Return of Hans Staden, A Go-Between in the Atlantic World*, Baltimore, 2011.

Doursther, Horace, *Dictionnaire universel des poids et mesures anciens et modernes, contenant des tables des monnaies de tous les pays*, Brussels, 1840; 3rd edn, Amsterdam, 1976.

Dutra, Francis A., 'Evolution of the Portuguese Order of Santiago, 1492–1600', *Mediterranean Studies*, 4, 1994, pp. 63–72.

Elliott, J. H., *Imperial Spain, 1469–1716*, New York, 1964.

—, *Empires of the Atlantic World: Britain and Spain in America 1492–1830*, New Haven, 2006.

Fernández-Armesto, Felipe, ed., *The Times Atlas of World Exploration*, London, 1991.

Freire, Felisbello Firmo de Oliveira, *História de Sergipe (1575–1855)*, Sergipe, Brazil, 1891.

Gasparini, Graziano, *Los Antonelli: Arquitectos militares italianos al servicio de la corona española en España, África y América, 1559–1649*, Caracas, 2007.

Gonçalves, Regina Célia, 'Guerra e açúcar: A formação da elite política na Capitania da Paraíba (séculos XVI e XVII)' in Carla Mary S. Oliveira and Ricardo Pinto de Medeiros, eds, *Novos olhares sobre as Capitanias do Norte do Estado do Brasil*, João Pessoa, 2007, pp. 23–67.

Harley, J. B., D. Woodward et al., eds, *The History of Cartography*, Chicago, 1987–, vol. 3, Pt I.

Heawood, Edward, *Watermarks Mainly of the 17th and 18th Centuries*, Hilversum, 1950.

Hemming, John, *Red Gold: The Conquest of the Brazilian Indians*, Cambridge, MA, 1978.

Henderson, James D., Helen Delpar, Maurice Philip Brungardt, and Richard N. Weldon, *A Reference Guide to Latin American History*, New York, 2000.

Johnson, H. B., 'The Portuguese Settlement of Brazil, 1500–1580' in *The Cambridge History of Latin America*, ed. Leslie Bethell, 2 vols, Cambridge and New York, 1984, vol. 1, pp. 249–86.

Johnstone, Christian Isobel, *Lives and Voyages of Drake, Cavendish, and Dampier*, Ann Arbor, 2005.

Joyner, Tim, *Magellan*, Camden, ME, 1992.

Kelsey, Harry, *Sir Francis Drake: The Queen's Pirate*, New Haven, 1998.

Kupperman, Karen, 'A Continent Revealed: Assimilation of the Shape and Possibilities of North America's East Coast, 1524–1610' in John Logan Allen, ed., *North American Exploration*, 2 vols, Lincoln, NE, 1997, vol. 1, pp. 344–99.

Landín Carrasco, Amancio, *Vida y viajes de Pedro Sarmiento de Gamboa*, Madrid, 1945.

— et al., eds, *Descubrimientos españoles en el Mar del Sur*, 3 vols, Madrid, 1991.

Lokken, Paul, 'Angolans in Amatitlán: Sugar, African Migrants, and *Gente Ladina* in Colonial Guatemala' in Lowell Gudmundson and Justin Wolfe, eds, *Blacks and Blackness in Central America: Between Race and Place*, Durham, NC, 2010, pp. 27–56.

Lyon, Eugene, *The Enterprise of Florida: Pedro Menéndez de Avilés and the Spanish Conquest of 1565–1568*, Gainesville, 1976.

MacCaffrey, Wallace T., *Queen Elizabeth and the Making of Policy, 1572–1588*, Princeton, 1981.

MacDonald, Norman Pemberton, *The Making of Brazil: Portuguese Roots, 1500–1822*, Lewes, Sussex, 1996.

Marley, David F., *Wars of the Americas: A Chronology of Armed Conflict in the Western Hemisphere, 1492 to the Present*, 2 vols, Santa Barbara, CA, 2008.

Martin, Colin, and Geoffrey Parker, *The Spanish Armada*, London, 1988.

Martínez Shaw, Carlos, ed., *Spanish Pacific from Magellan to Malaspina*, Madrid, 1988.

Mauro, Frédéric, 'Portugal and Brazil: Political and Economic Structures' in Leslie Bethell, ed., *The Cambridge History of Latin America*, 2 vols, Cambridge, 1984, vol. 1, pp. 441–68.

McAlister, Lyle N., *Spain and Portugal in the New World, 1492–1700*, vol. 3 in the series Europe and the World in the Age of Expansion, Minneapolis, 1984.

McDermott, James, 'Fenton, Edward' in *ODNB*, Oxford, 2004; online edn 2008.

Meide, Chuck, and John de Bry, 'The Lost French Fleet of 1565: Collision of Empires', *Underwater Archaeology Proceedings*, 2014, pp. 79–91.

Merriman, Roger Bigelow, *The Rise of the Spanish Empire in the Old World and the New*, 4 vols, New York, 1962.

Moncada Maya, José Omar, *Ingenieros militares en Nueva España: Inventario de su labor científica y espacial Siglos XVI a XVIII*, Mexico D.F., 1993.

Monteiro, John, 'The Crises and Transformations of Invaded Societies: Coastal Brazil in the Sixteenth Century' in *The Cambridge History of the Native Peoples of the Americas*, vol. 3, pt I, pp. 973–1023.

Morineau, Michel, *Jauge et méthodes de jauge anciennes et modernes*, Paris, 1966.

Morison, Samuel Eliot, *The European Discovery of America: The Northern Voyages, A.D. 500–1600*, New York, 1971.

—, *The European Discovery of America: The Southern Voyages*, New York, 1974.

Muldoon, James, *The Americas in the Spanish World Order: The Justification for Conquest in the Seventeenth Century*, Philadelphia, 1994.

Olesa Muñido, Francisco Felipe, *La organización naval de los estados mediterráneos y en especial de España durante los siglos XVI y XVII*, 2 vols, Madrid, 1981.

Oyarzun Iñarra, Javier, *Expediciones españolas al Estrecho de Magallanes y Tierra del Fuego*, Madrid, 1976.

Pagden, Anthony, *The Fall of Natural Man: The American Indian and the Origins of Comparative Ethnology*, Cambridge, 1986.

Parkman, Francis, *Pioneers of France in the New World*, Lincoln, NE, 1996.

Parry, John H., 'Drake and the World Encompassed' in Norman J. W. Thrower, ed., *Sir Francis Drake and the Famous Voyage, 1577–1580: Essays Commemorating the Quadricentennial of Drake's Circumnavigation of the Earth*, Los Angeles, 1984, pp. 1–32.

Pérez-Mallaína, Pablo E., *Spain's Men of the Sea: The Daily Life of Crews on the Indies Fleets in the Sixteenth Century*, trans. Carla Rahn Phillips, Baltimore, 1998.

Phillips, Carla Rahn, *Six Galleons for the King of Spain: Imperial Defense in the Early Seventeenth Century*, Baltimore, 1986.

—, '"The Life Blood of the Navy": Recruiting Sailors in Eighteenth-Century Spain', *The Mariner's Mirror*, 87, no. 4, November 2001, pp. 420–45.

—, 'Spanish Mariners in a Global Context' in Maria Fusaro, Bernard Allaire, Richard J. Blakemore, and Tijl Vanneste, eds, *Law, Labour and Empire: Comparative Perspectives on Seafarers, c. 1500–1800*, London, 2015, pp. 236–55.

Phillips, William D. and Carla Rahn Phillips, *A Concise History of Spain*, Cambridge, 2010; 2nd edn 2015.

Quinn, David B., ed., *The Hakluyt Handbook*, 2 vols, Hakluyt Society, 2nd ser., 144–5, London, 1974.

Reinhartz, Dennis and Gerald D. Saxon, eds, *Mapping and Empire: Soldier-Engineers on the Southwestern Frontier*, Austin, 2005.

Roncière, Charles de la, 'Une carte française encore inconnue du Nouveau Monde (1584)', *Bibliothèque de l'École des Chartres*, 71, 1910, pp. 588–601.

Rubio Serrano, José Luis, 'Las unidades de medida españolas en los siglos XVI y XVII', *Revista de Historia Naval*, 6, no. 20, 1988, pp. 77–94.

—, 'Métodos de arqueo en el sigo XVI', *Revista de Historia Naval*, 6, no. 24, 1989, pp. 29–70.

Russell-Wood, A. J. R., *Fidalgos and Philanthropists: The Santa Casa da Misericórdia of Bahia, 1550–1755*, London, 1968.

Safier, Niel, *Measuring the New World: Enlightenment Science and South America*, Chicago, 2008.

Salomon, Frank, and Stuart B. Schwartz, eds, *South America*, Pt I and II in *The Cambridge History of the Native Peoples of the Americas*, vol. 3, Cambridge, 2008.

Schurz, William Lytle, *The Manila Galleon: The Romantic History of the Spanish Galleons Trading Between Manila and Acapulco*, New York, 1939.

Spate, O. H. K., *The Pacific Since Magellan*, vol. 1, *The Spanish Lake*, Minneapolis, 1979.

Thrower, Norman J. W., ed., *Sir Francis Drake and the Famous Voyage, 1577–1580: Essays Commemorating the Quadricentennial of Drake's Circumnavigation of the Earth*, Los Angeles, 1984.

Vicente Vela, V., *Índice de la colección de documentos de Fernández de Navarrete que posee el Museo Naval*, Madrid, 1946.

Wagner, Henry Raup, *Sir Francis Drake's Voyage Around the World: Its Aims and Achievements*, San Francisco, 1926.

Wallis, Helen, ed., *The Maps and Text of the Boke of Ydrography presented by Jean Rotz to Henry VIII*, Roxburghe Club, Oxford, 1981.

—, 'The Cartography of Drake's Voyage' in Norman J. W. Thrower, ed., *Sir Francis Drake and the Famous Voyage, 1577–1580: Essays Commemorating the Quadricentennial of Drake's Circumnavigation of the Earth*, Los Angeles, 1984, pp. 121–63.

Wilson, Derek, *The World Encompassed: Drake's Great Voyage 1577–1580*, London, 1977.

Wright, Robin M., and Manuela Carneiro da Cunha, 'Destruction, Resistance, and Transformation – Southern, Coastal, and Northern Brazil (1580–1890)' in Frank Salomon, and Stuart B. Schwartz, eds, *South America*, vol. 3, pt 1, pp. 287–381, in *The Cambridge History of the Native Peoples of the Americas*, Cambridge, 2008.

Zavala, Silvio A., *Las instituciones jurídicas en la conquista de América*, 2nd edn, Mexico D.F., 1971.

INDEX

Abarca, Héctor, captain, 69
accountant (contador) defined, 59n
Acosta, Melchor (Melchior), 142–3, 162
Acres (Acles), George, captain, 171
acuerdo y parecer (deliberation and accord), 150
adelantado, defined, 11n
Adorno, Giuseppe, landowner, 101n
adze (*azada*), 145
Alas, Alonso (Alonsso) de las, captain, 36n, 76n, 100, 106–7, 110, 112, 177
Alas, Esteban (Estevan) de las, captain, purveyor and keeper of munitions, 76, 89, 99, 100, 117n, 135, 152, 180
Alas, Esteban de las, the Elder, 76n
Alas, Gregorio de las, captain, 13, 16, 71, 90, 94–5, 97, 106–7, 135, 147, 154, 179
Alas, Martín de las, alférez, 180
Alas, Pedro Esteban de las, captain, 68–9
Alba, duke of, 17, 19–20, 33n
alcabalas, defined, 85n
alcaide, defined, 60n
Alcalá de Henares, city, 10
Alcega (Alciega, Alzega), Don Diego de, 44–7, 58–60, 102, 104, 106–9, 111–12, 116, 149, 151–2, 155, 187
alférez (pl. alféreces), defined, 72n
Algarve (Algarbes), 129
Algeciras, Bay of, 69n
alguacil, defined, 171
almirante, defined, 1n
almojarife, defined, 142n
almud, 52, 159
alquer (*alqueire*), xiv, 106, 143, 154, 159, 161, 166
Álvarez de Toledo y Pimentel, Don Fernando, 3rd duke of Alba, *see* Alba, duke of
Álvarez de Toledo, Don Francisco, count of Oropesa and viceroy of Peru (1569–81), 7–10, 12, 14, 15, 64n
Amsterdam (Mostradama), city, 129
Andrada, Francisco, 33n
Andrada, Gaspar de, 33n
angeo, defined, 164n
Angra (Angla), city, 128, 163–4

Antonelli (Antoneli), Battista (Baptista, Bautista), 33n, 34, 53, 89n, 99n, 102, 122n
Antonelli (Antoneli), Giovanni Battista (Bautista, Juan Baptista), 19, 20
António, Dom, Prior of Crato, 7n, 111n
Aramburu, Marcos de, overseer and accountant, 106
arca de tres llaves, defined, 32n
Arenas Gordas, 69
arroba (pl. *arrobas*), xiv, 12n, 52, 133n, 144–5, 159, 161–2, 164
Arze, Pedro de, 163
Asencion, island, Ilha da Trinidade, Trinity Island, 74
Asencion, Islas del, islands of, 92
Asturias, 10, 20, 39, 50, 69n, 85n, 96n, 108n
Asturias, Prince of, defined, 11
Asunción, city, 83n
Atlantic Ocean (Mar del Norte, Mar Océano, Northern Sea), defined, 61n
auto, defined, 149n
ayuda de costa, defined, 18
Azores, islands, 7n, 14, 16, 26, 37, 45, 48, 51
azumbre, defined, xiv

Badajoz, city, 14, 64
Bahía (Vayya) de Caballos, Bay of Horses, likely the bay at Dahkla, Western Sahara, 71
Bahía de Cádiz (Baya de Cadiz), 32, 48, 50, 57, 59, 68, 70, 129, 166, 185
Bahia (Baia, Baya, Bayya) de Todos os Santos del Salvador (del Salvador, los Sanctos, Todos Santos), viii, ix, 5, 33, 46–8, 59–61, 77, 107, 110–12, 129, 155, 157–8
Baia da Traição (Baya de la Traicion), Bay of Treachery, Bay of Treason, 121–2
Baia de Paraíba, 122n
Barbary (Berbería, Berveria), 71, 173
Barbosa (Barboso, Barbozo), Fructuoso (Frutuoso, Frutuoso), 111–24, 159–60
barley, seed for planting, 168
barlovento (upwind), 71n
Barreto (Bareto), Manuel (Manoel) Tellez (Teles), 47, 60, 110, 113, 115n, 155, 163
battle centre, 135

195